Pan-African Protest:
West Africa and the
Italo-Ethiopian Crisis, 1934-1941

LEGON HISTORY SERIES
General Editor A A Boahen PhD

Pan-African Protest:
West Africa and the
Italo-Ethiopian Crisis, 1934–1941

S. K. B. Asante
Department of Political Science
University of Ghana, Legon

Longman

Longman Group Ltd
London

*Associated companies, branches and representatives
throughout the world*

© Longman Group Ltd 1977

First published 1977

ISBN 0 582 64194 2

Printed in Great Britain by
Western Printing Services Limited, Bristol

To my wife and children:
Adwoa Agyeiwa, Kwabena Botwe, Yaa Amoah,
Abena Konadu, and Kwame Annor

Contents

Acknowledgements

The author and publishers are grateful to the following for permission to reproduce photographs in this book:

Ghana Information Services for plates 10 and 11; Historical Picture Service for plate 9; The Mansell Collection for plates 1 and 2; Moro Archivo Fotografico for plates 3 and 4; Paul Popper Ltd for plates 6, 14 and 16; Radio Times Hulton Picture Library for plates 5, 7, 8, 12 and 13.

The publishers are unable to trace the copyright owners of plate 15 and apologise for any infringement caused.

Abbreviations

Acc. no.	Accession number
Adm.	Administration
ARPS	Aborigines' Rights' Protection Society
CMS	Church Missionary Society
CO	Colonial Office
Conf.	Confidential
CSO	Colonial Secretary's Office
EDC	Ethiopia Defence Committee
Encl.	Enclosure
FO	Foreign Office
GCYC	Gold Coast Youth Conference
IAFA	International African Friends of Abyssinia
IASB	International African Service Bureau
LCP	League of Coloured People
NAO	Native Administration Ordinance
NNDP	Nigerian National Democratic Party
NCBWA	National Congress of British West Africa
NYM	Nigerian Youth Movement
SNA	Secretary for Native Affairs
UNIA	Universal Negro Improvement Association
WASU	West African Students' Union
WAYL	West African Youth League

Preface

One of the most significant but relatively neglected external factors and in-fluences which stimulated national consciousness in West Africa to an almost unprecedented degree and kept the spirit of Pan-Africanism from becoming dormant during the 1930s was Italy's lawless and cruel invasion of Ethiopia, one of the oldest African states and one with an ancient and proud history. Technically, the issue was an international one involving the sovereignty of a small member state of the League of Nations. West Africa became seriously involved, not directly in the diplomatic aspects of the crisis, but indirectly, and much more importantly from the African viewpoint, in the impact which the conflict had on the development of nationalist movements in this region. For, in the eyes of the most articulate West Africans and pan-Africanists of the 1930s, the Italo-Ethiopian struggle represented Fascist aggression against a 'black' state and Europe's cynical connivance at such a flagrant breach of international law. In their view the conflict was essentially a racial war; what occurred in Ethiopia directly concerned other parts of Africa and peoples of African descent throughout the world. It was another aspect of white aggression upon black, the final 'Caucasian victory'. Emotions were thus aroused by the sense of common race with distant and unknown Ethiopia, emotions in which Italy's offence was in some way merged with West African opposition to British imperialism. The conflict was, therefore, portrayed by West African nationalist politicians as an important aspect of the nationalist cause in West Africa.

Many more people than I can list here have, in one way or another, been of great assistance to me in my research for and preparation of this book, and I am deeply indebted to them all. However, I owe my principal thanks to Mr D. H. Jones of the School of Oriental and African Studies, University of London, who unofficially supervised this work in its earlier form as a London doctoral thesis; his frank and penetrating criticism as well as his friendly advice and encourage-ment have been invaluable. One of my greatest debts is to Mr Christopher H. Fyfe of the Centre of African Studies, University of Edinburgh, who not only provided invaluable help and encouragement in the early stages of my research, but also read the whole manuscript and offered some highly constructive criticisms and comments. Among those to whom I am especially grateful are Dr Christopher Clapham, Department of Politics, University of Lancaster; Mr John Dunn of the African Studies Centre, Cambridge; Professor B. J. Dudley, Department of Political Science, University of Ibadan; and Professor A. A. Boahen, Department of History, University of Ghana, Legon, who read the original manuscript, and suggested improvements covering matters of style, fact and logic; their advice, opinions and criticisms were of crucial help in creating the framework of the book. I owe much to the helpful comments and corrections made by Professor J. E. Wiredu of the Department of Philosophy, University of Ghana, Legon, and Professor Claude Welch, Department of Political Science, State University of New York at Buffalo, United States. Any errors or absurdities which remain are entirely my own responsibility. I also profited greatly from my contact with the following friends and fellow-re-searchers whose sense and criticism I deeply respected: Dr J. Ayodele Langley, formerly of Edinburgh University, but now in the public service of his country, the Gambia; Dr P. O. Esedebe, University of Sierra Leone, Freetown; and Professors T. N. Tamuno and E. A. Ayandele, both of the University of Ibadan, Nigeria. At an earlier stage of the work I was able to interview, and in some cases re-interview, several people who had participants' views of the events I wished to study, and I am deeply indebted to these protagonists, some of whom also placed at my disposal their private papers on the subject.

Still another, and substantial, acknowledgement is due to the Research Grant Committee of the University of Ghana, Legon, and the British Council for their financial assistance during the final stages of writing the original manuscript. I am also appreciative of the co-operation and kindness received from the staff of the following: the Public Record Office, the British Museum, the Royal Institute of International Affairs, Rhodes House Library, Oxford, and the National Archives of Ghana, Nigeria and the Gambia. The substantial task of typing the earlier drafts of the manuscript was undertaken, very willingly and between other duties, by Mr S. A. Ofei of the Institute of Adult Education and Mr Paul Affum of the Department of Political Science, both of the University of Ghana, Legon. The finishing touches of this work were undertaken in the State University College at Brockport, State University of New York, where I spent the 1975 Fall Semester as a Fulbright-Hays Scholar. Special thanks are due to Mrs L. Rhody of this institution for typing the final drafts. I am also particularly grateful to my friends and colleagues of the Department of African and Afro-American Studies at Brockport for providing me with accommodation and office facilities, and many other forms of assistance throughout my stay.

Some of the material used in this work has appeared in different form in articles I have written for the *Journal of African History, African Affairs, Race, Research Review* and the *Transactions of the Historical Society of Ghana*. I wish to express my gratitude to the editors of these journals for permitting me to re-use that material in this present form.

Finally, I should like to record my sincere thanks to my wife and children who were patient enough even to put up with the long enforced separation during my various research trips to the United Kingdom and the other West African countries. The dedication of this book to them can hardly pay for the great debt of gratitude I owe them.

Introduction

Although numerous studies of world reaction to the Italian invasion of Ethiopia in 1935 have been made, most of them have dealt primarily or exclusively with the reaction of white communities to Italy's act of aggression.[1] For the most part, scholars have neglected the role played by black peoples in the affair.[2] As a consequence, it is not well known that Africans on the continent even took a significant interest in the Italo-Ethiopian conflict. The fact that black peoples all over the world were deeply concerned about the plight of the only truly independent black kingdom in the world and made sincere efforts to aid that beleaguered country is very little known. Although there exists an established generalisation that the conflict had a profound impact on the growth of nationalist movements in West Africa and development of pan-African thought and politics,[3] there has been very little investigation of the precise nature of this impact, and of the response which it evoked from political organisations.

The primary aim of this book, therefore, is to throw greater light on this much neglected aspect of the Italo-Ethiopian conflict and to stimulate further research on the subject. It seeks to present the precise nature of the impact of the Italo-Ethiopian struggle on West African nationalist thinking and movement, and to examine, particularly, the extent to which the Ethiopian question influenced the ideas of West African nationalists and fired their ambition to end colonialism. The study is limited to English-speaking West Africa, in fact to the former British colonies on the West Coast of Africa, although for purposes of comparison a brief review of the reaction of the French-speaking West Africans resident in Paris at the time[4] has been attempted.

Nationalism in British West Africa was far more vigorous than in any other colonial area south of the Sahara. Popular movements of comparable character and strength did not exist in the neighbouring colonies of France, Belgium, Portugal and Spain or in the British East African colonies where European settlers advocated white supremacy. Whereas, for instance, in English-speaking West Africa, newspapers developed as a voice to express the protest of the ruled, in East Africa they were from the beginning vehicles for the culture and concepts of the rulers; and in French-speaking West Africa, the laws concerning the press and liberty of association were very harsh. Applied vigorously, as Michael Crowder has said, 'they could lead to exile or imprisonment, a fate that befell several critics of the administration.'[5] French laws required that before anything could be published in French West Africa it must first be passed for publication by a government officer. As the British administrators in West Africa were quick to note, 'no newspaper is published' in French West Africa, despite its large European population. They were fully convinced that French colonial officers in West Africa would not pass for publication the 'type of propaganda which we allow against ourselves in the Gold Coast'.[6] Not only did the British West African colonies enjoy a considerable, though not unlimited, freedom of the press; they were also granted the rudiments of a parliamentary system (through the institution of Legislative Councils) and some measure of personal liberty and political opportunity. It was this basic difference in development of national awakening which, to a large extent, accounted for the respective attitudes of French and British West African nationalist politicians to the Italian invasion of Ethiopia.

One thing, however, must be stressed, even *ad nauseam*. It would indeed be far beyond the scope of this book to attempt an exhaustive study of the complex nature of West African nationalism as it developed during the inter-war period. Its aim is more modest: to concentrate on the Ethiopian crisis as an episode in the growth of West African political awareness. Considering the early growth of nationalist feeling in this part of Africa, it would be presumptuous to regard the Ethiopian question as a real independent factor in creating attitudes which might otherwise not have been formed. Our object is to view the crisis as a reinforcing rather than an innovative factor in the development of West African nationalism, and it is within this context that the Ethiopian episode decisively affected the fate of colonialism in West Africa. Ethiopia was employed selectively to attack specific aspects of the colonial system, the more so as it heightened still further the disillusionment of West Africans under British colonial rule.

As Peter Buckman has argued, 'Mankind is animated by discontent.'[7] Although Buckman's argument is in regard to conditions prevailing in 'advanced capitalist' societies, the question of 'discontent' or disillusionment was even more crucial and perhaps more widely felt in colonial African territories where the political, social, and economic parameters of the colonial subjects were defined by people other than their own. As a manifestation of their profound disaffection with the existing situation, Africans throughout the colonial period expressed resentment at their subjugation and domination by the European powers in diverse ways. Colonial rule introduced unwelcome changes that upset their traditional, social, economic, and political systems. Even when, at the turn of the nineteenth century, Africans were reconciled in 'a fatalistic way to the fact of subjugation', the articulate groups and individuals 'resented that conciliation, the nature of compromises that were daily made, and, perhaps most of all, the gross failures of colonialism to validate its own self-proclaimed moral justification for the assumption of hegemony.'[8] Although colonialism was questioned everywhere in Africa by the peoples affected, responses to the complexity and authoritarian nature of the colonial regime were most intense and pervasive in the British colonies along the West Coast. In this part of Africa there were a group of highly educated colonial subjects who controlled the press and who, it is important to note, had also been influenced by pan-Negro ideas which had given them a strong sense of racial self-awareness. The educated elite in this region, who later established associations, congresses and pressure groups, sought in various ways to reform the alien framework of their subjugation, redress grievances endured by Africans, and claimed the right to participate in the making of decisions that affected them, if not in the whole governing process. Hence throughout, the political history of colonial West

Africa was dominated by the conflict of interest between the coloniser and the colonised, or, as René Maunier would have it, 'a clash of traditions, aspirations, feelings and judgements'.[9] Generally, this conflict revolved around the broad issues of economic resources and political order, and was aggravated by the question of race which was used as a tool in exploiting the colonial peoples through imposing upon them a system of discrimination.

It might be useful at this point to recall what Buell Gallagher said a long time ago:

> When two groups of people are engaged in a chronic conflict of interests, largely economic, centering around the problems of security and status, each group having a high degree of visibility in skin color or other group characteristics there is a conscious drawing of racial lines of demarcation and the use of the concept of race as a tool in the struggle.[10]

Although in British West Africa racial tension was not as acute as it was in other parts of Africa, where it was intensified by problems of white settlement, race was nevertheless an important factor in colonial politics. For not only was race made the symbol of cultural status, it also provided distinctions which Europeans did not hesitate to use as grounds for social discrimination against Africans. Being a symbol of cultural status, it served to classify individuals, and so to retard their advance by limiting their freedom and determining the cultural values to which they had access. In many fields, especially during the early decades of the twentieth century, race evidently provided in West Africa a rationale for promotion, domination and competition, and race prejudice also served as a convenient device for European exploitation. Colonialism was thus all the more obnoxious because of its identification with race and the systematic expropriation of the local human and natural resources without corresponding compensatory advantages to the African. Frantz Fanon typified this mixture of race and economics when he argued that in the colonies, 'the economic substructure is also a superstructure. The cause is the consequence; you are rich because you are white, you are white because you are rich.'[11]

The concept of the 'colour-line' as the foundation of the entire colonial system led inevitably to an emotional attitude of protest by the nationalist intelligentsia in West Africa who were determined to 'prove their humanity and assert their racial and cultural equality with Europeans'. It was this tendency which awakened in them the spirit of race consciousness. For not only did they become conscious of the existence of people of African descent who lived outside Africa; they also established contact with them and identified themselves with the oppressed black groups both in and outside the African continent. Such contacts and identification had a profound effect on the thinking and politics of the West African nationalists. In the first place, it broadened their intellectual horizon and led to an intensification of their political consciousness which took on a more pan-African perspective. Secondly, the manifestation of the consciousness of a common origin, a common destiny and a common purpose inspired movements of protest and threats of revolt against anything that seemed to impugn the status of the African race. Small wonder, then, that the brutal Italian attack on Ethiopia provoked vehement pan-African protest among politically conscious groups.

It is worth noting that protest and threats of revolt were not infrequent in West African colonial history. They were in fact an indirect form of defence, a verbal means of projecting violent reaction which could not be realised physically. Professor Ali Mazrui has suggested four broad categories of protest in African history: 'protests of conservation, protests of restoration, protests of transformation, and protests of corrective censure.'[12] The West African reaction to the Italo-Ethiopian conflict may be considered as a 'protest of conservation', which is defined as 'those acts or movements which are aroused by a sense of impending peril to a system of values dear to the participants'. The reaction 'is a defensive action to conserve that system of values.'[13] What West Africans in this situation wanted to 'conserve' was the symbolic significance of the ancient kingdom of Ethiopia, the metaphysical black heaven, her historic independence and her proud traditional institutions and values which were worthy of emulation. Although the protest did not achieve its desired objective, as Ethiopia was eventually conquered by Italy, nevertheless it was unique and singularly important because of its profound impact on the political aspirations of the protesters themselves.

The protest against the Italian aggression on Ethiopia was also unique and significant in another important respect: it was pan-African in sentiment, scope and activity. In other words, this kind of protest was not in the same category of traditional acts or movements of protest in African colonial history which were generally confined to a specific territory and limited to a small portion of the population. The Italian 'imperialism' in Ethiopia stimulated all-African sentiments: it was a protest of the black world. For the tales of the unjust war in Ethiopia were told not only in British West Africa, but also in the neighbouring East African colonies of Uganda, Kenya and Tanganyika,[14] in the vast territory of Egypt,[15] in the far minority, white-ruled southern Africa,[16] in the West Indies, as well as among the black communities in America,[17] Britain and Europe,[18] with varying degrees of intensity and motivation. This protest, therefore, was a practical expression of the pan-African consciousness of Africans and peoples of African descent. It was also an expression of the unity of purpose and action existing among the black peoples of the world.

However, this work is devoted essentially to a detailed assessment of the pan-African protest of the British colonies on the West Coast of Africa. Much of the discussion of pan-Africanism in this study is somewhat different from the traditional approach to the subject. For we are concerned not with the complex problems of pan-Africanism, its origins, evolution, and ideas,[19] but with practical pan-Africanism, or a variety of pan-African activity. To a great extent, therefore, this study attempts to illustrate much of T. Ras Makonnen's view of pan-Africanism when he writes: 'At the grassroots, pan-Africanism meant that, whatever their country, blacks should be able to look after each other.'[20] This practical aspect of the pan-African concept has hitherto not received adequate attention from scholars.

II

The sources used for this study may be grouped into three categories; first, the nationalist press in West Africa; secondly, printed primary sources, official archival as well as published material; and thirdly, private papers and interviews.

The press in British West Africa which had flourished for many years provided a valuable source of information for the present study. It was the main factor which determined the popular view of the crisis and its significance,

Stating the case for the suitability of the press as source material for writing the story of the events in colonial Africa, Christopher Fyfe has written:

> The historian of a Colony has to draw much of his information from dispatches or reports written for the Government at home. They often tell a one-sided story. A governor may spare the Secretary of State unpleasant details that might lead to unwelcome inquiry; the authors of official reports often tend to have an eye fixed on objects beyond their immediate terms of reference. A country may be on the verge of revolution yet not a hint of it appears officially. But the Press, if not deliberately silenced, speaks with no such muted voice; the undercurrents officials conceal, bubble openly in the newspapers.[21]

I am anxious to stress that this is particularly relevant to the West African reaction to the Italo-Ethiopian dispute. Throughout the period of the crisis the press revealed many important details of which the official despatches omitted to take notice. The governors tended to ignore the intensity of the nationalist attitudes to the Ethiopian question, even though this was often detailed in the reports of the police, district and provincial commissioners submitted to them from time to time.

That the newspapers studied for this work are emotional expressions of deeply-felt grievances of the colonial subjects there can be no doubt. The press was perhaps the only imported institution which was almost exclusively in the hands of the educated class who were thoroughly dissatisfied with the colonial establishment and were therefore impatient for change and reform. It was the most potent instrument used in the propagation of nationalist ideas and racial consciousness, and thus performed a crucial role in the nationalist awakening in British West Africa. Throughout the period covered by this study, the press appeared to take its job very seriously, and quite openly regarded itself as filling the role allotted to it by Burke – 'the fourth estate of the realm'. Editorially, this claim was often made by implication and sometimes directly, and a strong sense of responsibility, and of vocation was frequently noticeable. It was sometimes claimed that in the absence of representative government the newspapers were the voice of the people. Supporting this claim by the press, Dr J. B. Danquah, the remarkable Ghanaian traditionalist, lawyer, philosopher, scholar and nationalist politician, declared in a public speech on 6 March 1934 that the duty of a newspaper was to 'serve as a linguist, an intermediary between the Government and the people, the people and the Government'. A newspaper proprietor himself, Danquah held that it was the responsibility of the press to interpret 'the doings and goings on of the Government to the people' and to express 'the wishes and desires of the people to the Government'.[22] Characteristically, Danquah was arguing from the concept of liberal democracy.

Intensive press campaigns in the cause of nationalism undoubtedly gave articulation to existing sentiment; with equal certainty they strengthened such sentiments as already existed and propagated more. Thus, in spite of the accusation by the Colonial Office that the press was highly emotional, prejudiced, biased, and that it generally lacked objectivity in its attitudes towards the white man and the whole colonial society, the West African press nevertheless served as a useful vehicle for the expression of nationalist feelings about the Ethiopian affair. Although physical, psychological and legal factors impinged on its efficiency and on its freedom, it would appear from the bold and forthright statements made therein about the colonial administration that the press operated in an atmosphere of considerable freedom. The study of it is thus able to give us an appreciable insight into the African thinking about the Ethiopian conflict. For this reason much use has been made of the West African nationalist press, although I have tried to avoid the error of taking its utterances at face value.

The second category of sources are the official documents at the national archives of the West African countries, printed primary sources mostly at the British Museum and the Royal Institute of International Affairs (London), together with the Colonial Office and Foreign Office records at the Public Record Office in London. I have relied heavily on both the Colonial Office and Foreign Office records for information on colonial governments' regulations and attitudes towards the West African reaction to the Ethiopian crisis in particular, and the West African nationalist movements in general. The material at the national archives of West Africa has varied in richness and quantity, according to specific countries, and this appears to have been so because of the different stages of national consciousness in the four British colonies on the West Coast of Africa.

Thirdly, much use has also been made of private papers, many of which have hitherto not been consulted, and still remain in the private possession of friends and families of those West African nationalist leaders who were active at the time of the Italian invasion of Ethiopia. Apart from allowing me to consult their respective papers, interviews with some of the key protagonists still living proved extremely valuable sources of information. The two informative private papers consulted in Britain were the 'Creech Jones Papers' at the Rhodes House Library, Oxford, and the 'Reginald Bridgeman Papers' in the owner's possession in Middlesex.[23]

Born in 1891 in Bristol, Arthur Creech Jones, a Labour M.P. who was keenly interested in colonial matters, succeeded G. H. Hall as Secretary of State for the Colonies in October 1946, and remained in the post until his defeat in the General Election of 1950. In 1940, as a member of the executive Committee of the Fabian Society, Creech Jones became the first chairman of the Fabian Colonial Bureau, formed at the instigation of Dr Rita Hinden, who became its secretary, to encourage research into colonial problems. Since entering Parliament in 1935, Creech Jones received copies of letters, petitions and memoranda sent to the Colonial Office by the nationalist leaders of almost all the British colonies and dependencies. The 'Creech Jones Papers' thus contain very useful material about such nationalist agitators as Wallace Johnson, Nnamdi Azikiwe, and J. B. Danquah, and organisations such as the West African Youth League and the International African Service Bureau. Reginald Francis Orlando Bridgeman (1884-1968) was a former British diplomat, who moved by way of the anti-imperialist left to the British Communist Party (CPGB) and the League Against Imperialism. His private papers contain some correspondence from the West African Students' Union and Marcus Garvey; newspaper cuttings and speeches on the Italo-Ethiopian crisis; some publications of the West African Students' Union and Marcus Garvey's Universal Negro Improvement Association and African Communities League. The 'Bridgeman Papers' also contain some early numbers of *The Negro Worker* edited by George Padmore, as well as a substantial amount of material on the League Against Imperialism of which Bridgeman was the secretary of the British section.

This book on the whole is an attempt to illustrate how an external issue can be used in domestic politics to advantage. It is the West African counterpart of Professor George Shepperson's observation of the importance of external factors in the development of nationalism in British Central Africa.[24] Chapter 1, which is also a background chapter, examines the symbolic significance of the concept of Ethiopia, while Chapter 2 surveys the initial West African reactions to the crisis against a broad background of protests organised in Britain and France. Chapter 3 deals with the attitudes of colonial subjects to crisis diplomacy. In Chapters 4 and 5 the actual movements of protest are discussed in greater detail. Chapter 6, the concluding chapter, raises several interesting issues which decisively reinforce the observation of A. G. Hopkins that the political reactions of the West African colonial subjects during the inter-war period must not be considered merely as a 'background' to the more publicised events of the post-Second World War period,[25] but in fact as the same generic type of phenomenon. For, indeed, a full understanding of the post-1945 political conditions in West Africa must inevitably entail an appreciation of this period of 'political incubation'.

1 For example, see F. D. Laurens, *France and the Italo-Ethiopian Crisis, 1935–45*, The Hague, 1967; also, Brice Harris, Jr, *The United States and the Italo-Ethiopian Crisis*, California, 1964.

2 As far as I can discover the only works dealing exclusively with the reaction of persons of African descent to the crisis are the two rather sketchy articles by Robert G. Weisbord entitled, 'British West Indian Reaction to the Italian-Ethiopian War: An Episode in Pan-Africanism', *Caribbean Studies*, x, 1, April 1970 pp. 34–41; 'Black American and the Italian-Ethiopian Crisis: An Episode in Pan-Negroism', *The Historian*, xxiv, 2 February 1972, pp. 230–41. These two articles have recently been reprinted in R. G. Weisbord, *Ebony Kinship: Africa, Africans, and the Afro-American*, Westport, 1973, ch. 3, pp. 89–114. Another study on this subject is R. W. Stott's unpublished M.A. thesis, 'The American Negro and the Italo-Ethiopian Crisis, 1934–1936', Howard University, Washington, D.C., 1966.

3 See, for example, Vincent B. Thompson, *Africa and Unity: The Evolution of Pan-Africanism*, London, 1969, pp. 31–2; James Coleman, *Nigeria: Background to Nationalism*, Berkeley, 1958, pp. 209–10; J. B. Webster and A. A. Boahen, *The Revolutionary Years: West Africa Since 1800*, London, 1967, pp. 304–5.

4 Nationalist activities of French-speaking West Africans before 1945 were mainly centred in France, and were carried out by those West Africans living in France. J. S. Spiegler has completed an unpublished doctoral dissertation in Oxford on this subject entitled 'Aspects of Nationalist Thought Among French-speaking West Africans, 1921–1939' (1968). Also, J. Ayo Langley has treated this subject in ch. 7 of his *Pan-Africanism and Nationalism in West Africa, 1900–1945*, London, 1973.

5 M. Crowder, *West Africa Under Colonial Rule*, London, 1968, p. 438.

6 H. S. Newlands, Chief Commissioner of Ashanti, Gold Coast, for example, made this clear in his despatch of 5 January 1933 to the British Under Secretary of State for Colonies; C.O.96/707/21613.

7 Peter Buckman, *The Limits of Protest*, London, 1970, p. 13.

8 Robert I. Rotberg and Ali Mazrui (eds.), *Protest and Power in Black Africa*, New York, 1970, p. xxiii.

9 René Maunier, *The Sociology of Colonies: An Introduction to the Study of Race Contact*, London, 1949, p. 81.

10 Buell G. Gallagher, 'American Caste and the Negro' in Alain Locke and B. J. Stern, eds, *When Peoples Meet: A Study in Race and Culture Contacts*, New York, 1959, p. 244.

11 Frantz Fanon, *The Wretched of the Earth*, New York, 1968, p. 40.

12 Ali A. Mazrui, 'Toward a Theory of Protest' in Rotberg and Mazrui (eds.), pp. 1185–96.

13 *Ibid.*, p. 1185.

14 Details of the reaction of the East African Colonies to the Italo-Ethiopian War are available in F.O. 371/20154.

15 For the response of Egypt to the conflict, see *The Round Table* (London), No. 102, March 1936. Also, F.O. 371/19073; F.O. 371/19064; and F.O. 371/19116.

16 Reactions of South Africa is detailed in House of Assembly *Debates* (South Africa), vol. 26, 31 January 1936. Also, F.O. 371/20155; F.O. 371/20156, etc.

17 For details, see Weisbord, *Ebony Kinship*, pp. 89–114.

18 The black protest in France and Britain is discussed in ch. 2, sections 2 and 3 above.

19 For a recent full-scale study of pan-Africanism, see I. Geiss, *The Pan-African Movement.*, London, 1974.

20 T. Ras Makonnen, *Pan-Africanism From Within*, London, 1973, p. xvi.

21 Christopher Fyfe, 'The Sierra Leone Press in the Nineteenth Century', *Sierra Leone Studies*, new series, 8, June 1957, p. 226.

22 'Danquah Papers', in private custody of Mrs Elizabeth Danquah, Accra, Ghana.

23 The author gladly acknowledges his gratitude to his friend and fellow-researcher, Dr Peter Esedebe of the University of Sierra Leone, Freetown, for making the Bridgeman Papers available to him in London in 1967.

24 George Shepperson, 'External Factors in the Development of African Nationalism, with Particular Reference to British Central Africa', *Phylon*, xxii, 3, 1961.

25 A. G. Hopkins, *An Economic History of West Africa*, London, 1973, p. 267.

CHAPTER ONE

Ethiopianism in West African political thought

To appreciate the extent of West African response to the Italian invasion of Ethiopia in 1935, it is vital to understand the concept of Ethiopianism in West African nationalist thought and politics, as well as the factors which heightened this concept at the time of the Italian attack on Ethiopia. A study of these factors is essential because racial sentiment alone cannot explain the attitudes of West Africans to the conflict. Their reaction to the Ethiopian question was no isolated event, but the culmination of a long period of agitation against European domination and exploitation. Towards the end of the nineteenth century, European racism, heightened by the racial theories associated with the long debate on the abolition of the Slave Trade and by European imperialism, gave West Africans a new conception of themselves: they began to see themselves in some kind of world perspective, and to think of themselves no longer in terms of small communities but as people belonging to a despised 'race'. This increased racial awareness found expression throughout the inter-war years, particularly during the period of the Great Depression and the ascendancy of Fascism and the doctrine of racial superiority in the 1930s. It is against this background that the West African conception of Ethiopia assumed a wider dimension.

Political symbolism of Ethiopia

The inferior status imposed upon Africans in several parts of the world, and the social discrimination which acted against nearly all Africans who had been in contact with European societies, evoked in response a psychological complex which fastened strongly upon the compensating idea of an independent African kingdom of Ethiopia under an African Christian king. The maintenance of Ethiopian independence was therefore of vital importance for the entire African continent. Although Ethiopia herself was largely isolated from most of the continent by the facts of geography and by the colonial domination of the rest of Africa, her existence as the oldest African state, and one with an ancient and romantic history, was of symbolic significance to all black peoples. To many of them, the black race, because of a colour distinction established by a 'bitter armed' white race, 'finds itself an exploited mass'; and Ethiopia, sole remnant of black greatness, as 'Italy is of Roman power', became a symbol, a rallying point of the black race.[1] Thus, although there was little chance of Ethiopia interesting herself in other African countries during the pre-colonial and colonial periods, the concept of 'Ethiopia' had a significant meaning for the black peoples as a whole. It was first employed to refer to the darker-skinned peoples in general, and Africans in particular. It was also used in the literature of the eighteenth and nineteenth centuries as synonymous with Africa.[2]

Ethiopia's status and value in the eyes of the blacks was enhanced by Biblical authority, especially the oft-quoted 68th Psalm: 'He hath scattered the peoples that delight in war. Princes shall come out of Egypt; Ethiopia shall haste to stretch out her hands unto God.' These revolutionary words, which gave additional impetus and rationalisation for 'Ethiopia', became a message of hope, a standard slogan for Negro aspirations, and the passage was echoed and re-echoed in black nationalist literature.[3] Indeed, all 'Ethiopian' references in the Bible which had a 'liberatory promise' greatly appealed to all black peoples, especially those in America and the West Indies, as these references 'showed the black man in a dignified and humane light.'[4] It is not at all surprising, then, that writings of such eminent blacks as the brilliant pan-Africanists Edward Wilmot Blyden, W. E. B. DuBois, Marcus Garvey and J. A. Rogers are replete with reference to Ethiopia's legacy.[5] By the early nineteenth century, at a time when the Negro anti-slavery movement was developing in America and the West Indies, the term 'Ethiopian' seemed to have become associated with ideas of liberty and liberation.[6] Conceived in the Biblical sense, then, the concept of 'Ethiopia' came to have a deep sentimental connotation.

It was natural, therefore, for Africans to describe the independent African churches which emerged throughout many areas of Africa at the end of the nineteenth century as 'Ethiopian Churches'. 'Ethiopianism' was the term used to describe the Ethiopian Church movement, that is, the establishment and operation of Christian Churches according to 'African ideals, methods and objectives, by and for Africans'.[7] The fact that 'Ethiopia' is mentioned in the Bible gave antiquity to the claim of the new African churches, and was thought of as a sanction of this claim. Although there is no single explanation of 'Ethiopianism',[8] the term was applied originally to the secessionist and independent native churches in South Africa in the 1890s.[9] To the whites of southern Africa, the Ethiopian Church movement was nothing less than a pan-African conspiracy under the guise of religion. An intelligence report on the movement stated, among other things, that evidence was 'constantly coming to hand that the Ethiopian movement continues to extend, not as a religious one but a secret political organisation'.[10] This is not surprising for Ethiopianism in this region was fundamentally racial, arising out of the colour-bar policy of the white rulers. The racial policy of the white rulers drove the 'separatist' churches to become media for distinct anti-white or anti-government movements employing 'terrorism and persecution'. Later, during the early decades of the present century, various groups in the United States, such as the Peace Movement of Ethiopia, the Back-to-Abyssinia Movement,[11] and the Ras Tafari Movement in Jamaica,[12] were organised around the concept of Ethiopianism. To these groups, Ethiopia, the ancient empire, stood for an inheritance of which they felt they had 'been defrauded'. They felt themselves denied a full share of citizenship in the country of their birth; Ethiopia 'is the nation to which they really belong; here is the culture truly their own.'[13]

It can be seen from this that the concept of 'Ethiopia' was used rather loosely by Africans and peoples of African descent which makes it difficult to make a clear distinction between 'Ethiopia' as a specific African country, and Ethiopia as mentioned in the Bible. For example, in the United States, the Back-to-Abyssinia Movement, a semi-religious and nationalistic organisation founded in 1919, claimed that its mission was 'marked in the Bible' and that one of its principal goals was emigration to Africa, particularly to Ethiopia.[14] However, awareness of Ethiopia as an independent African state was heightened considerably by the country's triumphant success in repelling invasion, and in having remained unconquered throughout the centuries. This made the identification of Ethiopia as an African country with 'liberated Africa', as evidenced in the Biblical references not only comprehensible but also reassuring. This identification was also spurred by an increasing African interest in, and knowledge of, the ancient kingdom.

After the victory over Italy at Adowa in 1896, Ethiopia acquired a special importance in the eyes of Africans as the only surviving independent African state, just as Japan was to become psychologically important to Asians when it defeated Russia, a 'white' nation, in 1905.[15] After Adowa, Ethiopia became emblematic of African valour and resistance, the bastion of prestige and hope to thousands of Africans who were experiencing the full shock of European conquest, and were beginning to search for an answer to the myth of African inferiority. The fact that Ethiopia had a long recorded history, an ancient Coptic Christian faith, a monarchy which claimed descent from King Solomon, and internationally recognised diplomatic status, also helped to increase her prestige.

To the articulate West African nationalist intelligentsia of lawyers, merchants, journalists, doctors and clergymen, who had since the turn of the century persistently sought to share political power with the colonial ruler, the role of 'Ethiopia' or 'Ethiopianism' in nationalist thought and politics was great and inspiring. In this part of Africa, both the political and religious importance of 'Ethiopianism' were in evidence. West African 'Ethiopianism', therefore, acquired a different meaning from that prevalent in South and Central African settings, where the whites saw it as a movement which was propagating 'detrimental racial doctrines' incompatible with loyalty and peace.[16] Although in West Africa also, Ethiopianism became fundamentally racial, this was in a peculiar way. West African Ethiopianism never became anti-government, and although it was anti-white, it was not on the same scale as in Central and South Africa, probably because West Africa did not experience white settlement. Generally, Ethiopianism was viewed in West Africa as forming a major ingredient of early African nationalism. In separate African Churches, Africans did and could protest against imperial rule and build articulate leadership to oppose the domineering and discriminatory actions of the colonial officials.

The West African concept of Ethiopianism as a religious basis for African nationalism has been ably dealt with in detail and need not detain us.[17] Quite recently, Professor Ayandele has expanded his view on this subject, and has convincingly traced the roots of Ethiopianism in West Africa to the establishment of the Native Pastorate in Sierra Leone in 1861 by the Church Missionary Society as an attempt to expand the missionary work in Africa.[18] Bishop James Johnson, undoubtedly one of the leading pioneers of West African Ethiopianism, saw in this establishment the opportunity of expounding his politico-religious beliefs and of setting up an independent pure Native Pastorate, but this did not mean a breakaway from the Anglican Communion. The process towards the development of a native Episcopate was to be an evolution, rather than a revolution. He saw in the Native Pastorate infinite possibilities for the emancipation of Africa from alien rule and the training of Africans in the art of self-government. Above all, the Native Pastorate was in James Johnson's view 'the

11

first institutional process in the evolution of Pan-Africanism'.[19] James Johnson employed the term 'Ethiopianism' to describe his 'nationalistic thoughts and activities'. He and his followers saw Africa as the 'Biblical Ethiopia which "shall soon stretch forth her hands unto God" ' and Africans as 'Ethiopians.'[20]

Ethiopianism in West Africa, then, was seen as a mark of self-assertion against foreign control, and a mark of racial adolescence. It was a symbol of freedom and emancipation. West African Ethiopianism 'awakened the dream of a nation-state to be controlled ultimately by Africans'. It thus claimed a share of political power, and, in some West African countries, it took its place in those political associations that had been founded and led by educated Africans. In the Gold Coast, for instance, the educated leaders of the Aborigines' Rights' Protection Society, a proto-nationalist movement founded in 1897, took a keen interest in Ethiopianism. S. R. B. Atto-Ahuma, an early Gold Coast nationalist and journalist, who was at one time secretary of the Aborigines' Rights Protection Society, showed the authentic Ethiopian historical spirit in his writings on the African past.[21] It is in this sense, too, that we can appreciate Omoniyi's defence of Ethiopianism as a struggle between those who recognised their claims to an equal participation in social and political rights with others, and those who for themselves and their order asserted 'a certain fictitious superiority of race, and claim for it as a consequence of causes, however accidental, exclusive consideration and special privileges. . . .'[22] A Yoruba student of the University of Edinburgh, Prince Bandele Omoniyi, who was disgusted about such phrases as the 'partition of Africa from the philanthropic or humanitarian motive', was one of the early uncompromising critics of British colonial administration in West Africa.

Another distinctive feature of Ethiopianism in West Africa was the desire to save cherished indigenous values from what were considered to be the disintegrating influences of the various European missions. Many West African nationalists such as the Sierra Leonean Rev. Orishatuke Faduma, challenged the general assumption that in order to civilise and Christianise the African, 'he must be foreignized'.[23] As one who believed in 'native Christianity', Faduma at the Congress on Africa held in Atlanta in 1896 vehemently deplored the tendency of 'native' converts and evangelists to abandon their indigenous names, dress and food in favour of foreign ones.[24]

This view was expounded with greater force and emphasis in the writings, speeches and sermons of the two staunchest disciples of Edward Blyden – Mojola Agbebi, the renowned Yoruba Baptist minister, divine church reformer and political agitator, and J. E. Casely Hayford, the eminent Gold Coast nationalist politician, patriot and a leading pan-Africanist of the period. As spokesmen for early African nationalism on an international plane, Agbebi and Hayford frequently invoked the concept of Ethiopianism as a defence of Africa's traditional institutions and culture. Founder and first President of the Independent Native Baptist Union of West Africa, and of the Native Baptist Church, the first breakaway independent African Church in Nigeria, Mojola Agbebi held that the Christian religion introduced by missionaries was foreign in thought and practice, and that what Africa needed was a religion with roots in the teaching of Christ but African in conception, interpretation and control. Also, because of the narrow-minded restrictions of much white missionary activity and its frequent racialism, he lamented that African Christians had become strangers in their own country and 'aliens at their father's house'. Agbebi considered this to be a disgrace of Africa which the sons of Africa were duty bound to wipe off. Christianity was not driven to Africa, it came as an 'interested friend to reside in the realms of the blacks', for the prophecy was that 'Ethiopia shall *suddenly* stretch out her hands unto God, not that someone will stretch out her hands for her. . . .'[25] He lucidly expatiated on this theme in his most impressive and widely publicised sermon of 21 December 1902, on the occasion of the first anniversary of the African Bethel Church in Lagos, when he declared, among other things:

> African Christians dance to foreign music in their social festivities, they sing to foreign music in their churches, they march to foreign music in their funerals, and use foreign instruments to cultivate their musical aspirations. . . . We are come to the times when religious developments demand original songs and original tunes from the African Christian . . . (for) no one race or nation can fix the particular kind of tunes which will be universally conducive to worship. . . . In the carrying out of the function of singing, therefore, let us always remember that we are Africans, and that we ought to sing African songs, and that in African style and fashion. . . . The vernacular of a country is the proper vehicle of thought of that country. Cultivate and make effective use of your mother-tongue.[26]

Thus, Agbebi attacked the superimposition of European standards upon African ways of life. He believed that the adoption of some features might tend to stifle the creativity of the acculturating group with regard to that feature and because of this view he believed it judicious to use original hymns in worship. Similarly, he questioned the right of one nation to name the particular tune which would be conducive to worship in another. In his view, tunes and songs 'depend on the frame of mind, the breadth of soul, the experiences of life, the attitude of faith, and the latitude of love of the individual.'[27] Mojola Agbebi argued that it was not until after Christianity had ceased to be 'London-ward and New York-ward but Heaven-ward' that Downing Street or the Colonial Office would be absent in the political polemics of the West African native. The concept of independence from alien control was at the centre of Mojola Agbebi's exposition of the African Church. He strongly believed that any form of control of one people by another could not be supported on Christian grounds, and it was in the Church that he believed the emancipation of Africa should begin. Thus, like James Johnson's, Mojola Agbebi's Ethiopianism was both a religious and political concept with greater emphasis on the latter.

Similarly, in the Gold Coast, a number of separatist churches, entirely West African in inspiration and membership, were established in the latest part of the nineteenth and early twentieth centuries. In 1898, for example, the African Methodist Episcopal Zion Church, which was classified as 'Ethiopian' in that it rejected Mission Church authority, was brought to Cape Coast from America on the initiative of Bishop John Bryan Small. But its rapid spread on the coast was largely due to the evangelistic zeal of the Rev. Frank Atta Osam Pinanko, who became founder of the Church in Cape Coast in 1903 and remained the Presiding Elder for forty-three years. In the same period, the Rev. Mark Christian Hayford commenced work for the establishment of the Baptist Church and Mission in Cape Coast, the first African Church to be founded in the country, out of the funds he had raised in Britain, Canada, and America. The Rev. Hayford received much inspiration and support from Mojola Agbebi,

Chief Coker, Dr A. Savage, and also from his brothers J. E. Casely Hayford and Ernest James Hayford. Author of *West Africa and Christianity*, published by the Baptist Tract and Book Society of London in 1900, and of *The Baptist Church and Mission and the Christian Army of the Gold Coast*, also published in London in 1913, the Rev. Hayford, who was ordained by Mojola Agbebi in 1898, was the Secretary of the Native Baptist Union of West Africa of which Agbebi was the President, and the Rev. M. T. C. Lawson of Sierra Leone, the Vice-President. This was constituted in 1899 and comprised twenty-one churches. Most of these small churches aimed at complete independence of European authority and standards of conduct.[28]

The concept of Ethiopianism formed the basis of the philosophy of Casely Hayford, as it did for Mojola Agbebi. In *Ethiopia Unbound: Studies in Race Emancipation*, published in London in 1911, he gave the concept of Ethiopianism 'something of a new ideological dimension'. This volume contained Casely Hayford's personal profession of faith in the black race. Like Mojola Agbebi, Casely Hayford believed that Africa's redemption was to be its own work. He saw colonial Africa as 'Ethiopia chained'; but he contended that, with Africans assuming control of their own affairs and developing their indigenous institutions, fettered Ethiopia would be unbound and eventually emerge as a giant among other nations.

The term 'Ethiopia' also found currency in speeches and writings of the later West African nationalists. Whenever they referred to the destiny and aspirations of the black race, or to the special qualities and abilities of the African, these nationalists invoked Ethiopia as a symbol of hope, and linked it with expressions of faith in the survival and development of the African. As Casely Hayford's nationalist newspaper said in an editiorial in 1924, 'Today when we speak of our prospects we speak of the prospects of the entire Ethiopian race. By the Ethiopian race we mean the sons and daughters of Africa scattered throughout the world.'[29] Besides, to many nationalists, the term 'Ethiopia' was symbolic of African pride and racial achievements. Hence, in his poem entitled *ACHIMOTA*, written in commemoration of the opening of the school, J. B. Danquah, the great Ghanaian nationalist politician about whom much will be said later, declared:

> Return, Ethiop, the dark age is past
> That veiled renown appraised at birth of time
> And kept from view thy science and arts sublime
> By this age claimed for beauty unsurpassed.[30]

Using 'Ethiopia' in the Ethiopianist manner as a synonym for black Africa, and the 'Ethiopian' for the African or Negro, Danquah proclaimed that there was hope for the black race. He was of the view that given adequate opportunities, a congenial environment and better conditions of life, the Ethiopian would not only attain the high level of progress found in the modern world, but would also emerge under the pressure of necessity, as the leading light in the world in generations yet unborn.[31] Like Casely Hayford and Mojola Agebi, Danquah incessantly repeated that Negroes had a history and a culture of which they could be proud. He dismissed the idea of inherent Negro inferiority to other races which was the major theme of social Darwinism in the latter part of the nineteenth century. He argued that actively as well as passively the Negro had contributed much to the world. He had aroused the world to a higher level of ethical idealism and to a far deeper humanitarian conception of life. Danquah held that the Negro had shown that slavery was no attribute of the civilised, that lynching was a perfected form of barbaric savagery, and that nothing had led more swiftly to degeneration than the assumption of racial superiority. Danquah lamented that wherever a Negro made a distinctive contribution to knowledge, or civilisation, he was looked upon by the other races as 'an exception . . . a remarkable exception', for the general view was that the African or the Negro 'cannot be human, he cannot be ordinary, he cannot be just a plain man or just a great man. He is either a plus one or a cipher, either a genius or a dunce.'[32]

Besides, in the early years of the twentieth century, not only did many West African nationalists look upon themselves as 'Ethiopians', but they also used the term 'Ethiopian' to describe the various organisations which they formed at home and abroad. In 1905, for example, West African students and their West Indian colleagues at various colleges in Liverpool formed an organisation known as the 'Ethiopian Progressive Association'. This association, which interested itself in coloured peoples, aimed at creating a bond of union between all members of the 'Ethiopian race at home and abroad'. Its other objective was to further the interest and raise the social status of the Ethiopian race, and to try to strengthen the friendly relationship of 'the said race and the other races of mankind'. Finally, the Ethiopian Progressive Association aimed at discussing matters of vital importance concerning Africa in particular and the Negro race in general.[33] While there is no evidence that this association was in touch with the nationalists at home, the 'Rising Ethiopian Development Association' which was formed in the late 1920s in Chicago in the United States, was in regular correspondence with such an important Gold Coast chief as Prempeh I, the exiled King of Ashanti. This association, comprising the Fanti and Ashanti students of the Gold Coast studying in Chicago, was founded by Kwesi Nyamikye Kuntu, who became its president. In August 1927, the Rising Ethiopian Development Association sent to Prempeh, Kumasihene, 'a gold watch with your royal name inscribed on', and welcomed him from his return from the Seychelles Island where he had lived in exile since 1900. In return, King Prempeh sent the president of the association a pair of Ashanti sandals.[34] Throughout many of these West African associations used the term 'Ethiopia' or 'Ethiopian' without any reference to a particular African country.

However, to such politically-minded nationalists as J. B. Danquah, Ethiopia as a country was a symbol of political independence. As he proudly wrote in 1927, Ethiopia 'is a purely independent African Kingdom' which shared equality of vote with Britain and France in the Assembly of the League of Nations.[35] Many articulate nationalists therefore identified Ethiopia with the Ethiopia of the Bible and the Queen of Sheba, an identification reinforced by the news of the Emperor Haile Selassie's coronation in 1930. It was not un-natural, therefore, that West African nationalists identified the future in-dependence of African countries with Ethiopia, 'the only oasis in a desert of rank subjugation from the avaricious hands of a foreign domination'.[36] By the time of the Italian invasion of Ethiopia, Haiti and Liberia, the other two in-dependent black nations in the world, were virtually disregarded as sources of inspiration and hope to black peoples. Haiti, for instance, gained her freedom from the United States at the price of shouldering an enormous debt which threatened to 'enslave her for many decades'. Liberia, too, was practically mortgaged to the Firestone Rubber Company after being threatened with absorption by both France and Great Britain.[37] And, as will be discussed later, just before the Ethiopian crisis there was an open demand that Liberia be placed under the League of Nations or under the control of foreign commission, a demand repeated during the House of Lords debate on the Liberia question in March 1932.[38]

Thus, neither Liberia nor Haiti appealed to the West African nationalist thoughts and politics. This was brought home by William Esuman-Gwira Sekyi, popularly known as Kobina Sekyi, one of the leading figures of the Gold Coast nationalist intelligentsia, a remarkable lawyer, writer, traditionalist and controversialist.[39] Sekyi argued that Liberia and Haiti had failed in the task of nation-building precisely because they were 'artificial' states created by 'artificial' means and maintained by methods equally 'artificial'. He felt that both countries lacked the impulse to remain truly sovereign in a world dominated by Europe. According to him, Haiti found it very difficult to maintain herself in the 'foreign and unsympathetic environment in which she found herself when unfree'. Liberia, too, was weighed down by her American training and her inevitable idea that she was a 'better person than the aboriginal whom she was to treat with as little consideration as possible'. Sekyi further argued that Liberia and Haiti, being primarily African and only secondarily American, 'should have sought to Africanise America instead of Americanising Africa.'[40] Because of this peculiar position of the two independent black states, Sekyi held that Ethiopia was undoubtedly the 'only country of promise' to West Africa:

> In Abyssinia we are likely to discover a great deal even in the nature of tradition that cannot but be useful to us in our present condition, and it is a country well worth a visit. Visits to Abyssinia are likely to be beneficial in many other respects.[41]

Moreover, unlike Haiti or Liberia, Ethiopia had kept comparatively free of debt, had preserved her political autonomy, had begun to reorganise her ancient polity, and was in many ways an example and a promise of what 'a native people' untouched by modern exploitation and race prejudice might do.

In 1935, therefore, Ethiopia had become in the words of Jomo Kenyatta 'the sole remaining pride of Africans and Negroes in all parts of the world'.[42] She was a spiritual inspiration. The future of the whole of the black race was therefore seen to be involved with the destiny of Ethiopia. The great importance which West African nationalist politicians at the time attached to this ancient kingdom was better expressed by Nnamdi Azikiwe, one of the pioneers of post-1945 African nationalism. In an illuminating study, Azikiwe referred to Ethiopia as representing the type of government which the 'forefathers of Africans established on this continent'. To him the continued existence of Ethiopia after its contemporaries and their descendants had vanished from political history, 'is, and should be, an object of admiration'. It also showed that black man, as demonstrated in the political history of the Ethiopians, 'has political capacity'.[43]

Thus, to the articulate colonial West African, the existence of African freedom somewhere, anywhere, was a relevant, nay a vital, fact. Apart from striking deep chords of racial awareness, Ethiopia was 'the shrine enclosing the last sacred spark of African political freedom, the impregnable rock of black resistance against white invasion, a living symbol, an incarnation of African independence.'[44] For Africans and peoples of African descent, Ethiopia had become 'the living exponent and testimony of the innate puissance of the black race'.[45] The Italian invasion of Ethiopia brought about the closer identification of Africans and peoples of African descent with Ethiopia, a country which they had at last learnt to see as a solid island of freedom in the stormy waters of colonial oppression against which they were themselves struggling. This identification of the Ethiopians with the oppressed peoples of Africa and the oppressed peoples of Africa with Ethiopia was a significant factor in the response of West Africans to the Italian attack on Ethiopia. The Italian action provided a unity of feeling among the blacks, for the African Negro seemed to possess a certain rudimentary sense of race-solidarity. It was considered immediately as an attack against the whole black race. For the 'whole of the Black World feels itself affected when one of the Black peoples is attacked. The law of tomorrow is the universal.'[46]

Growth of pan-African consciousness

West African nationalists' conception of Ethiopia was reinforced by one dominant strand in early twentieth century West African thought: pan-African consciousness, the consciousness of belonging to the African continent and the Negro race and the awareness of membership in that distinctive race, and the desire to maintain the integrity and assert the equality of that race. The whole continent of Africa was looked upon as a national homeland and, in consequence, West African nationalist politicians identified themselves with the problems affecting the African continent and developed a sense of affinity with national movements in other parts of the world. It was this pan-African thought which, to a large extent, formed the basis of pan-African organisations which became active instruments of protest and propaganda against colonial abuses and the rallying point for West Africans both at home and abroad during much of the inter-war years. By this time, Pan-Africanism had developed into what Wallace Johnson, who will be considered later, termed the 'opposition to the danger of "Pan-Europeanism" which was a union of all European nations who were united for the purpose of exploiting Africa'.[47] In this section, we will attempt a brief review of the institutionalised expressions of pan-Africanism which among other factors, generated the forces against the Italian attack on Ethiopia in 1935.[48]

Although West Africa had only just been subjected to white rule, the idea of pan-Africanism, however vague, had already taken some root by 1900.[49] The Pan-African Conference held in this year in London through the intitiative of Henry Sylvester Williams, a Trinidad barrister practising in London, was attended by such notable West Africans as Bishop James Johnson, J. Otonba-Payne and N. W. Holm (Nigeria), G. W. Dove (Sierra Leone), and F. R. S. Johnson, a former Liberian Attorney-General.[50] The significance of this conference was that for the first time a group of people, motivated by a common experience and emotions that befell people of their colour, were able to meet and think and feel in unison. The conference greatly impressed the budding nationalists in West Africa who gave wide coverage to it in the nationalist press.[51] These press comments, together with the intensity of interest shown by the nationalists in this first pan-African conclave, are evidence of the growing awareness of pan-African thinking in West Africa during this first decade of the present century. The nationalism of the twentieth century was becoming more complex than that of the nineteenth century; its leaders thought of themselves as belonging to a race which would, in due course, try conclusions with the white peoples of the world. Though still fragmentary and incomplete in the sense that it left untouched the teeming masses of illiterate Africa, progressive nationalism was no longer confined to one country. It was in this context that the Gold Coast Aborigines' Rights' Protection Society held a series of discussions on the possibility of convening a pan-African conference in the Gold Coast in June 1905.[52] This, however, did not materialise, as it did not succeed in arousing more than nominal interest. Nevertheless, the idea of participating in a pan-African activity or attending a pan-African gathering occupied the thoughts of many of the leaders of the Gold Coast Aborigines' Society.[53]

It was not at all suprising, then, that the Aborigines welcomed Booker T. Washington's small-scale pan-African conference on the Negro held at Tuskegee on 17–19 April 1912. The society sent as its delegate to the conference the Rev. F. A. O. Pinanko, an American-educated clergyman, and as we have noted already, the pioneer of the African Methodist Episcopal Zion Church in the Gold Coast who made 'most interesting and satisfactory reports with respect to the work being done under the general supervision of the Gold Coast Aborigines' Rights' Protection Society'.[54] The Rev. Mark C. Hayford also attended the conference as delegate of the Aborigines Society, and gave a lengthy and interesting address on the 'Progress of the Gold Coast Native', as well as a letter from his brother, J. E. Casely Hayford, the leading advocate of African self-assertion. Commenting on the 'great work' that was being done at Tuskegee as 'a mighty uplifting force for the race', Casely Hayford declared in this letter that there was 'an African nationality', and when the Aborigines of the Gold Coast and other parts of West Africa had joined forces with their black brothers in America in arriving at a national aim, purpose and aspiration, 'then indeed will it be possible for our brethren over the sea to bring home metaphorically to their nation and people a great spoil. . . .'[55] Booker T. Washington wrote to inform the Gold Coast nationalist leaders that the Gold Coast delegates made 'very fine impressions upon the delegates assembled'.[56]

Earlier, another West African, Mojola Agebi, director of the Niger Mission, had attended the First Universal Races Congress held in London in 1911. This was not really a pan-African affair, but rather a sentimental and well-wishing attempt to make for a better understanding between the various races, including the white, without challenging colonialism.[57] Pastor Agbebi, very much in the mode of the then dying Edward Blyden, presented a paper, 'The West African Problem', in which he strongly and proudly asserted the fine and distinctive attributes of the Negro race.[58] The congress brought together such members of the burgeoning pan-Africanist Movement as Tengo Jabavu from South Africa, Duse Mohamed Ali from Egypt, and ex-President Legitime of Haiti.[59]

Thus, before DuBois convened his first Pan-African Congress in Paris in 1919, pan-African movements and ideas had had a significant impact on West Africa. This had been manifested not only in the press but also in actual contributions to pan-African gatherings and activities. Contrary to the view of certain European observers,[60] West Africa was not unconcerned about the pan-African sentiments outside the confines of the African continent, neither was it outwardly acquiescent and politically passive. In general, West Africans looked beyond their borders and proclaimed the ideals of racial unity. To this may be added the role of West African delegates like L. B. Agusto, Peter Thomas, A. O. Olaribigbe, and Ibidunni Obandele (Nigeria); the Rev. E. G. Granville Sutton and the Rev. W. B. Marke (Sierra Leone) in the DuBoisian congresses.[61] The proceedings of these congresses stimulated among West Africans an awareness of belonging to a wider cause. An even greater stimulant was Marcus Garvey's movement, which excited much more interest and controversy among West African nationalist groups than DuBois's congresses. In the view of Casely Hayford, for instance, Garvey did more than any other agency to bring to the notice of world opinion 'the disabilities of the African race'.[62] In Nigeria, Garveyism attracted considerable attention, and a local branch of Garvey's Universal Negro Improvement Association was formed in Lagos in 1920.[63] Even West African businessmen became highly interested in the economic schemes of Garvey. In the Gold Coast, G. Ashie-Nikoi, later to become president of the Gold Coast Farmers' Union and a delegate to the 1945 Pan-African Congress, wrote several letters in an attempt to buy shares of the Black Star Line of Marcus Garvey.[64] Garvey's slogans such as 'Ethiopia Awake', 'Africa for Africans', and his universal Ethiopian anthem – 'Ethiopia, Thou Land of Our Fathers' – not only stirred the hearts of West Africans but also created a feeling of international solidarity among Africans and many peoples of African descent. Race consciousness was intensified, and the nationalist intelligentsia in West Africa identified themselves with this growth of 'colour consciousness' in the 1920s. To this intelligentsia of 'displaced and blocked persons', nationalism meant glorification of the Negro race. The result of all this was a growing sense, on the one hand, of hope for the coloured peoples of the world, stimulated by such news as that of Adowa and Port Arthur (where the Japanese defeated imperial Russia), and a widespread feeling, on the other, of belonging to a suffering race, including Congolese, Bantus, Japanese, Ethiopians and West Africans alike.

One other significant strand in the pan-African thought of West Africans which greatly influenced their attitudes towards the Ethiopian question was their assumption of leadership of the black world. The West African intelligentsia saw themselves as the advance guard in the awakening of racial consciousness in Africa, and as a distinct group within the British empire. Hence the political and national aspirations of the National Congress of British West Africa, which was formed during this period, were directed far beyond the boundaries of West Africa to the ideal of a larger pan-African movement, although for practical purposes, these larger and long-term objectives – the racial belligerence – were neither clearly expressed nor adequately spelt out in the London petition of the congress.[65] The West African press, on the other hand, gave repeated attention during the post-war years to evidences of Negro world solidarity.[66] Casely Hayford, the chief architect and theorist of the congress, was fully aware of the 'psychological potentialities' of the congress movement, and in his presidential speeches he repeatedly stressed its role not only in unifying the black race, but in establishing leadership for the world Negro cause at its source – that is, in Africa itself:

> . . . As a Congress, we must be in advance of the current racial thought of the day. We must, to a certain extent, be able to guide and control it. There is intense activity in racial progress in the United States and in the Islands

of the Sea. But, admittedly, in the last analysis, the right inspiration must come from the mother continent; and in no part of Africa can such inspiration be so well supplied as in the West. . . .[67]

Under West African leadership the Negro race would come together to harness the discoveries of science and make them work for the emancipation and prosperity of those who had too long been the burden-bearers for others. He told the congress members not to make the mistake of thinking that the general 'disabilities of our race in the four corners of the Earth do not concern us. . . .' On the contrary, he urged them to realise that the duty was cast upon 'us in West Africa' to lead the way in making suitable suggestions for 'amelioration of African disabilities'.[68]

West African leadership of Afro-centric thought was indeed a significant element in the early twentieth century West African nationalist activities. J. W. Quye of Gambia, another congress man,[69] and J. B. Danquah, then a student in London, expressed similar thoughts. Welcoming some distinguished West African intelligentsia to an 'At Home' function of the West African Students' Union in Great Britain, Danquah, as president of the union, remarked that West Africa had far-reaching responsibilities in regard to the future of Africa for there was more knowledge, more general advance, more material progress, and above all, more happiness in West Africa than could be found in either East or South. This being so, he maintained that the larger future of Africa could be read in the light of West African progress and prosperity. 'You cannot make a nation of Africa,' declared Danquah, 'but by securing unity in West Africa, and by securing African rights in the Western portion, you thereby raise the general standard of African welfare and lay down an ideal of life which the African in East and South will strive to realise.'[70] Like Casely Hayford, Danquah argued that if Africans were to survive, West Africa must become a nation and that it must unite under the sentiment of national progress.[71]

West African nationalist intelligentsia clearly saw the National Congress of British West Africa as a force not only in British West African affairs, but also in the affairs of the African world. They looked upon themselves as the champions of the African cause. They believed that the survival of Africans everywhere depended upon the progress and leadership of West Africa, and it was in this pan-African sentiment that the National Congress was born. The congress was not to stop at West African unity but must also give a lead in making constructive proposals for the attainment of African emancipation and redemption. Its political horizons were therefore wider than those of any other national group in Africa at the time. It was concerned with the pursuit of an African nationality which would tend to focus world opinion upon African interest generally. It was also concerned with the fortunes of Africans in various parts of the world. In short, it was a pan-African venture.

By the mid-thirties when Italy invaded Ethiopia, this pan-African consciousness in West Africa, the concept of 'we are all Africans'[72] and 'brothers in race, brothers in conflict' had received tremendous encouragement from the close contact that had developed between West Africa and the growing anti-imperialist sentiment and movement in Europe, Great Britain and other parts of the world. West African nationalist leaders were in frequent correspondence with such outstanding pan-Africanists as George Padmore,[73] and anti-imperialists like Reginald Bridgeman of the International League Against Imperialism,

Ronald Kidd of the National Council for Civil Liberties, Arnold Ward of the Negro Welfare Association and N. B. Hunter of the British Movement Against War and Fascism. These contacts were greatly stimulated by the Gold Coast agitation against the enactment by the local colonial government of the Criminal Code (Amendment) Ordinance or Sedition Bill of 1934 and the Waterworks Bill of the same year,[74] so that the constitutional fight of the Gold Coast became a point of contact between radical groups in the Gold Coast, African students' organisations in Britain and the British left wing.

The responsiveness of the left in England to the requests of the West African protest groups must be seen in terms of the prevailing political situation in England. In 1927 a Comintern-inspired world anti-imperialist conference held at Brussels had established a League Against Imperialism with branches throughout Europe. Fenner Brockway, an Independent Labour Party representative, was elected international chairman, later succeeded by James Maxton. Reginald Bridgeman was the secretary of the British section of the League. As the communist-oriented wing of the Labour Party, the Independent Labour Party had been engaged in a struggle during the early 1930s to move Labour Party opinion toward a more socialist, anti-imperialist stance on such issues as unemployment, nationalisation, Fascism and colonialism. There is no indication that Independent Labour Party leaders such as Maxton or even such anti-imperialist organisers as Bridgeman and Ward went out to West Africa, tried to encourage protests there, or were even aware of conditions there. The initiative was entirely from the African side, but, once representations were made by West African protest groups, the British left wing was happy to assist. These socialist anti-imperialist groups were anxious for any evidence to substantiate their anti-colonial protests.

Through the efforts of Wallace Johnson and Bankole Awoonor Renner of the Friends of Ashanti Freedom Society in the Gold Coast, as well as L. Odunsi of the African Hostel Defence Committee in London, the Gold Coast nationalists were put in touch with the anti-imperialist groups in England. Wallace Johnson solicited the assistance of Bridgeman who put the Aborigines' Society Delegation in contact with the National Council for Civil Liberties, a group greatly concerned about the growth of depression-bred authoritarianism in England. It had a number of Vice-Presidents well-known in British public life. They included, as well as members of the Conservative Party, the Leader and Deputy Leader of the Opposition, and also some Liberals – Dingle Foot, M.P., Bertrand Russell, Dr Ivor Jennings, D. N. Pritt, Dr G. P. Gooch, and Professor Harold Laski. The council responded very favourably to the protest against the Sedition Bill. In July 1934 Kidd wrote to inform Kobina Sekyi that the National Council for Civil Liberties had taken a serious view of the increasingly repressive legislation which was being passed in British colonial territories. He assured Sekyi that the council, which had played an important part in the campaign against the English Sedition Bill, would continue to do all in its power to safeguard the rights and liberties of the African people.[75] With the help of Sekyi's old contacts which were established during his visits to England in 1930 and 1932, and through Bridgeman, the Gold Coast delegates solicited assistance from a wide variety of sources with influence in the British political system. Through the press, through Parliamentary questions, and through informal personal persuasion, these contacts stated the case of the Gold Coast people.[76]

Outside the anti-imperialist circles in Britain and Europe, further encouragement came from such organisations as the Universal Legion of Marcus Garvey's
Universal Negro Improvement Association in New York and the All India
Congress Committee. This latter body wrote to the Gold Coast nationalist
groups about the 'common-enemy-Imperialism' which, as the congress
described it, had bound a 'mighty chain of slavery around the world surface . . .
the weakening or snapping of a link of this chain either in India or in West
Africa,' it concluded, would be of natural advantage to both.[77] Thus, although
the two 1934 Gold Coast Delegations were a failure, they were not an unqualified one, in so far as the campaigns in Britain and in West Africa not only
exposed colonial repression and injustices but also intensified anti-imperialist
sentiments in the 1930s.

It is important to note that the agitation over the Sedition Bill was not
limited to the Gold Coast. Nationalists in Nigeria, Sierra Leone and the Gambia
considered the issue as one which affected all the West African colonies, and
similarly expressed their vehement disapproval of the action of the colonial
government in the Gold Coast. During much of the inter-war period, the
nationalists tended to manifest in their actions the feeling that West Africa
should not be regarded as composed of separate colonies but as one self-
conscious and articulate community. As J. W. Quye, the nationalist agitator in
the Gambia, told the Congress Session at Bathurst in 1925: 'In visions of the
future of West Africa, I behold her people everywhere inspired with the consciousness of one common brotherhood from the hinterland of mighty Nigeria,
through the diamondiferous districts of wealthy Gold Coast, past the salubrious
hills of progressive Sierra Leone, on to the peaceful banks of secluded Gambia. . . .'[78]

Until the era of depression when a narrower conception of nationality became
dominant, the nationalists viewed matters, particularly those concerning
colonialism and imperialism, from a wider, West African point of view rather
than from the point of view of individual colonies. Hence in Sierra Leone, the
agitators against the Gold Coast Sedition Bill strongly believed that their
colony would suffer the next attack.[79] The Gambian agitation was initiated by
E. F. Small who, during this same period, was himself leading the Gambia's
protest against the introduction of code legislation into the colony. Small
offered to join forces with the Gold Coast nationalists, telling them that, in
view of the 'fact that the progress of code legislation threatens to lower the
legal status of West African subjects,' he had considered it his duty to 'offer
whatever services I can render in support of Gold Coast and Gambia protests.'
He indicated his willingness to come to the Gold Coast and to take part in any
delegation the nationalists were sending to England 'to champion their protests
in defence of the legal rights of loyal West African subjects of the Empire.'[80]
So far as the interests in the other West African colonies were concerned, the
1934 Gold Coast delegations to England were not unlike the 1920–21 Delegation of the National Congress of British West Africa to London. The Gold
Coast Colony and Ashanti Delegation was enthusiastically welcomed when
passing to and from London by the Sierra Leone section of the Congress movement.

The intensification of anti-imperialist attitudes in West Africa, and the
attendant growing awareness of pan-African thinking throughout the inter-war
years was effectively fostered by the press which published articles dealing

with lynchings in America, the bullying of Liberia by the European powers and the treatment of black men in Kenya and South Africa. The aspirations of the press as fighters against colonialism and imperialism were soaring during this period. It was the chief means of self-expression for the politically active urban intelligentsia in West Africa. It reflected the outlook of radical or discontented elements in society, with their hostility to the government and their strong feeling about colour. As was evidenced in an official report during this period:

> There is little doubt that the power of the Press is growing daily, and it is upon the young men of education that it exerts greatest pressure. Distrust of government has been its continued keynote with no counter-balancing policy of construction. . . . Personal contact is the best, if not the only weapon there is with which to fight the present wave of distrust which is sweeping the country.[81]

Sir Shenton Thomas, the Governor of the Gold Coast, felt that reckless statements or misinformation could mislead or inflame the people and undermine the basis of colonial power. In his opinion, therefore, the local press was harmful to the colony.[82] Besides the increasing official concern over communist-inspired subversion in the colonial world – particularly with the formation of the League Against Imperialism and of the Sixth Congress of the Comintern in 1928 – there was also the fear about the increasingly blatant appeals to race-consciousness. In a private despatch to the Colonial Office while on leave in England in January 1933, Harry Scott Newlands, the Chief Commissioner of Ashanti, referred to this fear, and stated, *inter alia*, that 'During the past few years the press, which had hitherto being singularly free from it,' had commenced writing on 'racial subjects, that is, the colour question.'[83]

The 'colour question' was indeed reflected in most of the editorials of the West African nationalist press, and this became intensified during the period of severe economic depression. Even as far back as 1920, the *Colonial and Provincial Reporter* in Sierra Leone was writing about the 'servility' under which the black in South Africa was groaning: 'In certain parts he is denied the right to own land upon which to live or to be buried.'[84] And just before the outbreak of the Italo-Ethiopian dispute, the radical newspapers were telling their readers that the Negro was being treated 'with so much contempt, so much brutality, so much disregard for his rights as a human being, nay, so much hatred and prejudice because and just because he is a Negro.'[85] During this period newspaper readers in West Africa were fed regularly and extensively upon the dogma of the oppressed, exploited condition of their race. Moreover, the West African press looked beyond its immediate confines and concerned itself with the Negro affairs in general, and kept a jealous and careful watch over the rights of all black men everywhere. The entire white race was frequently credited with an immoral outlook making them eager to oppress black men. Black peoples all over the world were seen as suffering under systems of downright injustice amounting sometimes to absolute cruelty, and the whole African race as groaning under the iniquitous tyranny of foreign conquerors. Africans were consistently taught to see themselves as a race in bondage. The representation of whites as oppressors and blacks as oppressed, the claim that blacks were equal in all ways to whites, the demand for equal opportunity and equal pay for blacks and whites, the reaction against the treatment of the blacks in Kenya, South Africa and America, were all illustrative of the general attitude of the West African newspapers to the colour question during this period.[86] Such press comments greatly sharpened the pan-African outlook of West African nationalist leaders, and did much to foster racial solidarity.

This racial solidarity strongly expressed itself against the proposed League of Nations control of Liberia, as a result of the British, French and American press charges of slavery and forced labour levelled against this only independent state in West Africa. To remove the discrediting effect of the press campaign, the Liberian Government requested the League of Nations to appoint an International Committee of Enquiry to investigate and report their findings. In 1929, therefore, the League of Nations appointed a commission under Dr Cuthbert Christy, an Englishman, to investigate the allegations. The commission's report, published the following year, found that although 'classic slavery' with slave markets and slave dealers no longer existed, a considerable measure of inter-tribal domestic slavery flourished. The commission was also satisfied that domestic slavery received no encouragement from the Liberian Government and that there was no evidence that the leading citizens participated in it.[87] Despite the cautious tone of the findings, many white critics, including a number of liberals, saw the report as confirmation of the earlier allegations that the Liberian Government had reduced the natives to oppression and servitude. The result was that condemnation of Liberia increased in volume and bitterness. So widespread and sometimes sweeping were the criticisms that several observers openly demanded that the country be placed under the control of a foreign commission.[88]

The eyes of the coloured world, particularly of the nearby West African colonies, were set on the black Republic of Liberia. In view of the conditions in South Africa, Portuguese Africa and the Belgian Congo where whites were in charge, the nationalist press felt that the scathing attacks on Liberia were a sheer exhibition of white hypocrisy:

> If these detractors of Liberia will only see themselves as others see them, they might not have been so quick and carping in condemning her in the way they do in being blind to their own vices whilst they denounce the no less abominable sins of their neighbour which they behold with magnifying glasses . . . seeing that she is not the only delinquent, can her denouncers honestly condemn her? Which of them is innocent and blameless? If any there is, let him cast a stone against her. Thou hypocrite. . . .[89]

In the view of the nationalists, therefore, Liberia was not the only sinner. As the only Black Republic in Africa struggling for existence against many and great handicaps, Liberia needed correction rather than censure. Other highly incensed nationalists like Wallace Johnson felt that the Western powers wanted Liberia because they saw in her a future of progress for the oppressed people of West Africa; they saw in Liberia's valuable resources the great possibility for 'Ethiopia once again to stretch forth her hands unto the God of Peace and Liberty and be free'.[90] The strongest protest, however, came from Nnamdi Azikiwe in an address delivered at the annual meeting of the Association for the Study of Negro Life and History in New York City on 10 November 1931:

> Men without appreciation for the contribution of the Negro to modern statesmanship are content to criticise this African Republic without deep

thought as to the onerous duty of statecraft. Greedy nations are lurking and watching Liberia with hawk-like dexterity. . . . I submit that eighty-four years of political autonomy are not sufficient to pass a final judgement as to the political incapacity of the Liberian Negro. And let it also be remembered that it took Great Britain about fourteen hundred years [*sic*] after the conquest of Boadicea to draft the Magna Carta. It took her several centuries later to pave way for the English Revolution which established a constitutional democracy.[91]

Thus, in the view of Azikiwe, because of the evolutional nature of modern democracies, Liberia should not be so hastily condemned. The reaction of Azikiwe was a measure of the feelings of nationalism which the debate on the Liberian crisis engendered in West Africans both at home and abroad. Such a debate could not but foster a corresponding feeling of solidarity among the black peoples for it was conducted on racial lines. The suspicion that the white critics' allegations stemmed from racial prejudice was reinforced by the fear that a bad reputation for Liberia would be exploited by racists to further discredit peoples of African extraction and to prove their 'incapacity' for self-government.[92] The bitter irony of the situation is that while the League of Nations was strong enough to bully Liberia it was quite ineffective to protect Ethiopia. Moreover, by attempting to control Liberia because of slavery and other 'barbaric' features associated with the country, the League of Nations laid down not an unwelcome precedent for Mussolini. As we shall see, Italy's 'civilising mission' was similarly motivated by allegations of slavery in Ethiopia.

The Ethiopian crisis was indeed a repeat performance of the Liberian episode. The reaction of West Africans to the latter in retrospect appeared to be a full dress-rehearsal of their response to the former. Those who staged the Liberian protest drama in West Africa – the Azikiwes, Wallace Johnsons, and the nationalist press – were set to repeat their play in a grander style, and in a more serious, widespread and spectacular performance during the Italo-Ethiopian crisis. The politically-minded nationalist leaders in West Africa were now more than ever deeply concerned about East Africa or South Africa and wherever they looked, from the Cape right up to Kenya, they saw the white man and the black man in terms of exploiter and exploited.

West African politics and the economic depression

We have already mentioned that, besides the growth of pan-African consciousness, the reaction of West Africans to the Ethiopian crisis was closely interwoven with their general response to the 'colonial situation'. To a great extent, the former was inspired by the latter, and thereby added a significant impetus to it. One important element of the 'colonial situation' in West Africa, as elsewhere, was the economic relationship between the colonial power and the colonial subjects. The West African anti-imperialist agitations were in most cases engendered by the nature of the colonial economics which they saw as a mixture of self-interest and paternalism. The economic relations between them and the colonial administration were generally expressed in terms of racism and exploitation which, as one scholar has recently argued, 'are absolutely the same thing', for colonialism needed racism to maintain itself.[93] There was, therefore, the close interaction 'between economic status and race', making the latter indeed an economic factor. Throughout the inter-war period identification between race and economic and social status was most stark in West Africa. In the view of most of the radical anti-colonial nationalists, to be 'black in skin and African in appearance was to be poor.'[94] As Casely Hayford told a joint meeting of the Gold Coast Farmers' Association and the Executive members of the Eastern Province branch of the Aborigines' Society in Accra, 'the idea of a white man is that a black man is always to work for him, and we are not supposed to know the worth of money; three pence a day is enough for a black man whilst 20 shillings is not sufficient for a white man for a day.'[95] Race and economic necessity thus interacted with one another in West Africa during the period under review.

Significantly, the imperialistic adventure of Fascist Italy came at a critical juncture in the history of West Africa. The Great Depression was ravaging the living conditions of people, many of whom were already frustrated and anguished by economic privation and racial discrimination in the colonial establishment. Local economic problems therefore became an aggravating factor which rendered the nationalists particularly sensitive about their subjugation, economic and political, by the colonial power. In this section, we shall attempt a brief discussion of the economic, social and political grievances which functioned as the driving force behind the West African agitation over the Italian attack on Ethiopia. As there have been recent studies on West African colonial economics,[96] we shall only be concerned with those aspects which engendered the nationalists' opposition to the colonial administration.

The economic situation in British West Africa from the period 1914 to 1939 was on the whole one of instability. There were violent fluctuations in which 'depressions followed booms at regular intervals'. The post-war boom of 1919–1920, for example, was followed by the severe slump of 1920–21, which was signalled by a dramatic fall of export prices. In the Gold Coast, this collapse of export prices led in 1921 to the first of the series of cocoa hold-ups. Indeed, the price fell so dramatically that many West African farmers, traders and merchants were ruined. They reacted with anger and frustration. Few could read and write, much less comprehend the subtleties of the laws of supply and demand. Such abstract theories meant nothing to them. They wanted renewed prosperity. Apart from a slight recovery of the cocoa market in 1927 and 1928, prices of West African export crops showed a marked decline as the period advanced. The dangerous insecurity of a cash crop economy became more than ever apparent and general disruption of commerce forced itself upon the notice of everyone. British West Africa, like many other parts of the world, was shocked and alarmed by the economic chaos and stagnation. From 1930 to 1937 it was quite clear that British West Africa was in the midst of a tremendous slump and economic crisis, and that the future was doubtful and devoid of hopes of immediate recovery of prosperity. The general price trend was downward throughout this period. For example, the price for Gold Coast cocoa in 1919–20 when the freak boom occurred as a result of pent-up wartime demand rose to as much as 125s 6d per cwt. in February 1920 but slumped badly to 31s per cwt. in 1923–24. Prices rallied during the 1920s to a peak of 79s 6d in 1927 but then began an extended decline in response to enormous plantings. This price decline due to increased supply was reinforced by the depression induced collapse of world demand. By 1930–31 price had fallen to the 20s–30s range. The trough was reached in December 1933 at 17s. 3d. Despite an unusual year in 1936–37 when prices rose momentarily to 55s and memories of the good old days rekindled, the price for an entire decade remained 20s to 30s.[97]

What greatly intensified the resentment among the West African entrepreneurs was the fact that the economic structure, like the political one, was subordinate to alien domination. African entrepreneurs found themselves unable to compete successfully against European import-export firms which were backed by enormous overseas capital. The domination of trade by expatriate firms was deeply feared and resented by African producers and shippers. It was widely believed that low prices resulted from manipulation of overseas markets by the pool firms through the use of forward contracts. Even though local price-fixing and oligopolistic practices had only a minimal effect on price, the pool firms were blamed for the serious fluctuations that caused so much injury to Africans.

The European commercial formations such as combines and rings therefore became the target of attack during the depression years. These were frequently attacked as being economically unfair and dangerous but there was also the nationalist aspect of the attack which sought to represent such commercial constructions as the special instrument of white men expressly designed to crush and subdue the Negro. Hence, in Sierra Leone, it was generally felt that the 'Financial Monopolist in a Crown colony' always claimed the right to treat the African peasant labourer in any manner he thought fit to secure his own interests: 'he grabs, he exploits, he bleeds him, and regards in a long run that his economic success is mainly the reward of his achievements.'[98] Alfred John Ocansey, through whose efforts and initiative the Gold Coast Colony and Ashanti Cocoa Federation was formed in 1930, attributed the big drop in price of cocoa not to overproduction nor the general depression all over the world but to 'the free gambling with our labour by irresponsible gamblers and greedy Pools'.[99] The Gold Coast farmer, it was generally believed, was being forced to live in a degraded and depressed economic condition planned by some white cocoa speculators, who had become such a powerful force that they actually dictated to the farmer what price to pay him.[100] Throughout, the African entrepreneurs seriously, and naturally, resented their subordinate status in the colonial economic organisation.

It is worth stating that the Western economic forces also had a tremendous impact on the structure of West African traditional societies. Not only did the European economic penetration with its attendant monetary economy and expanded commerce transform the tribal societies, but it introduced social classes, notably the lawyer-merchant class. The interests of these classes were based mainly on the new socio-economic system characterised by commercial agriculture, trade, and industry. As a social elite in the African society, these aspiring entrepreneurial groups had set 'imitable standards and patterns' for the rest of the population, and in general had spearheaded the drive for modernity in West Africa. Their social and economic status were immediately threatened by the economic crisis of the 1930s. They felt themselves denied opportunity they regarded as theirs, and the responsibility for such a denial was projected first upon the alien oligopoly and later upon the colonial administration. More importantly, these groups were strong and active in the nationalist movements of the time. They organised themselves as a political pressure group and as a means of finding a solution to the economic plight of the African merchant, producer and business man. In other words, in their efforts both to protect and advance their socio-economic and political status in a colonial situation, these groups turned to nationalism as one means of attaining these ends: 'What we have got to remember is that economic and industrial independence is a necessary step to our political freedom.'[101] In the view of the West African middle class, economic self-determinism could be effected only through an increased responsible status in government. This meant that the balance of political power had to be altered before the economic structure could be changed, since the colonial powers would not willingly act against their own interests.

In the 1920s it was the middle class nationalists, or the would-be entrepreneurial groups, who formed the core of leadership of the National Congress of British West Africa. Thus, when the conference which later resolved itself into the National Congress of British West Africa held its first meeting in Accra in March 1920, the delegates were preoccupied with economic relations between Britain and West Africa. For, as Casely Hayford later summed it up, 'We are powerless if we are moneyless, whether we are politically powerful or not. . . .'[102] The congress delegates in Accra demanded trade subsidies, export privileges, anti-monopoly legislation, free trade, limitations on Syrians, restrictions on profiteering, and control of the colonial budget. The congress urged creation of a British West African Co-operative Association to form banks, promote shipping facilities, and establish co-operative stores and produce buying centres.[103] These plans came to nothing as the glowing optimism of the 1919–20 boom, as we have noted, gave way to sudden depression.

Although the sweeping plans of the congress were never implemented, individuals continued to develop private schemes. For example, in 1922, some entrepreneurs in the Gold Coast – I. F. Ofori, Dr F. V. Nanka Bruce, C. J. Reindorf and S. O. Akiwumi – joined to form the Association of African Shippers and Planters to promote African markets.[104] Also, in 1924 the West African Credit Association was announced by a group of Accra, Addah, and the Quittah brothers with a nominal capital of £40,000 to aid in the establishment of various productive and commercial projects.[105] Similarly, the National Co-operative Society of Nigeria Ltd was formed on 29 November 1929, with a capital of £5,000 aimed at fostering in the young Nigerians 'the spirit of thrift and industrial co-operation'. Its directors were: Stanislaus Idowu Moses-Johnson (farmer), G. E. Cole (clerk), George Akintude Taylor (merchant), George Bandele Amancio Santos (clerk), E. O. Idowu Onitiri (merchant), J. Adebayo Abomire (clerk), and Abraham O. Shaw (trader). Soon after its formation the society issued a public statement on the prevailing conditions in West Africa, adding that 'those on whom we rely treat us as mere chattels and playthings and cast us aside at pleasure'. The statement then called on the sons of Africa, particularly Nigerians, to seize the 'splendid opportunity' offered by the society 'for emancipation from industrial thraldom'.[106] These endless schemes had little success; they added up, rather, to broken dreams and bad debts, even though the period of the 1920s was generally quite prosperous. While the expatriate firms grew fat and expanded, the African entrepreneurs did very poorly indeed.

Thus the economic grievances of the 1920s were carried over into the 1930s, a period of severe depression during which the price of cocoa, palm oil and other commodities fell considerably. This precipitous price decline, like that of 1920, set into motion certain activities in the farming and entrepreneurial community in West Africa to combat the expatriate exploitation or to cash in on farmers' frustrations about manipulated prices so as to establish control of marketing. Once again none of the efforts proved successful. The Gold Coast Colony and Ashanti Cocoa Federation (formed in 1930) found it difficult to challenge the European combines, as it was unable to secure financial backing from overseas interests. The birth of the Federation was attributed to the local belief that the cocoa pool entirely controlled the world price of cocoa. There was a firm conviction that the firms forming the pool were 'exploiting the cocoa farmer and making unjustifiably high profits by expanding the margins between the price arranged with the purchasing manufacturer and that dictated to the selling farmer'. It was held that it was the system of marketing by 'Forward Contract' and the helplessness of the African farmer which rendered possible the alleged extortionate process.[107] Both the 1930–31 and the 1934–35 cocoa hold-ups, 'as an economic strike for higher prices' directed against the large expatriate buying firms and their monopoly control over the Gold Coast economy were half successful.[108] When the hold-ups failed to bring relief, the shipping schemes were given a trial, but these also proved to be unsuccessful. Similarly, the several co-operative economic schemes inspired by Winifried Tete Ansa, a critical figure in the development of early co-operative economic enterprises in British West Africa soon collapsed.

It is pertinent to point out, however, that much of the failure of the efforts of the African entrepreneurs to break into trade in a big way can be attributed to the activities and attitudes of the colonial government during this period. In the first place, the colonial administration on the whole appeared indifferent not only to the economic plights of the African farmer or trader, but also to the relations between the expatriate companies and the indigenous peoples. Secondly, and what seems to be more serious, the Colonial Office was acutely biased against the educated elite. The officials at the Colonial Office were frequently mis-informed of the activities of their colonial subjects and reached opinions of sub-stantial importance, as often on the basis of preconceived notions as of analysis of fact. Thus, Africans by definition were viewed as would-be swindlers, and it is very difficult to escape the conclusion that they were proscribed because of the prejudices of a racialist-imperialist officialdom. British banks and invest-ment houses traded information with the colonial government on third-party questions. At the same time it was the practice of the colonial government to exchange intelligence abut African entrepreneurs with banks and investment houses. As a result of such exchanges the aspirant African commercial interests were almost uniformly viewed with hostility by both the Colonial Office and many of the investment houses. In very quiet, unobtrusive ways the colonial regime destroyed the prospects of would-be borrowers by suggesting that they were 'shady characters', 'swindlers' and 'men of dubious characters'.[109] The result of this was that legitimate African entrepreneurs could not get loans through established commercial channels and had to turn to high-cost, informal loan sources. This greatly increased the cost of borrowing and encouraged them to engage in creating fanciful images of their own commercial prospects. In informal loan channels, wealthy patrons, after dabbling in amusing specu-lation, had to be enticed with prospects of enormous profit. Thus, rejected at the loan counters of established banks and investment houses, the African entrepreneurs often resorted to exaggerated claims which bordered on fraud and misrepresentation. In Nigeria, the unwillingness of the European banks and investment houses to grant credit to Africans led to the formation of the first indigenous bank, the National Bank of Nigeria, in 1933. Also, the cocoa hold-ups in the Gold Coast became ineffective largely because of government pressure. In the 1930–31 hold-up, the government remained neutral, but, as Rhodie points out:

> Despite all official protests of neutrality, justice and fairness, the colonial administration chiefly served the interests of the large European firms. Neutrality was an argument for maintaining the *status quo*; in the inequitable conditions of the Gold Coast, such a policy left the field open to the most powerful. Moreover, the colonial bureaucracy, through its various departments, daily supplied information on crop movements, prices, rents and cocoa cultivation to the merchant firms. . . . Such information was not available to the farmers or to the Africans in general. When Africans protested or made requests, they were ignored or turned down.[110]

All these grievances led to the cry of exploitation, and something more than that, subjugation of the African. As one Nigerian nationalist somewhat exaggeratedly characterised the situation:

> The economic history of Nigeria is a narration of shame and exploitation. It is the story of a handful of fortune seekers, with the blessing of England, coming to Africa under the guise of trusteeship only to strangle the goose that lays the golden egg. Instead of educating the people to stand on their own feet, the foreigners aim at the economic deformity of the people.[111]

Throughout, the nationalists maintained that there was high overall identity of interest between the imperial power and the European firms in West Africa. Hence, they denounced not only the European pools but also the imperial power itself, whose 'principle' in their view, was 'focused on pure investment' which had led to a 'callous' and 'ruthless' exploitation of the African. It was believed that the imperial power and the expatriate firms had formed 'a class detrimental to our progress', and that their powerful 'combination' paid respect to neither conscience nor any development programme of the trusteeship. It was further held that because of the enormous financial interests which the imperial power derived from its close association with the European firms, it had 'allowed commercial representation on our Legislative Councils'.[112] The whole argument was reduced to a basic form of black versus white, with the dominant white depicted as struggling desperately to quell a rising nationally conscious black population.

By 1935 when the Italo-Ethiopian crisis broke out, West Africa had not yet recovered from the depression. Trade still lagged, revenue was down and money scarce. Many African traders and middlemen had been ruined, while the larger European firms had combined on the wrecks. Unemployment had become acute and critical, as Africans had been forced out of trade. Cocoa farmers, of course, had been very hard hit, and all the latent defects in the industry (in Gold Coast and in Nigeria) which had been shielded by prosperity had now become glaring weaknesses: unstable land tenure practices, increasing debts of farmers reliant on cash, immigrant labour problems, technical inefficiency, and unhealthy marketing patterns were painfully apparent in the throes of a world depression. All this led to strikes, destoolments and disturbances in the country-side. Besides, there were demonstrations and protests in the main centres of trade such as those in Freetown, Sierra Leone, in 1926 and 1931, and in Bathurst, Gambia, in 1929. In Nigeria, the attempt by Sir Graeme Thomson, the Governor of the colony, to introduce direct taxation in 1927 was met by vehement mass protest at the Glover Memorial Hall in Lagos in January 1928. This was followed in Eastern Nigeria by the more spectacular Aba Riot of 1929.[113] In the Gold Coast, a widespread opposition to Governor Sir Alexander Ransford Slater's imposition of an income tax in 1931 manifested itself in disorderly demonstrations at Sekondi, Cape Coast, Accra and Shama, and threatened at other coastal towns.[114]

As in the 1920s, so in the 1930s passionately felt economic grievances were accompanied by moderate constitutional demands. The constitutions granted in 1922–25 to Nigeria, the Gold Coast and Sierra Leone were regarded as most unsatisfactory by the nationalist leaders, and much wider franchise and elected African representation were repeatedly demanded. In the Gambia, a petition was sent to the House of Commons in August 1934 complaining bitterly against the Governor's power to control the groundnut trade. This was accompanied by a demand for a new constitution.[115] Similarly, the formidable Nigerian Youth Charter of 1938 – the official programme of the Nigerian Youth Move-ment – accompanied its constitutional reforms with a comprehensive economic charter in which the movement pledged itself 'to demand for our people eco-nomic opportunities equal to those enjoyed by foreigners'. It urged the govern-ment 'to protect our people against unequal competition by foreigners, if necessary by Legislation'.[116] This economic charter touched on many aspects of the Nigerian economy. It was a positive economic scheme designed as a panacea to the economic distress of the people of Nigeria in the 1930s. Although the charter was accepted by the Colonial Office as 'everywhere reason-able', because of Britain's own economic problems during this very period, its expressed aims were considered unacceptable.[117] It became one of the casualties of the depression.

In the Gold Coast, the two delegations to London in 1934 included economic proposals in their respective petitions. The delegation led by Nana Sir Ofori Atta petitioned that a special commissioner with a business experience be sent out 'to the coast to find a way of adding to the wealth of the country in addition to the cocoa they now cultivate'.[118] As we have seen, the two delegations were a dismal failure, and none of the economic proposals was granted by the Colonial Office. Similarly, a petition by the Sierra Leone Section of the National Con-gress of British West Africa to Governor Henry Moore in 1936 asking for constitutional, judicial, and municipal reforms was refused.[119]

Thus the depression years of the 1930s remained a period of economic and political frustration throughout the British West African colonies. The economic distress brought political discontent, which in turn greatly worsened Afro-European relations, and in particular increased the hostility of the people towards the expatriate government, which was regarded as supporting the expatriate firms and the existing marketing system. Even such a loyal and influential representative of the traditional elite as Nana Sir Ofori Atta of the Gold Coast could not help remarking bluntly in the Legislative Council that the Gold Coast could no longer boast of any co-operation between the colonial administration and the people.[120] Both the moderate and radical groups in the

Gold Coast generally held that the colonial government was not only 'gallivant-ing' with the finances of the country, but also that its general outlook was decidedly against the people.[121] The coastal elite in particular felt that they were suffering social humiliation as well as economic defeat which stemmed from racial prejudice. The colonial administrators themselves were aware of the fact that their colonial subjects in the West Coast of Africa had during this period become 'more than usually suspicious' of their governments and 'more critical' of their value.[122] In Nigeria, for example, the objection to the 1927 direct taxation was not primarily economic but rather nationalistic. The ob-jection was, as Dr Afigbo has argued, a proof of 'Nigerians' dislike of alien rule at this time'. To impose a direct taxation even in time of severe economic depression was taken as a proof of the 'fact' that alien rule 'cannot be other than oppressive'.[123] The Aba Riot in Eastern Nigeria was essentially anti-British and anti-alien rule, and not, as the British administrators contended, a rising against iniquitous Warrant chiefs.

Thus, when the Ethiopian crisis broke out in this atmosphere of economic exploitation and political distress and exhaustion, it was interpreted by the nationalistically conscious West Africans as a part of the total complex of European domination aimed at enslaving the African. What occurred in Ethiopia directly concerned them and those in other parts of the African conti-nent who were suffering under the same colonial regime. They saw the Italian brutalities in Ethiopia as the common lot of the black man. Hence their protest against injustices and exploitation in West Africa was invariably a protest against the disabilities of all black men. Thus in presenting the grievances of the Gold Coast people during this period, George Moore, leader of the 1934 Aborigines' Society Deputation to England, told Malcolm MacDonald that the people of the Gold Coast sincerely hoped that the Secretary of State for the Colonies 'will make a clear pronouncement on Liberty for Africans, whether in the Gold Coast or Abyssinia'.[124]

In this chapter I have attempted to analyse the main factors which form the background to the West African response to the Ethiopian crisis. During this period, apart from the symbolic status of Ethiopia, the sentiment of African race and African nationality became more important than ever. Although West Africans had 'become British by alliance', yet they were not unAfrican in inspiration. They had secured the benefits of the Pax Britannica, but they also wanted to preserve their race individuality. As one observer has noted:

> Today we realise that in the coloured race a new feeling of community is awakening, a feeling which has been possible only by the influence of the colonial powers; it is the same education, the same language, the same views which they learned from the nation of their masters; the hard, externally benevolent, but in reality suppressing treatment, intended to exploit them, which asked for protest and made them form a bond of unity.[125]

Thus, increasingly, by virtue of their colonial education, Africans came to think of themselves as Africans first, any other allegiance taking second place. For the continent of Africa was the only one in which the people's interests were identical in that they were geographically united, while from an ethnological point of view they were of one race. The rise and fall of one of her peoples, therefore, affected all others. The 'colonial situation', then, not only created 'a sentiment of oneness',[126] but also reinforced the racial feeling of many of the peoples on the West Coast of Africa, where there had been intense national awakening and pan-African consciousness as early as the 1800s when Edward Blyden's pan-Negro ideas spread throughout English-speaking countries in this region. As a result of their race pride, West Africans bitterly resented the Italian attack on Ethiopia, partly because it was an attack which appeared to impugn the status of the African race. The race-conscious West African posited his race as an entity to which he had obligations. He had a conscience about it. He must serve it, fight for it, be loyal to it.[127] Hence the intensity of West African interest in the international diplomatic setting in which dispositions touching Ethiopia's future were to be made. It is this diplomatic aspect of the Italo-Ethiopian crisis, and the responses which it provoked, that will be discussed in the following chapter.

1 Joel A. Rogers in *The Pittsburgh Courier* (New York), 20 July 1935. Rogers, traveller and chronicler of Negro achievements, was the historian-news analyst of this widely-read influential Negro weekly in the United States.
2 See Geiss, *The Pan-African Movement*, p. 32.
3 For instance, in Nigeria, when the Rev. S. A. Coker, President of the Congregational Union of West Africa, delivered a lecture in Lagos entitled, 'The Rights of Africans to Organise and Establish Indigenous Churches . . .', *The Lagos Weekly Record* of 17 April 1917 hailed it as advent of the period in which 'Ethiopia shall stretch forth her hands unto God.' Also, *The Lagos Standard*, 18 April 1917.
4 George Shepperson, 'Ethiopianism: Past and Present,' in C. G. Baeta, ed., *Christianity in Tropical Africa*, Oxford, 1968, p. 249.
5 For details, see Weisbord, *Ebony Kinship*, pp. 89–90. See also W. A. Shack, 'Ethipoia and Afro-Americans: Some Historical Notes, 1920–1970', *Phylon*, xxxv, 2, 1974, pp. 142–55.
6 Thomas Hogkin, *Nationalism in Colonial Africa*, London, 1962, p. 180.
7 Clarence G. Contee, 'The Emergence of Du Bois as an African Nationalist', *The Journal of Negro History*, lix, 50, 1969.
8 For the various uses of the term, see Ken Post, 'The Bible as Ideology', in C. Allen and R. W. Johnson, eds, *African Perspective*, Cambridge, 1970, pp. 187–88.
9 The Ethiopian movement originally started in the Transvaal by M. M. Mokone and J. G. Xaba about 1893, as Ethiopian Church. Details are provided in the 'Intelligence Report on the Ethiopian Movement', prepared by Major R. H. Massie, Johannesburg, December 1903. C.O. 537/513.
10 *Ibid*. See also, G. Shepperson, 'Pan Africanism and "Pan-Africanism"': Some Historical Notes', *Phylon*, xxiii, 4, Winter 1962.
11 E. V. Essien-Udom, *Black Nationalism: A Search for an Identity in America*, Chicago, 1962, pp. 46–9. Also, Weisbord, *Ebony Kinship*, p. 91.
12 Garfield Smith, *The Rastafar Movement in Kingston, Jamaica*. Also, Weisbord, *Ebony Kinship*, pp. 123–5.
13 Czeslaw Jesman, *The Ethiopia Paradox*, London, 1963, foreword.
14 Grover Cleveland Redding, a co-founder of the Back-to-Abyssinia Movement in Chicago, not only claimed birth in Ethiopia, but also declared at his court trial in Chicago in 1920 that the adherents of his movement, who referred to themselves as 'Ethiopians' or 'Abyssinians', did not belong to the United States and 'should be taken back to their country'. Chicago Commission on Race Relations, eds, *The Negro in Chicago: A Study of Race Relations and a Race Riot*, Chicago, 1922, pp. 59–60; also, Arna Bontemps and Jack Conroy, *Anyplace but Here*, New York, 1966, pp. 204–5.
15 The interest of the Gold Coast nationalists in this event is detailed in *The Gold Coast Aborigines* (Cape Coast, Ghana) 7 January 1905.
16 C.O. 537/315; Ethiopianism in Eastern, Central and Southern Africa has been studied by scholars like G. Shepperson and T. Price, *Independent African*, Edinburgh, 1958; B. G. M. Sundkler, *Bantu Prophets in South Africa*, London, 1964; W. C. Willoughby, *Race Problems in the New World*, Oxford, 1923.
17 E. A. Ayandele, *The Missionary Impact on Modern Nigeria, 1842–1914: A Political Analysis*, London, 1966, pp. 175–238.

18 E. A. Ayandele, *Holy Johnson: Pioneer of African Nationalism, 1836–1917*, London, 1970, pp. 34–47.

19 *Ibid.*, p. 42.

20 *Ibid.*, p. 44.

21 ACC. 91/65, *Gold Coast Aborigines Society Papers*, Ghana Regional Archives, Cape Coast, Ghana.

22 Prince Bandele Omoniyi, *A Defence of the Ethiopia Movement*, Edinburgh, 1908, p. 4.

23 J. W. E. Bowen, ed, *Africa and the American Negro: Address and Proceedings of the Congress on Africa*, Atlanta, 1896, p. 127.

24 Like the other early nationalists such as D. B. Vincent, who took his native Yoruba name, Mojola Agebi, and the Ghanaian S. R. B. Solomon, who became Attoh Ahuma, Orishatuke Faduma originally had a 'European' name: William James Davies.

25 Mojola Agbebi's inaugural sermon delivered on 8 May 1892 and published in *Sierra Leone Weekly News*, 12 November 1892; also, *West African Mail* (London), 25 August 1903.

26 *Inaugural Sermon*, December 1902. For biographical sketch of Mojola Agbebi, see E. A. Ayandele, *A Visionary of the African Church: Mojola Agbebi (1860–1917)*, Nairobi, 1971. Also, L. C. Gwam, 'Dr Mojola Agbebi' a seminar paper at the Institute of African Studies Library, University of Ibadan, Ibadan, Nigeria.

27 *Ibid.*

28 *Gold Coast Aborigines*, 25 February 1899.

29 *Gold Coast Leader* (Sekondi), 1 November 1924, editorial. In Sierra Leone, the C.M.S. Grammar School founded a monthly journal in 1872 called *The Ethiopian* which devoted itself to educational matters.

30 *Wasu* (Journal of the West African Students' Union in Great Britain), nos 3 and 4, March 1927. A similar reference can be found in the same journal, nos 6 and 7, August 1928.

31 J. B. Danquah, 'Is the Negro a Dead Letter?', *Danquah Papers*.

32 *Ibid.*

33 *The West African Mail*, 19 May 1905.

34 Case No. 5/1929, Kumasihene's Affairs, Office of D.C., Kumasi. I am grateful to A. B. Holmes, a colleague researcher, for sending me this reference.

35 *Danquah Papers*.

36 *Gold Coast Independent* (Accra), 18 January 1936.

37 *Gold Coast Spectator* (Accra), 23 November 1935. For other West African press comments on the Firestone Lease, see *Gold Coast Leader*, 14 November and 5 December 1925 and 11 September 1926. It should be noted, however, that although Liberia fell prey to the Firestone enterprise, the name of Liberia, for a while, spelled romance for some West African nationalists such as Azikiwe, who devoted a whole book to it, *Liberia in World Politics*, London, 1934. Members of Garvey's mass movement also viewed Liberia as a land of hope and promise. It was held that Liberia's existence gave the Negro race a foothold in Africa and that its destruction would mean the abandonment of the hopes of 'African redemption'. A. J. Garvey, *Garvey and Garveyism*, Kingston, 1963, p. 101. By 1935, however, the romantic aura of Liberia would seem to have been evaporated.

38 Parliamentary *Debates*, House of Lords, 5s, vol. 83, 1931–2, pp. 912–38.

39 For a recent biographical sketch of Sekyi, see J. A. Langley's introduction to *The Blinkards by Kobina Sekyi*, London, 1974, pp. 1–17.

40 The writer has discussed Sekyi's correspondence with Kwame Nkrumah in 'The Aborigines Society, Kwame Nkrumah and the 1945 Pan-African Congress', *Research Review*, Institute of African Studies, Legon, vii, 2, Lent Term 1971, pp. 47–72.

41 Kobina Sekyi, 'The Parting of the Ways' (1927), pp. 28–9. This unpublished manuscript was discovered among the *Sekyi Papers*, ACC.464/64, Ghana Regional Archives, Cape Coast. Similarly, Garvey declared, 'We have great hopes of Abyssinia in the East – the country that has kept her tradition even back to the days of Solomon.' *The Black Man* (a monthly magazine of Negro thought and opinion edited by Garvey in London), 25 October 1930.

42 Jomo Kenyatta, 'Hands Off Abyssinia', *Labour Monthly* (London), xvii, 9 September 1935, p. 536.

43 N. Azikiwe, *Renascent Africa*, London, 1968, pp. 163–4. Concluding this study in the Ethiopianist manner, Azikiwe said: 'And the God of Ethiopia cleared my vista as I see

a noble race of Renascent Africans. And the history of this great race was unfurled to me.' *Ibid.*, p. 310. See also James Coleman, *Nigeria: Background to Nationalism*, p. 209.

44 Daniel Thwaite, *The Seething African Pot: A Study of Black Nationalism, 1882–1935*, London, 1936, p. 207.

45 *Ibid.*

46 René Maunier, *The Sociology of Colonies: An Introduction to the Study of Race Contact*, p. 417.

47 *Wallace Johnson Papers*, Institute of African Studies Library, University of Ghana, Legon. It is worth noting that the term 'Ethiopianism' never ceased to be employed in its pan-African sense as 'a general reference to the programme "Africa for Africans", with a corresponding aversion to white domination', Sundkler, p. 56; see also Shepperson, 'Pan-Africanism and "Pan-Africanism" ', p. 352.

48 Though certain aspects of this ground have recently been covered in such studies as Langley, *Pan-Africanism and Nationalism*, it is necessary to repeat, where possible, some of the relevant details in order to create the framework in which this work is cast. This will also provide the psychological background to the political and emotional effects of the Ethiopian crisis.

49 It must be noted that pan-African consciousness of West African nationalists is not, however, entirely a twentieth-century phenomenon but in fact has its origins in the social and political thinking of Edward Blyden. See Hollis Lynch, *Edward Wilmot Blyden: Pan-Negro Patriot, 1832–1912*, London, 1967; Langley, *Pan-Africanism and Nationalism*, pp. 26–33. Note also, that the Pan-African Association formed in 1897, which organised the 1900 Pan-African Conference, included members from West Africa such as James Johnson and Mojola Agebi.

50 A good account of the conference has been detailed in Langley, *Pan-Africanism and Nationalism*, pp. 27–30; P. O. Esedebe, 'A History of the Pan-African Movement in Britain 1900–1948', unpublished Ph.D. thesis, University of London, 1968, pp. 40–1; I. Geiss, 'Notes on the Development of Pan-Africanism', *Journal of the Historical Society of Nigeria*, iii, 4 June 1967, pp. 726–8; also, Geiss, *The Pan-African Movement*, pp. 176–92.

51 See *The Lagos Standard*, 17 October 1900; *Gold Coast Chronicle*, 18 August 1900; and the *Gold Coast Aborigines*, 31 August 1900. The symbolic value of Ethiopia, Haiti and Liberia clearly came to the forefront at the conference.

52 J. E. Caseley Hayford, *Ethiopia Unbound*, London, 1911, pp. 182–3; *Gold Coast Leader*, 11 March 1905 and 13 May 1916.

53 See my article, 'The Aborigines' Society, Kwame Nkrumah and the 1945 Pan-African Congress'.

54 ACC.91/65, *Aborigines' Papers*, Ghana Regional Archives, Cape Coast, Booker T. Washington to Attoh-Ahuma, Secretary of Aborigines' Society, 22 April 1912.

55 Cited in Louis R. Harlan, 'Booker T. Washington and the White Man's Burden', *American Historical Review*, lxxi, 2, January 1966, pp. 441–67.

56 ACC.91/65, *Aborigines' Papers*, Booker T. Washington to Atto-Ahuma, 22 April 1912.

57 The broad aims of the First Universal Races Congress are detailed in preliminary circular of the Executive Council. See G. Spiller, ed *Papers on Inter-Racial Problems*, xiii.

58 *Ibid.* See also Akinsola Akiwowo, 'The Place of Mojola Agebi in the African Nationalist Movements: 1890–1917', *Phylon*, xxvi, 2, 1965, pp. 122–39.

59 For a recent detailed study of the Congress, see D. Diddiss, 'The Universal Races Congress of 1911', *Race*, xiii, 1, 1971, pp. 37–46.

60 For example, Michael Crowder has argued that it was after the First World War that the pan-African movement had an impact on West Africa. See M. Crowder, *West Africa Under Colonial Rule*, p. 140.

61 *West Africa* (London), 3 September 1921. See also, 'West Africa and the Pan-African Congress', supplement to the *African World*, 30 September 1921. For a detailed discussion of the Du Boisian Congresses and the African responses to them, see Langley, *Pan-Africanism and Nationalism*, pp. 58–103. Another interesting account of the London 1921 Congress is provided in P. O. Esedebe, 'A History of Pan-African Movement', ch. 2.

62 Casely Hayford, *The Disabilities of Black Folk and their Treatment with an Appeal to the Labour Party*, London, 1929.

63 C.O.583/109/28194, a confidential memorandum on Garvey's Universal Negro Improvement Association in Lagos prepared by G. H. Walker, Deputy Inspector-

General of Police, Southern Provinces, Nigeria, on behalf of Governor Sir Hugh Clifford, 27 February 1922.

64 *Ibid.* G. Ashie-Nikoi's letters are contained in Walker's confidential memorandum. For the impact of Garveyism on West African nationalists, see A. J. Garvey, *Black Power in America: Marcus Garvey's Impact on Jamaica and Africa*, Kingston, 1968, pp. 29–34; A. Edwards, *Marcus Garvey, 1887–1940*, London, 1967, pp. 37–9, and Jacob Akinpelu Obisesan Diary, 1920–1960, Ibadan University Library.

65 Details of the Congress Petition are provided in C.O.554/54/2760, 'The Humble Petition of the National Congress of British West Africa by its Delegates in London'.

66 See for example, *The Times of Nigeria* (Lagos), 1 March 1920, 'One lesson above all others which the results of the late world upheaval have taught the African races is the need for organising an African Brotherhood.'

67 Magnus Sampson, *West African Leadership*, London, 1969, pp. 78–9.

68 *Ibid.*, p. 79.

69 *The Gambia Outlook and Senegambian Reporter* (Bathurst), 21 November 1936, reproduction of the speech by J. W. Quye at the Third Session of the National Congress of British West Africa held in Bathurst, Gambia, December 1926.

70 *Wasu*, No. 2, December 1926.

71 *Ibid.* For the views of Kobina Sekyi on this subject of West African leadership, see 'The Parting of the Ways', p. 72.

72 Kwame Nkrumah, *I Speak of Freedom*, New York, 1961, preface, p. xi. The concept of 'We are all Africans' is discussed in detail in Ali A. Mazrui, *Towards a Pax Africana: A Study of Ideology and Ambition*, London, 1967, pp. 42–58.

73 For Padmore's correspondence with the Gold Coast nationalists during the early 1930s, see Samuel Rhodie, 'The Gold Coast Aborigines Abroad', *Journal of African History*, vi, 3, 1965, pp. 389–411. West African nationalists were also in close touch with the race-conscious organisation known as the 'African Churches Mission and Training Home' founded in 1931 by West Africans resident in Liverpool. The main purpose of this organisation, which was led by Rev. Daniel Ekarte, was to help raise to a more progressive level 'the endeavours to emancipate the Black Race from the present ignominious state of affairs forced upon it by a hydra-headed imperialism'. *Macaulay Papers*, University of Ibadan Library, Ibadan, Nigeria.

74 The Criminal Code (Amendment) Bill gave the government power to confiscate literature considered to be seditious. The Waterworks Bill provided for the collection of water rates in the principal towns of the Gold Coast Colony. C.O.96/714/21639/1934. See also, Stanley Shaloff, 'Press Controls and Sedition Proceedings in the Gold Coast, 1933–1939', *African Affairs*, lxxi, 284, July 1972.

75 ACC.94/65, *Sekyi Papers*, Kidd to Sekyi, 10 July 1934. For the reaction of the British Labour Movement to the Sedition Ordinance, see P. S. Gupta, *Imperialism and the British Labour Movement 1914–1964*, Cambridge, 1975, p. 262.

76 ACC.154/65, *Aborigines' Papers*, Danquah to Bridgeman, 9 July 1934; also, Bridgeman to Nana Sir Ofori Atta, leader of the 1934 Gold Coast Colony and Ashanti Delegation, 20 July 1934; Ward to Wallace Johnson, 9 May 1934; Sekyi to L. Odunsi, Secretary, African Hostel Defence Committee, 16 June 1934. For correspondence between Bridgeman and the Nigerian nationalists, see *Macaulay Papers*, Box 26, File 1.

77 ACC.109/65, *Sekyi Papers*, R. M. Lohia, Departmental Secretary, All India Congress Committee, to Sekyi, 28 May 1934.

78 *The Gambia Outlook and Senegambian Reporter*, 21 November 1936, reproduction of speech by J. W. Quye at the Third Session of the NCBWA, Bathurst, 1925–26.

79 *Sierra Leone Weekly News*, 16 June 1934. For the reaction of the Nigerian nationalist leaders to the Sedition Bill, see the *Comet* (Lagos), 27 June 1934.

80 ACC.154/65, *Aborigines' Papers*, E. F. Small to the Secretary, Gold Coast Aborigines' Society, 11 April 1934; also *ibid.*, the reply of Aborigines' Society to Small, telling him that their delegation would confer with him in Bathurst, 27 May 1934.

81 'Report on the Eastern Province of the Gold Coast Colony for the year 1934–35', enclosed in C.O.96/714/21639/1934.

82 *Ibid.* Sir Shenton Thomas, Governor of the Gold Coast, to Alex Fiddian, Colonial Office, London, 27 February 1934.

83 C.O.96/707/1613, Newlands to Under Secretary of State for the Colonies, London, 5 January 1933.

84 *Colonial and Provincial Reporter* (Freetown), 3 April 1920.

85 For example, *Times of West Africa* (Accra), 21 April 1932.
86 The attitudes of the West African press to the race question and to the other major problems agitating the minds of the nationalists are fully illustrated in W. D. Edmonds, 'The Newspaper Press in British West Africa, 1918 to 1939', an unpublished M.A. thesis, University of Bristol, 1951.
87 The report of the Commission is printed in the League of Nations, *International Commission of Enquiry in Liberia*, Official No. C.658, M.272, 1930, vi, Geneva, 1930. Also, Esedebe, 'A History of Pan-African Movement'.
88 Liberia's rejection of the League of Nations 'Plan of Assistance' is recorded in the British confidential 'Annual Report on Liberia', January 1934–May 1935, prepared by A. E. Yapp, British Legation at Monrovia, to Sir John Simon, Secretary of State for Foreign Affairs. F.O. 371/19235, 15 May 1935.
89 *Gold Coast Independent*, 22 June 1935; also, *Lagos Daily News*, 21 January 1931.
90 Wallace Johnson, 'Liberia: A Prodigy', *The Liberian Patriot* (Monrovia), vi, 12, 10 August 1935. For a similar criticism, see Harry W. Roberts, 'Liberia and the League of Nations', *The Keys* (organ of the League of Coloured Peoples), i, 3 January 1934.
91 N. Azikiwe, 'In Defense of Liberia', *Journal of Negro History*, xvii, 1, January 1932, pp. 30–50. See also N. Azikiwe, 'Liberia: Slave or Free', in N. Cunard, *Negro Anthology*, London, 1934, pp. 780–3.
92 This is clear from the reaction of Harold Moody, leader of the League of Coloured Peoples to the Liberian crisis. See Harold Moody, 'The Future of Liberia: Proposed League Control', *The Manchester Guardian*, 30 October 1932.
93 Han Suyin, 'Race Relations and the Third World', *Race*, xiii, 1, 1971, pp. 1–20.
94 Aspects of this subject in the case of Jamaica in the 1930s have been discussed in Ken Post, 'The Bible as Ideology'.
95 ACC.145/65, *Aborigines' Papers*, *Minutes* of 18 December 1923.
96 In particular, Hopkins, *An Economic History of West Africa* and Langley, *Pan-Africanism and Nationalism*, pp. 195–240.
97 University of Ghana, Legon, Institute of Statistics, Social and Economic Research, Department of Agriculture files on cocoa. Cited in A. B. Holmes, 'Economic and Political Organisations in the Gold Coast, 1920–1945', unpublished Ph.D. thesis, Political Science Department, University of Chicago, 1972, pp. 35–6.
98 *Sierra Leone Weekly News*, 14 August 1937.
99 *Macaulay Papers*, Box 26, File 9. On 27 October 1930, Ocansey wrote to Herbert Macaulay urging him to form a similar federation in Nigeria, adding, 'I feel that unless we stand up and fight for our rights, the end will find us in economic slavery.' Details of the Gold Coast Colony and Ashanti Federation can be found in ADM.11/1070, Ghana National Archives, Accra, A man of diversified interests and holdings, who not only owned the *Gold Coast Spectator*, but was also the proprietor of the *African Morning Post*, Ocansey was born in 1889 at Adda and educated at the Basel Mission, Accra. Thereafter he was a clerk with Messrs. F. and A. Swanzy for fourteen years, during which time he acquired a thorough knowledge of commerce in all its branches and bearings. Being of too ambitious a nature to spend his life as an employee, he started in business for himself in 1910 at Somanya, and met with such success that he was enabled to open from time to time branches at Adda, Akuse, Dodowa, Accra, Nsawam, Koforidua, Huhunya, Osiem and Brimso, making Accra branch his headquarters in 1918. A. Macmillan, *The Red Book of West Africa*, London, 1920, p. 203. Ocansey, a close associate of the West African Youth League in the Gold Coast, the body which spearheaded the country's reaction to Italy's invasion of Ethiopia, was alleged to be in frequent communication with a number of 'American agitators' and to be in receipt of numerous copies of the *Negro World* published by Marcus Garvey.
100 *Ibid.*, 'A Statement Issued by the West African Co-operative Producers Ltd. November 1931'. Also, ACC.583/64, *Papers of Farmers' Association*, Ghana Regional Archives, Cape Coast, the Gold Coast Farmers Association Ltd to E. Rodcliffe Clarke, Port of Spain, Trinidad, 12 April 1933.
101 *Vox Populi* (Accra), 23 April 1932.
102 ACC.145/65, *Aborigines Papers*, *Minutes* of a meeting of ARPS, Eastern Province branch, 18 December 1923.
103 C.O.554/54/2760, 'Resolutions of the Conference of British West Africa, Held in Accra, Gold Coast, 11–29 March 1920'.
104 ACC.806/56, Ghana National Archives, Accra.

105 *Ibid.* The other schemes announced in the Gold Coast during the 1920s included the Wilbambasu Consolidated Lands Co. floated by F. W. Dove in 1924; Theodore Taylor and Co. in 1926; the Cooperative Producers Alliance and the West African Co-operative Producers Ltd.

106 *Macaulay Papers*, Box 29, File 2.

107 C.O.96/696/6844, Sir Alexander Slater, Governor of the Gold Coast, to Lord Passfield, Secretary of State for the Colonies, 24 December 1930.

108 For a good discussion of the 1930–31 Cocoa Hold-up, see Samuel Rhodie, 'The Gold Coast Hold-up of 1930–31', *Transactions of the Historical Society of Ghana*, ix, 1968, pp. 105–18. The severe trade depression was aggravated locally by the boycott of imported articles which accompanied the farmers' 'hold-up' of cocoa in the first three months of the 1930–31 main season. C.O.96/696/6835.

109 Holmes, 'Economic and Political Organisations', p. 113. Homes reveals that there was an occasion when Barclays Bank in the Gold Coast informed the Colonial government of the financial status of all the directors of the West African Co-operative Producers Ltd, *Ibid.*

110 Rhodie, 'Gold Coast Cocoa Hold-up', p. 107.

111 K. O. Mbadiwe, *British and Axis Aims in Africa*, pp. 171–2. Cited in G. O. Olusanya, *The Second World War and Politics in Nigeria, 1939–1953*, Lagos, 1973, p. 19.

112 *Macaulay Papers*, Box 30, File 4. Tete Ansa, 'The Iniquities of the West African Trade Monopolists', January 1931.

113 *Ibid.*, Box 61, File 3.

114 C.O.96/699/7050A; also, file C.S.O.1403/31, Ghana National Archives, Accra, 'Demonstrations Against Income Tax Bill, 1931'.

115 C.O.87/240/33010. Incidentally, the Gambia was not granted a constitution in the 1920s.

116 'Nigerian Youth Charter', enclosed in C.O.583/234/30386.

117 *Ibid.*, minute by R. Turnbull, 23 December 1938.

118 C.O.96/717/21750/2, 'Papers Relating to the Petition of the Gold Coast Colony and Ashanti Delegation'.

119 C.O.267/655/32157/1936, A. B. Mathews, Colonial Secretary in Sierra Leone, to Joint-Secretaries, Sierra Leone Section of NCBWA, 13 August 1936.

120 Legislative Council *Debates*, (Gold Coast), 1931–32, pp. 241–2.

121 *Ibid.*, pp. 380–5.

122 C.O.96/699/7050A, Sir Shenton Thomas, Governor of the Gold Coast, to Sir Philip Cunliffe-Lister, the Secretary of State for the Colonies, 17 March 1933.

123 A. E. Afigbo, 'The People and the Introduction of Direct Taxation in 1928', Seminar paper, Institute of African Studies, Ibadan, Nigeria, 26 November 1964. For details of the riots, see H. A. Gailey, *Road to Aba: A Study of British Administrative Policy in Eastern Nigeria*, London, 1971.

124 C.O.96/723/31135/2, Moore to MacDonald, 9 November 1935.

125 Deidrich, Westermann, 'Ein Kongress der Westafrikaner', *Kolonial Rundschau*, pp. 167–8,

126 President Julius Nyerere once emphasised at a symposium that 'One need not go into the history of colonization of Africa, but that colonization had one significant result. A sentiment was created on the African continent – a sentiment of oneness.' Nyerere, 'Africa's Place in the World', in *Wellesley College Symposium on Africa*, p. 149, cited in Ali Mazrui, p. 46.

127 This does not imply that without the racial factor West Africans would not have taken interest in such a major international crisis as the Italo-Ethiopian conflict which involved their great colonial powers and the system of collective security. What is worth emphasising here is the intensity of their protest at the Italian action, and the degree of interest shown in the whole affair. As one scholar has rightly pointed out, 'closely associated with the oppression psychosis of the race conscious is their excessive sensitivity. Since the race conscious identify their personal status with that of their race any attack on the race is taken personally. The race conscious are aware of their status in relation to their race. They become "touchy" or supersensitive. To demean the race they feel is to demean every member of it. . . . The race conscious of the low status group are aware of past and present exploitation. They recall with bitterness the limitation of their freedom and their debasement. Grievances are formulated, becoming part of their ideology'. W. O. Brown, 'The Nature of Race Consciousness' in Locke and Stern, *When Peoples Meet: A Study in Race and Culture Contacts*, pp. 523–5.

CHAPTER TWO

West African responses: The early phase

Although this study deals essentially with West African attitudes to the Italian invasion of Ethiopia, it is important to reappraise the general diplomatic background within which the crisis was cast, as well as the activities of private international organisations in relation to the conflict, especially those of coloured groups in Britain and France, which were in close contact with West Africans. The crisis, and the way Africans saw it, cannot be adquately treated in isolation from this background. In this chapter, therefore, we shall review the initial West African responses to the Italo-Ethiopian question against the background of what was happening outside the confines of West Africa.

Diplomatic background

Ethiopia was an independent sovereign state: but her foreign relations were complicated by the fact that she was the only surviving independent state in the vast African continent, and surrounded by the European colonial powers who had made many treaties with or concerning her since 1889. She had been the subject of what colonial peoples regarded as the usual imperialist manoeuvres and machinations of the great powers seeking to acquire or control her. Thus, towards the close of the nineteenth century, when colonial expansion of the European powers in Africa reached its height. Ethiopia was swept into the full current of international politics. Her natural resources and temperate climate invited foreign exploitation, while her possession of Lake Tsana, the source of the Blue Nile, rendered her strategically important to any nation controlling Egypt and Sudan.[1]

Thus, although the curtain was raised at Walwal in 1934, the Italian attack on Ethiopia began in 1869 when an Italian shipping firm first established itself at Assab on the Red Sea. By 1890 Italy's possession on the Red Sea had developed into an Italian colony of Eritrea. The expansion of Italian possessions southward brought them into direct contact with Ethiopia. In March 1889, Menelik, Emperor of Ethiopia, entered into negotiations with Italy which culminated in the signing of the notorious treaty of Wichale of 2 May 1889, over some of whose provisions much controversy arose between Menelik and the Italians.[2] The thinly-veiled purpose of Article 17 of this treaty was to make of Ethiopia an Italian protectorate. When Menelik discovered this claim of Italy he repudiated the whole treaty, and it was this which led to the Battle of Adowa in which Italy suffered a crushing defeat on 1 March 1896. This defeat at Adowa therefore concluded Italy's first attempt to conquer Ethiopia.

But although the treaty of Addis Ababa signed after Adowa on 26 October 1896 recognised 'the absolute and unreserved independence of the Ethiopian Empire as a sovereign and independent state', in Europe the question of what country's influence was to predominate in Ethiopia was reopened. For neither Italy nor the other great powers had finally abandoned their intention to 'partition' Ethiopia. Hence, since that date, and especially in 1906, 1915, and 1925, the three limitrophe powers – Great Britain, France, and Italy – made unsuccessful attempts to carve Ethiopia up into spheres of influence.

By 1934, Benito Mussolini, who had assumed power in Italy in late 1922, had become completely disillusioned with European diplomacy: his grand European plan, the Four-Power Pact, which he regarded as an alternative to the League of Nations, had received but little encouragement from the other powers; his disillusionment with conference diplomacy had been confirmed by the failure of the Disarmament Conference in the late spring of 1934; Hitler was daily becoming a threat to the Italian position in the Danube and to all South–East Europe; a Nazi *putsch* had been attempted in Austria in July 1934 and the Nazification of Austria and subsequent *Anschluss* was almost in sight. Frustrated by these complicated affairs and the inhospitable political climate in Europe, Mussolini turned in 1934 to imperialism in Africa as a field for dramatic action; he put aside his plans to establish Italy's influence in Europe and looked now across the Mediterranean for the field in which to assert the power and prestige of Fascism: 'I have always held that having broken the pride of Bolshevism,' Mussolini declared before the march on Rome, 'Fascism should become the watchful guardian of our foreign policy,' and the 'future progress of the Fascist ethos demanded the avenging of Adowa.'[3] The mirage of a modern Roman empire beckoned: and if Italy was to match the position of Britain and France in the world, she must also possess overseas territories. Moreover, Ethiopia was one part of Africa not under control or virtual protection of another European power. The continued existence of Ethiopia as 'an independent native state in Africa' was a 'nuisance to Powers with colonial possessions in that continent',[4] as it would act as a focus of national feeling and an encouragement to subject races in the neighbourhood to assert themselves against the white powers under whose tutelage they had come.

The pretext for the Italian invasion of Ethiopia came at the end of 1934 when on 5 December sharp fighting broke out between an Italian contingent occupying Walwal in Ogaden and the Ethiopian military escort of an Anglo-Ethiopian boundary commission.[5] Italy demanded that the Ethiopian Government should apologise and pay heavy compensation, including a salute to the Italian flag at Walwal, and punishment of the responsible Ethiopian officers. Ethiopia rejected these demands, proposing instead that the dispute be referred to arbitration in accordance with the Italo-Ethiopian treaty of friendship of 1928. Mussolini refused the suggestion, whereupon on 3 January 1935, the Emperor of Ethiopia formally appealed to the League of Nations, asking that every measure should be taken to safeguard peace. There then followed ten months of fruitless negotiations at Geneva, while Mussolini frantically pushed forward his war preparations, turning Italian colonies of Ethiopia's seaboard, north and south, into bases for the coming war.

On 3 October 1935, without any formal declaration of war, Italian planes bombed the Ethiopian towns Adowa and Adigrat as the start of her 'civilising mission' in Africa. In resorting to this act of war Italy violated the covenant of the League of Nations, the Kellogg Pact, and the string of treaties from 1896 onward in which she had admitted the independence of Ethiopia. It was flagrant aggression. On 5 October, the Ethiopian delegate to the League of Nations, Tecle Hawariat, declared on behalf of the Ethiopian Government: '. . . Ethiopia asks the League of Nations to declare, with all the authority conferred on it by its mission of peace, that treaties must be respected, and the pledge word must be kept, that wars of aggression are outlawed and that force must give way to justice.'[6]

The League Council declared on 7 October 1935 that Italy had resorted to war 'in disregard to its covenants under Article 12 of the Covenant of the League of Nations', so that, for the first time in its history, the League had declared one of its members to be an 'aggressor'. On 11 October, fifty members of the League Assembly concurred with this declaration and on 18 November invoked a scheme of financial and economic sanctions against Italy. No embargo, however, was placed on oil, and the Suez Canal was not closed to Italian military shipments. Consequently, the sanctions imposed on Italy by the League proved to be ineffective. By 5 May 1936, Addis Ababa had fallen, marking the formal, but not actual, end of hostilities. The Italian conquest of Ethiopia was given recognition by the powers in 1938.

The various coloured groups in Europe, America, West Indies, as well as the pan-African conscious nationalist leaders in Africa, viewed the Italo-Ethiopian conflict of 1935 as a racial war. To them all Africa was involved and the whole relation of black and white. Mussolini had seen to that: 'Has the League of Nations become the tribunal before which all the Negroes and un-civilised peoples, all the world's savages, can bring the great nations which have revolutionalised and transformed humanity?'[7]

The unprovoked Italian attack on Ethiopia created one of the most disturbing crises that rocked the international world during the 1930s. The reaction was intense, for the Italian aggression became a burning question everywhere, and Ethiopia the 'hub of the wheel of world affairs'. It was discussed by illiterate Negro villagers in West Africa as eagerly as it was debated in the press and in the parliaments and on the radio networks of the great cities of the world. It provoked an eruption of international interests, sympathy, and in some instances, vehement protest. People all over the world read accounts of the horrors of the war – the machine-gunning of defenceless Ethiopians, the choking by poison gas, the mutilation of bodies – and were outraged. With no official prompting, and, moreover, while governments were holding back, world opinion demanded action by the League of Nations. As the collective system began to function, every move was commented upon. Pressing appeals came pouring in from nearly every country, adjuring the League to fulfil the hopes of humanity and safeguard the peace of the world. Some religious groups condemned the Italian aggression as an outrage against universal Christian morality, and denounced it as an intolerable wrong to mankind, and a 'sin against the laws of Christ'.[8] International peace organisations – such as the Women's International League for Peace and Freedom, International Federation of League of Nations Societies, International Student Service, and international labour groups like the International Federation of Trade Unions and the Labour and Socialist International – all regarded the crisis with serious concern and united in general condemnation of Italian agression,

In Paris, the *Rassemblement Populaire,* consisting of fifty organisations, held mass demonstrations and passed resolutions favouring economic boycott of Italy. In New York, the Friends of Ethiopia and the African Welfare Committee of the Federal Council of the Churches of Christ in America mobilised sentiment on a national scale in favour of Ethiopia. This body circulated an article entitled, 'Ethiopia – Still Proud and Free'.[9] In Trinidad, West Indies, a group of demonstrators pulled down the Portuguese national flags in the colony, thinking that they were Italian flags.[10] In London, the campaign in Ethiopia was severely criticised as a deliberate war of aggression and plunder by many organisations, including the British League of Nations Union, the Abyssinian Association, the New Commonwealth Society, and the National League of Young Liberals.

Undoubtedly the greatest single force in rallying British opinion to the League standard was the Peace Ballot organised by the British League of Nations Union. The results of the Peace Ballot were actual proof of where the country stood, and were accompanied by a very definite change in the tone of official references to the League which had often been politely sceptical. The reaction of the various groups and societies in Britain was sustained throughout the conflict. And when Addis Ababa finally fell, resolutions were passed urging the British Government to refuse recognition of the conquest of Ethiopia and to take no action which would compromise the right of the Emperor of Ethiopia to be represented at Geneva.[11] The Abyssinia Association formed in March 1936 by a group of British people particularly interested in Ethiopia, such as Sir George Paish, the economist Professor Stanley Jevons, the pacifist Norman Angell and Muriel Blundell repudiated outright the policy of the British Government in the following resolution:

> ... For Britain, trustee of millions of Indians and Africans, to proclaim to the world that she is prepared to sell a small independent African nation of great antiquity in order to buy from a cynical, unscrupulous adventurer a precarious peace is as shameful as it is suicidal. . . . We refuse to betray our trusteeship and have this crime upon our consciences.[12]

To many of these groups, the idea of Britain bargaining away the full rights of Ethiopia to existence as an independent state, however important the concessions which it was believed might be obtained in return, was absolutely contrary to the immutable principles of the League of Nations and to general treaties, such as the Pact of Paris, signed by all the principal countries of the world. Interest in the conflict was particularly intense, however, among Africans and peoples of African descent resident in Paris and London during this period.

Protest of Francophone West Africans in Paris

There was in Paris at the time of the Ethiopian crisis a small but articulate West African community which was for the most part a result of the First World War. Added to this were some radical groups of French Negro West Indians. These supported a number of organisations, radical anti-colonial newspapers and periodicals, some of which were vehicles for nationalist ideas.[13] Among the most important of the Negro political organisations in Paris which reacted violently against the Italian attack on Ethiopia was the *Ligue de la défense de la Race Nègre* (LDRN) led by Tiemoho Garan-Kouyaté of Soudan Français (modern Mali), who was closely associated with the League Against Imperialism and George Padmore's *The Negro Worker*, and after his dismissal in 1931, by Emile Fauré of Senegal. The LDRN had a branch office in Berlin and also attempted to establish an English Section through Reginald Bridgeman of the League Against Imperialism. It was committed to an ideal of international Negro solidarity, and specifically, to the defence of the 'absolute national independence of Abyssinia and Liberia with the utmost watchfulness'.[14] Thus the Ligue, like the nationalist groups in British West Africa, expressed serious concern over press campaigns against Liberia in the early 1930s. Emile Faure referred to Liberia as 'our only Republic on the West Coast of Africa, the only place where we can breathe the air of freedom'.[15] In a very prophetic tone, the *Race Nègre*, the organ of LDRN, wrote in 1931 that if Ethiopia 'were attacked, all Negroes worthy of the name would rally to her defence. . . .'[16]

Four years after these words were written, the military threat to Ethiopian independence materialised, and many Negro organisations in Paris rallied to the Ethiopian cause. The misfortune of Ethiopia reawakened in them the 'secret nostalgia, the mysterious bond of race which now links these "savages" of all colonised Negroes, no matter how loyalist, assimilated, or conformist they might be'.[17] While calling attention to the great movement of sympathy and support for Ethiopia, the Negro press in Paris such as *El Ouma, Cri des Nègres* and *Race Nègre*, also interpreted the symbolic value of Ethiopian independence more widely in terms of the right of all colonial peoples, and especially other Africans, to self-determination. The conflict was seen as a war for self-determination.

The Ethiopian question brought about a collaboration of groups and individuals among French-speaking Africans and West Indians previously estranged. It ushered in possibilities for co-ordinated activity by Negro organisations in France and internationally in a common cause. The moderate and radical elements, who had previously been attacking each other, now began to sink their differences and to sponsor joint demonstrations, and form common fronts.[18] This turn of events gave Kouyaté, who had for some time been in 'apparent political limbo', a springboard; he 'rode back into political activity on the Ethiopian wave'. As President of the *Comité de Défense de l'Indépendance National de l'Ethiopie*, Kouyaté, who was identified by the French as a Communist linkman, organised meetings in conjunction with the *Etoile Nord-Africaine* and the LDRN. The Negro press appealed to Africans to resist their own rulers if these gave any help to the Italian aggressor, and stressed the equivalence between the Italian intentions to subjugate a free African people and French colonial conquest in the past. Militant articles on protest demonstrations against the Italian action were frequently published by *El Ouma, Cri des Nègres* and *Race Nègre*. In July, for example, *Race Nègre* came out with a comprehensive list of names of local Negroes, mainly Africans, ready to fight in Ethiopia if called.[19] Similarly, Kouyaté's *Comite* claimed that it had recruited a hundred volunteers – Negro reserve officers, commissioned and non-commissioned. North African volunteers were reported to have come 'by thousands', all of them ready to fight in defence of Ethiopian independence, if only their transportation could be arranged. According to *Race Nègre*, most of the people who attended a mass meeting organised by the LDRN on 2 June 1935 were not members of the LDRN, but they now called on the oldest Negro political association to unify and lead 'the whole movement now developing in Paris in favour of Abyssinia'.

Resolutions calling on the LDRN leadership to constitute a broadly based committee to this end were passed. Other resolutions appealed to Haiti and Liberia to support Ethiopia in the League of Nations, to boycott Italian goods and expel Italians from their territory 'until this movement could extend to the West Indies and Africa'.[20] But the black protest demonstrations which had most impact on the nationalists on the West Coast of Africa were those organised in the metropolitan capital of London.

Black Protest in Britain

The Ethiopian conflict acted as a catalyst to unite many Afro-Americans, West Indians and Africans resident in Great Britain, who shared the belief that the League of Nations had been partial in its handling of the Italo-Ethiopian dispute. These young educated elite and agitators of African descent were exposed during this period to critical studies of the competing political and social systems of the day: socialism, liberal capitalism, and Fascism. The intellectual world was astir with the anti-Fascist struggle, and it was generally felt that the Fascist danger was threatening 'our racial extermination'.[21] The key figures in the radical protest movement against Fascism and colonialism were the voluntary exiles and 'professional' political propagandists like George Padmire, C. L. R. James, Jomo Kenyatta, Thomas Griffiths of British Guinea (better known by his adoptive Ethiopian name of T. Ras Makonnen), I. T. A. Wallace Johnson and Sam Manning of Trinidad. To the members of this intellectual clan the Italian invasion of Ethiopia was a great shock. It was no less than a second invasion of their homelands. They realised at once that Italy's aggression symbolised not only the powerlessness of the League of Nations but also the triumph of Machiavellism and the 'betrayal of the black race'. This brought about a spirited intensification of political activities of Padmore and his group in defence of the Ethiopian cause, a cause which they as Africans naturally saw as their cause. They became disenchanted not only with the League and Western powers, but also with the performance of the Comintern in the colonial sphere. Hence they challenged Communism and all the then existing ideological systems.

In response to the Ethiopian question, Padmore and his radical intellectual group published articles and studies in which they devoted pages to the conflict, and condemned not only the imperialist powers but also the Catholic Church and the role of the Vatican in the Ethiopian crisis. In his *How Britain Rules Africa*, Padmore wrote that he could not 'help but indict the Church (Roman Catholic) as an institution which has definitely identified itself with Western Imperialism against the coloured races'. He contended that because this was the attitude of the Catholic Church towards the coloured races of Asia and Africa, it was not surprising that the Pope had remained silent in the face of the Italian aggression in Ethiopia, and that the *Osservatore Romano*, the official organ of the Vatican, had openly endorsed the war.[22] Although he was a former Executive Secretary of the International Trade Union Committee of Negro Workers, Padmore charged in a similar thesis as early as May 1935 that the Soviet Union would be quite willing to sacrifice Ethiopia to Italy if Soviet interests would be served. Such an act, in his view, would well fit into the pattern of the desertion of colonial peoples which Russia had followed since Hitler's rise to power. He recounted numerous examples of Communist cynicism and opportunism.[23] George Padmore, who had tried for seven years to work for colonial liberation through the Comintern, and at one time was the most trusted Negro leader in the Comintern apparatus, vehemently denounced the failure of Communist Russia in coming to the aid of Ethiopia. None of the pan-Africanists at the time seemed to be aware that, with the Japanese threat in Asia and the emergence of the Nazi power in Germany, Russia found her isolation in Europe dangerous to her national security. This fear of isolation compelled the Soviet Union to join the League of Nations which she had earlier denounced as a mere mask, designed to deceive the broad masses, for the aggressive aims of the imperialist policy of certain great powers or their vassals. From 1934, therefore, the Soviet Union began to collaborate closely with the Western powers, much to the disappointment of Wallace Johnson and, in particular, Padmore, who broke with the Comintern.

Further criticism of the powers during this period came from the West Indian historian, C. L. R. James, who was uncompromising about external domination. James asserted that Africans and peoples of African descent, especially those who had been poisoned by 'British imperialist education', needed a lesson. This much needed lesson, he claimed, had been provided by the Italian aggression in Ethiopia. James argued that every succeeding day showed exactly the real motives which moved 'Imperialism in its contact with Africa'; it also showed the 'incredible savagery and duplicity of European Imperialism' in its quest for markets and raw materials.[24] A few years later C. L. R. James, who was dedicated to the twin ideals of African independence and pan-Africanism,[25] wrote his little known pamphlet entitled *Why Negroes Should Oppose the War* in which he again contributed to the debate on the Ethiopian crisis.

In anticipation of the Italian attack, James, together with several people of African descent, formed in the summer of 1935 in London an organisation known as the International African Friends of Abyssinia (IAFA) to arouse the sympathy and support of the British public for Ethiopia. A statement issued by Jomo Kenyatta, its honorary Secretary, said that the main object of the organisation was 'to assist by all means in their power in the maintenance of the territorial integrity and political independence of Abyssinia'. The Executive Committee included J. B. Danquah, S. R. Wood and G. E. Moore (members of the 1934 Gold Coast Delegations to England); Amy Ashwood Garvey, the ex-wife of Marcus Garvey who served as honorary treasurer; Peter Milliard, a medical practitioner from British Guiana who later became President of the Negro Association in Manchester, vice-chairman; T. Albert Marryshow, a trade unionist and member of the Grenada Legislative Council who had attended the 1921 London Pan-African Congress, second vice-chairman; Samuel Manning of Trinidad, secretary of propaganda; and the most prominent of them all, C. L. R. James, also a member of the League of Coloured Peoples, chairman. When George Padmore settled permanently in London later in the year, he joined the IAFA. Contrary to popular impression, Padmore, who eventually dominated the IAFA, was only a member of the organisation, and not the one who formed it.[26]

On 28 July 1935, the Executive Committee of IAFA issued a manifesto and an appeal at a public meeting held at Farringdon Hall, Ludgate Circus, London, which declared that Africans and persons of African descent all over the world had always looked with 'jealous pride at the Kingdom of Abyssinia', which alone of the ancient African kingdoms still maintained its independence. They had therefore viewed with alarm and indignation the desire openly expressed by Italy of conquering Ethiopia and the concentration of large 'masses of Italian troops and quantities of armaments on the Abyssinian frontiers'. After this preamble, IAFA demanded that the League of Nations should take measures to restrain Italy from 'this gross infringement of international law and agreements', assured the Emperor and people of Ethiopia that it wholeheartedly supported them in their efforts to preserve and maintain their rights, protested to the Italian Government against its 'immoral and barbarous attitude to Abyssinia', and finally demanded that the British Government should use all their efforts and influence in the League of Nations to assist Ethiopia to defend herself against 'this unwarranted attack'. The organisation then called upon Africans and peoples of African descent all over the world 'to represent the above sentiments to their respective governments', and to pledge themselves to assist Ethiopia in her struggle by all the means at their disposal. [27]

In seconding a resolution which was subsequently adopted at the meeting, S. R. Wood, Secretary of the 1934 Gold Coast Aborigines' Rights' Protection Society Deputation to England, repeated that Ethiopia was the 'idol of Africans the world over, and spiritually, their "Tower of Refuge".' He reminded the imperialist powers that the days of the scramble for Africa were past, for the watchdog of Africa was 'now awake, awake to her duties and responsibilities'. [28] This meeting was followed on 16 August 1935 by another impassioned appeal by the chairman of IAFA, C. L. R. James, in which he said that if in their fight for their independence, Ethiopians were to be defeated, 'we look to them to destroy their country rather than hand it over to the invader'. The radical and revolutionary James then declared: 'Let them burn down Addis Ababa, let them poison their wells and water-holes, let them destroy every blade of vegetation.' [29] The IAFA also proposed to organise a legion of volunteers composed of men of African descent to send to Ethiopia to assist the Emperor in the defence of his country. This proposal did not materialise, as the Foreign Enlistment Act of 1870 forbade British subjects to join forces of countries – in this case Italy and Ethiopia – which maintained friendly relations with Britain. The IAFA was, however, among the other coloured organisations in Britain which, under the auspices of the Pan-African Federation, organised a reception for Haile Selassie and the Ethiopian Royal Family when they arrived in London on 3 June 1936 to spend their years of exile.

Besides the IAFA which functioned for only a short period, were other pan-African oriented coloured organisations in Britain such as the League of Coloured Peoples and the West African Students' Union which took a very keen interest in the events of Ethiopia. The LCP was inaugurated in 1931 through the initiative and efforts of Harold Moody.

A native of Kingston, Jamaica, Harold Arundel Moody was born on 8 October 1882 and from boyhood developed an interest in the Christian religion. He arrived in England in September 1904 and enrolled at King's College, London, where he obtained a degree of Doctor of Medicine in 1919. [30] His scientific studies could not repress the religious fervour in him so that Christianity continued to loom as large as ever both in his private and public life. In 1936 he was elected President of the Christian Endeavour Union of Great Britain and Ireland, becoming the following year a member of the executive committee of the British and Foreign Bible Society. Harold Moody was 'very conscious of the need to bring together all the members of his own race resident in Britain for personal intercourse and consultation.' The LCP which he founded, and presided over until his death in 1947, was perhaps the first conscious and deliberate attempt in Britain to form a multi-racial organisation, led by blacks, although with a membership that for its first ten years was predominantly white.[31]

Among the West Africans who at various times became members of the executive of the League, and regularly expressed their resentment at the Italian aggression on Ethiopia were Louis Mbanefo and H. O. Davies of Nigeria; W. B. Van Lare, J. D. K. Gwira, J. E. Sackeyfio, A. H. Koi of the Gold Coast; and Miss Vida Thompson of Sierra Leone. Other West Africans who took an interest in the activities of LCP were Stephen Peter Thomas, a Nigerian law student who became secretary of the organisation in 1934, and Stella Thomas, his sister, who was called to the bar in 1933. Their father, Peter J. C. Thomas, attended the 1921 London Pan-African Congress. One of the main aims of the LCP was to interest its members in the welfare of coloured peoples in all parts of the world, and to improve relations between the races. As was explained in the editorial of the maiden issue of its organ, *The Keys*, the LCP had as its 'object the purpose of stating the cause of the Black Man'. The editorial further stated that apart from the coloured peoples within the British empire, the LCP also supported the claims of the peoples who owed 'allegiance to a flag other than our own', for 'all along the line there is the same tale'.[32] The Ethiopian question gave the League the opportunity to express in violent terms its ideas about colonialism and imperialism.

At a general meeting held on 4 September 1935, the League passed a resolution which not only expressed an opinion upon the impending conflict but also laid down a policy concerning the future of Africa as a whole. It identified itself with the Ethiopians and expressed its utmost co-operation with the Emperor and the Ethiopian people in the deep shadow of war which hung over their beloved country. The League felt that the attitude of Mussolini towards Ethiopia was expressive 'of a deeply seated conviction in the minds of most European peoples that African peoples were ordained to be their serfs'. It hoped that this long cherished idea should be dispelled once and for all. Europe should begin to recognise Africa and African peoples as equal partners with her in the great task of human development and cease to 'look upon Africa and the Africans as a country and people merely to be exploited'. It remarked that the African like the European was created in the 'image of God' and rightfully 'demands the privilege of directing its own affairs'. The LCP finally urged upon the metropolitan powers and the League of Nations that the time was 'now ripe for them to consider a plan for the future of Africa which plan should be nothing less than the ultimate and complete freedom of Africa from any external domination whatsoever'.[33] Although there is no evidence that the LCP set up an Ethiopia Defence Committee as did the West African Students' Union in Great Britain, Harold Moody and his West Indian and West African group continually expressed their indignation at the Italian action in Ethiopia throughout the period of the crisis. *The Keys* published such articles as 'What is the Ethiopian Sin?', 'Abyssinia and the Imperialists', and 'Abyssinia or Amharaland?'.[34] And when Ethiopia was finally conquered the League claimed that it was 'Italian poison gas and British oil' which had defeated Ethiopia. Hence at its annual general meeting held on 11 March 1938, the LCP called the attention of the British Government and Parliament to the great movement of solidarity which the Italian attack on Ethiopia had 'brought about among the African and African-descended peoples in reaction against European violence, conquest and domination'.[35]

But the focal point of the protest of West Africans in Britain to the Italo-Ethiopian conflict was the West African Students' Union (WASU) founded in August 1925. Its chief architect was H. C. Bankole-Bright, a medical doctor and member of the Sierra Leone Legislative Council and of the National Congress of British West Africa. A meeting of about a dozen West Africans, most of them law students, held on 7 August 1925, adopted a resolution to inaugurate a West African Students' Union.[36] At that time, there existed three African students' organisations in England: the Union for Students of African Descent formed in 1917 primarily for literary and social activities; the Gold Coast Students' Association and the Nigerian Progress Union established in 1924. Although Bankole-Bright appreciated the efforts of these organisations, he nevertheless urged greater unity, which he said had proved productive in other civilised countries.[37] He stressed that what the NCBWA had accomplished could not have been independently attained by each colony and advised the young men to improve not only their intellectual but also their moral development. The NCBWA, he went on, preached liberty and leadership. West Africa must study her own psychology and hasten the pace for constitutional freedom. He then stressed the necessity for a union of West African students. It was out of this that the WASU was inaugurated with the following elected as pioneer officers of the union for the year 1926: W. Davidson Carrol, a Gambian law graduate of Oxford who later became a member of the Gambia Legislative Council (president); J. B. Danquah of the Gold Coast (vice-president); Ladipo Solanke, a Nigerian arts graduate of Fourah Bay College, Sierra Leone, from where he had come to Britain in 1922 to study law (honorary secretary); Kusimo Soluade, a Nigerian law student (assistant secretary); and J. Akanni Doherty, another Nigerian trained at Fourah Bay College who came to England in 1924 to study medicine at University College, London (treasurer and financial secretary). It is important to note that the WASU was the first significant exile organisation initiated and led by Africans as distinct from persons of African descent.

Like the NCBWA, WASU was founded on a basis of geography, race consciousness, and a communal sense of discontent. The members of the organisation saw themselves as representatives of the intellectual elite of West Africa. The union thus became the centre of the intellectual and cultural life of West African students in Great Britain and Ireland. Like the participants in the National Congress conference in Accra in 1920, the members of the union identified themselves and their goals with 'national consciousness'. The spirit of the union embodied the desire not to oust the white man but to speak on equal terms with him.

Besides the need for unity, the decision of these students to organise themselves from 1925 onwards was inspired by two main reasons: first, the colour prejudice that faced them in Britain and, secondly, the colonial status in relation to Britain. One writer has asserted that because of this determining characteristic of being an association of coloured colonial students, the WASU developed, throughout its history, certain features not usually found among students' unions, and which are reminiscent of 'protest movements'.[38] Like the Congress movement, the objectives of WASU far transcended the narrow limits of West Africa. Ladipo Solanke of Nigeria, the moving spirit of the union, wanted an organisation which could represent and speak for all the students from West Africa, as a step towards creating 'a united states of West Africa', which, so he hoped, would lead towards a 'United Africa' of all the African peoples.[39] It was this spirit of pan-Africanism which inspired J. W. de Graft-Johnson, a leading Gold Coast member of the union, to describe the hope of African youth as the great yearning for freedom, for emancipation from the yoke of centuries. As he expressed it, the youth of Africa everywhere was assailed by the 'alluring thoughts of a free Africa', of an Africa owing no foreign burden 'but stepping into her rightful place as a unit in the powerful army of the human family'. In the opinion of de Graft-Johnson, the first step toward nationhood was 'to change the attitude of the white man towards the educated African'.[40]

This was, in fact, one of the objectives of WASU. Another of its main aims was to rehabilitate the African past by acting as a bureau of information on African history and culture and in this way present to the world a true picture of the land and people of Africa. Apart from launching a periodical, *Wasu*, members of the organisation spoke regularly at meetings organised by London societies. The union also participated in many international gatherings to acquaint members with the racial issues of the day, as well as the political changes which were taking place in the international world. For instance, two of its members represented the union, and Africa generally, at the Liverpool International Youth Movement for Peace in January 1928. In that same year the union was represented at both the British Fellowship of Youth International Conference at Oxford and at the Hague International Conference.[41]

During its formative years the union was tremendously influenced by the racial and political philosophy of such African or Negro celebrities as J. E. Casely Hayford, J. E. K. Aggrey, and in particular Marcus Garvey, who was closely associated with the WASU throughout the thirties until his death on 10 June 1940. Addressing the union on 5 November 1926 on the subject 'Nationalism As a West African Ideal', Casely Hayford pointed out that it was the duty of all Africans to take up the work of correcting wrong impressions concerning the African race wherever and whenever they came across them. In his opinion, unless the African thought for himself and produced his own leaders in all walks of life, 'he would always remain a hewer of wood and drawer of water'. Concluding in his usual pan-African vein, Casely Hayford reminded members of the union that the time had come when Africans from the north, south, east, and west of the globe, should join together, not for struggle, but in the way of 'saying to other men, "We, too, are men; we, too, have found our place in the world".'[42] That WASU members took the inspiring appeal of Casely Hayford to heart and saw themselves as the means of enhancing the prestige and status of West Africans in particular and people of African origin in general was reflected in the union's activities during the latter part of the 1920s and throughout the 1930s.

On any topic which concerned Africa in any way members of the union became immediately vocal. On 3 March 1929, for instance, the union protested to L. S. Amery, the Secretary of State for the Colonies, against the arrangements of a Newcastle upon Tyne exhibition that year so far as they concerned Africans. The matter was pressed forward to the House of Commons where assurance was given that nothing in the arrangements would bring the African natives into contempt or ridicule.[43] But what galvanised the union into rebellion against European rule in Africa was the Italian invasion of Ethiopia. From the beginning of the crisis members of the union, being themselves under colonial subjection, were able to grasp the full significance. Their attention was focused on Ethiopia, for the horizon of international politics had now extended 'into our borders'.

The union at once described the Italo-Ethiopian dispute as the 'age-long conflict between Right and Wrong'. Opinions were at first divided among them concerning the conflict. One group felt that, as the power with the largest portion of Africa, Britain, in fairness to her subjects, would see to it that justice was done and honour upheld without fear or favour. There were others who reduced the affair to the question of white versus black. This group questioned whether in the event of war breaking out Great Britain would not unhesitatingly sacrifice the black race on the altar of injustice to preserve the superiority of the white race. And yet another group definitely conveyed the idea that Great Britain would conduct herself in such a way as to obtain the greatest benefit out of the situation. Events moved quickly, and, as we have noted, Italy invaded Ethiopia without any formal declaration of war. It was evident therefore from Italy's unwarranted aggression that members of the union would be in sympathy with Ethiopia. The different Orders in Council and the Foreign Enlistment Act of 1870 governing active service abroad were known to all of them. What then could they do to demonstrate to the Ethiopians their deep sympathy and also their wish that Ethiopians should make a determined effort to maintain unimpaired their territorial integrity and political independence even if it meant dying free men rather than becoming subjects of a nation they hated so intensely?

Members of the union immediately joined in the protest activity in Britain against the violation of Ethiopia's sovereignty. They could not understand why the Holy See appeared to acquiesce in Mussolini's 'civilising mission'. In its editorial notes, *Wasu* lamented how Italy, the home of Christendom, could attack innocent Ethiopians. It was alleged that the other religious sects were not in a position to point a finger of reproach, for 'here in England for instance, while the clergy prate about "peace and goodwill to all men",' they held chaplaincies in the army, the navy, and the air force, and wore military decorations on their vestments. The editorial concluded from this that the so-called crisis that had overtaken the modern world was nothing but the judgement of the 'Moral Order'.[44]

The union set up an Ethiopia Defence Committee for the purpose of raising funds chiefly among WASU members, to be forwarded from time to time to the Ethiopian Minister in London, to be utilised in Ethiopia in defence of 'the people of Ethiopia against the present Italian aggression'. The committee was an all-female affair. Mrs A. M. Cole was appointed chairman of the committee, supported by Mrs Irene Howe (vice-chairman), Omoba Remi Ademola (treasurer), and Miss Gladys Franklyne (honorary secretary). The committee was responsible to the executive committee of WASU.[45] In addition, a series of services was held at the union's hostel to invoke Divine guidance for a peaceful settlement of the Ethiopian dispute.

The reaction of the WASU, and of the various coloured groups in Britain and France, to the Ethiopian crisis formed the basis of the nationalist agitation at home in West Africa. For there was a close liaison between these 'voluntary exiles' in London and Paris and the West African nationalist leaders. George

Padmore, for instance, was since the early thirties frequently writing to encourage West African nationalists to 'hit at the system of imperialism'. He brought to their notice that British 'exploiters' were not only 'misgoverning themselves', but had gone around the world 'grinding the life blood out of the masses through economic exploitation'.[46] Padmore told Alfred John Ocansey, a keen supporter of the ARPS, and proprietor of the *Gold Coast Spectator*, edited by Benjamin Wuta Ofei, and the *African Morning Post*, which Azikiwe came from England to the Gold Coast to edit, that amid all the 'manoeuvres and counter-manoeuvres, intrigues and counter-intrigues' that went on among the European chancelleries regarding the Ethiopian question, the powers were agreed on one thing: 'to try and direct Mussolini's aggression towards Africa', in the hope of maintaining the *status quo* in Europe as long as possible.[47] After the annexation of Ethiopia by Italy, Padmore continued to inform the politically minded West Africans of the tensions in Europe. In October 1938, he wrote to emphasise that the 'colonial question is coming up before the statesmen of Europe', as a result of the demands of Hitler, and it 'is necessary for us to be on our guard'. In this respect, he concluded, the 'closest collaboration of our Bureau [International African Service Bureau] and the Aborigines' Rights Protection Society' would be of tremendous importance in making the voice of Africa heard in the councils of nations.[48] Many of Padmore's articles were reproduced in the local press in West Africa.[49]

Other anti-imperialists like Nancy Cunard, a devoted afrophile, were also in steady contact with the West African nationalist leaders on the Ethiopian question. Nancy Cunard sent them copies of the aims and objects of an Ethiopia Defence Committee which had been formed in Paris on 16 August 1935, a committee which, according to her, had already received pledges of support from 195 world organisations many of which were anti-war and anti-fascist.[50] Later in the year she despatched to T. K. Orgle, the editor of the *Vox Populi* in the Gold Coast, a 'Ballad of Ethiopian People' for publication.[51]

Similarly, T. Ras Makonnen, later of the Pan-African Federation, the body which planned the Pan-African Congress of 1945, was regularly drawing the attention of the West African nationalists to the treatment of Africans in Ethiopia, Kenya and South Africa by the colonial powers, and asking them to express their opinion on such matters to their respective local colonial authorities and to the Secretary of State for the Colonies.[52] The net effect of these contacts was to create an atmosphere in which nationalism and anti-imperialist sentiments could flourish, and to generate the forces against the attitudes of the European powers towards the Ethiopian question.

The local colonial governments in West Africa were not unaware of these contacts. For even before the outbreak of the Italo-Ethiopian dispute, Sir Shenton Thomas, Governor of the Gold Coast, was writing in a somewhat exaggerated tone to tell the Secretary of State for the Colonies that large numbers of 'subversive pamphlets of all kinds' were being addressed to Kobina Sekyi, and that each communistic centre in Russia, Germany, France, England, America, and South Africa had communicated with him. He added that among Sekyi's friends were Padmore, Nancy Cunard, Bridgeman, Ward, Wallace Johnson and others, and concluded that Sekyi was definitely anti-European.[53] Sir Philip Cunliffe-Lister, the Secretary of State for the Colonies, was himself equally disturbed by such contacts, and therefore made every possible effort to stop them. In a confidential circular marked 'SECRET', he told the British officials in West Africa, who had during the period of the Italo-Ethiopian crisis become paranoid in their fear of a communist plot behind the nationalist reaction to the conflict, that George Padmore had formed, in conjunction with Tiemoho Garan Kouyate, 'a prominent French Negro communist', an organisation for revolutionary work in Africa entitled the 'Pan-African Brotherhood'. The organisation, according to Sir Philip Cunliffe-Lister, had already issued a manifesto on behalf of Ethiopia, and it 'may be taken for granted that any publication which it issues will be wholly undesirable in tone'. He instructed, therefore, that all publications of the 'Pan-African Brotherhood' be prohibited from entry into the colonies.[54]

Such measures did not appear to have had any appreciable effect on the nationalist press which continued to give considerable coverage to the activities of the coloured organisations abroad about the Ethiopian crisis. Also, much information came from the Negro press in Paris. The *Agence Metromer*, a small news service run from Paris by Augustin Azango of Dahomey, for example, despatched news of the course of hostilities in Ethiopia and of work in France to West African papers and circulated to the Paris press items on pro-Ethiopian activities among the English-speaking Africans. Several hundred copies of each issue of *Cri des Nègres* were allotted to West Africa, although because of the multiple and often indirect channel of distribution used, it is difficult to determine the exact number. Like the British colonial administrators, the French authorities in West Africa became increasingly concerned about the newspaper items on the Ethiopian question which were being smuggled to their colonial subjects. The acting Governor-General in Dakar was therefore constrained to ban such Gold Coast newspapers as the *African Morning Post* and the *Gold Coast Spectator* from entering French West Africa. According to him, certain articles on the Italo-Ethiopia dispute published by these papers seemed to have as their main object 'the creation in the native of a state of mind' which would be 'hostile' to the close collaboration of Great Britain and France in West Africa. Some of the articles were found to be 'insulting or harmful to French colonisation'.[55]

Besides the news items on the Ethiopian crisis despatched by the Negro press in Paris, the proceedings and activities of the IAFA, LCP and WASU were subjects of free discussion in West Africa. Harold Moody's LCP established a branch office in Freetown under the chairmanship of Mrs Constance Cummings-John, who was a Councillor. This branch was in constant communication with the parent body in London, and gave publicity in the local press to the activities of the LCP in connection with the Italo-Ethiopian conflict.[56] Similarly, although WASU functioned away from the African political scene, it was a breeding-ground for African sentiments against European rule in Africa. Ladipo Solanke's tour of West Africa from October 1929 to September 1932 provided an opportunity for the formation of branches of the union in several parts of British West Africa.[57] Copies of *Wasu* were mailed regularly to these branches. Besides, the *New Times and Ethiopia News* founded in the spring of 1936 by E. Sylvia Pankhurst, the suffragette, achieved an extensive sale in Africa, particularly on the West Coast. This influential weekly was published to win sympathy for the Ethiopian cause. The first issue appeared on 9 May, the day that the invading Italian armies marched into Addis Ababa. A popular feature of this weekly was entitled 'Africa for Africans'. Many of the articles appearing in the *New Times and Ethiopia News* were reprinted in full by the local West

Emperor Menelik (above) repudiated the Treaty of Wichale, which led to the defeat of the Italian would-be conquerors of Ethiopia at the Battle of Adowa in 1896 (below)

Mussolini's propaganda poster triumphantly proclaimed 'Italy has her own empire at last'

African press, particularly by such papers as the *Comet* and Azikiwe's *West African Pilot*.

The *Comet* was a highly polished weekly paper launched in Lagos on 22 July 1933 by the pan-Africanist, Duse Mohamed Ali of Sudanese-Egyptian origin, who was a committee member of the African Progress Union founded in London in 1918 by Judge McCants Stuart, at one time Chief Justice of Liberia. Before coming to Lagos (1931) where he lived until his death in 1945, Duse Mohamed Ali, well known in official circles for his 'seditionist activities' and close association with Garvey in the United States,[58] had earlier published in London the *African Times and Orient Review* (July 1912–October 1918) and the *African and Orient Review* (January–December 1920). The *Comet* was of a high literary quality and gave considerable coverage to news of foreign affairs. Azikiwe's *West African Pilot*, which an eminent Nigerian politician has described as 'a fire-eating and aggressive nationalist paper of the highest order',[59] also gave detailed accounts about Ethiopia. In the Gold Coast the newspapers which waded into the agitation were A. J. Ocansey's radical *Gold Coast Spectator* and *African Morning Post*, as well as T. K. Orgle's *Vox Populi*. Owners and editors of these papers were well-known pan-Africanists who were closely in touch with Padmore, Nancy Cunard, Arnold Ward, and were receiving numerous copies of Marcus Garvey's widely read newspaper, the *Negro World*. The paper most active in the Ethiopian affair in Sierra Leone was Claudius May's *Sierra Leone Weekly News*, the oldest newspaper in West Africa, having been established in 1884. Claudius May, the editor-proprietor, was a leading Creole, who played a prominent part in the formation and in the politics of both the Sierra Leone section of NCBWA and the Sierra Leone West African Youth League. The only nationalist paper of note in the Gambia was E. F. Small's the *Gambia Outlook and Senegambian Reporter* which not only carried reprints from Padmore's *The Negro Worker* but also aroused sympathy for Ethiopia in the Gambia.

The whole West African press at the time of the Ethiopian crisis thus underwent a great transformation, becoming less parochial and much more pan-African in content. As a personal letter from a European resident in Accra to Arnold J. Toynbee in London claimed: 'In the absence of real news the native newspapers are filled with the wildest stories of Italian routs, and I should imagine that there are very few villages in West Africa in which the war and its causes are not known and discussed.'[60] Such themes as racial inequalities, injustices, and the need for positive action to right historic wrongs were kept vivid in public consciousness by the press. In so doing, the press played a tremendous part in moulding public opinion in the various West African communities against the Italian aggression in Ethiopia.[61]

Rejection of Italian Claims

Although a large percentage of West Africans could not read newspapers and were dependent upon rumours and oral reports for knowledge of what was going on outside their borders, many of them were aware of the crisis in Ethiopia. They could not know much about the circumstances that brought on the war, but they did know that white men were killing blacks by the thousands in East Africa with the object of 'imperialising' another African country.[62] As a result, indignation, resentment, and distrust began to seethe in the minds of many of the unsophisticated colonial subjects who had otherwise gradually been learning to trust the justice and honour of the white man. The various nationalist groups began to express their concern over the situation in Ethiopia in the press, at public mass meetings, and even in pulpits. They vehemently protested and demonstrated, and bitterly denounced what they deemed to be the un-Christian behaviour of 'Christian' Italy. They identified themselves with Ethiopia and demanded 'justice', both for the Ethiopians and for themselves. Reports were received in London that in the courts of the 'great Nigerian Emirs, in the compounds of the native traders, in the village market places throughout tropical Africa, the story of unjust war and aggression' was the subject of countless comments and conversation.[63] Appeals to mother love, Christian duty, racial pride, and the 'plighted word', as well as threats of impending world chaos and the doom of western civilisation should Italy be allowed to conquer Ethiopia were simultaneously made.

It should be emphasised, however, that before Mussolini's threats to conquer and annex Ethiopia, little was known in West Africa by the man in the street about Haile Selassie and his Ethiopian empire. In Sierra Leone, for instance, the 'public originally was quite ignorant of conditions in Abyssinia'.[64] But since the Walwal incident which sparked off the crisis, West Africans, like other persons of African descent all over the world, became so to speak, Ethiopia-conscious, and the talk about town was 'Abyssinia':

> Everywhere Geographies, Maps, Histories and other records are being explored daily to find out all there is to be known of this now famous country and its people. And thanks to the radio and daily papers, the man in the street is getting first-hand information as to the happenings among European nations with regard to this much coveted Empire of the black man.[65]

With this interest increasing so rapidly, West Africans began to clamour for more information about Ethiopia.

Among the educated groups in West Africa, the one dominant issue that became a subject of interest in the press and at centres of local political consciousness was the question about the true racial identity of the Ethiopians. Dispute over whether the Ethiopians were truly racial brothers had been raised not only in West Africa but also in both black and white circles outside the African continent. In the United States, for instance, it was argued that some Ethiopians had balked at being called Negroes, a designation which they associated with enslaved Africans, and that the term 'Abyssinian', derived from the Arabic and meaning 'slave', was also frowned upon. The Negro press, therefore, made strenuous efforts in their editorials to challenge the white propaganda that the Ethiopians were not Negroid. On 12 October, for instance the widely read *Afro-American* argued that, despite considerable miscegenation in the history of Ethiopia, 'Ethiopia at base' was predominantly African and black.[66] Similarly, in Haiti, which, apart from Liberia, was the only other black independent state, there was a long correspondence in the papers as to whether Ethiopians were or were not Negroes. This discussion aroused a good deal of interest; and when it was eventually concluded that Ethiopians, though 'black men, were not really Negroes', the growing interest in the Italo-Ethiopian conflict itself lapsed.[67]

In West Africa, too, the dispute over the true racial identity of the Ethiopians was provoked by the propaganda of the Italian and some other white journalists that Ethiopians were white people and considered themselves superior to Negroes. By spreading such stories, they hoped to dissuade Africans and persons of African descent from supporting Ethiopia. Lectures and study groups were therefore organised in various West African capitals and urban areas at which questions such as these were critically analysed: Of what race are the Ethiopians? Are the Ethiopians black, using the term broadly? Is it true that Ethiopians are contemptuous of Negroes? Do Abyssinians believe in Africans?[68] Since the racial factor formed much of the basis of the West African response to the Italo-Ethiopian conflict, these questions posed a problem which, on occasion, became a subject of controversy even among Africans themselves.

The view that the Ethiopians were a 'white' people was first given prominence by an editorial in *West Africa*, a European-controlled weekly devoted to West African affairs, and which, as it is today, was widely read throughout West Africa. This editorial regretted that no attempt was being made by the Colonial Office to convince the 'many African races of West Africa' of the emptiness of the 'notion that there is the least political call upon them from Abyssinia'. In the opinion of the editorial, Italy was not attacking the Ethiopians because they were black. It was attacking them because it hoped to get from them political and commercial benefits. West Africans, it contended, had nothing in common with Ethiopians. In respect of this, the editorial stressed that 'Abyssinians do not for a moment regard West Africans, Mohammedan, Christian, or Pagan, as friends of theirs. The Abyssinian Government has turned back many Afro-Americans who rushed to its aid just as it has refused the services of 3,000 European volunteers.' The reason for this attitude of the Ethiopian Government, the editorial explained, was that the Ethiopians were not 'black' for, it continued:

> The fact that Abyssinians occupy part of the same continent as West Africans, and that the sun's rays have had the effect they have upon their complexions, no more imply common action or fellow-feeling than do like facts as affecting Bulgarians and Russians or British and Albanians in the continent of Europe.[70]

Thus, in the view of *West Africa*, the Italo-Ethiopian dispute was not a question of colour against colour. It was not a racial conflict. It was an attempt on the part of Italy to use 'force as a means of progress'. For the same purpose Italy could have attacked 'one of the weaker Balkan countries, or another fellow-European'. All through the period of the crisis Cartwright, founder and editor of *West Africa* since its first appearance on 3 February 1917 appeared unsympathetic to the plight of the Ethiopians. In an editorial of 23 May 1936, for example, Cartwright attributed the failure of Ethiopians to resist the Fascist aggression to the fact that 'there was no Ethiopian nation' and no feeling of national independence. He concluded that Africans 'will have no moral right to blame Great Britain or any other Europeans' for the failure of Ethiopia. This attitude of Cartwright contrasts sharply with his earlier consistent support of African causes generally. Born in 1869, Albert Cartwright, who retired as editor of *West Africa* in April 1947, had vigorously commended the aims of the National Congress of British West Africa to British firms, and remained evidently sympathetic to the political programme of the Congress throughout the 1920s. Similarly, in an editorial of 11 August 1934, Cartwright had strongly backed the petition of the 1934 Gold Coast Delegations to the Colonial Office. Chief

Awolowo, who was in close contact with Cartwright in the early forties, has in his autobiography described him as 'a genuine believer in, and fighter for, accelerated political advancement for the Africans'.[71]

That Cartwright should turn sharply against African opinion in the case of the Italo-Ethiopian struggle was due mainly to the economic interest of this journal. Since its inception it had been the policy of *West Africa* to gloss over the racial barrier, and to unite Europeans and Africans in amicable commerce. The prospect of 'race war' as a result of the Italian action in Ethiopia was an alarming prospect for Europeans. For it was generally feared that the weapon of race, which they had used so successfully against Africans, might be used against them and their interests in Africa. Put in its crudest economic terms, racial antagonism of black against white, stirred up by resentment over Ethiopia, would subject the European firms whose interests *West Africa* cherished, to severe damage from boycotts and hold-ups. Cartwright was thus inevitably frightened at the prospect of a 'race war', which would divide Africans and Europeans, and did all he could to play down the racial aspect of the Ethiopian situation.

The reaction of the West African press to Albert Cartwright's editorial, which appeared at the critical period of the crisis when feelings of intense antagonism had developed among large numbers of West Africans towards Europeans, was immediate, vigorous, and incisively hostile. The question was asked as to whether this was an attempt on the part of some Europeans to delude West Africans at this crucial period of racial conflict. Or, as some viewed it, whether this was a projection of the divide and rule policy which had characterised the colonial administration in Africa. A section of the press also wondered to which type of people the *West African* was supposed to be more akin – the Ethiopian, the white man or the Afrikaner. To the radical *Gold Coast Spectator*, Cartwright's editorial was a 'riot of ignorance, and interesting too if only for this wicked ignorance it displays'. This paper condemned the editorial as a 'flagitious attack by the white man upon his own knowledge of facts around him, and it is monstrous in dullness if it is not dissimulation.'[72] What surprised the *Gold Coast Spectator* was that, throughout, Mussolini had himself put the Italo-Ethiopian conflict in the shape of a contest between the black and white races. He had manifested some surprise about the sympathy shown in England with Ethiopians whom he described as 'Negroid, savages, and slave-dealers'. His aggression had been inspired by the fact that Ethiopians were Africans, and he had many a time made direct references to this fact in his 'bombastic' speeches.

On the question of Negro volunteers, Wuta Ofei, the editor of the *Gold Coast Spectator*, explained that Ethiopia had not turned away Afro-American offers for the same reasons for which she had rejected 3,000 European volunteers. Most of the latter were adventurers who, naturally, were not and could not be moved by any patriotic feelings. In addition, European volunteers were really not wanted for they would be a burden on Ethiopia. On the other hand, any African who wished to serve in the Ethiopian army was not turned away on the same grounds. Many officers in the Imperial Army were Afro-Americans; among them were John C. Robinson, the 'Brown Condor of Ethiopia', and Hubert Fauntleroy Julian, the 'Black Eagle of Harlem'. But these had to be paid. At the moment, therefore, Ethiopia needed more funds than men, and for obvious reasons Africans would be of more use to Ethiopia if they remained where they were.

In conclusion, the *Spectator* advised that instead of the Colonial Office conducting propaganda to dissuade Africans from taking an interest in the affairs of the Ethiopians as attempted by *West Africa*, they should rather 'warn the English press to be sensible in these days' in their criticism of West Africans and their doings, particularly with regard to the Italo-Ethiopian struggle. For, as the editorial put it, West Africans had 'passed the fooling stage'. The Gold Coast 'man, down to the school-boy', knew that he had everything in common with the Ethiopians; and that 'No amount of propaganda and repression can alter the African's opinion in the slightest degree on this question.'[73]

To some extent, both *West Africa* and the *Gold Coast Spectator* appear to be right in their respective views on the relationship between Ethiopia and the West Africa of the 1930s. Ethiopia's interest in, let alone concern for, the rest of Africa is a post-Second World War phenomenon. Before then the Ethiopians had had a different conception of the rest of Africa, particularly the far West Coast. The great cultural centres of Africa were in the main too far away to be meaningful to the Ethiopians who, for practical purposes, were concerned with their immediate neighbours, in the main tribes with little civilisation. Ethiopia in the past tended to be largely self-sufficient; the Ethiopians had little knowledge of foreign languages; they had little interest in travelling – except on pilgrimage and this took them mainly to Jerusalem, not southwards or westwards into Africa. As Richard Pankhurst has rightly argued, historic Ethiopia was largely isolated from most of the continent of Africa not only by its geographical position but also by the 'swords of Islam and the machine-guns of the Imperialists'.[74] The scramble for Africa reinforced Ethiopia in her age-old isolation. Surrounded by the colonial powers, Ethiopia once again appeared different from other parts of Africa. In the age of Prester John she had seemed, and considered herself, an island of Christianity in a 'sea of Paganism and Islam'; during the period of the scramble she became an 'island of indigenous African rule in a sea of European colonialism'.[75] She was surrounded by 'a ring of iron'. In this situation there was little chance of her interesting herself in other African countries whose foreign rulers would have seized any excuse to attack the last 'citadel of free Africa'. It is worth emphasising that since Britain, France and Italy, as previously mentioned, coveted Ethiopia, any flirtation of the Ethiopians with the black subjects in the rest of Africa would have hastened the extinction of Ethiopia as an independent state – perhaps long before 1936. Such efforts would have been construed as a threat to the interests and purposes of the colonial powers. Thus Ethiopia in her mountains and in her independence remained aloof from the rest of Africa.

It was after the Second World War that Ethiopia moved from the periphery of the classical world to become, in a very real sense, a major capital and one of the most important centres in a new continent. In a geographical or political sense, Ethiopia is now an entirely new setting. Through the growth of independent states on the African continent and the creation of a continental organisation within which these states can work together, the horizons of the Ethiopian people have been extended and widened. All this has been reinforced by the recent communications revolution which have provided direct channels of contact between the various self-governing African countries. Thus, what *West Africa* said in the 1930s was factually true. However, in matters of emotional attachment, even where such attachment is unreciprocated, hard facts are often completely irrelevant or of little use. This was exactly the position of the West African nationalists. They had all along exhibited a strong emotional attachment to Ethiopia; so that, in effect, what the *Gold Coast Spectator* was saying was simply that what Ethiopians thought about West Africans did not matter as much as what West Africans thought about Ethiopia.

It was this emotional attachment which, as a reply to Italian propaganda and some sections of the white press in Europe on the question of Ethiopia's racial identity, inspired the efforts on the part of the West African press, and of some public or leading nationalist politicians, to publish a series of comprehensive studies about Ethiopia as a black African state, her ancient and romantic history and, particularly, her distinctive achievements and contributions to ancient civilisations. In the Gold Coast, for instance, Azikiwe's *African Morning Post* devoted a series of articles about Ethiopia in a special column entitled 'Nuggets of African History' contributed by a columnist under the pseudonym 'Antar'. Ethiopia's achievements in the realms of philosophy, architecture, literature, astronomy, and politics were glorified by this race-conscious newspaper. Ethiopians, for instance, were said to have influenced the founders of Greek philosophy before the great systematisers, such as Plato and Aristotle. Ethiopian epistemology, which was one of the earliest on record, argued the *African Morning Post*, influenced the students who came to Ethiopia and Egypt. It was the insights learnt by these students which formed the basis of the systematic philosophies which emerged in Greece several centuries later. This, the paper contended, was another palm of victory for the mentality of the black man. 'Antar' lamented that in view of the fact that modern Egyptological scholarship had become 'victimised by the forces of imperialism and social stratification, coupled with the ratonalisations of certain shibboleths of a prejudiced society' it had been difficult to convince the average scholar or student of history that 'black peoples have made definite contributions to the history of civilisation'. In anticipation of the present-day research in African studies at many centres of learning, the *African Morning Post* urged its readers that the task of African scholarship was to interpret African history to a sceptical world.[76]

It must be pointed out, however, that the Ethiopia to which the *African Morning Post* devoted its series was the classical Ethiopia which was Nubia on the upper Nile, and not the medieval or modern Ethiopia which is traceable to the ancient Kingdom of Axum. Ethiopia of the 1930s was therefore quite distinct historically from the classical Ethiopia widely referred to in the New Testament. Thus, the Ethiopians of the twentieth century have no direct historical claims to the glories of ancient Ethiopia. Yet the exaggerated claims about African achievements which were not infrequent during the period of the Italo-Ethiopian crisis were mostly based on the achievements of classical Ethiopia. What we see here, then, is a process by which a new legitimacy was being given by 'an ideology' which permits of an identification between Ethiopia, the historical kingdom, and Ethiopia as all black people to those who feel themselves to be deprived and oppressed. If Ethiopians were the brothers of all black people, then their historical achievements could be represented as the achievements of all. It was a not too difficult step from viewing Ethiopia as an ancient African Christian kingdom to representing it as the fount of civilisation. Such claims were significant for their propaganda value. For they inspired the average West African with a new hope, and widened his outlook to enable him to see the Italo-Ethiopian struggle from a new angle.

The appeal to the significance of their history and the encouragement of historical awareness as a means of heightening public consciousness about the glories of the African past was a theme which ran through nationalist thinking and argument, and which was given greater currency at the time of the Ethiopian crisis. It was an important asset to the African that in his confrontation with the white man he could say that he too had made contributions to the fund of human knowledge by extending the frontiers of art, culture and spiritual values. Duse Mohamed Ali had this in mind when he told Nigerians during the period of the Italo-Ethiopian conflict:

To understand more fully that Africa has had its contributions upon the science, philosophy and religion of the past, is to give the African a new basis upon which to build his future. It is to inspire him with his social, political, and economic life that he will not longer deplore his inferior place among the higher order of created beings. Ours was indeed a past rich in ignorance but richer, perhaps, in the things that have made civilisation; a past whose glories ought to accompany us across the bridge into the present and our torchlight on the highway of the future.[77]

To young West African nationalists it was clearly of great value to be free from the superstition which identified traditional African society with 'barbarism' and British rule with 'civilisation', and to realise that their peoples had possessed, and still possessed, their own distinctive forms of civilisation. Thus, in spite of the sometimes exaggerated tone of the accounts of the press and the nationalist leaders, this had the desired effect of encouraging the ordinary people to think again about the significance of the past. It was this aspect of the nationalist ideology – a rediscovery of African history, a renewal of interest in the traditions, culture, language, and the like – which Azikiwe in the Gold Coast and Duse Mohamed Ali in Nigeria worked hard to propagate at the beginning of the Italo-Ethiopian dispute. The progressive nationalists, who at this time were assiduously marshalling the necessary ammunition to disabuse people's minds of the Italian thesis that Ethiopia was a huge mass of savage people, seized upon the claims of the press. Moreover, such claims were valuable to the nationalists themselves at a period of their history during which there was much talk and publicity about the emergence of the 'new Africa':

All over the continent enthusiasm for new thinking and new living is in the air; and each African youth has certainly caught a vision of a regenerated Africa looming in the not-far distant future. We are now awake and are watching the hazy cloud disperse. We feel that every event of the hour points to the broadening of our outlook upon life. . . . The new Africa postulates researches into African history and civilisation.[78]

This talk about the 'New Africa' and 'Renascent Africa' was frequently referred to in many a West African nationalist press in the 1930s. Nnamdi Azikiwe was the exponent of the two terms which he used in a psycho-social sense, and he devoted a whole book to it – *Renascent Africa*.

Among the few educated West Africans abroad who were puzzled by the question of Ethiopia's racial identity was Chief Hezekia Oladipo Davies of Nigeria. Chief Davies, who was one of the founders of the Nigerian Youth Movement and one of the best known Nigerian nationalists during the mid-thirties and the forties, has recently narrated the story of how he confronted

Haile Selassie of Ethiopia when he arrived in London in June 1936 with this question of Ethiopia's racial identity. Having completed his secondary school education at King's College, Lagos, Chief Davies was during this period a student of the London School of Economics, and also a member of the League of Coloured Peoples as well as president of the West African Students' Union in Great Britain and Ireland in 1936. He had read a few odd articles in the press about Ethiopia and met some Ethiopian students like Bayana and the Martins, the latter being children of the Ethiopian Envoy Extraordinary and Minister Plenipotentiary to the Court of St James in London, Dr Azaj Workneh Martin. Chief Davies tells us that when the Italo-Ethiopian conflict began, he took part in a number of talks and seminars on the subject at the London School of Economics. Furthermore, as president of the Cosmopolitan Society of LSE, he had presided over some of the talks given to the society by experts on Ethiopia, but he has recently admitted that he knew very little about Ethiopia before the outbreak of the crisis.

On hearing of the arrival of the Emperor in London, Chief Davies went to interview him as press representative of the *Nigerian Daily Times*:

> What I was anxious to clear up was the accusation made by the Italians that there was colour bar and slavery in Ethiopia. It was reported that the ruling class did not regard themselves as Africans, being lighter of skin, and that they looked down upon and oppressed the black population. I naturally laid emphasis in my questions on these accusations.[79]

On the question of colour bar and slavery, Chief Davies tells us that the Emperor dismissed the allegations as an Italian fabrication. He affirmed, however, that the Ethiopians were not, and did not regard themselves as Africans (or Negroes) as they were 'a mixed Hamito-semitic people'. In saying this, Haile Selassie was merely confirming what his predecessor, Emperor Menelik, was reported to have declared to a West Indian pan-Africanist, Benito Sylvain, who went to Addis Ababa to enlist his support for a society for the 'amelioration of the Negro Race'. Menelik replied, 'Yours is an excellent idea. . . . The Negro should be uplifted. . . . I wish you the greatest possible success. But in coming to me to take the leadership, you are knocking at the wrong door, so to speak. You know I am not a Negro at all; I am a Caucasian.'[80]

Chief Davies discloses that after this interview his 'enthusiasm for the Ethiopian cause became somewhat attenuated, but I continued to hate Fascism and all that it meant'.[81] In the course of the interview, Emperor Haile Selassie also said that whatever the Africans and other sympathisers did should be in co-operation with the British Government for 'the British Government and the British people have been very great friends and of enormous help to us in our struggle'.[82]

To H. O. Davies, as well as his West African student colleagues in Britain, the report of the interview with the Emperor was not comforting. But unlike Marcus Garvey who, in reacting to the Emperor's attitude, unsparingly censured Haile Selassie in the press for his reliance on the white race and white institutions,[83] these West African students debated among themselves a number of perplexing questions. In the first place, they were not quite sure whether the Emperor was not lending credence to the Italian propaganda that Ethiopians were a white people. Secondly, the Emperor's profuse gratitude to the British Government was disappointing to these students who had been equally profuse in their criticism of the role of the British Government in the Italo-Ethiopian imbroglio. Some wondered whether Haile Selassie was trying to be diplomatic in view of the fact that he was speaking on British soil and as a guest of the British Government and British people. Chief Davies told me in an interview that his confrontation with the Emperor was reported in detail to a meeting of the West African Students' Union. The consensus of opinion was that, in spite of what the Emperor said, the Italian aggression was an ugly manifestation of totalitarianism in Europe in which Africa was tragically involved as the victim.[84]

The perplexing question about the racial identity of Ethiopia was generally confined to the few sophisticated and intellectual groups in West Africa. It was these groups who could read and fully understand the dire consequences of the Italian propaganda and were puzzled by it. But by the time Mussolini moved from threats of aggression to actual aggression on Ethiopia, West Africans at home and abroad, literates as well as illiterates, had become fully convinced that Ethiopians were black Africans like themselves. At the beginning of the crisis Nnamdi Azikiwe had gone to the extent of adducing etymological evidence in the columns of the *African Morning Post* to reinforce this conviction that Ethiopians were 'black Africans or what we call Negroes'.[85] Besides, various authorities such as Professors Eadie and C. J. Prichard were freely cited in support of Ethiopia's black racial identity.[86] These authorities were, however, hopelessly outdated. It was argued that the Greek word 'Aithiopon' meant a person with a sunburnt face, and the skin of the Ethiopians, or perhaps Egyptians, 'was dark even to a proverb'. The *Morning Post* authoritatively concluded that Ethiopians were proclaimed by the 'voice of antiquity to have been a black and a genuine African race'.[87]

A detailed analysis of the black racial identity of Ethiopians was provided at an unprecedented crowded public lecture at the Wilberforce Memorial Hall in Freetown on 30 September 1935 by C. D. Hotobah During, a leading nationalist politician and barrister in Sierra Leone. The lecture, which was interspersed with lantern slides of the Emperor and Empress of Ethiopia, leading statesmen and soldiers, the different tribes and other aspects of life in Ethiopia, was said to have lasted for over two hours during which During gave his audience the information on the geographical and historical background so essential for a thorough understanding 'of the present famous dispute'. A close associate of Wallace Johnson in the late thirties and an enthusiastic follower of the Sierra Leone Section of the West African Youth League, Hotobah During was one of the foremost supporters of the Ethiopian cause, and a leading member of the Ethiopia Defence Committee in Sierra Leone. He had a reputation for having original ideas and for bold utterances which he brought into play in this public lecture on the 'Historical Sketch of Abyssinia'.[88] Holding 'his audience spellbound', During traced the ancient history of Abyssinia and how it was referred to in the Bible as Ethiopia. He explained that Abyssinia was from the Arabic word 'Habesh' meaning mixed, on account of the mixture of races in the Abyssinian people who were partly Semitic, partly Hamitic and partly Negro. He asked rhetorically: Why was Haile Selassie Emperor of 'Ethiopia' and *not* of 'Abyssinia', as his predecessors often called themselves? This, he said, was because Abyssinia was a word of Semitic origin, but Ethiopia was Negro. If there was a black race they belonged to it. Of course, he argued, there were not and never had been any 'pure' Negroes any more than there were 'pure' whites or 'pure' yellows.[89]

Not only did West Africans identify themselves with Ethiopia as an independent black state, but they also argued that the affinity which they bore to the Ethiopians was one of blood relationship. Realisation of this fact acted as a catalyst to unite all shades of opinion in West Africa and inspired the protest demonstrations against the Italian rape of Ethiopia. A section of West African intellectuals delved into history to cite evidence of historical connection between West Africans and the East Africans through Ethiopia and Egypt. In his 'The Solidarity of the African Race', Prince Adetokunbo Ademola, the son of the Alake of Abeokuta, who later became a justice of the Supreme Court of Nigeria, dwelt extensively on this subject.[90] This view was supported by the *Comet* when it stressed that Africa was one and indivisible; its ethnic strains were so universally blended that the same blood passed through the veins of all.[91] Hotobah During vigorously reinforced this thesis of West African blood relationship with the Ethiopians in his lecture and declared that the Hausa people were connecting links between the Ethiopians and the people of Nigeria: 'I make bold to say that Nigeria at the time formed part of Ethiopia as also the Gold Coast which historians have proved to be Ophir.'[92] Furthermore, in Nigeria the ancient trade route to the East including Egypt and Abyssinia 'is still in existence' and this accounted for the 'industries coming to the present-day Nigerians and Egyptians and Abyssinians particularly the pottery and leather work'. In conclusion, During affirmed that the 'Great Kingdom of Ethiopia' in the early days 'no doubt covered the great part if not the whole of Africa'.[93] It was further claimed that the Southern Nigerian Ibibio had at some time in their history constructed tomb chapels and the tomb chamber which originated from Ethiopia and became connected with the early Egyptian dynasties.

It can be argued that though some of these historical expositions have not been fully borne out by recent research, they served the desired objective at the time of the Italo-Ethiopian conflict. Emotions and racial sentiments were aroused to such an extent that anything that might favour the Ethiopian cause was devoured at its face value. The pan-Africanist Duse Mohamed Ali, for example, convincingly argued that Haile Selassie had reportedly declared himself 'not alone Emperor of Ethiopia, but of all Africans throughout the world irrespective of what Government may now control them'.[94] The accusation that the ruling classes of Ethiopia were contemptuous of Negroes made little impression among West Africans during the critical stage of the Italo-Ethiopian struggle. It was emphatically countered that the so-called spirit of contempt alleged to be shown by Ethiopians 'may be no more than the prejudices, traces of which still survive in Nigeria between the Yorubas and Ibos or the Fulanis and the Hausas'. It was nothing so deep-seated as that between two utterly distinct types as the Caucasian and the Negro. The former was an entirely superficial feeling which would disappear with growing opportunities of contact.[95] Moreover, it was frequently argued that Ethiopians were far from knowing anything about racial inferiority; they were indeed 'true believers in the African'.

Above all, the fact that the West African intelligentsia jealously looked upon Ethiopia 'as the last vestige of pride we possess' was enough to whip nationalist forces. The resistance of Ethiopia to further foreign intrusion of the African continent was, therefore, to many West Africans, not a national or local affair. It was more than that: all Africa was involved, and with it the destiny of the great black race. This was a question of the white man 'attempting to keep the black man in servile fearfulness, in eternal slavery and abject submission from which no human efforts can deliver him'.[96] Thus, in launching an Ethiopia Relief Fund in Lagos, Ernest Ikoli, known as the 'Father of the Nigerian Youth Movement', declared that the future of the black people was closely bound up with the Ethiopian crisis for, in his view, the prestige of the black man would either rise or suffer 'according as whether Abyssinia comes out of the contest victorious or beaten'.[97]

This involvement of the rest of Africa in the crisis was more clearly expressed in Azikiwe's *African Morning Post*, when it wrote: 'Let Abyssinia, the only black kingdom . . . be shattered and all our hopes will be doomed and our aspirations curbed. Let the Abyssinians be slaughtered and we shall become slaves . . . the progress of Africa will be delayed a thousand, if not a million years. . . .'

On the other hand, if Ethiopians should successfully repel the attack of Mussolini's onslaught, there could not be the slightest doubt that the whole Negro race would gain greatly in prestige. For 'Ethiopia shall then raise her hand unto God and Africa shall rise . . . the New Africa shall have been ushered in wherein grateful and kind Africans will be able to cooperate with all sincerity with all men, black, white, yellow, or red who had proved themselves our friends indeed.'[98] Hence the articulate nationalists made it unmistakably clear that though the battle was being waged in Ethiopia, 'it is our own battle, because it is an African battle'. Consequently, the bombardment of Adowa and Adigrat by the Italians must be considered in the same light as the bombing of any West African town by a hostile enemy. Throughout the period of the crisis, therefore, nationalist feelings in West Africa were aroused and there was grave spirit of unrest, of fear for the future, and an increasing distrust of the intentions of Europeans. It was this feeling of helplessness, humiliation and betrayal that underlay all the protests to the crisis in West Africa.

Another major concern in West Africa at the beginning of the crisis was to attempt a detailed criticism of the Italian aggression in Ethiopia. Mussolini had declared to the world that Italy's motive in attacking Ethiopia was to 'carry civilisation' to that 'savage' country and to stop the slave traffic. He cited lavishly the chronic state of internal disorder in Ethiopia, the inability of that country to progress and the cruel treatment of subject races which enabled Italy to pose as the champion of white civilisation against a state given over to barbarism and incapable of discipline. The cluster of Italian charges was later presented to the Council of the League of Nations on 4 September 1935, in an immense printed memorandum.[99] This memorandum depicted barbarities calculated to end any image of Ethiopia as a land of noble savages, of free and simple people. It stated that Ethiopia's admission to the League of Nations was a political act, inspired by confidence that 'the country could be led to make the efforts required gradually to attain the level of civilisation of other nations belonging to the League'. But, the memorandum contended, Ethiopia had shown that she was unable to find in her membership the impulse to make a voluntary effort to raise herself to the level of other civilised countries.[100] Thus the Government of Ethiopia was indicted in a long catalogue of slavery, cruelty, and injustice. This was indeed 'a tendentious and badly prepared document' complete with meticulous accounts of a whole series of alleged treaty violations, frontier raids and atrocities the blame for all of which was laid on the Ethiopian Government.[101]

These Italian allegations provoked a number of West African nationalists, especially those who were keenly aware of what was going on in European-controlled territories in Africa. It was these who, after viewing the Italian allegations against the background of the European record in Africa, vehemently denounced the hypocritical character of Mussolini's 'civilising mission' in Ethiopia. What disturbed many of them was that none of the so-called civilised countries could produce a record which was free from guilty association with, or participation in, the slave trade. Hence, they taunted: 'People, especially Europeans, who talk about abuses in Abyssinia must have very short memories or have different standards of evil in different races.'[102] As evidence of European 'plunder' in Africa, the radical nationalists not only cited the 'native policy' of South Africa, but also declared on many occasions that if Mussolini was really interested in preserving the respect of human personality, then he might as well declare war against South Africa.[103] Furthermore, the brutalities in the Portuguese colonies, particularly the 'various forms of slavery' existing in Angola, were referred to as more barbarous than any type of slavery existing in Ethiopia at that time. Nationalists like George E. Moore, leader of the 1934 Gold Coast Aborigines' Rights' Protection Society Deputation to England, described in detail the atrocities in Europe as well as those in European-ruled colonies:

> To say nothing of the horrible murders and other hideous crimes daily perpetuated in so-called civilised Europe, we know of the atrocities perpetrated on the natives of the Belgium Congo by members of the civilised race, we know of the dastardly and barbarous acts done in the Great War, and we know of the deadly instruments of war being amassed for the destruction of human life by all the so-called civilised nations. Can anything be more barbarous? Then they talk of slavery in Abyssinia. There is much more slavery in the colonies under the government of the so-called civilised nations than you can find in Abyssinia. In the colonies there is the tendency of the natives being autocratically ruled, ruthlessly exploited and politically and economically enslaved. . . .[104]

It is pertinent to point out, however, that the passionate refutation by West Africans of the Italian charges does not seem to be based on any concrete or accurate information about the actual state of affairs in Ethiopia. It was, to say the least, based on their emotional attachment to Ethiopia and the exaggeration of the trickle of news they might have obtained from some Ethiopian sympathisers abroad who, during the crisis, tended to paint a favourable picture about the country. Hence some nationalists went so far as to claim that the Emperor had improved his capital by building good roads and lighting by electricity.[105] Similarly, nationalists like Robert Broadhurst, formerly of the African Progress Union in London, who commented in glowing terms on the Emperor's edicts of 1924 and 1931 respectively which forbade 'slave-raiding, slave markets, and all further enslavements except in war',[106] made no effort to distinguish between policy and achievement. The Emperor had to face a great deal of opposition from the old Rases, and very little was achieved. Haile Selassie's adviser on abolition of slavery and servitude, the British ex-official de Halpert, felt compelled to resign in 1933 on the grounds that anti-slavery measures were not being enforced vigorously enough.[107]

This is also confirmed by the 1934–35 'Third Annual Report on Slavery in

Ethiopia' prepared by Sir Sidney Barton, the British Minister in Addis Ababa. This report stated, *inter alia*, that the Slavery Department inaugurated in August 1932 had, 'so far as can be judged', been reduced to a shadow of a department. The judges of Slavery Court had a 'well-nigh impossible task to fulfil', for they rarely enjoyed the support of the Provincial Governors and 'must often face the open hostility of their fellow officials'. Generally speaking, concluded the British report, public opinion was still strong against the abolition of the domestic slavery on which the structure of the society was founded.[108] There is indeed sufficient evidence that the veneer of civilisation had not yet spread very far or penetrated very deeply in Ethiopia in the early decades of the twentieth century. The Emperor himself, according to his biographer, was only too well aware of 'the backwardness of his country and the weakness and rapacities with which the regime was riddled'.[109] It was therefore inaccurate for the West African nationalist leaders to pretend that Ethiopia was a civilised nation in any real sense. The plain fact is that, as has been noted elsewhere, just as the Ethiopians in the 1930s did not know what was happening in far-off West Africa, so the West African protesters, almost to a man, knew next to nothing about the social, economic, or political realities of Ethiopia. What they wrote or said about the country was at best a manifestation of their emotional state at the time of the crisis. Apart from foreign news media and friends of Ethiopia abroad, the only source of information for the West African nationalists was that provided by such West African adventurers and Ethiopian apologists as Thomas B. Allotey.

Allotey, a Gold Coast native, was trading in Addis Ababa at the time of the Italian invasion of Ethiopia. He came of a family of merchants. His forefathers were leaders in the barter trade in cocoa, hides, and other Gold Coast produce before the establishment of the European trading companies. On leaving school Allotey joined his father in business, and having gained considerable experience, started as a merchant on his own account on the eve of the First World War. In the course of business, Allotey made many journeys to England during one of which he met Ras Haylu of Ethiopia and 'learnt much of the ancient realm of Abyssinia', which gave him a great desire to travel there. In 1931 Allotey left the Gold Coast for Ethiopia and established himself as a trader dealing in hides and coffee and other produce. In his view, Ethiopia was still backward in many respects and largely feudal, but the Emperor's reforms were modernising it, 'and whatever might be said of the comfort and cleanliness of an Abyssinian town', they were, in his opinion, '100 per cent cleaner than those of Persia'. The Emperor was working hard for education, and though some of the old Rases cared little for that, the younger people appreciated it.[110] When after the Walwal incident it became clear that the Italians were intent on war, Allotey and other West Africans formed a society called 'Sons of Ethiopia', and some of the men volunteered to travel in Africa and Asia lecturing on the Ethiopian case. Allotey volunteered for India, China, and Japan. In Japan he founded an Ethiopian society, and later returned to England. It is not quite clear to what extent Allotey became a source of information for those West Africans who desired to know the truth about Ethiopia, but significantly, there appears to be no evidence in any of the nationalist newspapers mentioning him or even referring to his trading adventures in Ethiopia.

Besides their outburst about slavery in Ethiopia, the nationalist intelligentsia regarded Mussolini's 'civilising mission' as a violation of the fundamental principles of international law. As Azikiwe put it at the time, 'International Law reached a milestone in its development (or devolution) on 3 October 1935, when Italy undertook to contravene all the legal doctrines of international relations which made a reign of law between States possible, since the days of Hugo Grotius.' The Italian action, in the view of Azikiwe, was in direct violation of the sacred principles and stipulations not only in the Covenant of the League of Nations but also of the Hague Convention of 1899, the Geneva Convention of 1906, the Washington Convention of 1922 and finally the Pact of Paris of 1928.[111] He argued that both Italy and Ethiopia were independent sovereign states, as well as members of the League of Nations, an international organisation which represented 'a new deal in international politics'. If Ethiopia really stood in need of a 'civilising mission', Italy was not the one to decide how this could be attained. Pursuit of a 'civilising mission' in Ethiopia by Italy was therefore a violation of the territorial integrity, and, more so, of the sovereign rights, of Ethiopia. It was a reversion to the 'lamb and wolf diplomacy' of the days of Niccolo Machiavelli, an Italian political machinator.[112]

Azikiwe's arguments were reinforced by a series of 'open letters' published in Freetown by C. B. R. Wright, a well-known Sierra Leonean barrister and radical nationalist politician, who cited a number of authorities to prove that the Italian 'civilising mission' did not accord with the accepted principles of International Law. Wright contended that nearly all the writers on International Law – Grotius, Pufendorf, Phillmore, Oppenheim and many others – agreed that 'only civilised nations and sovereign states could be subjects of International Law and now members of the League of Nations'. Once a state had been accepted as a member of the League of Nations she became entitled to all the privileges of a member of the League, and was subject to all duties. It was incumbent upon each of the state members of the League to respect the sovereignty and independence of the others. This sovereignty of a state extended to and included the right of a state to organise itself in such a manner as it might choose; it could do within its dominions whatever acts it might think calculated to render it prosperous and strong. It also included the right to peaceable possession and enjoyment of that which it had legitimately obtained. To foreign states the political and social doctrines which might be exemplified in it, or might spread from it, were legally immaterial. Wright inferred from this that Ethiopia, being a sovereign state, had the right to be under whatever government she chose, and do whatever she pleased within her territory with any of her property or her subjects:

> Even in the case of trafficking in slaves Abyssinia could be called to account only by the League of Nations, and that only to this extent that the League would offer an alternative to Abyssinia that she should either give up trafficking in slaves and continue as member of the League or cease forthwith to be a member. But there is no record that the League of Nations ever believed that Abyssinia trafficked in slaves. . . .[113]

Contrary to Wright's assertion, however, there is some evidence that the League members believed that there was slavery in Ethiopia, and it was this which provoked the British initial opposition to Ethiopia's membership of the League of Nations. During the discussion in 1923 of the admission of Ethiopia to the League Great Britain strongly insisted that a thorough enquiry should first be made into the desire of the Ethiopian Government to abolish slavery within its territory.[114] France similarly submitted to the League on 18 August 1923 a detailed memorandum on slavery in Ethiopia.

On the whole, however, in the view of the West African nationalists, it might be true that Ethiopia was a socially backward state, but to argue that Italy was justified in conquering the country to impose a more advanced civilisation was to go against the established view of international law. To suggest that Italy's invasion would be in the best interest of the League of Nations, was in their opinion, not only an act of effrontery – it was also ridiculous, For, as they pointed out, no fact or argument presented by Mussolini gave Italy the slightest moral or legal right to act unilaterally against Ethiopia. Nothing, they said, allowed Italy the freedom to cross Ethiopia's border without breaking the Covenant of the League of Nations. If Italy wanted further civilisation to come to Ethiopia, the proper method of helping a country toward internal reform was to co-operate with it, not to threaten it with national extinction. Italy was therefore described as an 'avowed international criminal', for she had 'signally failed to live within the ambits of international law', and 'violated the fundamental canon of international society'. Moreover, by 'harpooning the foundations of international ethics and morality', she had disrupted the comity of nations.[115] Thus, to the nationalist leaders in West Africa, the 'civilising mission' was tendentious in character; it was rightly denounced as an example of puerile tactics to attempt to discredit one whom it is intended to despoil or destroy. All this, in their view, was a pretext and a lame excuse: it was 'all moonshine', a Machiavellian strategem in action in Africa.[116] Mussolini's motive was therefore dismissed as essentially a case of imperialism veiled in the garb of a 'civilising mission'. In this line of criticism the nationalists were obviously on firmer ground. It is against this background that the politically-minded West Africans violently criticised the diplomacy of the colonial powers in relation to the Italo-Ethiopian conflict.

1 British interests in Ethiopia, for instance, were centred on Lake Tsana. In his memorandum to the British Minister at Addis Ababa on 21 July 1926, Sir Austen Chamberlain, the British Foreign Secretary, stressed that it was essential in the interests of Egypt and the Sudan to prevent outside interference with the sources of the Nile. He concluded that this consideration had governed the policy of the British Government 'for the past thirty years'. F.O.371/19175. This was reinforced in 1935 by the Maffey Committee on British interests in Ethiopia. F.O.371/19184.

2 For a good discussion of this controversy see C. Giglio, 'Article 17 of the Treaty of Uccialli', R. Caulk trans., *Journal of African History*, vi, 2, 1965, p. 221; Sven Rubenson, 'The Protectorate Paragraph of the Wichale Treaty', *ibid.*, v, 2, 1964, p. 243; Sven Rubenson, 'Professor Giglio, Antonelli and Article xvii of the Treaty of Wichale', *ibid.*, vii, 3, 1966, p. 445.

3 Cited in Christopher Hibbert, *Benito Mussolini*, London, 1962, p. 66.

4 F.O.371/19184, Minute by O. St C. O'Malley on his conversation with Signor Leonardo Vitetti of the Italian embassy in London.

5 League of Nations, *Official Journal*, February 1935, Annex 19530, Communication No. 10. For a very recent discussion of the Italo-Ethiopian conflict, see Frank Hardie, *The Abyssinian Crisis*, London, 1974.

6 F.O.371/19142, P. Tecle Hawariate to the Secretary General of the League of Nations.

7 Mussolini in an interview with Henry de Kerillis of the *L'Echo de Paris*, 21 July 1935. This paper, which was published in Paris, was distinctly pro-Italian in tone during the crisis. See F. D. Laurens, *France and the Italo-Ethiopian Crisis, 1935–36*, p. 161.

8 Church action on a national scale is believed to have been particularly noteworthy in England. For details, see Helen Hiett, 'Public Opinion and the Italo-Ethiopian Dispute', *Geneva Special Studies*, vii, 1, February 1936, p. 3. This article discusses the reaction of the various international organisations and societies to the Ethiopian crisis.

9 The reaction of the Afro-Americans to the crisis is detailed in my article. 'The Afro-American and the Italo-Ethiopian Crisis, 1934–36', *Race*, xv, 2 October 1973, p. 167. Also, Weisbord, *Ebony Kinship*, pp. 98–114.

10 F.O.371/20154, A. C. Hollis, Governor of Trinidad, to J. H. Thomas, Secretary of State for the Colonies, 6 January 1936. Also, Weisbord, 'British West Indian Reaction to the Italian-Ethiopian War: An Episode in Pan-Africanism', *op. cit.*

11 F.O.371/22397, 'Ethiopian Resolutions Received During 1938'.

12 *Ibid.*

13 I am greatly indebted to Dr J. S. Spiegler whose detailed analysis of this subject has been of immense help.

14 The Statutes and Aims of LDRN can be found in the *Bridgeman Papers*.

15 *Race Nègre*, November–December 1934.

16 *Ibid.*, August 1931.

17 Paulette Nardal, 'Levée de Races', *Periscope Africaine*, (Dakar), 19 October 1935.

18 Spiegler, 'Aspects of Nationalist Thought Among French-speaking West Africans', unpublishsed thesis, p. 266.

19 *Race Nègre*, July 1935.

20 *Ibid.*

21 George Padmore's letter to W. E. B. Du Bois, 17 February 1934. Cited in J. R. Hooker, *Black Revolutionary: George Padmore's Path from Communism to Pan-Africanism*, p. 39.

22 George Padmore, *How Britain Rules Africa*, New York, 1936, pp. 389–90.

23 George Padmore, 'Ethiopia and World Politics', *Crisis*, xlii, 5, May 1935, p. 1387. The reaction of the West African nationalists to the Catholic Church is discussed in detail in Chapter III. Also, see my article, 'The Catholic Missions, British West African Nationalists, and the Italian Invasion of Ethiopia', *African Affairs*, lxxiii, 291, April 1974, p. 204.

24 C. L. R. James, 'Abyssinia and the Imperialists', *Keys*, iii, 3, January–March 1936, p. 32.

25 I have discussed James's dedication to the cause of pan-Africanism in my article, 'C. L. R. James: Pan-Africanist', *Africa*, No. 30, February 1974, p. 25.

26 For details about IAFA, see Kenyatta, 'Hands Off Ethiopia', *op. cit.*

27 *Times* (London), 29 July 1935.

28 ACC.75/64, *Aborigines Papers*.

29 *Daily Mail* (Freetown), 17 August 1935. For a discussion of the activities of the blacks in Britain in the 1930s, see C. L. R. James, 'Black Intellectuals in Britain', in Bhikhu Parekh, ed., *Colour, Culture and Consciousness*, London, 1974, p. 154–63.

30 For the biography of Moody, see D. A. Vaughan, *Negro Victory: The Life Story of Dr. Harold Moody*, London 1950, Also Esedebe, 'A History of the Pan-African Movement'.

31 For a recent detailed account of LCP, see Roderick J. MacDonald, 'Dr. Harold Arundel Moody and the League of Coloured Peoples, 1931–1947', *Race*, xiv, 3, January 1973, p. 291. Also, Geiss, *The Pan-African Movement*, pp. 340–50.

32 *The Keys*, i, 1, July 1933.

33 *Ibid.*, iii, 3, January–March 1936.

34 *Ibid.*, ii, 2, October–December 1934 and iii, 3, January–March 1936.

35 *Ibid.*, v, 4, April–June 1938.

36 *West Africa*, 15 August 1925. For details, see Esedebe, 'A History of Pan-African Movement'.

37 *Ibid.*

38 P. Garigue, 'An Anthropological Interpretation of Changing Political Leadership in West Africa', unpublished London Ph.D. thesis, 1952–53, p. 393.

39 *Ibid.* See also, Garigue, 'The West African Students' Union: A Study in Culture Contact', *Africa*, xxiii, 1, January 1953, p. 55. For details about the thoughts of the West African students at this time, see Ladipo Solanke, *United West Africa (or Africa) at the Bar of the Family of Nations*, London, 1927.

40 J. W. de Graft-Johnson, *Towards Nationhood in West Africa*, London, 1971, p. v.

41 *Wasu*, 11, 1, January 1933, p. 2.

42 The address is detailed in *Wasu*, December 1926, pp. 23–8.

43 House of Commons *Debates*, 8 May 1929; also *Wasu*, 11, 1, January 1933, p. 19.

44 *Wasu*, iv, 5, November 1935, p. 5.

45 *Ibid.*

46 ACC.74/64, *Aborigines Papers*, Padmore to Sekyi, 15 July 1932.

47 *Ocansey Papers*, Padmore to Ocansey, 14 February 1935.

48 ACC.156/65, *Sekyi Papers*, Padmore to Sekyi, 4 October 1938.
49 See, for instance, *African Morning Post*, 11 February 1935; and also *Gold Coast Spectator*, 10 September 1938.
50 Nancy Cunard, 'Ethiopia Defence Committee in Paris', *Vox Populi*, 16 November 1953. For a brief biographical sketch of Miss Cunard, see J. R. Hooker, pp. 27–8.
51 *Ibid.*, 27 November 1935.
52 ACC.77/64, *Aborigines Papers*.
53 ADM.12/3/103, Ghana National Archives, Accra, Sir Shenton Thomas to Sir Philip Cunliffe-Lister, Secretary of State for the Colonies, 3 January 1934.
54 C.S.O.1/36, Nigerian National Archives, Ibadan, Sir Philip Cunliffe-Lister to Officers Administering British Colonies in West Africa, 3 June 1935. There is no evidence that such a body as 'Pan-African Brotherhood' was created during this period. James Hooker, pp. 43, 50–1.
55. C.S.O.400/35, Ghana National Archives, Accra, the British Consulate General at Dakar to Sir Arnold Hodson, Governor of the Gold Coast, 10 September 1935.
56 Details of the Sierra Leone Branch of the LCP is given in the LCP Ninth Annual Report for the Year 1939–1941. *Macaulay Papers*, Box 26, File I.
57 Among the branches formed as a direct consequence of Solanke's tour were those of Cape Coast, Elmina, Nsawam and Sekondi in the Gold Coast; Aba, Abeokuta, Ebute Meta, Jos, Port-Harcourt and Zaria in Nigeria. ACC. No. 617/56, Ghana National Archives, Accra; also *Macaulay Papers*, Box 18, File 7.
58 Special Branch Report, S.B.320/ABD/93, 14 October 1922 encl. in C.O.554/57/2760. I am grateful to Dr Ian Duffield of the Department of History, University of Edinburgh, for sending me a copy of Vol. II, Chapter VIII, 'Back to Africa 1933–1945', of his unpublished Edinburgh Ph.D. thesis, 'Duse Mohamed Ali and the Development of Pan-Africanism 1866–1945'.
59 O. Awolowo, *Awo: Autobiography of Chief Obafemi Awolowo*, Cambridge, 1960 p. 84.
60 Cited in Toynbee, ed., *Survey of International Affairs*, Vol. 11, 1935, pp. 110–11.
61 The Gold Coast newspapers increased in circulation during this period as follows: *Gold Coast Independent* – 1,995 (1933–34), 2,240 (1935) and 2,100 (1936). *Gold Coast Spectator* – 2,800 (1933–34), 2,900/3,000 (1935) and 2,500 (1936). *Vox Populi* – 1,000 (1933–34), 2,000 (1935) and 2,000/2,500 (1936). ADM.7/1/67, 68, 69, Ghana National Archives, Accra, *Blue Books*. *African Morning Post* increased its circulation from 2,000 in 1934 to 10,000 daily in 1936. See Azikiwe, *My Odyssey*, p. 259. In Nigeria, from circulation of 5,200 in 1934 the *Nigerian Daily Times* 'rocketed' to 5,700 in 1936; and the *Nigerian Daily Telegraph* from 1,500 (1934) to 3,000 (1936). *Nigerian Blue Books*, 1934–36.
62 The West African governors indicated in their respective secret despatches that in the view of the people of West Africa the Ethiopians were fighting for life and liberty 'against white imperialism', F.O.371/20154.
63 *Times* (London), 25 October 1935.
64 F.O.371/20154, Henry Moore, Governor of Sierra Leone, to J. H. Thomas, Secretary of State for the Colonies, 30 December 1936.
65 *Sierra Leone Daily Mail*, 2 July 1935.
66 *Afro-American* (Baltimore), 12 October 1935. Cited in Weisbord, *Ebony Kinship*, footnote 34, p. 112.
67 F.O.371/19164, British Legation in Port-au-Prince to Sir Samuel Hoare, Secretary of State for Foreign Affairs, 8 November 1935. For Marcus Garvey's criticism of Ethiopia's attitude towards the black race, see *The Black Man*, July–August 1936. Also E. D. Cronon, *Black Moses*, Madison, 1955, p. 162.
68 This last question was, for instance, the subject of a crowded lecture in Lagos, Nigeria, given by a young Oxford graduate, Miss K. Moore, daughter of Eric O. Moore, one time Vice-President of Macaulay's Nigerian National Democratic Party. For a report of Miss Moore's lecture, see *Nigerian Daily Times*, 11 December 1935.
69 A Nigerian, who signed himself 'Kritikus', argued that West Africans were wasting their sympathy on Ethiopia whose ruling classes had been credited with being contemptuous of the Negroes. *Nigerian Daily Telegraph*, 23 December 1935.
70 *West Africa*, 12 October 1935.
71 Obafemi Awolowo, *Autobiography*, p. 91.
72 *Gold Coast Spectator*, 12 November 1935, editorial entitled 'We are Ethiopians'.
73 *Ibid.*

74 Richard Pankhurst, 'Ethiopia and Africa: The Historical Aspects', *Ethiopia Observer*, viii, 2, 1964, p. 155.
75 *Ibid.*
76 *African Morning Post*, 29 and 30 January, and also 6 February 1935. Details about the nationalists' discussion of Egyptian civilisation during this period are contained in ACC.716/56, Ghana National Archives, Accra.
77 *Comet*, 26 January 1935. For a discussion of this aspect of nationalist ideology, see Hodgkin, *Nationalism in Colonial Africa*, pp. 172–4.
78 *Ibid.*, 26 January 1936, 'Is "The New Africa" a Utopia?'
79 *Service* (Lagos), Vol. 1, No. 13, 17 December 1960.
80 Cited in Pankhurst, p. 156. For a brief reference to the pan-African activities of Benito Sylvain at the 1900 Pan-African Conference, see Geiss, *Pan-African Movement*, pp. 182–92.
81 *Service*, 1, 13, 17 December 1960.
82 H. O. Davies, 'A Talk with Emperor of Ethiopia', *West Africa*, 27 June 1936.
83 Marcus Garvey, 'Italy's Conquest?', *The Black Man*, July–August 1936.
84 Interview with H. O. Davies, Lagos, Nigeria, 2 May 1969.
85 *African Morning Post*, 23 January 1935.
86 Extracts from Eadie's *Oriental History* (1852) and Prichard's *Researches Into the Physical History of Mankind*, Vol. ii (1841), were quoted. *Ibid.*
87 *African Morning Post*, 23 January 1935.
88 *Sierra Leone Daily Guardian*, 1 October 1935.
89 *Ibid.*
90 See Nancy Cunard, *Negro Anthology*, p. 612.
91 *Comet*, 10 December 1935.
92 *Sierra Leone Daily Guardian*, 1 October 1935.
93 *Ibid.*
94 *Comet*, 14 September 1935.
95 *Nigerian Daily Telegraph*, 23 December 1935.
96 *African Morning Post*, 1 October 1935.
97 *Nigerian Daily Telegraph*, 5 October 1935.
98 *African Morning Post*, 24 October 1935.
99 'Abstracts from the Memorandum of the Italian Government to the League of Nations', League of Nations, *Official Journal*, 1935, xiii, pp. 1355–1416.
100 *Ibid.* See also F.O.371/19184.
101 British Foreign Office commentary on the Italian Memorandum; F.O.371/19149, 14 October 1935.
102 *Nigerian Daily Telegraph*, 20 November 1935.
103 *Sierra Leone Daily Guardian*, 13 August 1935.
104 ACC.75/64, *Aborigines Papers*.
105 *Sierra Leone Daily Guardian*, 21 March 1935.
106 *West Africa*, 6 June 1936.
107 Leonard Mosley, *Haile Selassie: The Conquering Lion*, London, 1964, p. 174.
108 F.O.371/20185, 'Third Annual Report on Slavery in Ethiopia,' 10 August 1936.
109 L. Mosley, p. 172.
110 *New Times and Ethiopia News*, 14 November 1936.
111 Azikiwe, *Renascent Africa*, pp. 220–9.
112 *Ibid.*
113 C. B. R. Wright, 'The Italo-Ethiopian Dispute and International Law: An Open Letter to My Countrymen and Members of the Negro Race', *Sierra Leone Daily Mail*, 12 October 1935. Also, *ibid.*, 10, 11, 15, and 17 October 1935.
114 League of Nations, *4th Assembly 6th Committee*, 1923, p. 15.
115 *African Morning Post*, 30 October 1935.
116 *Comet*, 6 July 1935. See also, *African Morning Post*, 29 December 1934; *Gold Coast Independent*, 21 September 1935 and *Sierra Leone Daily Mail*, 10 October 1935.

CHAPTER THREE

Appeasement, Christianity, and West African reactions

The Italo-Ethiopian conflict marked a significant stage in the attitudes of West Africans towards international diplomacy of the great powers. It greatly widened the outlook and horizon of the nationalist leaders who, almost for the first time, became increasingly critical of the diplomacy of their colonial over-lords. It also gave them – after the Liberian episode – another altogether disagreeable taste of League of Nations' intervention in matters affecting an independent African state. Hitherto, as Margery Perham has argued, the handful of pioneer nationalists had known little beyond the boundaries of West Africa and Britain, and 'for all their resentments, Britain still seemed unassailable.[1] For the most part it was against the local colonial administrators that the articulate nationalists directed their attack on the administrative and economic regime which had been imposed on them by the colonial powers. They tended to believe that it was 'the men on the spot' – and not the officials at Whitehall – who were generally unsympathetic to the African cause. In their view, the British Government *per se* knew little of what was taking place in West Africa, and they felt that it was the 'doctrine of the man on the spot' which invariably compelled the Colonial Office 'to back up the governor of the Colony when people oppose his will or ordinances'.[2] This tendency, coupled with the belief in the British 'gospel of equity and fair play' was effectively exposed by the vacillating British and French attitudes towards the Ethiopian question, and their resultant 'failure of nerve' to meet the Italian challenge. The Ethiopian experience convinced the anti-colonialists that, so far as the fate of the African was concerned, there could be no appreciable difference in the attitude between the 'men on the spot' and the officials at the Colonial Office. They realised with surprise the fact that the 'scramble for Africa' was still the basis of European diplomacy. This bitter realisation constrained them to follow closely and criti-cally the international complexities in which the Ethiopian question was cast. And, as a consequence they vehemently protested against the action of their colonial powers whom the crisis had exposed to the ignominy of failure, to a loss of prestige, to contempt for inconsistency, and to charges of immorality. The League of Nations' handling of the crisis, and the uninspiring role of the Vatican and the Christian Church as a whole in the Ethiopian affair, similarly became targets of the nationalists' attack and condemnation.

'What Ails the British Lion?'

The West African criticism and general denunciation of European diplomacy with regard to the Italo-Ethiopian conflict were centred initially on the

European conspiracy to starve Ethiopia of arms or ammunitions of war as the danger of Italian aggression grew. By July 1935 the Ethiopian supply of arms and ammunition was 'in quantity hopelessly inadequate for a campaign of moderate length, and in quality incapable of carrying a campaign to a speedy victory'.[3] It was obvious, then, that if Ethiopia was to have a fighting chance, the Emperor, Haile Selassie, must have more arms at once. A 1930 treaty had regulated the importation into Ethiopia of arms, anmunition, and implements of war.[4] This treaty was an attempt on the part of the three Western powers (Great Britain, France and Italy) to give some proof of their desire to assist what appeared to be the programme of Haile Selassie by reserving to him alone the power to receive and control imports of arms. But in spite of this agreement, the Emperor's sources of supply were cut off during the initial stages of the conflict. Britain and France were reluctant to live up to the spirit of the 1930 treaty, which had been signed to help Haile Selassie 'obtain all the arms and ammunition necessary for the defence of his territories from external aggresion'. The two leading members of the League, as well as the small European states such as Belgium, Switzerland, Czechoslovakia, bowed to Mussolini's request that they stop selling arms to the Emperor. This meant that at the most vital moment of her preparations to defend herself Ethiopia was starved of arms. The attitude of the powers placed Ethiopia in a difficult position as she possessed no local manufacturers:

> There is no manufacturer in Ethiopia, either public or private, of arms or ammunitions of war. The Imperial Ethiopian Government today finds it absolutely impossible to obtain means of defence outside its own frontiers. Whenever it attempts to obtain them, it meets with prohibitions and export embargoes. Is that real neutrality? Is it just?[5]

Since, on the other hand, Mussonlini's arsenals were quite capable of supplying his requirements, the embargo penalised only Ethiopia. It was not until Italy had invaded Ethiopia that Britain hesitatingly changed her policy, and raised the embargo.

The refusal of Britain and France to supply arms to Ethiopia was to the nationalists both morally and legally indefensible, and it was not surprising that it provoked a great deal of resentment and violent criticism in West Africa. For, in their opinion:

> While the world feeds and arms the bully that insults it, it piously refused to send arms to the bully's practically unarmed victim. We may send Welsh coal to drive the bully's ships, but we must not send aeroplanes to give the victim a fighting chance of defending himself against the aggressor whom we denounce. . . .[6]

If the two leading members of the League had raised the embargo, as requested by the Emperor, Ethiopian resistance would have been immeasurably stiffened. The arms embargo issue was indeed the primary cause of 'the nation's ultimate defeat'.[7] It was not only inequitable, but a 'cardinal error of policy'. To the nationalist leaders in West Africa this was concrete evidence that Britain and France were 'privy to a secret plot for the murder of Abyssinians',[8] the more so as Britain had already supplied arms to Italy. Anthony Eden, the British Minister for League of Nations affairs at the time of the Ethiopian crisis, confessed that the Ethiopians seemed to him 'to have had a consistently raw deal from us in the matter of arms'. He minuted that for many months the British Government 'maintained an arms embargo which had no justification in equity', but seriously handicapped the Ethiopians and made it almost impossible for them to win a victory.[9] Eden could not find any justification – even were there no treaty – for the refusal of arms to the victim of an aggressor. He was as highly critical of his government's policy as were the West African nationalists.

The arms embargo question formed the basis of West African belief in British treachery, duplicity and perfidy in the Ethiopian affair,[10] a belief which was confirmed by the abortive Hoare-Laval plan of December 1935. This peace plan originated from the fear of war with Italy should an impending oil embargo be imposed on her, and from the French and British reluctance to go to war in the circumstances.[11] The plan was a complicated scheme which proposed immediately to hand over half of Ethiopia to Italy and added conditions respecting the other half which indicated that it too would soon be absorbed.[12] The Emperor of Ethiopia rejected the scheme as 'the negation and abandonment of the principles upon which the League of Nations was founded'. He was also reported to have been very much 'bewildered by the association of His Majesty's Government with these proposals'.[13] The storm of indignation in Britain when the plan was leaked to the press obliged Sir Samuel Hoare to resign as Secretary of State for Foreign Affairs.[14] In the House of Lords, Lord Davies, the most eloquent critic of the plan, argued persuasively that the Hoare-Laval scheme was inconsistent with the principles of equity and fair dealing and 'our obligations under the Covenant of the League of Nations'.[15]

In West Africa, the ouburst against the Hoare-Laval episode was tremendous. Nnamdi Azikiwe, then resident in the Gold Coast, taunted in the editorials of his *African Morning Post* that the formulation of the Hoare-Laval peace proposals, 'immoral and unmoral as are its principles', was an index of the inability of Great Britain to be morally consistent when faced with the contigencies of world politics, especially when these affected a state 'peopled by the lesser breeds'. He wondered whether Great Britain had the weakness to urge Sir Samuel Hoare to arrange with Laval to carve half of Ethiopia for the gratification of Italy, and later to denounce her Foreign Minister.[16] When British public opinion torpedoed the plan on the verge of its acceptance by Italy, nationalists sighed with relief: 'Thank goodness the still-born agreement has been buried. Curse be unto its ashes.'[17] In Nigeria, the Hoare-Laval peace scheme was labelled as a 'prize for aggression', a 'ridiculous plan', and the climax of British betrayal of Ethiopia and the black race in order to save the face of the League. It was generally questioned whether there was any morality in European diplomacy. For to the incensed nationalists in Nigeria, the Hoare-Laval plan was a 'humiliating peace', and a shock to the decency and morality of all right-thinking men and women.[18] Similarly, in Sierra Leone, radical nationalists like Hotobah During described the plan as a 'caricature' and a 'fallacious exchange', and wondered whether there was any sense of 'honesty left in the souls of France and England', or whether British justice and French fair play – virtues world-famous for centuries – had given 'pride of place to baser national traits'.[19] As was repeatedly emphasised in secret confidential despatches at the time, the Hoare-Laval scheme was everywhere regarded in West Africa as 'surrender to Italian aggression'.[20]

On the whole, then, the Hoare-Laval peace plan, as the nationalists saw it, was something incomprehensible, utterly at variance with all the assurances and declarations of the British Government. In their opinion, it was outrageous and an 'indelible stain upon honour and reputation' of Great Britain. Apart from being a travesty of justice, the plan seemed to be a delightful invitation to other nations to take the law into their own hands and to resort to violence for the attainment of their ends. The scheme was thus generally regarded as the latest manifestation of imperialism under the cloak of the League and with the connivance of two of its members. Nationalist agitators lost no time in comparing the Hoare-Laval plan with the various agreements which the British had signed with her West African colonies. Samuel Wood of the 1934 Gold Coast Aborigines' Rights' Protection Society Deputation in England, for instance, recalled at a protest meeting organised by C. L. R. James and some Africans in London how the 'same British Government had repudiated agreements' signed with the people of the Gold Coast. 'The apparently disowned Bond of 1844 stands gaunt like a tall pillar in evidence, made unsightly still by the unredeemed word of Governor Clifford about water taxation.'[21]

The terms of the Franco-British compromise scheme created a sensation at various political centres both in Britain and France, and in West Africa. It was the most dramatic event in the Anglo-French diplomacy in the mid-thirties. It was also the turning-point in the reaction of the articulate West Africans to the crisis diplomacy of the period. West African press comment regarding the Ethiopian question reached its climax both in intensity and in volume during December 1935 and January 1936. It centred on the Anglo-French fiasco and the abandonment of the League. The Hoare-Laval episode proved to the nationalists that their colonial powers were not all-powerful. It further made it evident that Britain had neither adequate military strength, nor the decision and willpower to oppose aggression, either alone or at the head of a collective coalition under the League of Nations, against any future 'rape' of another African territory. For, in their opinion, the mere bluff of Mussolini was sufficient to send the government helter-skelter on the path of appeasement. They argued that it ought to have occurred to Britain that without the co-operation of any of the League members, she could easily have engaged and annihilated the Italians.[22] The nationalists' view of British policy appeared to be shared by Frank P. Walters who, as Deputy Secretary-General of the League of Nations, was intimately connected with the diplomacy of the powers. In a private and strictly confidential despatch to Anthony Eden in June 1935, Walters, like the nationalists in West Africa, advised that Britain should take strong measures against Italy without French support, even if such an action would lead to war. France and other League powers, he said, would 'very soon follow enthusiastically a clear lead from the British Government', and the League could 'quite well survive the loss of Italy' in circumstances which were entirely to its credit.[23] But the British cabinet, as the articulate West African nationalists saw it, could bring only a divided mind to the problems of the day. No definite lead could come from Stanley Baldwin, the British Prime Minister, during the period of the crisis. The outcome of all this, in their view, was a policy which lacked conviction, and which throughout appeared to be sterile, unimaginative, and confused in a period of grave international crisis.

The disillusionment of the West African nationalists and their condemnation of the British and French handling of the Ethiopian question would seem to have been largely a sharp reaction against the false assumption long held by them that Britain and France, as the only two powers which exercised control over large non-European populations, would not dare to 'let Mussolini pull them into any conflict with the coloured races'.[24] The nationalist leaders claimed that historically the Negro race had for centuries regarded Great Britain 'with filial affection' as the champion of the weak against the oppressor, and recalled that Britain was chiefly responsible for 'the repression of the international wrongs done to the Africans in slavery in the West Indies, America and other places'. As the 'God mother of the African and coloured races', they hoped that Britain would take up the mantle of the past and protect the territorial integrity and political independence of Ethiopia, a kingdom 'dear to all Africans and revered by all coloured races'.[25]

Apart from this claim to special relationship with Britain, there were other considerations which seemed to strengthen the conviction of West Africans that the United Kingdom was the only country which had the power and authority to stop Mussolini decisively, and to impose the sanctions demanded by the Covenant of the League of Nations. Geographically, Ethiopia lies close to the main sea-route that passes from the Mediterranean through the Suez Canal and the Red Sea into the Indian Ocean and beyond, an area in which Great Britain would be able to exercise her sea-power effectively in the event of concerted action by the League. The strategic position of Great Britain was considered to be enough to dishearten Mussolini. Furthermore, many West Africans shared the belief that as Great Britain was the only power with ubiquitous interests, preservation of international peace through the Geneva system was identical with her political interests. Sentiments such as these were expressed in diverse ways with a view to inviting the attention of Great Britain to the impact which the Ethiopian crisis had had on her subject peoples in West Africa.

On the other hand, the more radical groups in West Africa tended to regard with the utmost distrust the good faith of Great Britain and France in their efforts to seek a negotiated settlement of the Italo-Ethiopian dispute. These uncompromising nationalists felt that, in view of their own colonial holdings, Britain and France might not be effective or disinterested peace-makers, as both powers looked 'like those accused at the bar of their own conscience . . . the very wrong they were desirous to condemn in others seemed to testify against themselves. . . .' As Chief Awolowo recalled in the late 1940s, the statesmen of Europe knew that to condemn Fascist imperialism in Ethiopia 'would be the case of the stove accusing the kettle'.[26] Yet, in spite of such misgivings about British and French sincerity, these radical groups ultimately came to believe that 'one word from England could dispel all the war-clouds gathering anywhere and bring contending nations back to the sober ways of peace'. Britain was to some of them 'God's policeman on earth', and others felt that the British Empire could shape international policy as it pleased.[27] The West African attitudes to the British and French diplomacy during the period of the Italo-Ethiopian conflict were dominated by this ambivalent belief and confidence in British power and justice, and by their historical association with Britain and France. It was against this background that they waited with breathless anxiety to see what effective steps the two colonial powers would take on their behalf in the Ethiopian affair. Thus, when they realised by mid-September that Britain in particular had not taken any decisive and effective measures to meet the Italian challenge, they taunted:

What ails the British Lion that instead of roaring with the full volume of the voice, he purrs like a cat before ignoble Italy? And cringes to the proud Mussolini? If Britain is indeed the defender and protector of the weak peoples of the earth, we want to see her extend her protective hand to Abyssinia. . . .[28]

Coupled with such sentiments about the past record of Great Britain was the inability of the nationalist leaders to appreciate the full weight and implications of the international situation in which the Italo-Ethiopian conflict was cast. This failure to comprehend the exigencies of international politics deepened their conviction that the Italo-Ethiopian affair was 'a simple problem' which did not need, as they described the League procedures, 'all these serpentine circuitous methods' for solving it.[29] Hence in utter disgust at the diplomacy of the League powers some radical nationalists impatiently burst out: 'Look at the Great Powers on the stage of the Italo-Ethiopian drama. What means all these strutting and fretting with all the ravings of shallow diplomacy – mere sound and fury which have hitherto achieved nothing? Decidedly there is something radically wrong with these Powers. . . .'[30] Evidently, the various nationalist groups tended to approach international politics from the point of view of general and ideal concepts rather than concrete political circumstances, largely ignoring power relations, particular interests and commitments of nations, and specific responsibilities stemming from geographic location, resources, and capabilities.

So far as Britain and France were concerned, the determining factors in the Italo-Ethiopian affair were not African. In the months after the Walwal incident of December 1934, European politics exerted a specially strong pull on international affairs owing to pressures for a united Anglo-French-Italian front against the comparatively new menace of Hitler. Hitler's declaration of German rearmament in March 1935 (like his entry into the Rhineland a year later) intensified the determination of British and French politicians to keep in with Mussolini, who had only recently struck an anti-German attitude on the Brenner at the time of the murder of Dollfuss, the Austrian Chancellor. The so-called Stresa-Front, which was formed in April 1935 after the German denunciation of the Versailles settlement, may have been an illusion, but on the British and French sides there was a genuine attempt to form an anti-German alliance with Italy, and this attempt, as Peter Calvocoressi has argued, 'entailed a conscious or half-formed resolve not to allow the League of Nations to intervene in Africa to the extent of damaging a possible accord between London, Paris, and Rome'.[31] Mussolini was able 'to exploit the European situation and hold Britain and France captive', because he wanted only one thing, the conquest of Ethiopia, while they wanted two incompatible things, to protect Ethiopia and the Covenant but, still more, to protect themselves against Hitler. Hoare made this clear to the various High Commissioners in London that the British Government could not accept any solution of the Italo-Ethiopian dispute which would imply the renunciation of Ethiopian sovereignty. Yet, at the same time he was greatly concerned as to what would happen if Italy left the League.[32]

That the appeasement of Italy was a cardinal element in British policy during this period of international crisis was confirmed by the British Foreign Office commentary on the Franco-Italian Agreements of January 1935. Soon after the conclusion of the 'Rome Agreements', V. E. Sergent of the British Foreign Office stressed that in any examination of the Ethiopian question the Foreign

Office should bear in mind that the success of 'our European policy, based as it is on co-operation between ourselves, France and Italy, may be seriously prejudiced if we give even the impression that we are trying to block Italy's expansionist schemes in Africa.' He warned that Britain should be careful not to oppose the extension of Italian influence, even territorial extension in directions where such extension 'will not clash with our interests'.[33] The Foreign Office took note of this and agreed that it be kept 'constantly in mind' by Sir John Maffey's Committee, which had been set up to investigate British interests in Ethiopia.[34] In almost any calculation of Britain's strategic interests, Italian friendship was invaluable. A friendly, or at least a neutral, Italy would assure a stable Mediterranean, which meant that extra units of the British fleet would not have to be tied up there. On the continent, an Italian ally, maintained in the spirit of the Stresa-Front, might provide an opposing force to Germany in the south. Thus appeasement – the attempt to 'purchase peace by making concessions to an aggressor' or a desire to 'make the best of difficult times by offering the hand of friendship'[35] – was very much the guiding principle of the British conduct of the Italo-Ethiopian conflict.

As for the French, the theory of ensuring national security through the maintenance of the Geneva system was never orthodox in their forumlation of foreign policy. What France cared for and placed reliance on was not so much a peace machinery to deter any would-be aggressor, irrespective of geographical or other considerations, as a set of alliances with states in Europe which entertained the same kind of apprehension about a concrete potential enemy. The French were inclined to the belief that the collective security system was essential for Europe. It meant a protection against Germany destroying the provisions of the Versailles Peace Settlement. France thus regarded the League as another instrument to keep Germany in her place and to deter or defeat another German aggression. Aggression elsewhere was not considered to be of vital importance. Thus the French cared little or nothing for the fate of Ethiopia, but only considered it in so far as it affected French security in Europe. In view of the French fear and weakness in the face of Germany, the French did not like to do anything which might destroy the Franco-Italian Agreement of January 1935. The press in France during the period of the crisis therefore urged with significant unanimity the importance of not losing Europe for the sake of Africa.[36]

Thus, in the Italo-Ethiopian dispute West African expectations appeared to be at variance with the political objectives of Britain and France. While the nationalists were anxious to see swift and decisive action initiated against Italy, their imperial overlords, tied to their respective national and security interests in Europe, hesitated and wavered. They had looked to Britain and France for action, but saw only prevarication, self-interest and unwillingness to stand firmly by the League of Nations. Neither Britain nor France was prepared to be drawn into war for the sake of Ethiopia. On 10 June 1936, for example, Neville Chamberlain, the Chancellor of the Exchequer and future Prime Minister, declared at the 1900 Club that to advocate the maintenance of sanctions against Italy was 'the very midsummer of madness'.[11] This was reinforced by Sir John Simon, Hoare's predecessor in the Foreign Office, when he told the House of Commons on 23 June 1936 that he 'was not prepared to risk a single ship to preserve Abyssinian independence'.[38] The phrase was illuminating. It breathed the essential spirit of 'appeasement'. In view of the impending grave international crisis occasioned by resurgent Germany under Adolf Hitler, the Ethiopian question could only be considered as a matter of secondary importance. Ethiopia thus remained throughout the thirties as the 'living symbol of violated right'. Her ancient and jealously guarded independence was sacrificed in a welter of conflicting interests and obligations.

Ethiopia and the 'League of European Brotherhood'

It was not unexpected, then, that West Africans tended to express doubt about their confidence in the League of Nations as an instrument that could safeguard the rights of coloured peoples. Much as they would have preferred to ventilate their grievances under the colonial system in the open forum of the League, the West African educated elite, like their opposite numbers in other colonial territories, were excluded from membership of the 'Great Experiment', primarily because West Africa was not a 'nation' in the Western sense of the word. This exclusion from the Geneva institution caused a great deal of disillusionment among the nationalist intelligentsia of the 1920s. In their opinion, the Western definition of the word 'nation', which denoted 'the possession of military, naval, and air power', had deprived many groups and communities of people, particularly coloured, of the privilege of the status of 'nationhood', and therefore of membership of the newly established international forum.[39] They argued that although the description given by Europe to the word 'nation' might 'not apply to us', yet if the name was inapplicable 'the thing is there'. From Nigeria to Sierra Leone 'we are one people', and what applied to one portion should also apply to the other.[40] Furthermore, in their view, it would have been expedient inasmuch as the various groups and communities were racial entities with social, economic, and religious systems of their own to have been accepted as 'racial or national units' within the League. As early as 1928 J. W. de Graft Johnson, an ardent nationalist at the time, argued:

> A League of Nations properly so-called should be an institution to safeguard the rights of all nations and to guarantee to the people of the earth international equality status. It should have as members, not only representatives of nations so-called but also of various groups each forming one social organic whole. In short, it should in essence be a League of Races, and the youngest and most helpless member of the international population of the world should have as much equal right to be heard at its assemblies as the most powerful and most wealthy.[41]

This view of the League does not appear to take into consideration the obligations of the Covenant which member states of the organisation were called upon to assume, particularly since most of these racial groups, though of different entities, were militarily and economically weak and ineffective. Moreover, it poses the question as to how such groups, most of whom were subject peoples, could reconcile League membership with their dependent status. In spite of these inherent problems de Graft Johnson's view would seem to have formed the basis of West African reaction to the League when the Ethiopian crisis broke out.

For as soon as Italy attacked Ethiopia the contention in West Africa was that the League, as it was constituted, had no meaning for other than European peoples. It was a 'League of European Brotherhood', and 'black' Ethiopia would not get the justice she deserved in such a predominantly white club. For the Geneva institution, in their view, was set up for realisation of European ambitions at the expense of the 'dear lives and rightful possessions' of the weaker and darker races. It was a body united together in acquiescing, and putting into practice the infamous doctrine of 'Might is Right'. Because Ethiopia was a 'black' state, sanctions, the most effective weapon in the hands of the League, to be used against the adjudged aggressor, had become a matter for committees of experts and non-experts.[42] Africans should not therefore have any faith in the League for it was 'a child born bad, and it was the circumstances of its birth that made them have their doubts as to its ever turning out to be any good at all to non-Nordic peoples'.[43]

The failure of the League to take up arms on behalf of Ethiopia was thus immediately viewed by the nationalists as a predetermined policy 'to cheat the ends of justice'. Hence the denunciation of the League in most derogatory terms. To the *Gold Coast Times*, the League should be properly styled as 'The League of Abominations'.[44] To the *Gold Coast Independent*, the League was not merely an 'abomination'; it was also destined to go down in history as the 'greatest joke which depicts the results of man's effort to tread the paths of righteousness without the inspiring and directing force of the Golden Rule'. It was a 'tragic farce'.[45] It was also a 'League of Cowards', for at the mere threat of a bully it decided to lift sanctions. It was described as a 'hypocritical' organisation which did not deserve the task of keeping world peace. For it preached disarmament while its members manufactured arms. It claimed to assure security while it betrayed this same security that it professed. It accommodated impiety, such as the Italian atrocities, while its members claimed to be Christian and civilised.[46]

All the evidence seems to point to the conclusion that to the West Africans the failure of the League in Ethiopia was due to the fact that the conflict was between the white and black races, and this was made clear in the official despatches at the time.[47] Thus, the question whether sanctions were effective or not was immaterial, for:

> It cannot be disputed that had Ethiopia been a European country, or a country inhabited exclusively by the caucasoid races, the League of Nations would have been much more energetic in its policy. . . . We make bold to say that had Ethiopia been a white country like Belgium, Holland, or Greece, not only would the League have imposed economic and financial sanctions, but military and diplomatic sanctions would have been in order. . . . But a country which is populated by a black race has no rights which Italy, a white race, must respect, and it has no influence to challenge the League of Nations, an organisation whose membership preponderantly belongs to the white race, to live up to the terms of its covenant.[48]

In utter dismay, many argued that the Negroid races had committed no crime to warrant 'this prejudice'. They were not responsible for their colour which 'Nature has devised in order to protect them from the active rays of the sun', and other destructive forces of the physical world. Yet those who formulated the League, despite their intelligence, were so biased that the colour of one's skin was used to prejudice the application of measures stipulated in treaties.[49] The nationalists leaders inferred from all this that there was no sincerity 'left in the world', when the fate of Africa and the black man became the talk of the day. If anything at all remained, it was the old prejudice of superiority complex and colour which 'dies hard when the African or the Negro appears on the stage of life'.[50] The conclusion reached was that Mussolini had his way because the irony of the fate of Africa paved the way for him; and that the League could not do more than it did, because it was confronted with a problem which was 'accentuated by the blackness of the black man'.[51] In a defiant note, the nationalists leaders declared:

> A people so jealous of their independence cannot easily submit to the Fascist tutelage. It must be rightly understood that it was due only to the treachery of the League of Nations that the present situation has come about. . . . The League will collapse notwithstanding all the smooth assurances of Anthony Eden. . . . And when the next war comes, Europe will realise that the African has not forgotten the white man's treachery to him nor will he ever forget it.[52]

The integration of Ethiopia into Italian East Africa, and the subsequent assumption of the title of Emperor of Ethiopia by King Vittorio Emmanuele of Italy in May 1936,[53] did not cause any immediate loss of West African interest in the Italo-Ethiopian affair. In a very impassioned editorial bearing the long title, 'Injustice that shall be paid in blood and tears: The League completes betrayal of Ethiopia: Justice Murdered in High Places', the *Gold Coast Independent* mourned Ethiopia thus:

> The final curtain has been rung down over a dismal and disgraceful episode in world history. The Kingdom of Ethiopia, the lone bulwark of African sovereignty that had withstood the storms and blasts of a thousand years, is no more. The ancient Kingdom that had its roots deep in antiquity and existed when the world was young has crumbled under the heel of a conqueror. The rocky domain against which the Caesars of Ancient Rome's palmiest and mightiest days shattered their legions in vain, is now over-run by the effeminate soldiery of a puny imitation Caesar. . . . The League of Nations has formally handed over Ethiopia to Italy and the Kingdom of the Lion of the Tribe of Judah is no more: it has been sold, betrayed and done in by those whom it trusted and in the sanctity of whose pledged word it reposed the most implicit faith.[54]

On Christmas Eve, 1938, the people of Nigeria offered prayer for the cause of the brave Ethiopians who, 'although forgotten by the world Press', were stubbornly fighting to regain their lost independence.[55] All through the period up to the outbreak of the Second World War, the photographs of the Emperor and Empress of Ethiopia were boldly advertised for sale: 'ABYSSINIA! Get a framed picture of the Royal Pair. . . . Despite Recognition by the League, the WAR IN ETHIOPIA IS NOT ENDED! ETHIOPIA STILL fights.'

The Italian declaration of war on Britain and France in June 1940 was hailed throughout West Africa as the much needed opportunity for the British and West African forces to liberate Ethiopia from the Fascist occupation of the country. The war was welcomed mainly because many felt that it might decide the fate of Ethiopia. For it was generally hoped that when the wrongs that had been committed by the 'brigands of the nations' came to be righted, and the independence of Poland, Czechoslovakia and Austria restored, Ethiopia too would be restored to the independence which she had enjoyed from time immemorial.[56] It was also believed that the failure of Britain to secure and maintain Ethiopian independence would evoke bitterness and cynicism, 'under-mining the confidence' which was the basis of British colonial rule, and 'render-ing co-operation with Africans more difficult in every British African territory'.[57]

The honour of making the final assault fell to West and East Africans, Sudanese and Ethiopians. According to the London correspondent to the *West African Pilot*, General Sir Andrew Cunningham, Commander-in-Chief in the Abyssinian campaign, disclosed that until then 'all praise was given to the white South Africans and Rhodesians, but it can be revealed that it was the Natives of the Gold Coast, Nigeria, and the King's African Rifles, who broke the backbone of Italian resistance on the entire Kenya and Somaliland fronts after a series of brilliant attacks'.[58] General Sir Andrew Cunningham was said to have stated that it was the Nigerian troops who captured the capital of Somaliland; 'and these same Nigerian troops' through their 'lighting advance' recaptured Harrar, the birthplace of Haile Selassie, and the second largest city in Ethiopia.[59] The gallant part played by the officers and men of the Gold Coast Brigade in the liberation of Ethiopia was vividly described in two well-illustrated articles by Sir Arnold Hodson, the Governor of the Gold Coast.[60] Quoting from official reports from Headquarters and eye witness accounts, Sir Arnold disclosed that 'Officers and men from the Gold Coast have arrived in Kenya to play their part in the operations in East Africa . . . all ready and anxious to take their full share in the task of driving the aggressor from the continent.'[61] Special mention was made of the Kumasi Battalion of the Ashanti Province, who seized the rare opportunity they had long been waiting for since the Italian invasion of Ethiopia in 1935, to display their gallantry. The Kumasi Battalion was reported to have 'lived up to its tradition of discipline, efficiency, courage and willingness'.[62] To the Gold Coast Brigade went the credit of 'being the first of the overseas imperial troops to fight the Italians and to enter enemy territory'. The Emperor's return to his capital on 5 May 1941 – after exactly five years of exile – was 'more warmly acclaimed by the people of the West Coast . . . than his own people'.[63] And when Ethiopian independence was finally re-established in 1941, West Africans saw it as the righting of a great wrong to the African race, and the whole Italian onslaught as one of the blackest chapters in the history of European colonial expansion in Africa.[64] It was a shattering experience – the beginning of the end of British prestige as one of the props of colonial rule. As a corollary to the West African disillusionment with the League powers was their intense reaction to the role of the Pope and the Christian Church in the Ethiopian affair.

The Christian Churches, the Crisis, and West Africa

The Italian attack on Ethiopia became not only a direct challenge to the post-war system of collective security as established by the League of Nations, but also a problem of extreme delicacy for the Christian missions – and particularly those of the Catholic Church – and their endeavours in West Africa. The ethical basis of their teachings was variously challenged by the militant race-conscious groups of nationalists who during the crisis persistently argued that twentieth-century Christianity had no further value or relevance for the black man. The Catholic Church was the recipient of particularly harsh criticism. In their bitterness, the ardent nationalists denounced Roman Catholics over the studied reticence of Pope Pius XI and the Catholic hierarchy generally towards the wanton aggression of Mussolini's Fascist regime against Ethiopia. The unwillingness of the Papacy to intervene in the conflict deepened suspicions held by the nationalist groups of the existence of an imperialist conspiracy in Africa – supported by colonial governments and missionary societies. When it became clear that the Pope and the Catholic Church would not intervene or even protest against the un-Christian action of the Fascists, it was assumed by the nationalist politicians that the Holy See and the *Duce* were acting in unison against Africans. Italy after all was the home of the Pope and of Mussolini, and many West Africans concluded that both were working in connivance. Thus, the Italo-Ethiopian crisis had the unexpected result that the Pope and the Catholic Church were made responsible for Mussolini's brutal actions. This created a mood of disillusionment which tended to make the nationalist groups cynical about and critical of all white pretensions. And as Christian Italy continued to use poison gas on innocent women and children in Ethiopia, and the Pope remained conspicuously silent, this disillusionment became bitter and politically consequential. It provided another weapon for the war against colonialism in Africa. In their disenchantment the embittered radicals like Wallace Johnson and Nnamdi Azikiwe renewed the blistering attack of the nineteenth century on the Catholic Church in West Africa by such early national-ists as James Johnson.[65] It would be appropriate to discuss this interesting dimension of the West African reaction to the Ethiopian question against the background of the nationalist view of the activities of the Christian church in Africa prior to the outbreak of the Italo-Ethiopian dispute.

Long before Mussolini embarked on his fateful 'civilising mission' in Ethiopia, many West African nationalists had seen the role of Christianity in Africa from two main points of view. There was, on the one hand, a group of Africans who sincerely appreciated the work done in Africa by the various Christian missions. This group accepted the view that the history of West Africa was the history of missionary societies which had certainly done far more for 'our civilisation and religion' than all other agencies put together.[66] For, with the advent of Christianity in Africa a good many of the wicked institutions and practices which had once been rampant among the Africans 'in their pristine ignorance' had completely disappeared.[67] They believed that without Christian missionaries the African continent could not have developed a sense of social or moral stability. Christianity was to them 'a symbol of illumination and civili-sation' in the dark continent of Africa. They would argue that whatever progress Africans might have in Africa was due directly to the efforts of mission-aries. Although they agreed that the missionaries might have had their short-comings, they, nevertheless, felt that these could not overshadow the 'great emancipation of Africans, mentally and physically through the efforts of missionaries'.[68]

On the other hand, the majority of Africans looked at the missionaries with some suspicion. Christianity and Western civilisation were not infrequently identified by this group as just another form of 'Europeanisation' portrayed as possessing tendencies disruptive and antipathetic to the African way of life. To this group of people, Christianity and European culture became synonymous. As Ako Adjei, a leading post-1945 Ghanaian nationalist who was a student colleague of Kwame Nkrumah at Lincoln, Pennsylvania, once wrote, the divine duty of the Western world was to impose the Christian religion upon the Africans in order that they 'might evolve from their primitive stupidity to the golden age of civilised intelligence'. Through the Christian ideas of God, Africans would begin to acquire the 'morals of the civilised world'; and through civilised morality they would develop the character traits that were acceptable to the 'will of God and also the European world'.[69] For the missionaries brought not only the Christian religion, but also the institutional forms and moral and ethical concepts which were a necessary part of their background. They could not confine themselves to the introduction of the Bible; to ensure that it was read and understood they organised Christian communities on the lines of those in Europe, provided schools and organisations through which to disseminate their ideas and religious practices, and tried to enforce the moral code of Western Europe as universal standard. Acceptance of these standards by the African meant a wholly new way of life and rejection of traditional society. Those who conformed to the new standards were accorded a higher status, as Christians, enlightened and civilised. Thus the natural hierarchical order was upset and the traditional bases of authority were contravened. The 'missions therefore set in motion a politico-social revolution.'[70]

Thus, as the nationalists contended, to many missionaries the Christian creed was incompatible with any form of social organism which was non-European. To be Christianised one had to be Europeanised. This meant for the African a loss of his individuality, while his thoughts and aspirations became less and less Negroid. Hence, Christianity, as practised and presented by Europeans, had in it a germ of religious intolerance which was unknown and was undesirable in Africa. As a pioneer nationalist strongly protested in the thirties:

. . . We have no alternative than to state categorically that most Christian missionaries we have known, in their contacts with Africans and other religious groups, are apt to be intolerant and dictatorial, and these evidences of human weakness are usually the means towards the undoing of the noble work done by pioneering and tolerant missionaries.[71]

This evidence of intolerance was responsible for the scepticism of some Africans regarding the practicality of Christianity. Most progressive Africans became highly critical of the obdurate position of many of the missionary societies.

More importantly, many nationalists identified Christianity and Western civilisation with imperialism. In their view, the Christian missions were one agency (alongside the government and the foreign firms) through which Europeans exercised power over Africans. They held that there existed a latent but effective link between the missions and the imperial and colonial governments, and that the missionaries did collaborate in the conquest of Africa. Nationalists therefore attacked the missionaries as agents of imperialism who 'conditioned the minds of Africans to accept colonialism'.[72]

Not only was Christianity frequently denounced as virtually a hand-maid of imperialism and commercialism; it was also held by the militant groups that the churches were but 'veritable publicity bureaux where all sorts of European goods are advertised'.[73] Hence Orishatukeh Faduma attributed the failure of Christianity to make appreciable inroads in Africa to its close association with imperialism. The white man, he said, belonged to an imperial race. His form of Christianity was imperial, and partook of his nature. Therefore it was not Christianity but the form it took when it was 'presented by the white man', which failed to attract the many in Africa. The same ship that carried the missionaries of the cross carried also millions of 'demijohns of rum and whiskey' from Christian countries.[74]

This suspicion of a missionary–government conspiracy was reinforced by another important and persuasive factor: the silence of the missionaries on such widely felt grievances as racial discrimination, inequality, exploitation, denial of opportunity, and all the other features identifiable with colonial rule. Although these evils were patently un-Christian and contrary to missionary teachings, yet, in the eyes of the Africans, they were glossed over by the European missionaries.[75] To most nationalists, therefore, Christ, Western civilisation, and colonisation were so bound together as to be indistinguishable:

> The word 'Christ' has always been identified here with the British Empire . . . [and] the general feelings are that the Missionaries have been the front troops of the Government to soften the hearts of the people and while people look at the cross white men gather the riches of the land.[76]

It was this apparent alliance between commercial interests, government circles and missionaries which strengthened the conviction of many nationalists that white men irrespective of their different endeavours in Africa, were allied in some way against Africans. They felt with Nehru that the Church had 'served the purpose of British imperialism and given both capitalism and imperialism a moral and Christian covering. . . .'[77] Italian aggression against Ethiopia appeared to confirm the nationalists' view that Christianity as a whole, especially the Roman Catholic Church, and the Vatican in particular, had conspired with the Fascists against Africans. This view was reinforced by the unwillingness of the Holy See to become involved in the conflict, owing to the extreme delicacy of its position.

For after the annexation in 1870 of the sovereign state of Rome by the newly united Kingdom of Italy, a Law of Guarantees of 1871 was imposed upon the Papacy. Under this law the Pope occupied an anomalous position in international law; the Papacy thereupon protested against this unilateral act of Italy and refused to co-operate formally with the Italian Government until 11 February 1929 when the Lateran Accords were signed by the two parties.[78] With the Lateran Treaty and Concordat the Pope was re-established in his dual capacity as spiritual leader of a universal church and a parochial temporal prince. In his political capacity the Pope, by Article 24 of the Treaty, agreed that the Papacy should remain 'extraneous to the temporal competition between other states and to the international conferences summoned for such an object, unless the contending parties agree to appeal to its mission of peace'. It was this aspect of the Lateran Treaty which the Catholics in West Africa frequently quoted in their defence of the silence of Pope Pius XI during the crisis.[79] Tradition as well as treaty obligation led the Vatican to stand apart from what in the political sphere could be construed as a purely secular dispute.

However, in spite of the independence of the Holy See, which the pro-Catholic writers in West Africa constantly emphasised, the exclusive jurisdiction of the Papacy was advantageous to its taking a definite stand in the cause of international morality. The Papacy indeed had this right, because in the same Article 24 of the Lateran Treaty that restricted its political activities the Holy See had reserved to itself 'the right to make its moral and spiritual protest heard', and this was the clause through which Pope Pius XI might speak out for the cause of justice and peace. Although it was the custom of the

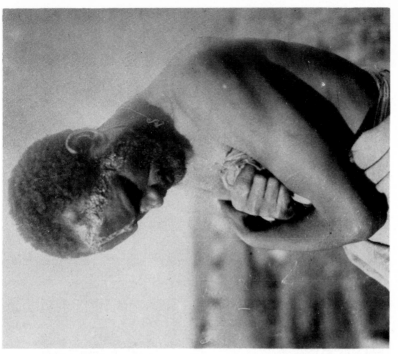

Terrible damage was inflicted by Italian planes and tanks and many Ethiopians were injured by the use of mustard gas

Emperor Haile Selassie appealed to the League of Nations in vain Pope Pius XI remained conspicuously silent about the ethics of the Italian invasion

Papacy not to intervene and denounce any particular war as unjust, for this would mean passing judgement on secular causes and events, peace was important to the church. As Professor Binchy argued, 'The greater the war the greater the disaster to the church, and in particular a European war in which Italy was involved would be a calamity of the worst kind. . . .'[80]

It is significant to observe, however, that neutrality did not imply complete indifference, at least before the outbreak of the Italo-Ethiopian war in October 1935. For, in spite of its ties with the Italian nation and its connections with the Fascist regime, the Holy See viewed Mussolini's aggression in Ethiopia with deep concern and made this known in a number of public speeches and private interviews.[81] In July 1935, for instance, Pope Pius XI was reported to have expressed at a private audience his disapproval of the threatened war. The Pope said that a war of the kind being prepared by Mussolini would be 'abominable', and that he still refused to believe that it would really take place; he further stated that he could not understand a civilised nation setting out to conquer another country in complete disregard of all existing laws and rules. It was like 'going and taking something out of someone else's safe'. The Pope told his interlocutor that he could not bring himself to believe that Italy would really seek to destroy a country which for thirteen centuries had defended Christianity against Islam. He concluded solemnly: 'If a war does break out, which I still do not believe, I shall be obliged to take a very serious step which I have been thinking over for a long while.'[82]

If this reported interview were correct, the Pope would seem to have supplied proof of his independence of judgement and moral courage. Pius XI was obviously vehemently opposed to the settlement of a quarrel between two members of the League of Nations by methods of 'Blood and Iron'. This private disapproval of Mussolini's action was followed on 27 August by a public address to the Catholic Nurses Congress at Castel Gandolfo in which the Pope condemned wars of conquest in an obvious allusion to the Ethiopian crisis:

> Already we see that abroad there is talk of war of conquest, of a war of aggression. . . . A war which is only a war of conquest would be clearly an unjust war. . . . One thing seems to us beyond doubt, that is, if the need for expansion is a fact with which we must reckon, the right of defence has its limits and its qualifications, and if the right of defence is to be blameless it must observe a certain moderation. . . .[83]

This address was the Pope's most complete and definite statement of the Italo-Ethiopian crisis before the outbreak of war. It was addressed not only as a warning to the Fascist regime but also as an encouragement to those who were seeking a negotiated settlement. The passage concerning the limits of the right of defence was widely quoted as having increased the moral authority of the Papacy before international public opinion, and Pius XI was acclaimed as a fearless leader not subservient to Mussolini.[84] Elsewhere it was pointed out that the address was couched in terms that could not call forth Italian criticism. One thing, however, is clear. Pressure was exerted on the Pope by the Italian Government through the Vatican's secretary of state, Cardinal Eugenio Pacelli, to attenuate the harshness of his remarks and to counteract the bitterness they caused among the Fascist leaders.[85] The Italian Government's representations had their effect for, on 7 September, the Pope addressed a pilgrimage of Catholic ex-servicemen, and in reference to the Italo-Ethiopian dispute, said that he hoped and prayed for peace, but a peace that would satisfy the hopes and ends of a great and good people, which were his own people.[86]

This was the last public reference to the Italo-Ethiopian crisis made by the Holy See. And despite the growing seriousness of the Ethiopian affair and his own concern, Pope Pius XI did not further warn or condemn the aggressor or offer succour to the victim when the war finally broke out. What was more surprising, the Vatican did not encourage the various moves and attempts that were being made at settling the conflict on the principles of international law then universally accepted. The Pope remained studiously silent even though in his primary capacity as spiritual and moral leader he should have come out strongly and openly against what appeared clearly to be an unjust war. Throughout Pius XI seemingly endeavoured to maintain a stand as unobtrusive, and as enigmatic, as possible.[87]

It was this non-committal attitude of the Holy See which suddenly provoked a revival of the nationalist criticisms of Christian missions in Africa which had been voiced a few decades earlier. The general belief was that the Christian world – particularly of course the Catholic Church – was strongly in favour of Italy's blatant act of aggression. The whole Ethiopian question was viewed by nationalists not merely as a test of the utility of the League of Nations, but also as an acid test of Christianity and Western civilisation in Africa.

Viewing the role of Christianity in world affairs against the background of the Italian atrocities in Ethiopia, some West African nationalist leaders rashly claimed that most of the sorrows of the world had emanated from the church. In their opinion, Christian Europe had over the years used religion as a cloak to perpetuate the greatest injustice and persecutions. The fate of the Huguenots in seventeenth-century France and the activities of the Spanish Inquisition were cited as evidence of this contention. The Christian religion had used its influence not in the way of promoting peace, happiness and comfort but to create turmoil, dissensions and strife.[88] West Africans recalled that among the sins which the doctrines of Christianity counselled its adherents to denounce were selfishness and covetousness. But through covetousness Ethiopian women and children were hurried to death with all the speed which modern technology could command. Christianity also (it was held) advocated the brotherhood of men, and upon the principles of equality of rights of man every human being had the right to his possessions and property no matter what his race. The Ethiopian problem had shown that this principle was applicable to the white race only.[89]

After this sensational attack on the Christian Church, militant nationalists attempted to examine the record of Christianity in the light of Italian aggression in Ethiopia. They concluded that Christianity had failed, and with it the white man's civilisation. In their opinion, Hitler's Germany, the country which had given birth to Martin Luther proved this. John Wesley's England and David Livingstone's Scotland supported 'this universal conviction'. Mussolini's Fascist Italy by her barbarous, aggressive 'mission' in East Africa, supported as they felt it was by the Vatican, demonstrably confirmed it. The awful lynching practices in the United States of America showed what the 'supposed civilised countries could do under the banner of Jesus, the Christ'. Furthermore, it was widely argued that the 'colour' problem in the United States and Africa and other parts of the world and the countless instances of gross injustice to coloured peoples portrayed the failure of Christianity in the balance of religions. In all cases, it was stated, Africa had been the easy prey of Christian propagandists.

She had been the target of European 'imperialism and goal of insatiable capitalist government'.[90]

The denunciation of the Christian church, and some comments on Europeans' belief in God, was followed by a sharper and more serious indictment from Wallace Johnson, who always tended to 'equate European Christianity with colonial subjection'. Johnson, whose other activities will be discussed in the subsequent chapters of this study, was a major force in colonial politics in English-speaking West Africa. At the height of the crisis, in a series of editorials he strongly deplored whatever value that European religion and Christianity had had in Africa. In one of these editorials, he declared:

> The means whereby the Africans, particularly those of West Africa, have been kept in subjection under the European nations is religion and Christianity. The Italo-Ethiopian war is destined to prove to the African masses that Europe with all its civilisation is still enshrined in barbarism and that Western civilisation is sheer mockery. It is also destined to prove to the African masses that Religion, especially Christianity as it has been introduced by the whiteman to the blackman, is a heinous mass of deception. We must worship God according to our conviction, not according to the theory of the whiteman's Christianity. We must see Christ as a Blackman and all the Holy angels as Negroes. As for Western Civilisation, it has to be properly sifted. Take that which is good from it and throw the rest in the dustbin. . . .[91]

In another instalment Wallace Johnson asserted that the white man's Christianity and barbarism were identical. Europeans had also proved that their Christian faith and doctrine was 'Blessed are the strong for they shall weaken the weak'.[92] Wallace Johnson, who had received part of his education in Communist Russia, had earlier in a lengthy publication argued that in the Gold Coast Christianity existed under a different guise; it was capitalism and imperialism and nothing else:

> I find Christianity in the Gold Coast to be nothing but a capitalist group at work to exploit the toiling masses. Such being the case, it is clear that according to its protagonists, if Christianity should succeed in its aim, the only road whereby it could gain its ends is to keep the masses bound under the shackles of illiteracy.[93]

Wallace Johnson's other contention in this article – that the church was one of the stumbling blocks to Gold Coast education – can hardly be borne out by the available evidence. The contribution of the Christian church to education in the Gold Coast, and indeed in West Africa in general, is common knowledge. From the very first the spread of Christianity was bound up with the spread of literacy, because literacy was a vital means of evangelisation. The mission churches were therefore committed to the introduction of formal education wherever they went as the best means of disseminating their ideas, through the children, to future generations. Christianity in West Africa meant schooling to such a degree that the two were often accepted as inseparable. As early as 1902 a nationalist Gold Coast newspaper could observe that 'whatever there is of education that this country can speak of, has been the work of the Mission Bodies'.[94] In spite of his violent criticism of the role of Christianity in Africa, Ram Desai openly admits that Christian missionaries had the 'monopoly over education in almost all of sub-Saharan Africa'. No other force, he concludes, 'had done so much to educate the Africans'.[95]

Moreover, the missionaries helped to lay the foundations of nationalism in West Africa. It was the African ministers of the church who played an important role in the development of the nationalist movement. For the most part the leaders of pre-twentieth century Gold Coast nationalism were men who had ambitions in the church as well as in the state.[96] The training for leadership given to African ministers, and their growing self-confidence in working alongside Europeans, may be regarded as a positive stimulus to the development of the nationalist movement. The nationalist movement, in which Wallace Johnson was so much interested, could hardly have got under way had it not been for the remarkable work of the missions in the field of education. It was because Christianity was so much bound up with Western civilisation, and offered the introduction to ideas and technology necessary to the conception of a modern nation state, that it was so closely interrelated with nationalism in a colonial territory, and in fact to some extent generated the nationalist movement.[97] Thus, even if it is true that the Christian missionaries made the African soil fertile for the growth of imperialism, they equally helped to sow the seeds of destruction of imperialism and the alien rule. By superimposing the structural organisation of the mission churches and schools upon African society, they 'taught and trained Africans more than just to read the Bible and preach in their churches'. And, as the English historian Tanner rightly argued: 'From free speculation on matters religious there ran a broad and easy road to free speculation on matters political. Men who chose their own pastors naturally demanded the right to choose their own magistrates too.'[98] In Nigeria, the church was the only forum of 'nationalist expression until the beginnings of the Nigerian-owned press after 1879, and the main focus of nationalist energies until after 1914'.[99] Thus, so far as the growth and development of education in West Africa was concerned, Wallace Johnson's indictment of the church for gross dereliction of duty has hardly any basis in fact.

In the nationalist attack on Christianity the Vatican and the Catholic Church bore the greatest part of the approbrium. The radicals like Azikiwe, Wallace Johnson, Nwafor Orizu, and even such moderates as Isaac Delano, violently attacked the Roman Catholic Church, and contended that the *Osservatore Romano*, the semi-official organ of the Vatican, had openly endorsed the war.[100] To these uncompromising nationalists there could be no appreciable distinction between Roman Catholicism, Fascism and the Italian aggression in Ethiopia. Thus, as they argued, every African who supported the Roman Catholic Church supported Fascism, and this meant support for Italy's atrocities in Ethiopia.[101] As a reprisal against the role of the Catholic Church in the Italo-Ethiopian dispute, they campaigned for Catholicism to be entirely boycotted in Africa, for the following considerations. First, it was widely alleged that Catholic churches were harbouring Fascist agents in Africa, who should be denounced as spies. Secondly, there was a widespread view that Catholics in Africa were financially contributing to the victory of Italy in Ethiopia. The impression generally held was that the collections in Catholic churches in Africa were sent direct to the Vatican which, it was assumed, was controlled by Mussolini, particularly since everything in Italy was state-controlled.[102] Even some Protestant bishops in West Africa shared this belief, and supported the campaign against Catholicism. In Nigeria, for example, a Protestant bishop was said to have warned that, in view of the close relationship between the Vatican and Mussolini, further Catholic progress would be disaster to Nigeria.[103] A Miss Hebe Spaull of the League of Nations Union of Great Britain toured West Africa in 1938 to discover what Africans felt about the League of Nations' handling of the Italo-Ethiopian controversy. In her confidential report, Miss Spaull stated that at Kumasi in the Gold Coast the Protestant missionaries told her that Mussolini had given the Pope a million pounds on condition that he used 'the money to send Italian missionaries to Africa', adding, 'I was told that some of these missionaries had recently arrived but I heard no details.'[104]

Thirdly, the campaign on the theme 'Boycott the Roman Church' was inspired by the firm belief that the wavering attitude of the French towards the Ethiopian question was due to the fact that the French Government at the time was not only composed principally of Roman Catholics, but was also being strongly influenced by the Vatican.[105] The available evidence, however, would appear not to support this view. According to the confidential British Foreign Office despatches at the time, for instance, there were major difficulties in the way of the Catholic Church exercising political influence in modern France: the Third Republic recognised no state religion, and laicism had become an essential part of its doctrine. The Catholic Church in France was identified with 'reaction' and remained the object of profound and jealous suspicion to the government. Besides, there is evidence that even French Catholics had a strong strain of Gallicism, which would make them instinctively resent any attempt by the Papacy to influence French policy. Finally the bishops in France were reported to have received strict instructions to make no public reference to the Italo-Ethiopian conflict, owing to the latent anti-clerical movement from the Left.[106] Thus, the contention of the African nationalists that the French Government at the time was Catholic-orientated was an oversimplification of the realities of the French situation.

The seemingly weak stand of Pope Pius XI on the crisis also aroused deep hostility. The outspoken critics described the enforced silence of the Pope as 'odious' and an 'unrighteous approval' of Italy's hostilities in Ethiopia. Besides, the 'formalised political neutrality' of the Pope created the impression that Pius XI lacked the courage and fortitude of such tenacious early Christian fighters as John Wesley, Paul of Tarsus, John Calvin, and Martin Luther. It was even doubted whether the Pope really held the keys of Peter and whether he was truly the accredited representative of Christ on Earth. For if the Pope was 'a true Christian' he would have told the Italian Duce to abandon his course of action. Some inferred from this that the Christianity of Pope Pius XI was poles apart from the noble profession of John the Baptist who faced the tyrant Herod Tetrach and pointed a reprimanding finger at the obscene monarch. Evidently, the attitude of the Pope left much to be desired, and it was this that gave rise to a widespread rumour in Africa that Pope Pius XI 'blessed the sword of Mussolini to kill other human beings and to demolish Ethiopia'.[107]

There can be little doubt that the nationalists on many occasions acted with scant circumspection and discretion, and as a result, alienated the Catholics in West Africa and their sympathisers who pleaded for restraint and objectivity. The basis of the argument of the local Catholics was that such an open criticism of the Catholic Church and the Pope would not make for the much needed unity in West Africa to face the common foe, that is, Italy. For such cries and boldly printed posters as 'Down with Catholicism' would only tend to revive the religious feud of the sixteenth century that would not in any way 'help our brothers and sisters who daily swim in the pools of blood' at the hands of the Fascists.[108]

Considered in the light of what really happened, however, the contention of the Catholic organs in West Africa that the Roman Catholic Church and the Holy See strenuously worked towards peace throughout the period of the crisis, and even went to the extent of negotiating with Mussolini on the Ethiopian affair,[109] would seem to be overstated; the reality was significantly different. There is also no evidence, as incorrectly argued by the *Nigerian Catholic Herald*, that Pope Pius XI declared that in the event of war Mussolini could get no sympathy from him.[110] Besides, the fact that temporal powers such as Britain or France had failed to persuade Mussolini to desist from his wanton attack on Ethiopia, as emphasised by some sections of the Catholics press, did not preclude Pius XI from expressing moral concern about the Ethiopian question during the height of the crisis when he could be expected to do so, to serve as an encouragement to the efforts that were being made by these temporal powers to reach a peaceful settlement of the dispute. Certainly the Pope could have been much more energetic and unequivocal in committing himself against the imperialistic and militaristic ambitions of Fascist Italy.

The unwillingness of the Papacy to intervene in the Italo-Ethiopian dispute may be explained on an institutional level by its long-standing reluctance to involve itself in secular affairs, and by the particular acuteness of this reluctance when an issue involved the Italian state. The position of Achille Ratti – who was Pope Pius XI from 1922–39 – was rendered more difficult because his natural feelings were strongly Italian (he had scarcely spent three years of his life outside Italy), and because he owed his status as an independent sovereign to the Italian Duce.[111] Mussolini's skilful negotiation of the Lateran Accords in 1929 marked the high point of friendly relations between the Pope and the man 'whom Providence caused us to meet' (to use Pius XI's phrase).[112] The Pope was anxious that nothing be done to jeopardise the continuance of the Lateran Accords. His social conservatism, together with a penchant for authoritarianism, made him unsympathetic to the progressivism of the young but powerful Catholic Popular Party of Luigi Sturzo and the activities of the Catholic trade unions. Although hostile to Fascist encroachments on the spiritual and moral domain, he none the less saw much in the regime that he could approve. As early as 1924 the Vatican had concluded that Mussolini was the only man who could 'steer the ship of state into smoother waters, and give Italy the strong hand she needs'.[113]

Another important factor which influenced the attitude of the Pope was his belief that democracy was too feeble and incoherent to serve as a dam against the Communist tide; hence his attachment to the new form of authoritarian government of Italy as offering the only hope of successful resistance. The anti-clerical activity of the Communists in Russia, Spain and throughout Europe steadily drove the Holy See towards an uneasy alliance with the Fascist Dictator. Pope Pius XI regarded atheist Communism as the enemy most to be feared, and believed that the church should accept the aid of the Fascists in waging war against it. Thus throughout the period of the crisis, the whole point of view of the Pope was coloured by 'his dread of Bolshevism'. He was afraid that if the Italian people were driven to desperation by the combined effects of sanctions against the country and an unsuccessful war in Ethiopia, they would turn Bolshevik or at least anti-clerical. The Pope envisaged that the fall or transformation of the existing regime would encourage anti-Catholic propaganda, whether by Communists or American Methodists, and possibly even the denunciation of the Lateran Treaty and Concordat. All this made His Holiness dread the idea of giving offence to Mussolini.[114] The view commonly held that Mussolini won the Pope to his side by declaring the desire of his government to bring the Ethiopian church, which Catholics believed to be schismatic, under the rule of the Roman Catholic Church, can hardly be sustained.[115]

Moreover, the younger Italian clergy (with notable exceptions), as well as many of the older, were inclined to support the Fascist government. Indeed, it was the general attitude of the Italian clergy to the Ethiopian problem which seemed to justify the criticism levelled against the Catholic Church in West Africa. Most of these were reported to have been swept away by a wave of patriotic enthusiasm and, like the Pope, by the pathological dread of the possibility that the fall of Fascism might bring to power in Italy forces hostile to the Catholic Church. Thus, speaking of the war of aggression which Italy was conducting, Cardinal Ildefonso Schuster of Milan, one of the most prominent members of the Sacred College, went so far as to say that the Italian flag was bearing the Cross in triumph over the Ethiopian plains and that the Italian army was opening the gates of Ethiopia to Catholic faith and Roman civilisation.[116] Similarly, in a much publicised pastoral letter, Monsignor Cole, bishop of Nocera in Umbria, declared that the Ethiopian enterprise was 'just and holy' as well as necessary for the purposes of both defence and expansion. In his opinion, Italy was called upon to fulfil an important task, that of conferring the benefits of Catholicism on a backward people.[117] Other bishops were widely reported to have stated that the Italo-Ethiopian war was one at which all good Italian Catholics should be united in working for the success of Italian aims and the triumph of the Italian cause.[118] It was not surprising, then, that the reaction of the bishops to the sanctions policy of the League of Nations was very violent, and must have strengthened the hand of Mussolini considerably. Throughout the crisis the Church in Italy showed its solidarity with the national political, rather than with the universal religious community. The patriotic statements of the bishops were accompanied by equally patriotic acts. In many instances bishops and archbishops organised collections of gold for the state; the bishop of San Minito declared himself ready to melt down the precious objects of his churches and the bronze of their clocks for the fatherland.[119] All these seemed to lend some credence to the various remarks which were made in West Africa against the Catholic Church and its alleged conspiracy with Mussolini in the Italo-Ethiopian conflict. As we have seen, the Pope himself personally disapproved of the Ethiopian campaign, but he refrained from checking the martial ardour of the Italian bishops, on the ground that a national clergy must be permitted, so far as they conscientiously felt able, to espouse the national cause. It was not surprising, then, that throughout the period of the Italo-Ethiopian crisis the gap of misunderstanding and suspicion between the Christian missions and many West African nationalists was never bridged. The latter were bound by their solidarity with Ethiopia to regard the former as the agent of imperialism and thus committed to the support of Mussolini's action in Ethiopia.

The atrocities of Christian Italy in Ethiopia, and the failure of the Papacy to take a strong stand against Mussolini would seem to have shaken the foundations of the Christian faith in Africa, especially on the pan-African-conscious West Coast. The whole episode, as one anti-colonial nationalist contended, had a 'great effect on the minds of Christian Africans', and remained for a long time 'an important factor in determining the attitude of Africans towards the Christian church'.[120] Africans could hardly understand how a Christian people could be guilty of such horrors, be covetous of the national home of another people, and dishonour solemn pledges. According to T. B. Allotey, a Gold Coast adventurer in Ethiopia at the time of the crisis, this traumatic experience constrained 'thousands of Africans' to turn from Christianity to Islam.[121]

Apart from discrediting Catholic missions in Africa, there is evidence that the Ethiopian question caused a setback in a number of the missionary activities of the Roman Catholic Church. In Cape Coast, the headquarters of the Catholic Church in Ghana, some ardent young men were alleged to have openly announced severing their connections with the Roman Catholic Church.[122] Similar reports came from the Catholic centres such as Kumasi, Keta, Ho and Accra (Gold Coast) as well as Freetown in Sierra Leone. In Nigeria, one of Azikiwe's disciples, Nwafor Orizu, an Ibo militant nationalist, added 'Abyssinia' to his name and called himself Akweke Abyssinia Nwafor Orizu. He explained that his name 'Abyssinia' was taken after the Italian invasion, and that it reminded him of what European Christianity and diplomacy meant to the security of Africa. For 'Between expediency and remorse, appeasement and self-interest; between half-measures and callousness, unpreparedness and political astigmatism the Great Powers of Europe left the Lion of Judah and all his peace offensives and prophetic appeals to flee his throne from Fascist cruelty.'[123] Orizu leaves us in no doubt that his faith in man and European Christianity began to shake 'from its roots' as a result of what took place in Ethiopia; the attitude of the Pope 'imposed a heavy burden upon my idea of God'. These thoughts inspired him to travel to America in February 1939 to further his education, a venture which he felt might enable him to 'conquer my deficiency' and to study the American tradition of 'Liberty or Death'. With Christian Europe's treatment of Ethiopia in mind Orizu contended that it was not that Africa was 'backward' but that Europe had no 'discipline'. He declared that the Ethiopian episode should be a warning to Christian Europe that the 'soul of man in Africa is awake, and resolves to be free now and forever'.[124]

Interest in independent or separate African churches received fresh impetus as a result of the Italo-Ethiopian conflict. For instance, the African church in Nigeria was reported to have significantly increased its converts, for Africans could not forget what seemed to be the 'attitude of the Roman church during the Abyssinian matter'.[125] The *African Church Chronicle*, a quarterly bilingual magazine devoted to the affairs of the African church, declared in its editorials that the attitude of the Pope had gone far to confirm the viewpoint that the church was national and embodied in each state. Pius XI was an Italian and it was natural that he should be interested in, and not be indifferent to, matters affecting the destiny of his country. The *Chronicle* concluded that the silence of the Pope was a warning to the African 'to go back to the land, to the indigenous institutions of the land from which he has been hewn'. It also argued that the more Africans embraced foreign religions, the more they would be disposed to compromise in the face of the aggression of Christian European powers in Africa just as did some Catholics in West Africa with regard to the Ethiopian question.[126] The Italo-Ethiopian experience indeed played a part, even if only minimally, in stimulating separatism as an instrument of African liberation.

The Roman Catholic missions in West Africa were not unaware of the increasing hostility to the church during this period. Some missionaries were very much upset, and preoccupied by the repercussions of the nationalists' reaction on Catholic interests in Africa. For, as one Catholic organ admitted, 'the air was charged with Anti-Catholicism'.[127] In order to maintain their hold over their converts, and as a safeguard against the anti-Catholic campaign, Catholic priests at various centres in West Africa launched a sustained counter-attack to explain to their adherents the actual role of the Catholic Church in the Ethiopian conflict. At the gold-mining centre of Obuasi in Ashanti, for instance, a Catholic priest was said to have 'preached to his flock' about the sweeping condemnation of the Christian missions by the militant nationalists, and seriously advised a Catholic agent of the *African Morning Post* in the district to give up the agency.[128] Other strategies in the Gold Coast took the form of the inauguration of Catholic societies and youth movements. In Kumasi a Catholic Young Men's Society was begun in December 1935. Its main objective was to mobilise the Catholic youth in the Ashanti province to face stoutly the challenge on the Ethiopian question posed by the nationalists.

The polemics between the Catholics and the nationalists in West Africa reached such a disturbing stage that the Gold Coast Catholic Young Men's Society and the Catholic Women's League resolved at an extraordinary meeting at Cape Coast on 13 November 1935, that 'as long as the present policy continues' no Catholic should read any of the radical nationalist papers, especially the *African Morning Post* of Nnamdi Azikiwe. The meeting hoped that if the thousands of Catholics in the Gold Coast refrained from buying such papers it would tangibly show 'our strong resentment of their scandalous policy'. It was further decided that the illiterate members of the church, both men and women, should be enlightened about the true position of the Pope who had 'no voice in the quarrel between nations unless asked to arbitrate'.[129] It is significant that Bishop Porter, the head of the Roman Catholic Church in the Gold Coast, added his weight and influence to the campaign. He recommended to the Catholics during the period of the Italo-Ethiopian conflict the following words which were boldly printed in every issue of the main Catholic organ in the country:

> My dear children, I earnestly ask you to bear no malice against these misguided people. Like our Lord Himself, we must be ready at all times to love the sinner but hate the sin, and breathe with Him that Prayer of sublimest Charity – 'Father, forgive them for they know not what they do.'[130]

The Ethiopian question seemed to have posed an unprecedented challenge to the Roman Catholic missionaries in West Africa and indirectly to the other missionary societies. For decades, if not for centuries, the West African had been taught that the European race was superior because it was Christian; hence he was acutely conscious and critical of any un-Christian behaviour by a white man. When Christian Europe and the Pope appeared indifferent to the precepts of Christianity, the West African was not only disenchanted but infuriated at being duped by humbug and a holier-than-thou attitude. The crisis, therefore, tended to undermine the extensive evangelical activity of the Christian missionaries, their long monopoly in the field of education, and their critical role as torch-bearers of Western civilisation.

1 Margery Perham, *The Colonial Reckoning*, London 1962, p. 40.
2 J. B. Danquah's comments on the failure of the 1934 Gold Coast Colony and Ashanti Delegation to England of which he was the secretary. *Danquah Papers*.
3 George Steer, *Caesar in Abyssinia*, Boston, 1937, p. 53.
4 The terms of the treaty are available in League of Nations, *Official Journal*, 1935, pp. 1411–12 and 1601.
5 F.O.371/19125, Tecle Hawariate (Ethiopian delegate to the League of Nations), to the General-Secretary of the League, 12 August 1935.
6 *Sierra Leone Daily Mail*, 17 September 1935; also *African Morning Post*, 7 May and 10 July 1936.
7 George W. Baer, *The Coming of the Italian-Ethiopian War*, p. 224.
8 *African Morning Post*, 6 November 1935. The reaction of Nigerians to the arms embargo issue is contained in F.O.371/20154, B. H. Bourdillon, Governor of Nigeria, to J. H. Thomas, 27 February 1936.
9 Anthony Eden's minute of 29 November 1935. Cited in Lord Avon, *Facing the Dictators*, London, 1962, p. 290.
10 *African Morning Post*, 6 November 1935.
11 F.O.371/20155. Note of a meeting at the Foreign Office, 10 December 1935; also, F.O.371/19170, Sir George Clerk, the British Ambassador in Paris, to Hoare, 15 December 1935.
12 The text of the plan is provided in League of Nations, *Official Journal*, 89 Session of the Council, XVII (1936), Annex 1573, *Document* C.482, M.258, VII, pp. 39–41.
13 F.O.371/19170, Sir Sidney Barton, the British Ambassador in Addis Ababa, to Hoare, 16 December 1935.
14 For details, see Viscount Templewood, *Nine Troubled Years*, London, 1954, pp. 107–96.
15 Parliamentary *Debates*, House of Lords, Vol. 99, No. 9, Official Report, 19 December 1935.
16 *African Morning Post*, 11 January 1936.
17 *Gold Coast Spectator*, 18 January 1936.
18 *Comet*, 21 December 1935.
19 *Hotobah During Papers*, private possession, Freetown.
20 For example, F.O.371/20154, Governor Bourdillon to Thomas, 27 February 1936.
21 S. R. Wood, 'Lessons of the Peace Terms', *Gold Coast Spectator*, 18 January 1936.
22 *African Morning Post*, 24 March 1936; also, *Vox Populi*, 20 May 1936.
23 F.O.371/19114, Walters to Eden, 29 June 1935. For Frank Walters' study of the Italo-Ethiopian crisis, see F. P. Walters, *A History of the League of Nations*, London, 1964, pp. 623–91.
24 *Gold Coast Spectator*, 7 September 1935.
25 Hotobah During, 'England Awake', *Sierra Leone Daily Mail*, 15 August 1935. Hotobah During's claim was in no way exceptional; the same spirit, for example, can be found in the writings of such early nationalists as J. E. Casely Hayford who once wrote: 'Surely we can look to England for a certain amount of fair play. The history of your relations with the weaker races is not altogether such as to fill us with despair, or to make us think that you will go the way of all flesh. We believe that when the crooked has been made straight to your moral line of vision, you will stand corrected.' J. E. Casely Hayford, *Gold Coast Native Institutions*, p. 235.
26 O. Awolowo, *Path to Nigerian Freedom*, Lonon, 1947, p. 28.
27 *Sierra Leone Weekly News*, 26 June 1937.
28 *Vox Populi*, 11 September 1935.
29 *Ibid*.
30 *Ibid*.
31 Peter Calvocoressi, 'The Politics of Sanctions: The League and the United Nations', in Ronald Segal, ed., *Sanctions Against South Africa*, London, 1964, p. 49.
32 F.O.371/20155, 29 July 1935.
33 F.O.371/19184, minute by V. E. Sergent, 6 February 1935.
34 *Ibid*.
35 Martin Gilbert and Richard Gott, *The Appeasers*, London, 1963, pp. 34–5. For details about the policy of appeasement, see also, Martin Gilbert, *The Roots of Appeasement*, W. H. Chamberlain, *Appeasement – Road to War*, Anon.; 'Appeasement Reconsidered: Some Neglected Factors', *The Round Table*, 212, September 1963, pp. 358–71.
36 F.O.371/19127, Sir George Clerk to Hoare, 22 August 1935.

37 Cited in Keith Feiling, *The Life of Neville Chamberlain*, London, 1947, p. 296.
38 Cited in Viscount Cecil (Lord Robert Cecil), *A Great Experiment*, London, 1941. p. 278.
39 J. W. de Graft Johnson, *Towards Nationhood in West Africa*, London, 1971, p. 98.
40 *Sierra Leone Weekly News*, 12 March 1921.
41 J. W. de Graft Johnson, p. 98.
42 *Comet*, 30 May 1936.
43 *Sierra Leone Weekly News*, 9 May 1936.
44 *Gold Coast Times*, 9 May 1936.
45 *Gold Coast Independent*, 2 May 1936.
46 *Sierra Leone Weekly News*, 11 July 1936.
47 For example, F.O.371/20154, George London, Deputy Governor of the Gold Coast to J. H. Thomas, Secretary of State for the Colonies, 17 January 1936.
48 *African Morning Post*, 7 April 1936.
49 *Ibid.*, also, *Sierra Leone Weekly News*, 16 November 1935.
50 *Comet*, 23 May 1936.
51 *Ibid.*
52 *Gold Coast Spectator*, 9 May 1936.
53 On 9 May 1936, the King of Italy signed a decree-law of which Article 1 stated that the title of Emperor of Ethiopia had been assumed by the King of Italy for himself and his successors. League of Nations, *Official Journal*, Special Supplement, 151, p. 82.
54 *Gold Coast Independent*, 11 July 1936.
55 *Comet*, 11 February 1939.
56 *Gold Coast Independent*, 28 October 1939.
57 *West Africa*, 20 September 1941.
58 Cited in A. A. Nwafor Orizu, *Without Bitterness*, New York, 1944, pp. 42–3.
59 *Ibid.*
60 Sir Arnold Hodson, 'An Account of the part played by Gold Coast Brigade in the East African Campaign, August 1940, to May 1941', *Journal of the Royal African Society*, xl, October 1941, pp. 300–11, and xli, January 1942, pp. 14–28.
61 *Ibid.*, xl, October 1941, pp. 300–1.
62 *Ibid.*, p. 311.
63 *West Africa*, 17 May 1941.
64 For the West African comments on the Anglo-Ethiopian Treaty of 1941, see *Comet*, 24 January and 7 February 1942. Details about the re-establishment of the Ethiopian independence are provided in F.O.371/27516.
65 See Ayandele, *Holy Johnson: Pioneer of African Nationalism, 1836–1917*, p. 57.
66 *Sierra Leone Weekly News*, 4 September 1920.
67 *Nigerian Pioneer* (Lagos), 8 August 1920.
68 Nnamdi Azikiwe, *Renascent Africa*, p. 190.
69 Ako Adjei, 'Imperialism and Spiritual Freedom: An African View', in Ram Desai ed., *Christianity in Africa as Seen by Africans*, Denver, 1962, p. 68.
70 Mary J. Marshall, 'Christianity and Nationalism in Ghana', unpublished M.A. thesis, University of Ghana, Legon, 1965, pp. 11–12.
71 Azikiwe, *Renascent Africa*, p. 191.
72 Mary Marshall, p. 1; see also, J. E. Casely Hayford, *Ethiopia Unbound*, p. 158, W. E. B. Du Bois, 'Inter-Racial Implications of the Ethiopian Crisis: A Negro View', *Foreign Affairs*, xiv, October 1935, p. 85.
73 *Vox Populi*, 4 September 1935.
74 O. Faduma, 'Christianity and Islam in Africa', *African Mail*, 22 May 1914.
75 J. W. de Graft Johnson, p. 8.
76 Isaac Delano, *One Church for Nigeria*, London, 1945, p. 15. See also, Ayandele, *Missionary Impact*, p. xvii.
77 Cited in A. A. N. Orizu, p. 161. See also Marvin D. Markowitz, 'The Missions and Political Development in the Congo', *Africa*, x, 3, July 1970, pp. 234–6.
78 On the general course of relations between Church and State in Fascist Italy, see especially Anthony Rhodes, *The Vatican in the Age of the Dictators, 1922–1945*, London, 1973; Daniel A. Binchy, *Church and State in Fascist Italy*, London, 1941; Arturo Garlo Jemolo, *Church and State in Italy, 1850–1950*, Oxford, 1960; and Luigi Salvatorelli and Giovanni Mira, eds, *Storia d'Italia nel periodo fascista*, Rome, 1959. The Lateran Accords were incorporated into the constitution of the Italian republic that came into effect on 1

January 1948. For details of the Lateran Accords, see John W. Wheeler-Bennett, ed, *Documents on International Affairs, 1929*.

79 See for instance, the *Gold Coast Catholic Voice* (Cape Coast, Ghana), December 1935.

80 Daniel Binchi, p. 640.

81 The British Foreign Office reports on the official and private opinions of the Pope and the Vatican circles are in F.O.371/19227, 26 November 1935.

82 F.O.371/19135, Hugh Montgomery disclosed that this confidential despatch was based on information he obtained from his colleague, the French Chargé d'Affaires, François Charles-Roux, whose acquaintance held an audience with the Pope. It does not appear that it was Charles-Roux himself who personally had the interview with the Pope, as was stated in Baer, p. 284.

83 Pius XI, *Discorsi di Pio XI*, pp. 379–80; also, *The Times* (London), 29 August 1935.

84 See, for instance, a letter from the Archbishop of Westminster to the editor of the London *Times*. *The Times*, 2 September 1935.

85 François Charles-Roux, *Huit ans au Vatican, 1932–1940*, Paris, 1947, p. 137.

86 Pope Pius XI, p. 389. See also *The Times*, 9 September 1935.

87 The silence of the Pope puzzled not only the West African nationalists but also the British diplomats as discussed in F.O.371/19227, Montgomery to Hoare, 26 November 1935.

88 *Vox Populi*, 3 July 1937.

89 *Gold Coast Times*, February 1936.

90 Okoto-Brigya, 'The Imperialists at bay through their own acts', *Gold Coast Spectator*, 22 February 1936.

91 *Provincial Pioneer* (Koforidua, Gold Coast), 14 December 1935.

92 Wallace Johnson, 'League of Nations and the Italo-Ethiopian War clearly Tabled', *Gold Coast Spectator*, 16 May 1936.

93 *Ibid.*, 29 February 1936.

94 *Gold Coast Leader*, 1 November 1902.

95 Ram Desai, p. 28.

96 F. L. Bartels, *The Roots of Ghana Methodism*, Cambridge, 1965, p. 158.

97 Marshall, p. 2.

98 Tanner, *English Constitutional Conflicts*, p. 137, cited in F. B. Welbourne, *East African Rebels*, London, 1961, p. 26. For a discussion on the church and the growth of national consciousness in Togo, see Hans W. Debrunner, *A Church Between Colonial Powers: A Study of the Church in Togo*, London, 1965, pp. 122–42.

99 Ayandele, *The Missionary Impact*, p. 175; also, J. F. Ade Ajayi, 'Nineteenth-century Origins of Nigerian Nationalism', *Journal of the Historical Society of Nigeria*, ii, 2, December 1961, p. 197. In Ghana the Rev. Dovlo was reported as saying in Parliament that the mission churches '. . . . taught us that we are all children of God – a concept which is the very basis of our national revolution which spurred us to gain our independence'. Ghana Parliamentary *Debates*, 22 January 1965, Official Report.

100 A similar statement is reported to have been made in 1944 by Dr Henry Townsend, Moderator of the Council of Free Churches. See Anthony Rhodes, p. 11.

101 *Gold Coast Spectator*, 16 May 1936.

102 *Ibid.*

103 Cited in *Nigerian Catholic Herald* (organ of the Catholic Church in Nigeria), October 1935.

104 Conf. C.S.O., 361/38, Ghana National Archives, Accra, Miss Hebe Spaull to Sir Arnold Hodson, Governor of the Gold Coast, 1 September 1938.

105 *Gold Coast Spectator*, 16 May 1936.

106 F.O.371/19227, Sir George Clerk, British Ambassador in Paris, to Foreign Secretary Sir Samuel Hoare, 30 November 1935.

107 Nwafor Orizu, p. x. See also, *Vox Populi*, 31 July 1935; *Sierra Leone Guardian*, 27 September 1935.

108 A correspondent who styled himself 'Freedom', 'Must History Repeat Itself?', *African Morning Post*, 17 October 1935.

109 *Gold Coast Catholic Voice*, September 1935.

110 *Nigerian Catholic Herald*, October 1935.

111 F.O.371/19135, Hugh Montgomery to Hoare, 16 September 1935.

112 Cited in Charles F. Dalzell, 'Pius XII, Italy and the Outbreak of War', *Journal of Contemporary History*, ii, 4, 1967, p. 137.

113 F.O. Vatican relations with Italy, Annual Report for 1924, prepared by Sir Odo Russell, the British Minister to the Vatican, 25 February 1925. Cited in Rhodes, p. 26. Also see S. William Halperin, *Mussolini and Italian Fascism*, Chicago, 1964, p. 66.

114 F.O.371/19227, Montgomery to Hoare, 26 November 1935.

115 This view appears to be held by such writers as Anthony Rhodes. See Rhodes, p. 70. Rhodes also states that the silence of the Vatican over Mussolini's adventure in Ethiopia was partly due to its disapproval of the League of Nations' mediation in international disputes which the Holy See regarded as 'supererogation', since for centuries this had been the function of the Pope. Rhodes, p. 71. This view does not appear to be convincing since the Vatican totally committed itself to the Fascist regime on Mussolini's assumption of power in 1922. The *Osservatore Romano* was as early as 4 November 1925 writing favourably of 'the new currents, new forces, the new attitude of the government whose sense of historical reality and political influence stand out prominently and undeniably above all the old petty party notions'. Even if the League had not existed and mediated, the position of the Vatican on the Ethiopian affair would not have been in anyway different.

116 F.O.371/19227, Montgomery to Hoare, 26 November 1935.

117 F.O.371/19155, Montgomery to Hoare, 21 November 1935.

118 *Ibid.*

119 F.O.371/19166, Montgomery to Hoare, 29 November 1935.

120 Ako Adjei in Ram Desai, p. 73.

121 T. B. Allotey in *New Times and Ethiopian News*, 4 November 1936. The author has so far not discovered any evidence in support of this rather exaggerated claim of Allotey.

122 *African Morning Post*, 10 October 1935. The impact of the Ethiopian question on the Sierra Leone Christians can be found in *Sierra Leone Weekly News*, 7 September 1935; *Sierra Leone Daily Mail*, 28 and 30 September and 25 October 1935.

123 Orizu, pp. 55–6.

124 *Ibid.*, pp. ix–x, xii; Born in Eastern Nigeria in 1920, Orizu came under the influence of Nnamdi Azikiwe. He was one of the notable Eastern Nigerian nationalists during the early post-war period.

125 Isaac Delano, p. 16.

126 *African Church Chronicle* (Lagos), October–December 1935.

127 *Gold Coast Catholic Voice*, February 1936.

128 *Catholic Papers*, Cape Coast, Ghana.

129 *Gold Coast Catholic Voice*, November 1935.

130 *Ibid.*, February 1936.

CHAPTER FOUR

Protests of nationalist groups

In the preceding chapters, we have attempted to discuss the opposition to the Italo-Ethiopian imbroglio initiated mainly by the press and certain individuals. But as the crisis entered its crucial stages, expression of indignation and resentment came from the existing nationalist movements as well as the *ad hoc* committees and associations which were established in response to the conflict. The general belief among the nationalist groups was that, following the traditional method of airing nationalist grievances, organised protest demonstrations and the passing of resolutions on the crisis would be most effective. This would at least reinforce the similar action that was being taken by coloured groups in Britain, France, the United States, and the West Indies. From September 1935, therefore, one encounters in West Africa organisations of mass meetings and rallies, and a spate of correspondence between the nationalist movements, the local colonial administration and the Colonial Office in London. These were occasionally punctuated by interviews and confrontations. Besides this expression of black solidarity against the Fascist aggression, various attempts were made to recruit volunteers to bolster the fight of the Ethiopians against the 'imperialist exploiters'. When this latter action proved impracticable, the nationalist groups and the Ethiopia committees which had been set up at the time resorted to the widespread organisation of special prayers and a regular collection of relief funds for Ethiopia. The following two chapters will discuss the nature and activities of the West African nationalist movements and societies and their reaction to the Ethiopian question.

Nationalist Movements and Youth Leagues

The pan-African political dreams of the National Congress of British West Africa had begun to fade by the close of the 1920s. In fact, following the death of its chief architect and moving spirit, J. E. Casely Hayford the Congress was a spent force by about 1930. The decline of the Congress and the coming of the economic depression forced the attention of most nationalist leaders in West Africa closely upon their own respective countries. The concept of nationalism began to have a territorial rather than interterritorial basis. Thus, although in theory West African nationalists still thought in terms of pan-Africanism during this period, in practice the 1930s may be justifiably described as the period of the regionalisation of nationalism, during which nationalist politicians devoted themselves to the development of their own countries, rather than to West African progress as a whole.

One remarkable feature in the development of nationalism during this period was the reaction against the politicians of the Congress era which developed through the organisation of youth movements and leagues in Nigeria, the Gold Coast and Sierra Leone. Briefly stated, these movements 'opposed the conservatism' of the established elite, rejected their 'jaded' ideas, and sought to 'interest many more people than before in politics'. As Webster and Adu Boahen have argued, the youth movements 'tried to get away from the idea that political protest should be the monopoly of a top elite and confined to the cities of Lagos, Cape Coast and Freetown'.[1] They became in effect a convenient mechanism for a discussion of political, economic, and social problems of the period, and 'represented a more highly evolved form of political association than their prececessor: from an organisational standpoint, since they appealed to a wider, though still essentially an urban and educated, public, and were based upon local branches in the main towns . . . and from the standpoint of politics and programmes – since they put forward explicit demands for self-government'.[2] Although these political associations still lacked effective mass support, they at least began to recognise the need for it. This in itself marks a significant step forward. For, in the 1920s the elite's penetration of the mass elements in West African society was extremely limited. Despite Casely Hayford's assertion that it would never be possible to 'dissociate the educated African from his uneducated brother',[3] the Congress leaders showed little awareness of the problems and needs of the rural areas.

Like the Congress movement, however, the youth movements concerned themselves with issues of more than local significance. It is no wonder, then, that they seriously took up the Ethiopian cause in West Africa as part of their opposition to imperialism and colonialism, and their challenge to the established elite. The close identification of the youth movements and leagues with the fate of the Ethiopians made it increasingly difficult for some of the nationalists of the old leadership to show more than nominal interest in the Ethiopian affair. Such older politicians as F. V. Nanka Bruce in the Gold Coast, H. C. Bankole-Bright of Sierra Leone and Herbert Macaulay of Nigeria, occasionally reacted violently to the youth organisations and all that they stood for. Bankole-Bright, for example, was of the opinion that the 'good work' done by the Congress was 'being blurred due to the false vision and policy' pursued by certain Congress men in Sierra Leone who had joined Wallace Johnson's West African Youth League. In a mood of despondency, he declared that Sierra Leone 'of yesterday with its policy for order and good government is now converted by a new organisation', that is, the West African Youth League, to a 'Sierra Leone of Disorder and Lawlessness'.[4] The youth movements, which, on the whole, built up their stature at the time of the Ethiopian crisis, were able to capture the political initiative from the 'tired elite leadership' and win the Legislative and Municipal Council seats during the closing years of the 1930s. To appreciate these developments in relation to the Italo-Ethiopian question, it is important that we review briefly the political movements in the four British West African colonies during this period.

Professor James Coleman has referred to the 1930s as the period during which there 'was comparatively little nationalist activity' in Nigeria.[5] This assertion is not too far off the mark, at least before 1935. For the thirties on the whole were largely a period of 'nationalist gestation' during which new influences were being felt and new movements were being formed in Nigeria. Of the political associations which emerged during the period under review, the Nigerian Youth Movement was the most dynamic and the most broad-based nationalist organisation which lighted the flame of the new era of nationalism in Nigeria.[6] The NYM was a more radical form of political protest against the inadequacies of the colonial government. It was also directed against the 'accommodationist' attitude of Herbert Macaulay's Nigerian National Democratic Party.[7] A great deal of its 'militancy' derived from the many frustrated young men but its mass support still came from the native community many of whom had broken with the Democratic Party for a variety of reasons, not least being disillusionment with Herbert Macaulay.

Originally known as the Lagos Youth Movement, the NYM was formed in 1933 to oppose the local government's educational policy with regard to alleged deficiencies of the Yaba Higher College. Though the leaders were drawn from the same middle-class intellectuals of Lagos, they were younger men with a wider national outlook and social perspective than the older generation of politicians, who were basically satisfied with the tempo of economic and social progress of the country and Anglo-Nigerian political relations. The movement was founded by a few young men who, in response to 'an inner urge to serve their countrymen', came under the leadership of James Churchill Vaughan. As a correspondent put it:

These eager young men, representing several communities or tribes in Nigeria, began to dream dreams and to see visions – dreams of the great services rendered by their grandsires in the cause of their fatherland, and visions of a glorious future for a new and united Nigeria taking its rightful place in the British Empire and fulfilling its destiny among the nations of the world.[8]

The NYM claimed that its role was that of 'a sentinel guarding the interests of the people, voicing the feelings of the inarticulate public' and offering when necessary timely and constructive criticisms of government's policy. The response was reported to be spontaneous. Thousands of young folk throughout the country were said to have joined the NYM, which soon swept aside the older organisations. It was the first political movement in Nigeria to possess a Nigerian image with concern for a wider range of national interests, and thus the first genuine 'nationalist' organisation in Nigeria. The leadership was less exclusive than the NNDP and included non-Yorubas such as Ernest Ikoli and Azikiwe. Determined attempts were also made to broaden the base of the party by expanding into the hinterland of Lagos and winning over the cocoa farmers of the Yoruba interior.[9] The NYM addressed the government from time to time on questions 'which were worrying African opinion'.

The movement appeared first to come to the notice of the local government early in 1935. Its first president was Dr Vaughan, a local medical practitioner who was succeeded, on his death in December 1937, by Dr Kofo Abayomi, another local medical practitioner, According to Bourdillon, the Governor of Nigeria, Dr Abayomi's conduct of the affairs of the movement was exemplary; he appeared fully capable of maintaining discipline and exercising a restraining influence over the hot-headed members.[10] Bourdillon applauded the efforts of the NYM to bring the whole of the youth of Nigeria together and to make them think nationally rather than parochially. This view was shared by the permanent staff at the Colonial Office who hoped that while the movement was led by men who were sincere and more or less sound, it would provide an outlet for ideas and emotions which might otherwise find a much less satisfactory vent, 'as witness the unhappy Youth League of Sierra Leone'.[11] It was also felt that with proper handling by the government officials in Nigeria with whom the movement came in contact, it should serve not only as a useful safety valve, but in time also as a body capable of offering 'constructive as well as destructive criticism in local affairs'. The officials hoped that the NYM would manage to keep itself free from 'the extreme bias of the Wallace Johnson West African Youth League in Sierra Leone', which was endeavouring to affiliate to itself other youth movements on the West Coast.[12] In view of their communist tactics and the fact that they were markedly influenced by Marxism in their programme and terminology, Wallace Johnson's youth movements in the Gold Coast and Sierra Leone, which will be discussed later, constantly struck fear into the Colonial Office.

The NYM organised most of the protest demonstrations and Ethiopia relief fund campaigns in Nigeria. It whipped up considerable popular anger over the Italian attack on Ethiopia to stimulate political awareness and activity. According to one of the founders of the movement, Oba Samuel Akisanya, the Odemo of Ishara, the General-Secretary and later Vice-President of the NYM from 1933–40, the change of name from Lagos Youth Movement to Nigerian Youth Movement with its activities extending outside Lagos, was partly influenced by the movement's response to the Ethiopian crisis.[13] Thenceforth, the NYM assumed the character of a Nigerian-wide organisation with branches scattered all over the country.[14] Apart from establishing its own Ethiopia Relief Fund Committee in Lagos, the NYM was closely in touch with other Ethiopia relief fund committees and organisations interested in the Ethiopian affair, such as the Comet Abyssinia Relief Fund, the Enugu Ethiopia Relief Fund Committee, the Goodwill Society of Lagos, the Prominent Lagos Women Society as well as the Save Abyssinia Society.

Unlike Nigeria where, as Crocker observes, there were no economic or political problems and 'no problem of racial antagonism during much of the early thirties',[15] the political and economic situations in the Gold Coast were quite tense. Such a cautious historian as G. E. Metcalfe has described the 1930s as a period of 'hard feelings' among the Gold Coast nationalists.[16] On the basis of evidence drawn from a study of political activity in the Gold Coast during this period, Metcalfe's description has a certain validity. As we have noted, by 1930 the world slump had halved the price of cocoa and 'with the old prosperity went much of the harmony between Government and Governed that marked the Guggisberg era'. The Income Tax Bill of 1931, followed in 1934 by the 'obnoxious' Criminal Code (Amendment) Bill and Waterworks Bill, touched off a fresh explosion of Gold Coast opinion and greatly embittered the relations between the colonial administration and the nationalists. Nationalist politics at this time had assumed a different dimension. The reaction of the people to the Guggisberg Constitution of 1925 had created a split in the nationalist movement. The violent and persistent opposition of the ARPS to the new Constitution and the Provincial Councils which had been institutionalised by the Native Administration Ordinance of 1927 had driven the influential chiefs into an alliance with the government. The official hostility both in London and in Accra to the intransigence of the ARPS also split the leadership of the society. The majority of the educated elite, led by Casely Hayford (who had become reconciled with the chiefs) and F. V. Nanka Bruce, abandoned the policy of total opposition to the new Constitution and the Native Administration Ordinance. It was the intransigent anti-government and anti-imperialist wing of the ARPS – together with Wallace Johnson's hard-core anti-colonialist West African Youth League which, more than any other political organisation in the Gold Coast, championed the cause of Ethiopia in the country.

During the early years of the present century, the ARPS had been the foremost political organisation in the Gold Coast, both as a forum for developing policy and as an active group for promoting that policy. It was the pivot of all nationalist politics, and the recognised mouthpiece of the people and the medium of communication between the government and the people.[17] Constitutionally, the society had always claimed to be an organisation of the natural rulers of the country with the educated elite acting in an advisory capacity on the Executive Committee. Although this advisory capacity had always been a thinly transparent cover for manipulation of the chiefs by the educated elite, it served admirably in soliciting the patronage and co-operation of the chiefs. By the early 1920s, however, the government had begun to regard the society as a 'private Society' and to show signs of non-recognition of the ARPS. As early as 1912 Governor J. J. Thorburn had argued that the society existed primarily to oppose government measures, 'frequently stirring up prejudice by an absolutely distorted interpretation of the Government's intentions'.[18] The hostility of officials to the ARPS grew in proportion to the intransigence of the society's opposition to the Native Jurisdiction Bills of 1919–22, the Municipal Corporations Ordinance of 1924, the Constitution of 1925 and the Native Administration Ordinance of 1927. The formal establishment of the Provincial Councils in 1925 and the recognition of their consultative role in 1927 sounded the death knell of the society as spokesman of African opinion. It was argued that the Provincial Councils were now the official spokesmen of African opinion, while the ARPS was merely a private body, with no claim to represent African opinion in general. This distinction which was made very clear in 1928 by W. J. A. Jones, then the Commissioner of the Central Province,[19] was formally and finally communicated to the ARPS in March 1932, when C. E. Skene wrote to inform the society that the government did not recognise it 'as the medium of communication between Government and the Chiefs and People, the Provincial Councils having been established for that purpose'.[20]

After this crushing blow dealt by the institutionalisation of the Provincial Councils, the ARPS devoted most of its efforts either to destroying the Provincial Councils or to seeking government recognition of its long standing (since 1898) as the accepted intermediary between the chiefs and government. Three times, in 1926, in 1932, and in 1934–36, the society approached the government and the Colonial Office to request recognition. Unable to regain the government's favour, the ARPS was forced to seek an independent position of power by capitalising on popular discontent. It was this position which, apart from its pan-African consciousness[21] and its avowed opposition to colonialism and imperialism, reinforced the society's vigorous response to the brutal Italian attack on Ethiopia under the able leadership of Kobina Sekyi and his close associates, G. E. Moore and S. R. Wood. For the Ethiopian crisis offered them the opportunity to attack the colonial administration.

Kobina Sekyi (1892–1956) did not become president of the ARPS until 1946, but from 1928 onwards he was the dominant force in the society, the main influence in the formulation and execution of its policies.[22] A barrister by profession, he also held a B.A. and an M.A. in philosophy which he had taken at London University by 1918, as well as reading sociology and law at King's College, London. His extraordinary energy, intelligence, personal magnetism and charm made a strong impression on everyone who met him.[23]

From our point of view, however, the most important strand of Sekyi's character was his pronounced anti-colonialism, a factor which throughout influenced his view of politics. It was his utter dislike for colonial domination which made him so intensely hate Nana Sir Ofori Atta and the Provincial Council system which was essentially the latter's creation. In his opinion, the chiefs who co-operated with the government by supporting the Provincial Councils were destroying the hegemony of the educated elite against alien domination. Sekyi considered this to be a betrayal of the chiefs of their old allies, the educated elite, who had no place, or only a minor place as 'attendants', in the Provincial Council system, and who were left out of the machinery of indirect rule. A 'revolutionary conservative' and thorough-going elitist, Sekyi believed that political leadership in the Gold Coast must be based on the old 'alliance between the Natural Rulers and the educated conservative class of lawyers and doctors . . .' which had found its supreme expression in the Fante Confederacy and the early ARPS.[24] Secondly, in accepting the support of the colonial government the chiefs, as Sekyi argued, were becoming increasingly dependent upon the British, losing their autonomy and freedom of action and becoming the tools of the colonial administration, mere subordinates in the official hierarchy. His attack on the Provincial Councils reflected a transparently contrived interpretation of the democratic nature of traditional polity, but it was true to his distaste for alien domination. Having taken a stand against his African rivals – Ofori Atta and Provincial Councils – Sekyi adopted a rigid antagonism towards all those who accommodated chiefly paramountcy. He refused to work with either the Provincial Council chiefs or their collaborators, even when it meant weakening his African stance against colonial domination. And he consistently garbed his personal inflexibility with the highest of rationalisations. To work for fifteen years for a diamond-rich stool – the Asamankese Case – against Nana Sir Ofori Atta I, who was closely associated with the government, was anti-colonialism. To seek to get a foothold in the cocoa export trade was to break European domination of trade, as was the attempt to peddle gold mining concessions.[25] The racism and autocracy of the colonial government and expatriate firms were almost more than he could bear. And he seldom lost an opportunity to point out the weaknesses and failings of the colonial government. He described the colonial administrators in West Africa as mere 'pupil Governors', 'student magistrates' and 'officers-in-training' who were 'blundering through Affairs of state, uncouth like boys at school'. The depth of Sekyi's feeling about the colonial administrators sent to West Africa is most cogently expressed in one of his writings:

> Few will dispute that the sort of Europeans who seek employment in West Africa, whether as civil servants or in other capacities, are generally those who have no prospects of success in life in their own country, and who come out to West Africa, as a place where they will get extraordinary opportunities to improve their positions financially in a short time. . . .[26]

On the platforms of literary clubs and through the press Kobina Sekyi constantly advocated maintenance of tradition and independence from alien political and cultural domination. Small wonder, then, that Sekyi aligned his wing of the ARPS with Wallace Johnson's West African Youth League to organise a country-wide protest against the Italian rape of Ethiopia, a country which, as we have noted, he had held to be the only one 'of promise to West Africa'. However, the agitation over the Ethiopian question in the Gold Coast cannot be fully appreciated in isolation from the main trend of nationalist politics of the period as a whole. It is therefore worth casting it in a brief historical setting. This is also important because discussions relating to colonial politics in the Gold Coast in the mid-thirties have either been too general or have tended to concentrate exclusively on the period after 1945.[27]

We have mentioned that the Guggisberg Constitution cost the nationalist movement in the Gold Coast its unity. The Provincial Council system had drawn a wedge between the chiefs and the intelligentsia; the ARPS which was now confined to Cape Coast, the cradle of Gold Coast nationalism, was rapidly losing political influence; the established politicians, such as F. V. Nanka Bruce and K. A. Korsah, were rather concerned to preserve the position they had gained in the Legislative Council. This state of affairs was unfavourable for the development of nationalism in the Gold Coast, and the Gold Coast Youth Conference, inspired by J. B. Danquah, sought to remedy the situation.

Born on 21 December 1895, Joseph Boakye Danquah, described as the 'doyen of Gold Coast politicians',[28] was a central figure in the nationalist movements in the Gold Coast and a leading spokesman of the Gold Coast intelligentsia for more than three decades.[29] He was closely involved in the main trends of colonial politics in the Gold Coast during the period covered by this study: the demand for constitutional reform and the agitation for self-government, the Gold Coast youth movements which provided, as David Apter has put it, 'a basis for more serious political organisation along nationalist lines after World War II',[30] and the economic crisis which culminated in the cocoa hold-up of 1937–38.[31] The core of his political ideas was to bring the natural rulers and the non-traditional elites together. Before he left the Gold Coast for further studies in England in November 1921, Danquah had his first involvement with the nationalist movements which were beginning to gain currency in West Africa when he represented the Akim Abuakwa State (his native traditional area) at the conferences of the Aborigines' Society at Cape Coast. On his return from England in 1927, he found himself in the midst of a struggle between the intelligentsia, led by Casely Hayford, and the chiefs, led by his illustrious half-brother Nana Sir Ofori Atta I. Danquah's prime political motivation was to resolve this conflict, as it struck him that the country's future 'would be greatly endangered if the abysmal cleavage between chiefs and intelligentsia was suffered to continue and to embitter political relations or give rise to communal strife'.[32] For Danquah, who enjoyed affiliation both with the intelligentsia and with the traditional elite, nothing could appear more natural than trying to effect a reconciliation between these groups which had been at odds since the era of the National Congress. To further his aim of reconciling the chiefs and the intelligentsia, he called for a 'national assembly of youth' to consider the problems facing the young men and the need 'to think and act together as one people for the good of the country'.[33] It was out of this that the Gold Coast Youth Conference (GCYC) was born.[34]

Briefly stated, the GCYC was a convocation of the educated elite of the Colony and Ashanti for the purpose of developing a common platform of demands upon the colonial government. It attempted to do for the Gold Coast what the NCBWA had done for West Africa – to devise a generally acceptable programme of reforms. And, like the Congress, it was highly elitist in composition as well as attitude. By its nature and activities the Youth Conference was a revised expression of Ghanaian nationalism in the 1930s. In its aim, its implications were inevitably political, and it published schemes for constitutional reform. But unlike the ARPS and the West African Youth League, the Youth Conference was extremely moderate and constitutionalist in outlook, goals, and means. The restraining influence of generally apolitical or collaborationist chiefs and educated persons kept the inclinations of the more demanding and anti-imperialist factions from coming to the surface.

Although the first meeting of the Youth Conference held at Achimota in April 1930 created a new climate of opinion, the Conference did not reconvene until it was revived in 1938. On the whole, the conference had only a minimal impact and was little different in nature from the Achimota discussion sessions that had met on educational matters since 1926. The failure to publish the proceedings of the conference indicates its limited importance. Subsequent efforts to hold another conference during Easter of 1933 proved abortive.[35] During this time J. B. Danquah, the moving force of the movement, was absorbed in his newspaper activities, and in 1934, 1935, and early 1936 the attention of the Accra elite was entirely absorbed in the 1934 Delegation and the 1935 Legislative Council elections.

As noted elsewhere, Danquah, like Casely Hayford, had on many occasions expressed his belief in the concept of Ethiopianism and shown considerable interest in the pan-African cause. As a student in Britain he had played an instrumental role in the organisation of the West African Students' Union. On his return to the Gold Coast Danquah was elected president of the local branch of the society and occasionally referred to the pan-African mission of the WASU.[36] He was among the few nationalist politicians who collaborated with Wallace Johnson in his agitation in early 1934 about the Scottsboro Boys Case involving eight Afro-American youths from the Southern United States, who were falsely accused of having raped two white girls, and were consequently sentenced to death. Although he violently disagreed with the views held by the ARPS on the introduction of the Provincial Council system in the Gold Coast, and had referred to Sekyi and his dissident group as 'our *soi-disant* leaders in the Colony', Danquah found the pan-African platform of the Aborigines very attractive. He was full of praise for the society's racial and pan-African outlook and its contribution towards 'the racial and social emancipation of Africa'.[37] In 1938 he wrote to commend highly the foresight of Kobina Sekyi for the part he had played in making the rising generation race conscious, concluding, 'I love Africa and I am not afraid to call a spade a spade. This has caused me to lose a very lucrative job, but I do not mind.'[38] Again, in his 'Biographical Note' to Bankole Awoonor-Renner's *This Africa* (published in England in 1943), Danquah associated himself with the author in declaring that he was hoping for 'that Africa – the Africa liberated, the Africa of our dreams, the Africa that is sure to come, and is coming'.

However, unlike Casely Hayford, Danquah's pan-Africanism remained only a dream. He did not make any positive efforts to realise it in the 1930s. Thus, although Danquah was an Executive Committee member of C. L. R. James's International African Friends of Abyssinia Society formed in London as a result of the Italian threat to the independence of Ethiopia, there is no evidence that he actively participated in the protest demonstrations organised by the society against the rape of Ethiopia. Danquah focused his attention rather on the problems of the nationalist movement in the Gold Coast, and it was in this field that he became one of the dominant political personalities in Ghanaian politics. He was instrumental in stimulating a national consciousness in the 1930s, during which period he had a firm grip on the reins of the nationalist movement.[39]

In contrast to J. B. Danquah and the Youth Conference, the Aborigines' Society, both at home, and abroad in England, took a very keen interest in the Italo-Ethiopian conflict. To a great extent the Ethiopian question provided grist to the mill of the rival ARPS Deputation to the Colonial Office during the latter part of their campaigns in Britain to put the case of the Gold Coast people before the British public. G. E. Moore and S. R. Wood soon joined forces with the C. L. R. James International Friends of Abyssinia Society and, as we have seen, vigorously spoke on the society's platform against colonialism. During the period of the 1935 British General Election, the ARPS delegates went to Retford in the parliamentary constituency of the Secretary of State for the Colonies to ask Malcolm MacDonald to be good enough in his electioneering campaign to speak on 'Liberty and Justice' for the African colonial peoples and the inhabitants of Ethiopia.[40] They also urged him to make a firm declaration before his electorate on the question of the welfare and happiness of the colonial peoples in Africa and, especially, on the attitude of the British Government to the attack of Africans in Ethiopia. The delegates, accompanied by Ronald Kidd of the National Council of Civil Liberties and B. H. G. Bing, a man who later became more important to the Gold Coast as a legal adviser to Kwame Nkrumah, held a series of rallies in Retford and so persistently harassed MacDonald with Gold Coast and Ethiopian affairs that the Secretary of State was constrained to bring their action to the notice of the Gold Coast Government. In November 1935, he complained to Sir Arnold Hodson, Governor of the Gold Coast, that 'these gentlemen's incursions' into his constituency 'may have lost me a hundred votes. . . . I cannot remember a similar case in which Africans or others from the Colonies have taken a direct part like this in an election here.'[41] Although some other reasons might have accounted for MacDonald's loss of votes and defeat in the election, the visit of Wood and Moore to Bassetlaw which, according to the Secretary of State, 'was a clever move on their part', was perhaps a decisive factor. J. B. Danquah, who was still in England after the departure of the rest of the members of the Ofori Atta-led Gold Coast Colony and Ashanti Delegation to England in 1934 (of which Danquah was the Secretary), was very much impressed by the achievements of the ARPS Delegation. In a congratulatory note to the Delegation he declared:

I feel sure that your labours in carrying the case of the people to the supreme political tribunal of the Empire will, whatever the result, add to the honoured name of your Society and enshrine in the hearts of our people. . . . I can expect the people at home welcoming you with laurels of glory upon your return, for, truly, the effort you have made to assert and maintain the liberties of the people of Akan-land [Gold Coast] is unparalleled in our somewhat chequered and eventful history.[42]

Meanwhile, at home in the Gold Coast, it was in the wake of the general confusion resulting from Governor Shenton Thomas's 1934 Sedition and

Water-works Bills, and the excited condition of public feeling about the Italian invasion of Ethiopia, that Wallace Johnson, through his West African Youth League, and Nnamdi Azikiwe, through his journalism and public platform, attempted to give new direction to nationalist agitation in the country. For a comparatively short period of about four years (1933–37), radical nationalist movements in the country were centred around these 'two strangers', who shared the belief that the 'soil of Africa was now fertile for the struggle to redeem it from European imperialism'.[43]

Isaac Theophilus Akunna Wallace Johnson is no longer a neglected pan-Africanist or a 'forgotten' man, as he used to be. For, apart from the brief notices of him in West African historiography, there have quite recently been some detailed scholarly references to his pan-African activity and contribution to the rise of West African nationalism. However, these references have so far paid only marginal attention to one dominant strand in his pan-African activity during the 1930s: his sustained and persistent reaction to the Italian attack on Ethiopia. For example, while James Hooker's partial and incomplete sketch of him does not mention this aspect of Wallace Johnson's pan-African politics,[44] the recent contribution by Leo Spitzer and La Ray Denzer is rather sketchy and superficial in its reference to this subject.[45] Similarly, although Ayo Langley makes some illuminating references to Johnson's writings about the Italo-Ethiopian conflict, he does not focus any attention to his leadership of the African reaction to the crisis.[46] For Wallace Johnson did not merely comment upon every significant stage of the Italo-Ethiopian struggle; he also made sincere efforts to aid that beleaguered country. Furthermore, unlike any of his contemporaries in West Africa, Johnson did not confine his defence of the Ethiopian cause to one country; rather, he carried on the fight, from 1935 to 1938, in the Gold Coast, in England, and in Sierra Leone. The Ethiopian question greatly reinforced his opposition to colonialism and imperialism, and influenced much of his subsequent political activities. Because of Wallace Johnson's leadership and active involvement in the protest demonstrations and campaigns organised against Italy's assault on Ethiopia, we shall attempt to highlight those neglected aspects of this radical and tireless West African journalist, trade union organiser, politician and revolutionary pan-Africanist.

Born in 1895, I. T. A. Wallace Johnson, who preferred to describe himself as an 'International African' with ancestors from Abeokuta (Nigeria), West Indies and Nova Scotia, was a Creole from Wilberforce Village, near Freetown.[47] Completing his elementary education in the Centenary Tabernacle Day School, Freetown, in 1909, he entered the C.M.S. Grammar School and later the United Methodist Collegiate School where he finished his 'course in December 1911 with a Matriculation Certificate'. In 1912 he entered the Hunter's Commercial Class and 'graduated with a creditable certificate in the art of conducting both Government and Commerical Affairs'. Between 1926 and 1928, Wallace Johnson went through various courses of study in the United States and finally in England where he completed a 'course of Practical Journalism'. In January 1932 he entered the People's University in Moscow for further studies in 'Political and Natural Sciences as well as to have a clear insight of educational work in the Soviet Republics'. Johnson finished his studies there a year later with a Russian Certificate as a graduate of the 'XVI School' which, according to him, was equivalent to a Bachelor of Science degree in British Universities.[48]

The story of Wallace Johnson's experiences with a variety of jobs, as well as his movements and many travels abroad in Africa, Europe and the Soviet Union, has already been told in great detail.[49] All that will be done here is to give a brief account of his pan-African activities, particularly in relation to the Ethiopian question; in this case, material not available to either Spitzer and Denzer or Holmes will be used to clarify a few interesting points.

In 1931 Wallace Johnson joined the editorial staff of the *Nigerian Daily Times* and also acted as secretary to the newly formed Koffey African Universal Church Society in Lagos. It was under the auspices of this society that he undertook an extensive tour of Europe in 1932. While in England, Johnson was reported in February 1933 to 'have been speaking under the auspices' of the Negro Welfare Association,[50] and associating himself with its secretary, Arnold Ward, as well as other anti-imperialists like Reginald Bridgeman of the British Section of the League Against Imperialism, Ronald Kidd of the Council for Civil Liberties and N. B. Hunter of The British Movement Against War and Fascism. Returning to Freetown on 18 February 1935, Johnson was said to have observed that 'there was little response to his subversive propaganda'.[51] From his letters to the International Trade Union of Negro Workers at Hamburg, which were intercepted at the time, Johnson was again reported to have considered that in Sierra Leone the 'employed worker was not interested in the unemployed' while the unemployed struck him as 'very care free'.[52] After a short stay in Freetown, he left for Nigeria where, among other things, he assisted in establishing the Nigerian Workers' Union. The founder of the Nigerian Workers' Union, Frank Macauley, also had Communist affiliations, and therefore Wallace Johnson was probably engaged in Communist-connected work by this time.[53] In October 1933, a search was conducted at his premises in Lagos for copies of the *Negro Worker*, a prohibited journal and an organ of the International Confederation of Negro Workers dedicated to raising the consciousness of unity among black workers everywhere.

The search became a subject of a series of correspondence between the Nigerian Government, the Colonial Office, and Reginald Bridgeman.[54] There is no evidence that Wallace Johnson was deported from Nigeria as categorically maintained by Spitzer and La Ray Denzer and other writers.[55] Although during the search books and documents were found containing 'seditious sentiments or seditious intentions', he was not prosecuted. In March 1934, the Acting Chief Secretary to the Government of Nigeria wrote to inform Wallace Johnson in Accra that 'His Excellency is advised that no breach of the law has been committed' and that all the books and documents retained by the police had been 'carefully packed and sealed'. He added that on receipt of an expression of Wallace Johnson's wishes in the matter these would 'be sent to any address which you specify'. On the other hand, 'should no expression of your wishes in the matter be received' the books and documents would be retained in Lagos and 'handed to you personally when you *return* to the Colony'.[56] However, anticipating trouble, Wallace Johnson, who was already in touch with R. B. Wuta Ofei, editor of the *Gold Coast Spectator*, had left for the Gold Coast in November 1933, where he had his 'fingers in all the many pies available for him there'.[57] Here, indeed, was a promising area for revolutionary activity, a base from which he was to emerge as an agitator and leader of exceptional ability.

By the time that Wallace Johnson arrived in the Gold Coast, his early travels and acquaintance with the problems of the black peoples from various parts of the world had developed in him a radical pan-African perspective. Throughout this period he had talked on public platforms and published in the columns of the *Negro Worker*, under his favourite alias, Wal. Daniels, about the injustice and oppression which black peoples suffered in America, Europe and Africa, and how dangerous certain types of Africans were to the struggle against colonial domination and racial discrimination. Wallace Johnson tended to think and act along racial lines. Like DuBois, the 'father of Pan-Africanism', his basic pre-conception was that the struggle of the future was racial, between black and white, a preconception which was given tremendous impetus by Italy's blatant act of aggression against the 'coloured empire' of Ethiopia. Besides, Johnson was a man of unquestioned ability. He had the strength of a powerful alien perspective on West African conditions, while at the same time being firmly grounded in an intimate knowledge of those conditions. His experiences in London and Moscow aided him primarily through the connections he made there. Throughout his career, he relied heavily on his left-wing contacts in England and Europe to create an illusion of influence over colonial affairs. Bridgeman, Ward, and members of Parliament like Miss Eleanor Rathbone, J. P. Mallalieu, and Sorensen provided Wallace Johnson with the appearance of great influence over the colonial system. A powerful character with faults, Johnson illuminated but did not dominate the West African political scene during the 1930s primarily because the tendencies that he opposed were so powerful.

Before the outbreak of the Ethiopian crisis, Wallace Johnson was pre-occupied at the beginning of his stay in the Gold Coast first by the agitation over the Scottsboro Boys Case and subsequently, by the tremendous reaction which had been sparked off by Governor Shenton Thomas's Sedition and Waterworks Bills. The intense political conflict and controversy provoked by the Sedition Bill in particular brought Wallace Johnson into close contact with the opposition and 'non-collaborative' elements in Gold Coast society, especially the ARPS and its powerful leader and moving spirit, Kobina Sekyi. Contrary to the view of Spitzer and Denzer, who appear to have relied un-critically on Nanka Bruce's *Gold Coast Independent*, the Sedition Bill was not introduced in the Gold Coast in order to 'neutralise' Wallace Johnson's success or impact on a section of the Gold Coast nationalists.[58] The decision to intro-duce the Bill was taken long before the arrival of Wallace Johnson in the Colony.[59] It is true, however, that when the Bill was published, Wallace Johnson, according to Shenton Thomas, 'looked on it as a direct affront', and therefore instigated and directed the attack against it.[60]

The governor was probably right. For Johnson not only helped in the drafting of the ARPS petition to the Colonial Office, but he also addressed some cor-respondence to Bridgeman and Arnold Ward requesting them that 'they should be on the look-out' and render all possible assistance to the Aborigines' dele-gates.[61] He specifically asked Ward to arrange a reception for the delegates on their arrival in London. This, he said, would be a 'fine example of cooperation and it will help our work here greatly'.[62] Apart from the ARPS, Wallace Johnson came into contact with sub-elite groups, mostly in Accra, who had attained a certain anti-imperialist consciousness. Particularly noteworthy was a study group which met regularly at the house of John Joseph Ocquaye, manager of the *Vox Populi* and founder of the St John's School at Nsawam. This group of educated, mobile, and disgruntled men who were also members of the ARPS, included as well as Ocquaye, an ex-government teacher, A. Roger Dennis, a cocoa broker, J. B. Lartey, a pensioner and farmer, R. W. Amoah, a freelance journalist, Frank Duncan, a trader, and F. A. Bruce, a journalist. Dissatisfied with the possibilities for successful politicking through the ARPS, these men who were not a part of the top level of the African colonial elite, were anxious either to revive the political impact of the Aborigines' Society or to create a new organisation altogether. It was this group which later became the nucleus for the Wallace Johnson Youth League.

Wallace Johnson's first labour activities in Accra were with the Motor Drivers' Union, consisting primarily of lorry drivers unhappy with their treatment by the police, and with the Gold Coast Workers' Protective Union, a labouring class grievance articulation and mutual benefit organisation that failed to gain a wide following. In 1934 Wallace Johnson took up the case of the forty miners who lost their lives in a Prestea mine disaster and began to form close ties with some of the mining areas. He was able to enlist the support of miners by pressing accident cases and other grievances against the companies. Johnson used his parliamentary connections, especially in labour circles, to arouse concern over labour grievances in the Gold Coast.

Given the limited experience of Gold Coast workers in the status as employed labourers, consciousness of workers' rights was very imperfectly developed; Wallace Johnson had to prove to the workers that their grievances could be alleviated by collective action. Consequently, he spent most of his time not in union-organising but rather in communicating cases of injured workers for compensation and of dismissed employees for reinstatement or payment of back wages and pensions. Depressions are not encouraging periods for labour activity; so worker protests focused more on compensation and amelioration of abuses than on higher wages. Compensation and reinstatement were not sought through strike threats; instead Johnson appealed to law and conscience for compassionate grants and workman's compensation. These demands were made, not only directly to the companies but also to the Gold Coast Government, Members of Parliament, and parliamentary pressure groups in England.

The forces already set up in motion by the activities and speeches of Wallace Johnson, coupled with the effects of the ideas promulgated by Azikiwe, resulted in the creation of the West African Youth League (WAYL) in February 1935. Working from the nucleus of the Ocquaye group, Wallace Johnson sought to guide grievance articulation throughout the Colony and Ashanti into a more socialistic and anti-imperialist direction within the framework of an organised mass-membership party. Wallace Johnson became its organising secretary 'and virtually ran the whole show'.[63] Its executive consisted of Bankole Awoonor-Renner, R. B. Wuta Ofei, Ellis Browne, and J. A. Arbleh. Key supporters of the league's initial organisation were Azikiwe, Kojo Thompson, K. A. Bossman, and Kobina Sekyi. However, most of these individuals had serious reservations about Wallace Johnson's ideas and eventually withdrew their support. Some support also came from the chiefs: the *Ga mantse* of Accra, the chief of Asamankese (Sekyi's client), Chief M. D. Ankrah, and Chief Alhaji were all patrons of the league.

The Youth League, which represented chiefly the efforts of Wallace Johnson and the Ocquaye-ARPS groups to organise on a broader scale, is commonly considered the radical, socialist, anti-imperialist political organisation of the 1930s. On the other hand, it has frequently been dismissed as a one-man show of negligible importance.[64] Both of these views require substantial qualification. Although the Youth League, founded and driven by Wallace Johnson, derived most of its ideology and dynamism from him, it made a successful start within the decidedly non-socialist context of the Gold Coast and managed to enlist the efforts and attention of more than a minuscule number of educated and energetic sub-elite activists. Although the Youth League spoke the language of anti-imperialism and socialism and acquired through Wallace Johnson important socialist contacts overseas, it achieved its primary impetus from the articulation of local grievances, some anti-imperialist in nature, others more clearly based on self-interest. The leadership of the League responded primarily to anti-colonial themes, while mass support was attracted only by more tangible benefits such as workmen's compensation or protection from abuses of consti-tuted authority.[65] Through this dual appeal, Wallace Johnson managed to attract both sub-elite leadership cadres and mass support for his programmes. The rising sub-elite, denied status and influence by the colonial situation, and the workers employed by an alien government and by alien mining and mercantile enterprises rallied to Wallace Johnson's League. Although providing a potentially potent core of anti-colonialist movement, these groups required mobilisation through propaganda and organisation which involve no little effort.

The organisation of the League did not proceed very rapidly until late 1935 when Mussolini's threat to the independence of Ethiopia became evident.[66] By the end of the year the League had established over twenty branches in the Colony. Overtures were made to such principal towns of Ashanti as Kumasi, Bekwai, Bompata, Juaso and Konongo, but the League did not make as great an impact there as it did in the Colony. We lack evidence as to details about membership of the League. Up to 1937, the Colonial Office knew 'very little about the membership of the League'. Even the minutes of the proceedings of the League did not show membership.[67] According to an ex-policeman in the CID, those who showed enthusiasm for the League got into 'bad graces' of the government.[68] A foreign correspondent claimed a membership of 3,000 to 4,000 in June 1936 and 7,000 in twenty branches after the sedition trial of Wallace Johnson.[69] But that the League had any support at all was a major tribute to the energy of its leader. As Organising Secretary, Wallace Johnson toured the Colony, made speeches, held mass meetings, and extended the influence and organisation of the League to every major town. The League attracted trade unions, young people's clubs, literary societies and ex-servicemen's groups. An effort was also made to engage the Muslim communities.

Wallace Johnson explained that the aim of the League was to bring the masses together: 'the high and the low, the rich and the poor, the learned and the unlearned'. According to him, the League was organised to champion the cause of the people and particularly the 'less favoured and down-trodden' and to defend the natural and constitutional rights of the inhabitants of West Africa'.[70] He said that he had found it necessary to form the League because the 'Old School' could not be entrusted with the effective handling, reconstruc-tion and reorganisation of West African society. For this work 'needs new ideas and new vision; new determination and will'. These qualities, he said, were far more the 'virtue of the youth – the youth in age and the youth in mind – than of the old and decrepit'.[71] The League chose as its motto the slogan 'Liberty or Death', a phrase which caused some alarm among the Gold Coast elite and government officials. The League's manifesto, borrowing heavily from the preamble of the United States Constitution, set forth the following objectives:

> We the Youth of the Gold Coast and of West Africa in general, in order to form a more united body to watch carefully and sincerely, affairs political, educational, economical and otherwise that may be to the interest of the masses of the motherland, to sacrifice, if need be, all we have for the progress and liberty of our Country, and Race, and to ensure happiness to ourselves and our posterity.[72]

Wallace Johnson claimed that the League was not confined to the Gold Coast alone. It was the affair of the whole of West Africa. Furthermore, it had contacts outside British West Africa with French-speaking and Portuguese-speaking areas.[73] The League was, on the whole, concerned with the complete transformation of the colonial system rather than its gradual reform. Its broadly worded intention 'to safeguard the natural and constitutional rights, privileges and liberty of the inhabitants of the country' from the prevarications of whichever foreign power controlled them evoked the musty memoranda and petitions of the ARPS and the NCBWA. Nevertheless, the League was much more militant than either of these two organisations and envisaged the beginnings of a movement toward emancipation. It sought to establish a programme for the economic, social and political emancipation of the West African colonies in order to instil feelings of self-determination among the colonial subjects.[74] Writing in the *Negro Worker* about the aims of the League, Wallace Johnson stated clearly that the Youth League was striving for a drive towards the 'establishing of a foundation for national independence'.

The first major political campaign of the Youth League was in support of the candidacy of Kojo Thompson for the 1935 Legislative Council elections. This campaign not only increased the popularity of the League as a new pressure group in the country; it also enhanced the prospects of the Ethiopian cause which it subsequently championed. The League aligned itself with the *Mambii* or People's Party against the Ratepayers' Association in the struggle for political power in Accra. Augustus William Kojo Thompson, leader of the *Mambii* Party, who won the Accra seat in the Legislative Council in 1935 against Dr F. V. Nanka Bruce of the Ratepayers' Association, was the 'most talked of politician' in the Gold Coast in the mid-thirties. A close associate of radical Wallace Johnson, Azikiwe and Kobina Sekyi, Thompson was known in official circles as one who was usually found in the van of any agitation against the government.[75] He was described by the local colonial administrators as an unreliable man of questionable probity who suffered from an inferiority complex.[76] He was, however, one of the most enthusiastic supporters of the Ethiopian cause in the Gold Coast.

Born at Winneba in 1880, Kojo Thompson was educated at the Collegiate School in Cape Coast, the Wesleyan School in Accra, and the Wesleyan Boys' High School in Lagos. He was called to the Bar at Lincoln's Inn in 1914. On returning to Accra to practise law, he did not participate in the Congress movement in 1920 or its fight for elective representation during the years 1920–25. Instead he concentrated on his law practice, entering the political arena only in 1924 when he played a leading role in the fight against the Municipal Corporations Ordinance.[77] In 1926 he accepted nomination to the Legislative

Council, having been proposed by the Mantsemei, that is, the chiefs of Gbese, Asere, Sempe, and Akumanji. Thompson was defeated in the subsequent Legislative Council election of 1927 by Glover Addo of the Ratepayers' Association. The point at issue in the 1927 campaign was the character of Kojo Thompson, who was loudly attacked as a demagogue, a self-seeker, and an opportunist. Thompson's greatest asset – willingness to insult the colonial regime – was not as much in demand during the prosperous days of the late 1920s as it would be during the frustrating depths of the Great Depression.

In 1931 Kojo Thompson was again defeated in the Legislative Council election, having secured 558 votes against 806 of his political opponent, Nanka Bruce. Unlike Nanka Bruce, Thompson, an average lawyer, did not seem to have any tangible achievement to his credit. His anti-colonialist colleagues like Azikiwe and Wallace Johnson supported him in 1935 but seldom praised him for anything other than standing up against the Europeans. However, regardless of his motives, the causes that he espoused were of more than local interest. His two causes, those of the people against the elite and of Africans against the European colonial system, were the themes of a drama which was played out during the interwar years in Accra that would be carried to every town and village after World War II by Kwame Nkrumah's Convention People's Party.

On the other hand, Thompson's political opponent, Dr Nanka Bruce,[78] had received his political baptism through his involvement in the Congress movement, and had also served on the Accra Town Council for four years. Through his brother-in-law, Thomas Hutton Mills, he had become involved in politics and come into contact with men like Mensah Sarbah, Father Brown, Casely Hayford, and E. J. P. Brown of the ARPS.[79] Dr Bruce was of a generation and a section of the upper elite which saw colonialism from a different point of view. Being the political and social leader of a set of people who were intimately involved, as the highest African employees, in the colonial governmental and economic structure, he sought co-operation rather than conflict with the white man. He and his followers felt that the primary problem of the country was progressive development by adopting certain benefits of European civilisation to the best of African civilisation. Bruce was a supporter of, and apologist for, colonialism not because he preferred alien rule but because he sincerely believed that the great mass of people in the Gold Coast, 'the rabble', as Akilakpa Sawyerr would call them, were not yet ready for self-government. This viewpoint was deeply elitist and collaborationist, but it was based on a high standard of conduct that demanded responsible action.

By 1935 the political and economic situations in the Gold Coast had turned against the moderate wing of the upper elite to which Nanka Bruce belonged, and it was this which changed the balance of political power in Accra in favour of Kojo Thompson. The depression had become increasingly worse, and had raised frustrations among the people. Nanka Bruce neither caused the depression nor supported the government's tax proposals, but he was blamed because he was in office as member of the Legislative Council. Secondly, the conflict over the 1934 protest delegations against the Sedition Bill had divided the upper elite sharply along lines of collaborationist versus anti-colonialist. Nanka Bruce was a logical target for all the hostility of opponents of the Ofori Atta Delegation on which he had served. In opposing Nanka Bruce, the Youth League and the ARPS were joined by Tackie Oblie, the Ga Mantse (paramount chief of the Ga state), A. J. Ocansey, proprietor of both the *Spectator*, a weekly, and the *Morning Post*, a powerful daily edited by Azikiwe, and Nii Jacobus Vanderpuije, owner of the *Vox Populi*. Evidently, the Accra Legislative Council election of 1935 was waged at a time of great political ferment and division in the Gold Coast.[80] To a great extent, the same elements which were responsible for two rival delegations proceeding to England on similar missions in 1934 were behind the party and press rifts in Accra. The *Gold Coast Independent* and the Ratepayers preferred the path of moderation and gradualism, while the *African Morning Post* and the Mambii advocated the more aggressive, less conciliatory approach favoured by the ARPS. The latter group had joined forces with a new generation of political activists not cut in the collaborationist mould of the Congress. These young men had entered the scene during times of economic decline. They had read the anti-colonialist books and pamphlets which had induced government to pass the Sedition Bill. But they found their political ambitions blocked by an older generation of moderates of the Congress era.

As the Accra Legislative Council election was held soon after the Italian attack on Ethiopia, the victory of Kojo Thompson[81] was interpreted by the Youth League as victory for the youth, the masses, the anti-imperialist groups and, in particular, for the cause of Ethiopia in the country. The League thus composed the following poem, 'Stand Fast Youths', to commemorate their victory and to show their interest in the Ethiopian affair:

> Now the conflict is done, The Battle is won;
> The city is now in the hands of the youths.
> Unite, youths in the League, Listen! Your
> Mother Country Abyssinia sounds her bugle.
> Rally to her call.
> Youth League, Lead the battle, Fight for
> Abyssinia and for yourselves. Now that Kojo
> Has won, the battle is for us.[82]

It was under the banner of the Youth League that Wallace Johnson organised the Ethiopia Defence Committee, and rallied the Gold Coast Motor Drivers' Union, the Carpenters' Union, and the Gold Coast Workers' Protective Union, which he had helped organise in the country, together with the ARPS, the Ocansey and Vanderpuije groups of newspapers, the Ex-Servicemen's Union, the mine-workers, some dissident chiefs and the youth of the Gold Coast, against the invasion of Ethiopia.

Before Wallace Johnson's return to Sierra Leone in 1938, there was no country-wide militant political organisation like the Nigerian Youth League or the WAYL in the Gold Coast to whip up Sierra Leonean opinion against the Italian aggression in Ethiopia. Until the late 1930s political activity was confined to the Creole elite who as collaborators occupied a distinctive stratum within the social structure. Beyond the confines of the Creole elite there was an almost total lack of explicitly nationalist activity. The activities of the local branch of the Congress of British West Africa – the only branch in West Africa with a spark of life at all – were entirely limited to Freetown and the immediate surroundings, and did not in any way affect or interest the majority of the population of the country who lived in the Protectorate.[83] Despite the deep anti-colonial feeling in the hinterland which was made evident by the House

Tax war of 1898 and the Haidara (Idara) affair of 1931, the Creole elite in the Colony who dominated the Congress remained indifferent to the problems of the people of the interior whom they tended to treat with contempt. Because of the conservatism of the established elite, none of the younger members of the bar, with the exception of Benka Coker and O. T. V. Metzger, evinced any interest in the local branch of the NCBWA.[84] In general, until the late 1930s, very few of the younger generation took much interest in political affairs in Sierra Leone. Their imagination was reported to have been caught by football, cricket and tennis. All these games appeared to 'give them sufficient food for thought'. The various disputes, quarrels and controversies between the various clubs and players occupied 'most of their attention'.[85] Even such older politicians as J. G. Hyde and T. E. Nelson Williams were no longer active members of the local branch of the NCBWA; they both considered originally that the local branch might be of use to them. Similarly, the older members of standing and repute – such as T. J. Thompson, S. J. Barlatt, Hotobah During, Songo Davies, E. A. C. Noah – were reportedly no longer much interested in the affairs of the Congress. Personal animosities would seem to have been responsible to a certain extent for the lack of interest taken by some of these gentlemen. The local branch was entirely in the hands of Beoku Betts and Bankole-Bright, the two Urban Members of the Legislative Council, who used the Congress to 'emphasise the matters which they desire to bring to Government's attention'. Their built-in conservatism militated against any pressure for radical changes or for a hurried acceleration of political development. The Congress movement was also said to be bolstered up locally by a few persons with private ambition or who felt resentment against the local government for one reason or another.

By the time of the Ethiopian crisis, the Sierra Leone branch of the NCBWA had only forty members on its roll, and the average attendance at general meetings, which were held every six months, was about twenty. However, as a general rule, the Committee of the Congress met monthly. Public meetings of the Congress were held from time to time in the Wilberforce Memorial Hall. They were usually convened to protest against some government bill or policy. The speakers were usually Bankole-Bright, Beoku Betts, Tuboku Metzger, Dr Pratt and Eleady Cole. Thus, on the whole, the leadership of the political scene in Sierra Leone was predominantly middle class and conservative. The traditional social elite and the Westernised social elite had constituted themselves as a group of collaborators with colonial rule. As key collaborators they expected, on the eventual withdrawal of the British Government, to fall heirs to the colonial political structure of which they were now a part. However, in spite of the lack of enthusiasm, the general conservatism and lethargy of its leaders, it cannot be gainsaid that the Sierra Leone branch of the Congress movement 'kept the flag flying'.[86] Fed by press reports on the international situation with regard to the Italo-Ethiopian conflict, the Congress leaders took up the Ethiopian cause in Sierra Leone and organised Ethiopia Relief Fund Committees in 1935 and 1936.

When Wallace Johnson returned home on 23 April 1938, the dominant political mood in Sierra Leone, on the surface, still seemed placid, almost apathetic. But not far beneath the surface lay resentment and dissatisfaction ready to be tapped and exploited by anyone offering leadership and a new hope.[87] For the Sierra Leone economic situation during the post-depression years was changing fast. The country was developing into a mining centre – into the land of iron and diamonds – and job-seekers were rushing to Freetown and the mining areas in numbers far greater than the jobs open to receive them. Besides, the strategic importance of Freetown as a key port for British imperial defence had stimulated work projects aimed at improving strategically important marine and military facilities. Foreign technicians and soldiers working at the mines and the military installations often clashed with Africans, whom they treated as if they were sub-human.[88] Incidents in which African workers were subjected to flogging, stocking, and other forms of brutal treatment were common. Also, in spite of the new economic dynamism, working conditions and salaries for African workers were deplorably low. There was thus a popular sense of frustration with the imbalance between rising expectations and actual living conditions.

In view of his previous record in Nigeria and the Gold Coast, on his arrival in Freetown, Johnson's baggage was searched and three isues of the *African Sentinel* (a revolutionary journal edited by Wallace Johnson in London on behalf of the Gold Coast section of the West African Youth League),[89] about two thousand copies in all, were seized by the customs authorities and later handed over to the police. For, according to Governor Douglas Jardine of Sierra Leone, 'it is most undesirable that such nonsense should be circulated among the population of Sierra Leone'.[90]

The seizure of the *African Sentinel*, was a grave error on the part of British officialdom in Sierra Leone, for it not only focused public attention on Wallace Johnson; it also presented him with an issue to exploit. Soon he organised public meetings at the Wilberforce Memorial Hall in Freetown at which he exposed British imperialism and colonialism:

> In no other Colony in West Africa do I find the masses in such a miserable state of economic and social disabilities. Instead of progress, after a lapse of twelve years, I find conditions within the colony rapidly declining. . . . As a people, we have been too lethargic, drowsy and happy-go-lucky. . . . A very wide margin has been provided for the foreign exploiters – capitalists and imperialists alike – to drive the wedge of divide-and-rule within our social circle: and while we keep grasping at shadows, they [the foreign invaders] are busy rapidly draining out the natural resources of the land for their personal benefits, leaving us in poverty and want.[91]

After vehemently criticising the Sierra Leone administration for not allowing Africans to read what they wanted, Wallace Johnson then appealed to his enthusiastic audience about the need for organisation:

> Now is the time and now is the hour. There is only one way out of our difficulties, and that is to organise and move. Although it has always been asserted by our so-called benefactors that we should take what we get and be satisfied, I maintain as Aggrey did that we should not be satisfied with taking what we get or what has been given us but to use what we have been given to gain what we ought to have.[92]

Predictably in a short time Governor Jardine was informed of the establishment of the Sierra Leone branch of the West African Youth League (SLYL) and the West African Civil Liberties and National Defence League in accordance with a resolution passed at a mass meeting on 2 May 1938.[93]

Unlike earlier organisations, the Youth League spread beyond the colony boundaries, with branches throughout the Protectorate, particularly in the mining and ore-despatch areas as well as centres of local political consciousness. To provide a reliable following and a mechanism for involving it in political activity, the League established ties, often through overlapping leadership links, with a variety of voluntary organisations like the Women's Auxiliary of the League, the Sierra Leone branch of Harold Moody's League of Coloured Peoples, and such militant trade unions as the War Department Amalgamated Workers' Union and the Mabella Coaling Workers' Union. Using his past experience in the labour movement, Wallace Johnson quickly and successfully organised as many as seven trade unions throughout the Colony and Protectorate which were affiliated to the Youth League. The standpoint of the League was socialist and anti-colonial and it regarded itself as the mouthpiece of the toiling masses. Its membership was open to all sections of the community – wage-earners and unemployed, rich and poor, the educated and uneducated, men and women, Muslims, Christians, pagans, Creoles, and up-countrymen. But Wallace Johnson's appeal was definitely to the wage-earner who was then labouring under the 'heaviest strain of economic, social and political disabilities'.[94] He was thus frequently involved in political and industrial action against the colonial government. Wallace Johnson's concern with the fate of the toiling masses provided him with a popular base to project his personality into the labour movement in the country. The trade unions were the most important source of the political and probably the financial strength of the Youth League.[95]

At its peak during this period, the Youth League was large and dynamic, although probably not as large as the 25,000 paid-up Colony and 17,000 Protectorate members which Wallace Johnson claimed. It was bonded together into an ardent fraternity by the word *comrade* with which all members addressed each other, and by slogans which for the first time in Sierra Leone history, called for unity among all the oppressed in the country regardless of social, economic, or ethnic differences.

Under the banner of the Youth League, Wallace Johnson protested against a new Education Ordinance of 1938, the Rural Areas Ordinance of 1938 and the Mining Laws of Sierra Leone. He considered these enactments as 'dangerously inimical to the progress of the people' and the 'most oppressive' forms of legislation ever enacted in a British colony. To him, the mining laws of Sierra Leone had placed 'the whole of the material progress' of the country in the hands of foreign investors as their 'sole and bona fide property'. Earlier in one of his public platform addresses after his arrival in Sierra Leone, Johnson had declared:

> Today we have got to make a change on the Sierra Leone Government. . . .
> We have got to change the Legislative Council and make it better. . . . . If
> we look backwards in the history of Sierra Leone we shall find that . . .
> Sierra Leone is far back and below the standard of freedom as far as the
> government of the colony is concerned.[96]

Wallace Johnson therefore advocated the return of the Municipal Councils to African control and equal African voting power in the Legislative Council; he would even alter the British constitution by sending African representatives direct to the imperial Parliament at Westminster.[97] In a memorandum to Governor Sir Douglas Jardine he contended that when affairs were viewed from an economic, social, political and educational standpoint, the people of

Sierra Leone would realise that they were 'bound hands and feet together with the bonds of abject slavery', the chain of which were 'eating at the bones of our existence'. The thirty-five paragraphed memorandum expressed utter dissatisfaction with the whole machinery of government of Sierra Leone. The form of legislature was described as 'a mere farce', and the Legislative Council institution as 'a form of anachronistic machinery' which was an insult to modern democracy. The civil service machinery was similarly deplored as 'nothing but a vicious tool' in the hands of the government for the exploitation of labour.[98] Like the youth movements in Nigeria and the Gold Coast during this period, the Sierra Leone Youth League also agitated for self-determination and denounced the moderate approach of the Sierra Leone National Congress to this important question. The comprehensive memorandum which greatly disturbed the officials at the Colonial Office in London, as evidenced in the commentary of O. G. R. Williams,[99] ranged over a number of sensitive subjects in a somewhat vague and rhetorical manner. It finally called for the appointment of a special and independent commission of inquiry to investigate the entire state of affairs in Sierra Leone with a view to 'making such reconstructions to the machinery of Government' and for the establishment of a better and more democratic, just and sympathetic form of administration in the country.

It was with such an extremist or leftist point of view of politics that Wallace Johnson attempted to give a new and dynamic direction to the nationalist politics in Sierra Leone. Quite evidently, his conception of nationalist politics was strikingly different from that of his contemporary established elite and collaborators. Alone of the political activists, he drew upon the grievances of previously neglected groups of non-collaborators and, in strident terms, attacked real and perceived injustices of colonial rule. A strong believer in communist revolutionary methods, Wallace Johnson had a Marxist-Leninist interpretation of the West African colonial government, and spoke in terms of immediate radicalisation and politicisation of the masses, socialism, boycotts and strikes as the quickest means of seizing power.[100] Unlike the Sierra Leone branch of the National Congress movement, Johnson's Youth League did not confine itself to sedate constitutional language, but employed the tone of the radical and the revolutionary and used techniques of ridicule, caricature and lampoon to attack the government and personnel of the day and to undermine the long-standing respect they had engendered in the people. Through its organ, the *African Standard* (which was launched in January 1939), the Youth League agitated for greater African representation in the political order and the eventual withdrawal of the European element.

Such radical political development was unknown in the Gambia, where no youth movement was formed during this period. Almost as in Sierra Leone before the advent of Wallace Johnson, there was no significant measure of political activity in this smallest British colony on the West Coast of Africa. The older politicians, largely the dying members of the NCBWA, occasionally demonstrated through the medium of E. F. Small's radical *Gambia Outlook and Senegambian Reporter* against some government piece of legislation considered inimical to the interest of Africans. Although the local branch of the Congress was the only nationalist organisation in the country in the 1930s, it rarely met to pass resolutions; nor did it endeavour to influence government to any extent.[101] Influential but conservative politicians like Sir Samuel J. Forster, who had been a member of the Legislative Council for over thirty years, and Dr Tom Bishop, the second most leading African at the time, would have nothing to do with the activities of the local branch of the Congress in any shape or form. These two politicians were conveniently described by the colonial officials as 'shock absorbers', for representations to and agitations against the colonial government were 'absorbed' and 'toned down' by them.[102]

Also, not unlike Sierra Leone during much of this period, the protectorate part did not count politically; and there was no 'opinion' of any kind in that territory. In the colony, however, there were two different communities and body of thought which might be said to count so far as nationalist politics was concerned. These were first, the real Gambians – Joloffs and Mandigoes with a few members of the West Coast tribes who had been settled in the colony for many years. The second was the Sierra Leone clerical element – at one time very strong, but much reduced in numbers and influence during the thirties. The first group disliked the Congress and had little or no use for it, while the second gave it very lukewarm support.

Just before the coming of the Italo-Ethiopian war, the 'Citizens' of the Gambia had expressed their dissatisfaction with certain conditions in the country, and had agitated for reform. In August 1934, a petition which was said to have been signed by some 1,450 inhabitants of Bathurst, was presented to the British House of Commons touching on a variety of subjects: an appeal for a constitution; a recommendation that the Legislative Council should consist equally of Officials and Unofficials – the Governor having a casting vote; a request for unofficial representation on the Executive Council; a recommendation that 'Native' Councils should be instituted to function as advisory bodies to the Commissioner and the non-enforcement of the Criminal Code Ordinance and the Criminal Procedure Code Ordinance.[103] This petition was for the most part a re-statement of previous ones. For example, a petition dated 12 December 1933 had been sent to the Privy Council asking for the non-enforcement of the Criminal Code Ordinances.

In rejecting the 1934 petition, an official recommended that in view of the fact that the activities of Messrs Small and E. J. C. Rendall were well known to the Colonial Office, he did not think that it was necessary to regard the petition 'as a matter of any great importance'.[104] This was endorsed by Sir Philip Cunliffe-Lister who informed the House of Commons that he was satisfied that the petition proceeded 'from a very small minority of the inhabitants of the Colony'.[105] The refusal of the petition – a fate which befell the two Gold Coast Delegations of the same year – was a bitter disappointment to the politically-minded groups in the Gambia who felt that the Colonial Office had once more discriminated against them in the matter of granting elective representation to the Legislative Council. This episode, occurring at the time of the great depression, contributed in no small measure to the intense reaction of the few radical elements in the Gambia to the British role in the Italo-Ethiopian affair. It was these elements, led by Councillor H. Darlington Carrol, who set up an Abyssinia Red Cross Fund committee in the Gambia.

Demonstrations and Rallies

The first call in Nigeria to mass protest demonstration came in early July 1935 from the *Nigerian Daily Telegraph* under the editorship of Ernest Sisei Ikoli, a nationalist politician and pan-Africanist who had closely associated himself with the Garvey movement in Lagos in the 1920s as Secretary of the local branch of the Universal Negro Improvement Association. In the opinion of the *Telegraph*, only the mass protest action of the 'workers and intellectuals' could prevent the imminent 'predatory war'. It then urged that in all working organisations, trade unions, workers' clubs, fraternal organisations, co-operatives and churches, 'work must at once be started to organise and build up "Hands Off Abyssinia Committees" '.[106] The general belief in West Africa at this time was that a series of protest demonstrations by colonial or coloured groups in their various communities would either constrain Italy to withhold her hand on Ethiopia or move the colonial powers to intervene vigorously on behalf of Ethiopia. It was with this in mind that prominent Nigerians of all political parties, notably the Nigerian Youth Movement and Herbert Macaulay's Nigerian National Democratic Party, readily responded to the call of the *Daily Telegraph*, and on 20 September 1935, organised the first mass meeting on the Ethiopian question in Lagos at the Glover Memorial Hall, the principal arena of Nigerian nationalism. Over 2,000 people attended this widely publicised meeting to express publicly their real feeling about the Ethiopian affair.[107] At this time the war clouds were gathering over Ethiopia and Mussolini bombastically spoke of regaining the glory of ancient imperial Rome.

The chairman of the meeting was Eric Olawu Moore (later Chief Bagbimo of Oko), the Vice-President of the National Democratic Party, who was supported by Ernest Ikoli. These were among the few most articulate nationalist politicians of the 1920s and 1930s, the former having been an elected member of the Nigerian Legislative Council from 1923 to 1938.[108] Other supporters included J. C. Vaughan, founder and president of the NYM. Vaughan had previously played a prominent role in the Union of Young Nigerians formed in 1923 to support the NCBWA and the NNDP. Another enthusiastic member of the group was Dr Akinola Maja, medical practitioner and politician, who was one-time president of the NYM and member of the Action Group. Also present at the meeting were influential nationalist politicians like E. J. Alex Taylor, J. Alesinloye Williams, R. M. Macaulay and P. J. C. Thomas, a Sierra Leone businessman and nationalist resident in Nigeria who had made a significant contribution at the W.E.B. DuBois Pan-African Congress held in London in 1921. Thus, the organisers of the Glover Memorial Hall meeting represented a cross section of the notable personalities of Nigeria in the 1930s. It would appear from this that the view held by certain writers that members of Macaulay's NNDP did not support the 'Hands Off Abyssinia' campaign in Nigeria, should be modified in the light of the available evidence.[109]

In his opening address, Eric Moore remarked that there was greater race consciousness in Nigeria than previously, and that this had been demonstrated by the large attendance at the meeting. He said that the object of the meeting was to strengthen the hands of the British Government with regard to the Italo-Ethiopian dispute. Intense enthusiasm was reported to have marked every phase of the proceedings of the meeting. The following resolution which was moved by Dr R. M. Macaulay and seconded by Ernest Ikoli, was unanimously adopted:

That the African Community of Lagos in Mass Meeting assembled, representing all shades of opinion not only in the capital but throughout the greater part of Nigeria, hereby declare their feeling of deep appreciation of the stand taken by the British Government in the Italo-Abyssinian dispute as expressed at the League of Nations Assembly by the British Foreign Secretary, Sir Samuel Hoare, for the independence and integrity of Abyssinia. Opportunity is taken at this meeting to renew our loyalty to His Majesty the King and to express our whole-hearted support for any measures that His Majesty's Government might consider necessary to take to restrain Italy from military aggression on Abyssinia.[110]

As is evident in this resolution, most Nigerians, and indeed West Africans, thought highly of Sir Samuel Hoare's stirring address at the Assembly of the League of Nations on 11 September 1935, in which he pledged British support of, and belief in, the system of collective security.[111] This address caused a surge of hope among West African pan-Africanists for, in their exaggerated and ill-informed view, it meant that Britain had, after a period of uncertainty and vacillation, decided to stop Mussolini, even if that meant using force. Hence the profuse profession of loyalty among West Africans to the British Crown.

As chairman of the mass meeting, Moore forwarded the resolution to the Chief Secretary to the Government of Nigeria for transmission to the Secretary of State for the Colonies 'for the information of the Imperial Government'.[112] Three days later J. A. Maybin, on behalf of the Officer Administering the Government of Nigeria, forwarded the original text of the resolution to the British Government as requested by Moore. Maybin commented that the mass meeting which had passed the resolution was most orderly and well conducted.[113]

The Glover Memorial Hall meeting, however, provoked a rather unexpected polemic between the two leading newspapers in Nigeria at the time – the *Nigerian Daily Telegraph* and the *Nigerian Daily Times* – on the general attitude of Nigeria to the whole Italo-Ethiopian affair. Writing under the editorial, 'Is the *Nigerian Daily Times* Anti-Negro?', the *Daily Telegraph* bitterly criticised the somewhat indifferent attitude of the *Daily Times* to the Ethiopian question which had 'stirred deeply the non-European races throughout the world'.[114] Chief Obafemi Awolowo, who during this period was an employee of the *Nigerian Daily Times* as resident correspondent of the paper in Ibadan, has thrown considerable light on the basic difference in the outlook and orientation of the two papers. In his view, although the *Nigerian Daily Times* was technically the best paper then in circulation, yet, on a strictly professional assessment, it was 'an unpardonably dull journalistic and literary product: a veritable stagnant pool of stale, colourless news; and a musty reservoir of articles which lacked animation, pungency, and nationalist flavour'.[115] More relevant to our subject under discussion, Chief Awolowo discloses that the news that mattered most to the editor of the *Daily Times*, Chief C. A. A. Titcombe, was, in order of importance, that 'relating to the late Sir Adeyemo Alakija and his family, the Roman Catholic Church, and Egba affairs'. Any criticism of the Catholic Church 'was taboo'. Besides, unless any definite instructions 'came from the very top', nothing critical must be written about the Nigerian Government or expatriate officials.[116] Since, as we have noted in the previous chapter, many West African nationalist leaders generally blamed the Pope, the Catholic Church and the British Government for the Italian aggression in Ethiopia, it is quite evident that the conservative *Daily Times* would be unlikely to project what was happening in Ethiopia. On the other hand, in contents and style, the *Daily*

Telegraph was the very antithesis of the *Daily Times*, 'and therefore much better'.[117] Moreover, apart from the radical Ernest Ikoli, the pan-Africanist Duse Mohamed Ali, was an associate editor of this paper.

In the Gold Coast, too, the initial reaction of the Executive Committee of the Youth League was to despatch a cable message to the Secretary-General of the League of Nations emphasising that the youths of West Africa viewed the Italo-Ethiopian struggle with great concern. It also urged the League of Nations to use all its influence to settle the dispute and to 'repudiate any economic and political concession to Italy in Ethiopia'. The Committee finally declared that the 'League denounce aggressor or fail. African youths stand by Ethiopia.'[118] A day after Italy had attacked Ethiopia, a mass meeting was held (4 October 1935) in Accra at the Palladium, a popular meeting place of the nationalists, to protest vehemently 'against the rape of Abyssinia'. The news of the invasion was received with such indignation that over 3,000 people, including clergymen and teachers, thronged to the Palladium long before the meeting started. The protest meeting had been convened by the Gold Coast Section of the WAYL and the Ex-Servicemen's Union, and over thirty representatives from eleven branches of the Youth League attended.

The Gold Coast Ex-Servicemen's Union, like its post-1945 successor, was not an insignificant body in the Gold Coast politics of the 1930s. The idea of forming the Union originated with a few Gold Coast soldiers who were serving in the Nigerian army in the 1914–18 War. After the war was over, these soldiers, including Emmanuel Cobina Lartey, popularly known in Accra as 'Old Lartey', William Neequaye, Nortey Moffat and Kojo Sackey, returned home to the Gold Coast to form a nucleus of the Ex-Servicemen's Union in Accra in 1919.[119] These were later joined by Prince R. T. Dodoo and B. E. A. Tamakloe, who subsequently became president and secretary of the union respectively. On hearing about this private union of discharged soldiers, Governor Gordon Guggisberg, who was himself an ex-serviceman, took an extraordinary interest in the union and encouraged the formation of an officially recognised body of the ex-soldiers in the country. And so, on Poppy Day, 11 November 1920, the Gold Coast Ex-Servicemen's Union was inaugurated in Accra.[120] Guggisberg became its first patron-in-chief. The entrance fee was five shillings, and the association was limited to ex-soldiers who had actually been on 'Active Service'. It was discovered at the end of 1927 that several members had only had local service contrary to the rules of admission to membership of the Association and this had resulted in its division into two groups – Local Ex-Servicemen's Association and the Old Comrades' Association. In 1935, as membership of the Old Comrades' Association diminished 'due to deaths and transfers on business', the two ex-servicemen's associations amalgamated under a new name, African Ex-Servicemen's Union. Accra was the headquarters, and branches were established at the provincial capitals. In 1937 Governor Arnold Hodson honoured it by becoming its patron-in-chief with Colonel M. A. Green, M.C., Officer Commanding the Gold Coast Regiment and Inspector of Local Forces, as its patron, and Rev. Dr John O. Aglionby, Bishop of Accra, as vice-patron.[121] The enrolment fee was reduced to two shillings and sixpence.

The aims and objects of the Gold Coast Ex-Servicemen's Union were first, to 're-unite into a sacred link men who during the Great War I served together in truly wonderful spirit of comradeship for King and Empire'. Secondly, the union aimed at maintaining brotherhood by 'assisting one another in emergencies, and helping widows and orphans of members'. Thirdly, it was the object of the union to make representation to 'Government for consideration to be given to African Ex-Servicemen in the Gold Coast and to stand by Africa at all times, particularly Gold Coast'. Every member of the union took an oath and thereby pledged himself 'to be a good and true man as befitting a soldier and a loyal British citizen to the credit of my late Regiment and this Union'. He should be a peaceful citizen by conforming to the laws of the 'Government under which I am and not to be a party in any plot or conspiracy against the Government and rightful leaders'. Every member was expected not only to keep the 'secrets of this Union at all times' but also to fight to 'save the King of the British Empire, the Natural Rulers and Africa'.[122]

It was through the union that the government in the thirties got in touch with ex-soldiers scattered all over the country and was able to pay them their gratuities. In 1927 a labour bureau for the purpose of getting employment for ex-soldiers of the Gold Coast Regiment and the Royal West African Frontier Force was established. This bureau worked closely with the union for the interest of ex-servicemen. During the years 1935–37, the union was able to give financial assistance, obtain war gratuities and medals, as well as employments and pensions for its members. In August 1938 it initiated an industrial scheme with a training centre in Accra. This project was to enable the union to take over contracts for painting, roadmaking, weaving of baskets and cane chairs. The scheme was favourably received not only by the government but also the provincial councils, especially the Western and Eastern Provincial Councils. This 'excellent scheme' was not implemented as a result of the outbreak of the Second World War. During the hostilities the government got in touch with the union, and through it recruited many men. The union canvassed and lectured for recruits, and the Information Department of the Colony on several occasions called on union members to 'speak at recruiting meetings or on the Radio'. Many of its members and officers re-enlisted as an encouragement to the younger generation. But after its energetic Secretary-General, B. E. Ahmed Tamakloe, was re-enlisted, the union became moribund for the period of the war until he returned home in July 1946 from overseas service with the West African Expeditionary Force. Tamakloe quickly reorganised the union for the purpose of 'admitting Ex-Servicemen of both World Wars into the sacred link of comradeship'. He was still the General-Secretary of the post-war Ex-Servicemen's Union when the historic 1948 Gold Coast riots erupted. These riots led to a series of events culminating in the granting of independence to Ghana in March 1957.

The failure of the government in the early thirties to redress the grievances of the ex-soldiers inclined the union towards opposition to the colonial administration. The union eventually teamed up with the WAYL and the ARPS in the traditional garb of anti-colonial protest. The alliance between the Union and the Youth League was not difficult to establish since many ex-servicemen were already Wallace Johnson's close friends.[123] At the height of frustration, the union's hostility against the colonial government became racial. It consistently fostered racial awareness by focusing on such dramatic examples of racial injustice as the Scottsboro Boys Case and the Italian action in Ethiopia.

At the Palladium meeting of 4 October, Bishop Victor Pratt of the African Church led the audience 'for fifteen minutes in prayer for the defence of

Ethiopia'. The chair was occupied by Prince R. T. Dodoo of the Ex-Service-men's Union, and was supported by Wallace Johnson, himself an ex-serviceman, A. W. Kojo Thompson, who was at this time greatly in need of the Youth League and the various militant and literary clubs for his electioneering campaign in Accra scheduled for 8 October, Kobina Sekyi of the ARPS and Bankole A. Renner,[124] first President and foundation member of the Youth League, as well as President of the Ashanti Freedom Society, rival of the Asante Kotoko Society, of which I. K. Agyeman was the President. Also at the meeting were Nee Tackie Obli, Ga Mantse, A. J. Ocansey of the defunct Gold Coast Colony and Ashanti Cocoa Federation, Nnamdi Azikiwe and the executive members of the Ga Young People's Literacy Club led by J. Acquah, the club's secretary. It would appear that those who organised the meeting were among the opposition elements in Gold Coast society. All these, together with the ARPS, now formed the radical side of Gold Coast politics. Their action alarmed the colonial government who instructed the police that meetings organised in response to the Ethiopian crisis should be carefully covered. Hence a couple of 'plain clothes native policemen' were usually sent to Wallace Johnson's meet-ings to take notes.[125] The Palladium meeting advocated strong co-operation and a united determination in a country-wide protest against the events in Ethiopia. Following this, Wallace Johnson and some executive members of the Youth League travelled to Sekondi where he declared to his attentive listeners that:

> The Negro masses of the world have long been in subserviency under the white nations. The present war (Italo-Ethiopian) is designed to open the eyes of the whole Negrodom and lead the Negroes through the path of emancipation from European serfdom. . . . Some say we must respect the whiteman because he can make iron float and all the rest of it. The white man is a man – just as an ordinary man and the blackman is also a man. There is nothing that the whiteman can do which the blackman cannot do. All that is required is Resolution, a positive determination and the will to succeed.[126]

Unlike the Lagos meeting, resolutions on the Ethiopian crisis were not immediately adopted in the Gold Coast until 1936, when the Youth League held its first annual conference in Accra from 21 to 28 March of that year. By this time Wallace Johnson and his anti-colonialist groups had been touring almost the whole country, except the former Northern Territories, and making long speeches on the Ethiopian question, emphasising how the Italian aggression in the world's last remaining bastion of black power was reminding the colonial subjects of the way in which foreign rule had been imposed on them. Ethiopia indeed provided the radical nationalist leaders with a vivid example of the extreme harshness of colonial conquest, of the impotence of a courageous African army in the face of the overwhelming firepower of the imperialists, and of the inhuman practices of a so-called civilised people. The war thus offered an unparalleled opportunity to attack imperialism at length without risking sedition. All the speeches on the Ethiopian crisis sought constantly to enhance self-awareness and self-confidence along racial lines. In March 1936, at its first annual conference, the Youth League and its associated groups passed the following resolutions on the Ethoipian war:

> 1. . . . having carefully and seriously considered the after effect of the 1914–1918 World War [WAYL] hereby registers its protest against the

attitude of the fomentors of war and calls upon the League of Nations to use all the influence at its disposal against the plunging of Europe into another World War that would cause the unnecessary sacrificing of the lives of Youths and particularly those of West Africa, in another carnage.

2. That this Conference also registers its serious protest against Italian aggression in Ethiopia and the murderous slaughtering of innocent Ethiopian women and children by Italian invaders and calls upon the League of Nations to denounce the aggressor in a more practical form by the application of oil sanctions – the only effective means of putting an end to Italian hostilities in Abyssinia.

3. That this Conference calls upon all Youth Organisations, all associated and affiliated bodies of the West African Youth League to register their protest against war and against Italian aggression in Abyssinia by effective resolutions. . . .[127]

These resolutions were communicated to the Secretary-General of the League of Nations, the British Secretary of State for the Colonies, and to the various West African colonial governments for their information and whatever action they 'may deem necessary to take in connection therewith'. Also, at this conference life-size photographs of the Emperor and Empress and a large coloured map of Ethiopia were shown to the people.

The reaction of the nationalist organisations in Nigeria and the Gold Coast was vigorous, widespread and sustained throughout the period of the crisis. Protest demonstrations were reported to have been organised by both the Nigerian Youth Movement and the Youth League in the Gold Coast at their various branches. For example, agitations were organised at Ibadan and Enugu respectively.[128] In Lagos, an Italian firm of builders, Messrs Cupp d'Alberto, was victimised and its Italian employees were assaulted by some militant NYM members. In November 1935 the Youth Movement staged a mass protest against a contract granted to this firm for work on the Holy Cross Cathedral at Yaba, Lagos. The protesters declared that the employment of an Italian firm for work intended for the benefit of Africans was, on the face of the 'present crisis', a sheer insult to the intelligence of the Catholic community in Nigeria. They felt that this would be adding insult to injury while 'our kith and kin are being ruthlessly massacred in their own homes by Italian soldiers and airmen.'[129] The management of the firm complained bitterly of this assault which they termed the 'unjustifiably hostile attitude of the local public' to their firm for the action of their government with which they in their private capacity might not have been in sympathy.[130] Similarly in Accra, a group of young men believed to be members of the Youth League pronounced curses on an Italian ship, the S.S. Carnia, which docked at Accra harbour on 6 May 1936.[131] Two months later, the Italian Consul in Lagos lodged a complaint with Governor Arnold Hodson regarding the use of the Italian national flag to cover a chair in the Port Officer's boat at Accra harbour.[132]

The fall of Addis Ababa in May 1936, and the British Government's recognition of the Italian conquest, generated a series of resolutions, interviews and confrontations between the nationalist organisations, the local colonial governments and the imperial power itself. Although by mid-1936 Britain had not shown any definite sign of change of policy towards the Ethiopian question, many nationalist groups strongly suspected British intentions on the recognition issue. The first to confront the Nigerian administration on this subject was the Prominent Lagos Women Society led by Mrs G. S. Wynter Shackleford, an influential woman of Ebute Meta, Lagos. The Shackleford family appeared to be ardently pan-Africanist in outlook and activity, having played a prominent role in the local branch of Marcus Garvey's Universal Negro Improvement Association in the early twenties. The president of the Lagos branch of the Association was Wynter Shackleford, who sustained the movement while other members became 'lukewarm and the public no longer in favour of it'.[133] It is not surprising that throughout the thirties there was a close working relationship, as well as friendship, between Duse Mohamed Ali, the ardent Garveyite, and the Shacklefords.

West Indian by birth, Amos Stanley Wynter Shackleford, 'The Bread King of Nigeria', came to Nigeria as a railway clerk in 1913, became an entrepreneur in 1917, and in 1921 entered the bread trade in Lagos. By acquiring the services of an army-trained baker, and introducing both technical and distribution innovations, he made a fortune during the difficult inter-war years, also successfully operating ferry services and petrol stations, and expanding into the Gold Coast in 1934. He was so successful that the shares he privately sold to his friends at £50 each later sold for as much as £3,000.[134] But Shackleford was more than a businessman – he entered into Nigerian political life. He was a member of the Lagos Town Council, president of the Democratic Party in 1946, a cricketer, and a noted philanthropist. He and his equally enterprising and knowledgeable wife, G. S. Wynter Shackleford, played a dominant role in the agitation against the Italian invasion of Ethiopia.

On 10 June 1936, Mrs Shackleford sent round a special appeal she had received from Princess Tsahai of Ethiopia to all women in the world to help in getting the League of Nations to condemn and forbid the use of poison gas and other deadly weapons by Italians on the people of Ethiopia. Commenting on the appeal, Mrs Shackleford said that the women of Nigeria should support the Princess by sending through 'our Governor to the League of Nations our own agreement with the protest'. She added that the women should also urge the League not to allow Italy to annex Ethiopia as the Italian war 'was an aggressive one. . . . We hope to take our request to His Excellency in person and would like us all to go together'.[135]

In a subsequent interview with G. C. Whiteley, the Acting Chief Secretary to the Nigerian Government, Mrs Shackleford expressed the intentions of the Prominent Lagos Women Society and asked the permission of the government to present their protest in a procession to the Government House after prayers for Ethiopia at Breadfaint Church. The procession would consist of fifty children and at least two hundred women. Mrs Shackleford guaranteed that the procession would be orderly and that there would be no singing or noise-making. It was also agreed that if the Governor disliked the idea of such a large crowd in the vicintiy of the Government House, Mrs Shackleford said they were quite 'prepared for the procession not to proceed beyond half-way, or indeed to have no procession at all'. She added that the procession, however, appealed particularly to the market women who had shown 'great sympathy' for Ethiopia.[136]

Whiteley's report on his interview with Mrs Shackleford greatly embarrassed Sir Bernard Bourdillon, Governor of Nigeria, who had become apprehensive of the impact which the Ethiopian crisis had had on the ordinary people in

Nigeria. He could hardly understand how even market women should take such intense interest in foreign affairs – an event far beyond the confines of Nigeria. His first reaction was to refuse the women's request, but Whiteley repeatedly advised that Bourdillon should receive the deputation and their petition, for it 'would probably do more harm to refuse to see them', as Nigerians in general seemed to have lost their sense of perspective over the Ethiopian affair. After some hesitation, the Governor agreed that he would 'welcome a deputation without procession at 4:00 p.m. on 24 June 1936', and this was accordingly communicated to Mrs Shackleford.[137] The protest, which was addressed to the President of the League of Nations in Geneva, through Bourdillon, declared that the women of Nigeria 'join our voices with that of Princess Tsahai of Abyssinia', and that they most humbly and earnestly:

> implored the League to make definite pronouncement against the use of poison gas, etc. in war, and to refuse to recognise the annexation of Abyssinia by Italy as a result of an aggressive war, waged in violation of all rules of civilised warfare.[138]

The Governor forwarded this petition to the Secretary of State for the Colonies, W. Ormsby-Gore, with the enclosure that the petitioners desired that their message be transmitted 'by you to the appropriate quarter at Geneva'. He remarked that the signatories to the petition were ladies prominent in Lagos society but 'I am not, however, in a position to say how far feeling on this subject extends outside Lagos'.[139] In reply, Ormsby-Gore informed Bourdillon that a copy of the petition had been sent to Anthony Eden, the Foreign Secretary, with the request that, provided he saw no objection, the message be communicated to the League of Nations.[140] Mrs Shackleford was accordingly informed of the Colonial Office's acknowledgement of the receipt of the petition.

Most unexpectedly, however, a further despatch from Ormsby-Gore informed Bourdillon of Anthony Eden's rejection of the petition. In the opinion of the Foreign Secretary, it was not for the Government in the United Kingdom to undertake to forward to the League communications 'of this nature from private persons or organisations'. He therefore stated with regret that he did not see his way to forward the message. Eden requested that the Prominent Lagos Women Society be informed of the attitude of the British Government and that they be advised to communicate their message direct to the Secretary-General of the League of Nations, should they so desire.[141] This despatch put the Nigerian Government in an awkward position, the more so since the Governor's despatch of the petition to London had been widely publicised in the local press. The government was seriously concerned about the reaction that Eden's rejection of the petition would provoke should these 'excited women be so informed'. On the other hand, Bourdillon felt that it would be administratively improper on the part of the government to refuse to transmit the message of the Foreign Office to the women. The Governor remarked that 'in order not to hurt these people's feelings unduly', it would be preferable to inform Mrs Shackleford in an interview that a further despatch had been received from the Colonial Office, and to explain the situation verbally to her. Alternatively, a letter could be sent to her straight away to appraise her of the attitude of the British Government, and 'advise her to direct her message' to the League of Nations. Whiteley approved of the second alternative, and informed Mrs Shackleford accordingly.[142]

The confrontation between the Prominent Lagos Women Society, the Nigerian Government and the Colonial and Foreign Offices in London is not the only evidence illustrating the intensity of the feeling of West African women about the events in Ethiopia. For, in the Gold Coast, too, it was the women's section of the WAYL which carried the news about the Ethiopian conflict to remote areas of the country. At Osiem, a small village in the then Eastern province of the Gold Coast, for example, the villagers were reported to have 'rent their apparels and shed tears' when the news of the 'crucifixion' of Ethiopia was flashed there by a touring group of women belonging to the Youth League. A full two-minute silence was observed for those brave Ethiopian warriors who suffered death through the 'wicked machinations of the *Duce* and "Christian" Italy'.[143]

The recognition of the Italian conquest of Ethiopia by the powers engaged the attention of various groups in Eastern Nigeria, particularly the radical nationalists at Enugu, who had already established an active Ethiopia Relief Fund Committee with Bentum-Obrigya as secretary. At an all-night meeting on 20 June 1936 this committee finally adopted a resolution deploring the

. . . annexation of any part of Abyssinia by Italy as a result of aggressive war waged in violation of all human methods and international law, praying the League, as the only body destined to protect world peace, to refuse recognition of annexation and urge intensification of all sanctions covered by Covenant.

The resolution further desired that Great Britain be moved to pursue steadfastly 'all lawful means towards the vindication of the rights of Ethiopia and restoration of the sovereignty and independence of the Black Empire'.[144] As with that of the Prominent Lagos Women Society, this resolution which was sent to Bourdillon through the Secretary of the Southern Provinces, was summarily rejected by the Foreign Office. The recognition issue, however, took a dramatic turn in the Gold Coast. Here, it was something more than the question of registering a protest at the wanton violation of international law by Italy and requesting Great Britain not to recognise the Italian sovereignty over Ethiopia. At a crowded meeting in Accra on 15 May 1936, under the chairmanship of A. W. Kojo Thompson, an Unofficial Member of the Legislative Council, the Gold Coast Ex-Servicemen's Union passed what they termed 'a historic resolution' which declared that, should Great Britain refuse the Union's request, they would 'never again take up arms to defend European nations in the event of any future war which may arise out of their diplomatic bargains contrary to the spirit and letter of the Covenant of the League of Nations'.[145] The resolution which received wide publicity in the press, was read by B. E. A. Tamakloe, general secretary of the union, after a short but stimulating address by Sergeant Major J. Q. Allotey, in which he reminded the veterans of how African blood had been shed 'to make Belgium free'. Earlier, Nnamdi Azikiwe had delivered a lecture on 'The Crucifixion of Ethiopia'. Copies of the 'historic' resolution were sent to the Gold Coast Government, the Secretary of State for the Colonies and the British Ex-Servicemen's Union and its affiliated bodies. This attitude of the ex-soldiers was alluded to in the confidential report which Miss Hebe Spaull of the British League of Nations Union staff submitted on her tour of the Gold Coast and Nigeria in 1938 to which reference has already been made. Miss Spaull said that 'recruitment of Africans', especially the Hausas who had copied Arab culture and had become pro-Arab, in the event of war would be difficult, for Africans were very much dissatisfied with the attitudes of Great Britain towards the events in both Ethiopia and Palestine.[146]

The subject of recognition of the Italian occupation of Ethiopia was brought to the fore in early 1938. On 21 February of that year, Neville Chamberlain, the British Prime Minister, told the House of Commons that he had always taken the view that the question of the formal recognition of the Italian position in Ethiopia was one that could only be morally justified if it was found to be a factor, and an essential factor, 'in the general appeasement'.[147] The British Government subsequently entered into negotiations with Italy for a general 'settlement' of their relations. By the beginning of April they were ready to sign an agreement including the grant of full recognition to Italian sovereignty in Ethiopia. This change of British policy aroused a great deal of protest and indignation in West Africa. To the nationalist organisations, the British recognition of the Italian conquest was a great shock. In their opinion, it was destined to destroy British prestige throughout the world and be remembered against the British people, especially by coloured peoples who would never trust or honour Britain again. The resignation of Anthony Eden, the British Foreign Secretary, on the recognition issue was hailed throughout West Africa. In the Gambia, for example, E. F. Small's weekly, *Gambia Outlook and Senegambian Reporter*, devoted a series of editorial comments throughout February and March 1938 in praise of Eden's action. In the Gold Coast Eden's resignation was seen as 'worthy of true British character'. It was even predicted, and rightly too as latter events proved, that 'Eden may come back as a Premier of Great Britain, and early too; a terror to dictators, and a bulwark against attacks upon the traditional character of all Britons and the liberty of Britain'.[148] The British action was so deeply felt that in Sierra Leone a section of the community refused to participate in the celebration of Earl Haig's Poppy Day Fund. Wallace Johnson's Sierra Leone Section of the West African Youth League angrily reacted against an invitation to participate in a wreath laying ceremony which was intended to form part of Earl Haig's Poppy Day Fund celebrations fixed for 11 November 1938. The League unanimously resolved on 4 September:

> That in consideration of the attitude of the British Government in the recognition of the conquest of Abyssinia by Italy by means of force, murder, rape and robbery, which acts are contrary to all international laws of war and adverse to all human conceptions, morality and justice, which attitude of the British Government represents a condonation of the barbarous aggression of Italy against Abyssinia, thereby betraying the confidence of the African people in British equity and fair play, the League declares that not until Britain dissociates herself from this group of international aggressors and taken her stand on the pedestal of Justice and Equity as hitherto she has stood in the eyes of the African People, there should be expected no manner of co-operation whatsoever from its members in connection with any future celebration of the Armistice.[149]

Apart from the recognised and well-known nationalist organisations we have noted, there were some less organised bodies and groups such as the market-women associations in Ibadan and Lagos, the Sailors' Union in Freetown, the League of Coloured Peoples in Bathurst, and even schoolchildren, who in one way or other expressed their resentment at what was happening in Ethiopia. Nnamdi Azikiwe, for example, has narrated the excitement with which school-children in the Gold Coast learnt of the Italo-Ethiopian conflict. Azikiwe's account, which reveals the impact of the crisis on African thinking, tells how on being 'told of how black soldiers aided by the invisible hand of God, were out-witting and overthrowing their enemies', the children became 'heated up with pride'.[150] In a similar mood, some Sierra Leone crew members of the *S.S. Holmea*, one of United Africa Company's steamers which regularly called at Sierra Leone, protested against the Italian threat on Ethiopia in a resolution at North Shields, which the captain of the ship was made to sign before the ship could set out for Sierra Leone.[151]

The Ethiopian question was indeed the one single external episode in the crisis years of 1935 and 1936 that deeply touched the feelings of the common man, as well as the articulate nationalist intelligentsia or the progressive politicians in West Africa. The agitation became so intense, even in the inland Province of Ashanti in the Gold Coast, that at a meeting of the newly restored Ashanti Confederacy Council in February 1936, the Chief Commissioner for the Province, Major Sir Francis Jackson, was said to have seriously advised the chiefs and people of the Province to attach no importance to newspaper pub-lications and to stop reading them or getting them read and explained to them.[152] Such official pressure, coupled with the underground propaganda which was launched by Italians resident in West Africa, could hardly prevent the militant nationalist groups from backing their resentment and resolutions with some-thing more practical.

1 J. B. Webster and A. A. Boahen, *The Revolutionary Years: West Africa since* 1800, Longman, 1967, p. 312.
2 Hodgkin, *Nationalism in Colonial Africa*, p. 142.
3 M. Sampson, *West African Leadership*, London, 1969, p. 62.
4 C.O.267/669/32157, enclosure in despatch No. 537 of 21 August 1939. R. R. Blood, Deputy Governor of Sierra Leone, to Malcolm MacDonald, Secretary of State for the Colonies.
5 J. S. Coleman, *Nigeria: Background to Nationalism*, p. 201.
6 For a detailed account of the NYM, see Awolowo, *Autobiography*, pp. 113–32; Coleman, pp. 218–29; T. N. Tamuno, *Nigeria and Elective Representation, 1923–1947*, pp. 51–4; Azikiwe, *The Development of Political Parties in Nigeria*, pp. 7–8. Our brief discussion here is focused mainly on the activities of the NYM in relation to the Ethiopian question and the reaction of the Colonial Office to the movement during this period.
7 The Nigerian National Democratic Party (NNDP) was formed in 1923 by Herbert Macaulay, generally referred to as the 'Father of Nigerian nationalism'. This party dedicated itself mainly to the cause of Eshugbaiyi Eleko, the deported Head of the House of Dosumu. This dedication won the party the overwhelming support of the people of Lagos. The NNDP was generally a Lagos party and did not look outside the city. This, as well as its failure to take note of important social changes in the 1930s constituted a source of its weakness. For the constitution of NNDP, see *Macaulay Papers*, Box 61, File 8.
8 A. T. Ariori, 'The Significance of "Youth Day" 1935', *Service*, September 1936.
9 Arnold Hughes, 'The Nationalist Movement in the Inter-War Period: 1923–1938', Seminar paper, Institute of African Studies, Ibadan, November 1964.
10 C.O.583/234/30386, Governor Bourdillon to Malcolm MacDonald, 7 November 1938.
11 *Ibid.*, minute by R. Turnbull, 23 December 1938.
12 *Ibid.*, minute by Sedebotham, 23 December 1938.
13 Interview with Oba Samuel Akisanya, April 1969.
14 By 1938 branches of NYM had been formed at Enugu, Jos, Sapele, Kaduna, Port-Harcourt, to mention only a few. Tamuno, p. 154.

15 W. R. Crocker, *Nigeria: A Critique of British Colonial Administration*, London, 1936, p. 235. From the now available evidence – the Colonial Office records and the NYM 'Youth Charter' of 1938 – Crocker's observation appears to be an oversimplification.
16 G. E. Metcalfe, ed., *Great Britain and Ghana: Documents of Ghana History, 1807–1957*, London, 1964, p. 640.
17 The ARPS published its Constitution on 29 April 1909; ACC.73/64 and 89/65, *Aborigines Papers*.
18 J. J. Thornburn to the Secretary of State for the Colonies, No. 398 of June 1912. Cited in David Kimble, *A Political History of Ghana: The Rise of Gold Coast Nationalism, 1850–1928*, London, 1963, p. 369.
19 ADM.11/1/974, Ghana National Archives, Accra, W. J. A. Jones to Colonial Secretary, 29 May 1928.
20 ACC.74/64, *Aborigines Papers*, C. E. Skene, Commissioner, Central Province, to ARPS, 21 March 1932.
21 See my article, 'The Aborigines Society and the 1945 Pan-African Congress', *op. cit.*
22 There is no biography of Sekyi, but for sketches of his character and activities, see *ARPS Papers* and *Sekyi Papers*; also, Langley, intro. to *Kobina Sekyi: The Blinkards*, pp. 1–11; K. A. B. Jones-Quartey, 'Kobina Sekyi: A Fragment of Biography', *Research Review*, Institute of African Studies, University of Ghana, Legon, iv, 1, 1967; Langley, 'Modernisation and its Malcontents; Kobina Sekyi and the re-statement of African political theory (1892–1956)', *Research Review*, vi, 3, 1970; Samuel Rhodie, 'The Gold Coast Aborigines Abroad', *Journal of African History*, vi, 3, 1965; Holmes, 'Economic and Political Organisation in the Gold Coast, 1920–1945,' ch. x and R. L. Stone, 'Colonial Administration and the Rural Politics in South-Central Ghana, 1919–1951', Unpublished Ph.D. thesis, Cambridge, 1974, pp. 102–17. A full biography of Sekyi is being worked out by Dr J. A. Langley.
23 Stone, p. 105.
24 Langley, 'Modernisation and its Malcontents', p. 16.
25 Holmes, p. 478.
26 Kobina Sekyi, 'Official Encouragement of Official Recklessness', ACC.539/64, *Sekyi Papers*.
27 David Apter's *Ghana in Transition*, and F. M. Bourret's *Ghana: The Road to Independence*, contain some gaps and do not give the 'feel' of Gold Coast nationalist politics of the 1930s. On the other hand, the case of Nigeria has been fully covered in James Coleman, *Nigeria, Background to Nationalism*; that of Sierra Leone in Martin Kilson, *Political Change*, J. R. Cartwright, *Politics in Sierra Leone*, Leo Spitzer, *The Creoles of Sierra Leone: Responses to Colonialism, 1870–1945*, and Ayo Langley, *Pan-Africanism and Nationalism*.
28 *Report of the Commission of Enquiry into Disturbances in the Gold Coast, 1948*, London, 1948, p. 17.
29 A systematic treatment of Danquah's life is provided in a pamphlet, *Liberty: A Page from the Life of J. B. Danquah*, written by Danquah in prison in 1948 when he was detained by the government in connection with the 1948 Gold Coast riots. A biographical study, based mostly on secondary sources, has been attempted by Walter Hellerstein in an unpublished Honours thesis, Harvard University, 1967; also L. H. Ofosu Appiah, *Life and Times of J. B. Danquah*.
30 Apter, *Ghana in Transition*, New York, 1963, p. 128.
31 For Danquah's views on this, see his *Liberty of the Subject: A Monograph on the Gold Coast Hold-up and Boycott of Foreign Goods, 1937–38*.
32 *Danquah Papers*.
33 *Gold Coast Leader*, 20 March 1929. This call was repeated at the second annual meeting of the WASU branch in the Gold Coast held on 18 May 1929.
34 The originators of the GCYC were J. C. de Graft Johnson (President), Brakatu Ateko (Treasurer) and Danquah (General-Secretary). C.S.O.1324/31, sub. file 36, Ghana National Archives, Accra.
35 *Times of West Africa*, 17 March 1933. This paper was established by Danquah in 1931 and served as an effective instrument of his political ambition. It attacked different aspects of colonial policy in flamboyant language. C.O.96/717/21750.
36 ACC.716/56, Ghana National Archives, Accra.
37 ACC.378/64, *Sekyi Papers*, Danquah to Sekyi, 13 December 1938.
38 *Ibid.*

39 The GCYC which Danquah organised was the recognised hub of political activity in the Gold Coast in the early forties. A measure of its prestige can be seen in the careful consideration which the government gave to the Youth Conference's recommendations on constitutional reform embodied in a memorandum, 'Things to Change in the Gold Coast'. These recommendations, submitted in 1943, were largely the product of Danquah's labours. The Burns Constitution of 1946 which adopted many of the proposals owes much to Danquah's inspiration. Nevertheless, it is one of the ironies of Danquah's political career that his success in awakening his people to modern realities spelt his own political demise in the post-war period.

40 C.O.96/723/31135/2, Moore to MacDonald, 12 November 1935.

41 *Ibid.*, MacDonald to Arnold Hodson, 20 November 1935.

42 *Danquah Papers*, Danquah to the Secretary of ARPS Delegation, London, 7 June 1935.

43 Azikiwe, *My Odyssey*, p. 219.

44 Hooker, *Black Revolutionary: George Padmore's Path from Communism to Pan-Africanism*, pp. 49–52.

45 Leo Spitzer and La Ray Denzer, 'I. T. A. Wallace Johnson and the West African Youth League', *The International Journal of African Historical Studies*, vi, 3, 1973, pp. 413–52.

46 J. A. Langley, *Pan-Africanism and Nationalism*, pp. 330–43.

47 C.O.267/665/32208/1938, Douglas Jardine, Governor of Sierra Leone, to MacDonald, 30 June 1938.

48 C.S.O. 25/36, Ghana National Archives, Accra, Johnson's application to the Director of Education of the Gold Coast on 21 January 1936 for the establishment in Accra of a vocational class to be known as 'Westnel Vocational Class' gives details of his educational background. The application was rejected.

49 Particularly in Spitzer and Denzer; also Holmes, pp. 669–736.

50 C.O.267/665/32208/1938, Jardine to MacDonald, 30 June 1938.

51 *Ibid.*

52 *Ibid.*

53 For early trade union development in Nigeria, see Wogu Ananaba, *The Trade Union Movement in Nigeria*, London, 1969, ch. 2.

54 C.O.583/195/21029/1934.

55 Spitzer and Denzer, p. 422; Shaloff, p. 244.

56 C.O.583/195/21029/1934, A. C. Burns to Wallace Johnson, 29 March 1934.

57 C.O.96/731/31230, minute by Gerald Creasy, Colonial Office, London, 27 February 1936.

58 Spitzer and Denzer, pp. 427–8. For the claim of the *Gold Coast Independent*, see Wallace Johnson, 'The *Gold Coast Independent* and Myself', *Vox Populi*, 21 August 1935.

59 The decision to introduce the Bill was originally instigated by Harry Scott Newlands, the Chief Commissioner of Ashanti, in January 1933, and approved by Shenton Thomas in May of the same year. C.O.96/707/21613/1933; also, A.D.M.12/1/82, Ghana National Archives, Accra. For further details, see Shaloff, 'Press Controls and Sedition Proceedings in the Gold Coast, 1933–1939', *African Affairs*, lxxi, 284, July 1972, pp. 241–2.

60 C.O.96/714/21639/1934, Shenton Thomas to Alex Fiddian, Colonial Office, London, 27 February 1934.

61 ACC.96/65, *Sekyi Papers*, Johnson to Sekyi, 17 June 1934.

62 *Ibid.*, Johnson to Ward, 19 June 1934.

63 C.O.96/731/31230, 'Youth League: Activities of Mr. Wallace Johnson', minute by Alex Fiddian, 30 August 1935.

64 *Ibid.* This was the view originally held by Arnold Hodson, Governor of the Gold Coast. The Executive Council of the Gold Coast similarly dismissed the importance of the League at the beginning of its formation. See *Minutes* of Executive Council, 9 March 1936.

65 On behalf of the League Wallace Johnson complained on several occasions to the Colonial Office in London, and also to Arthur Creech Jones, the Labour M.P. interested in colonial matters, about treatment of African workers by expatriate firms and mines. For details see Mss. Brit. Emp. S.332, ACJ.18/3, *Creech Jones Papers*.

66 For example, during the week of 11–18 November 1935 inaugural meetings of the League were held at Suhum and Axim, while Ethiopia Defence meetings were held at Saltpond, Cape Coast and Sekondi to raise money for the Relief Fund. Branches of the League were established at Takoradi, Axim, Nsawam, Koforidua, Mangoase, Cape Coast, Nyakrom, to mention only a few. The headquarters was at Accra.

67 C.O.96/731/31230.
68 Interview with S. A. Amable, a retired Assistant Commissioner of Police, Ho, Ghana, 22 May 1971
69 C.O.96/740/31230, quoted from *Negro Worker*, May 1937.
70 *Wallace Johnson Papers.*
71 *Ibid.*
72 *Ibid*
73 *El Ouma* and *Cri des Negres* of the Negro press in Paris occasionally reported on the activities of Johnson's Youth League. As Spitzer and Denzer claim, Wallace Johnson maintained contact with the Paris headquarters of the International Bureau of Youth. Spitzer and Denzer, pp. 433–4.
74 Spitzer and Denzer, pp. 434–5.
75 C.O.96/740/31230/1, minute by C. Lambert, Colonial Office, London, 22 March 1937.
76 C.O.96/717/21750, Shenton Thomas to Fiddian, 23 June 1934.
77 *Gold Coast Independent*, 25 March 1931.
78 Frederick Victor Nanka Bruce was born at Accra in 1878. Educated at the Accra Government School and the Wesleyan High School in Lagos, Nanka Bruce subsequently studied medicine at Edinburgh Univerity from 1901 to 1907. On his return to the Gold Coast (1907) he served on a number of commissions on medical matters, and also fought as well as to keep the West African Medical Service open to Africans and for the improvement of health conditions in the Gold Coast. In 1918 he and J. J. Akrong of Labadi founded the *Gold Coast Independent*, and he served as editor despite his medical duties.
79 *Gold Coast Independent*, 14 September 1935 and 12 Spetember 1931.
80 For details of the Accra election, see Stanley Shaloff, 'The Press and Politics in Accra; The Accra Legislative Council Election of 1935', *Societas*, Vol. 1, No. 3, Summer 1971, pp. 213–19,
81 Thompson was elected by 1,030 votes to 926. At the subsequent election in April 1936 after Dr Bruce had petitioned the government to set aside the result of the October 1935 election, Thompson was again elected by 1,022 to 867. *Judgement Book*, Supreme Court, Accra, Vol. 13, 1936. Kojo Thompson served at the Legislative Council for eight years. His tenure was terminated abruptly in 1944 when he was convicted of soliciting a bribe of £25,000 from AWAM in return for which he would refrain from attacking them in the Council. *Gold Coast Independent*, 23 March 1944 and 20 May 1944.
82 *Vox Populi*, 16 October 1935.
83 C.O.267/655/32157, Ag. Governor, Sierra Leone, to W.G.A. Ormsby-Gore, Secretary of State for the Colonies, 20 September 1936.
84 *Ibid.* The officers of the Sierra Leone branch of the NCBWA in 1936 were: A. E. Tuboku Metzger (President), Dr H. C. Bankole-Bright and E. S. Beoku Betts (Vice-Presidents), the Imans of Fourah Bay and Foulah Town (Hon. Vice-Presidents), W. Baanah Davies (Treasurer), S. A. Hughes and T. J. Carew (Joint-Secretaries), A. Benka Coker and J. N Faulkner (Assistant Secretaries). Among the nine committee members were Beoku Betts, Bankole-Bright, Tuboku Metzger, Baanah Davies, S. A. Hughes, T. J. Carew and Benka Coker.
85 *Ibid.*
86 *Ibid.*
87 I am grateful to Spitzer and Denzer for the use of their discussion of the Sierra Leone economic situation in the late 1930s as provided in their paper, 'I. T. A. Wallace Johnson and the West African Youth League, Part II: The Sierra Leone Period, 1938–1945', *International Journal of African Historical Studies*, vi, 4, 1973, pp. 565–601.
88 *Ibid.*
89 There does not seem to be any evidence that the *African Sentinel* was ever published in the Gold Coast as claimed in Spitzer and Denzer, 'I. T. A. Wallace Johnson and the West African Youth League' (the Gold Coast Section), p. 430. It is true, however, that in spite of its prohibition by the Colonial Office, copies of this journal secretly found their way into West Africa.
90 C.O.267/665/32208/1938. Wallace Johnson failed in his claim of £100 damages against W. H. Eccles, Comptroller of Customs, for unlawful detention of copies of his journal. C.O.267/666/32216, Governor Jardine to Malcolm MacDonald, Secretary of State for the Colonies, 28 November 1938.
91 *Sierra Leone Weekly News*, 30 April 1938; *West Africa*, 11 June 1938.
92 *Ibid.* 30 April 1938.

93 C.O.267/666/32216, C. Tregson Roberts, joint secretary, West African Civil Liberties and National Defence League, Sierra Leone, to Colonial Secretary, Sierra Leone, 12 May 1938.
94 *Ibid.*, Youth League to the Colonial Secretary, Freetown, 18 June 1938. Encl. in Sierra Leone secret despatch, 4 August 1938.
95 C.O.267/666/32218, Governor Jardine to MacDonald, 8 November 1938.
96 C.O.267/665/32208, Wallace Johnson's address, 28 April 1938.
97 *Ibid.*, secret report, 20 June 1938.
98 C.O.267/666/32216, memorandum of Youth League to Governor Jardine, 16 June 1938.
99 *Ibid.*, minute by O. G. R. Williams, 18 August 1938.
100 In September 1938, Jardine alleged that Wallace Johnson addressed his audience at Pepel 'to strike if they wished to strike'. C.O.267/655/32210. On 25 September 1938 as many as 10,000 workers demanded the immediate recall of Jardine. C.O.267/672/32254.
101 C.O.267/655/32157/1936, report of the Ag. Governor of Sierra Leone on the Congress movement in West Africa in the 1930s to W. G. A. Ormsby-Gore, 20 September 1936.
102 *Ibid.*
103 C.O.87/240/33010, 'Note on Petition From Citizens and Inhabitants of the Gambia to the House of Commons', 14 August 1934.
104 *Ibid.*, minute by Fletcher Cooke, 18 February 1935.
105 *Ibid.*, Sir Philip Cunliffe-Lister to J. A. Parkinson, M.P., undated.
106 *Nigerian Daily Telegraph*, 5 July 1935.
107 *Ibid.*, 21 September 1935.
108 E. O. Moore was born at Abeokuta in 1878. He was educated at the C.M.S. Grammar School in Lagos. In 1899 he went to England to continue his studies, and in 1902 was called to the bar. He returned to Lagos to practise law, and in 1917 he was nominated an Unofficial Member of the Legislative Council, and an elected member from 1923. A Macmillan, *The Red Book of West Africa*, London, 1920, p. 134.
109 For the view that Macaulay and his NNDP did not support the 'Hands Off Abyssinia' campaign in 1935, see Webster and Boahen, p. 311; Crowder, *West Africa under Colonial Rule*, p. 472. There is indeed no evidence that Macaulay personally participated in any of the agitations over the Ethiopian crisis. This is because Macaulay was usually luke-warm towards the pan-African cause. He concentrated rather on local politics – 'Lagos, the Eleko and the Legislative Council'. He was even opposed to Garveyism as contained in local police report. C.O.583/109/28194.
110 C.S.O.26/30468, Vol. 1, Nigerian National Archives, Ibadan.
111 For the text of the speech, see League of Nations, *Official Journal*, Speczl Supplement No. 138, Records of the 16th Ordinary Session of the Assembly, Plenary Meetings, Geneva, 1935, pp. 43–6.
112 C.S.O.26/30468, Vol. 1, Nigerian National Archives, Moore to Chief Secretary to the Government of Nigeria, 24 September 1935.
113 *Ibid.*, Nigerian despatch No. 723, Maybin to MacDonald, 27 September 1935.
114 *Nigerian Daily Telegraph*, 25 September 1935.
115 Awolowo, *Autobiography*, p. 82.
116 *Ibid.*, p. 84.
117 *Ibid.*, p. 82.
118 *Wallace Johnson Papers.*
119 Interview with E. C. Lartey, a foundation member of the Ex-Servicemen's Union, Accra, 9 May 1970. Born in 1890, E. C. Lartey, who has seen service in Israel, Egypt and India, is one of the oldest ex-soldiers still living.
120 J. B. Danquah told the Watson Commission in 1948 that he knew the 'existence of the Ex-Servicemen's Union some time in 1920, after the first World War'. *Proceedings*, Watson Commission, 1948, Ghana National Archives, Accra. Danquah and Koi Larbi, one-time judge of the Supreme Court, were the honorary legal advisers of the Union after 1946.
121 *The Ex-Service*, official organ – a fortnightly of the Union, 25 April 1947: 'A brief history of Ex-Servicemen's Union'. Two issues of this newspaper were discovered at the Cape Coast Regional Archives, ACC.599/64.
122 *Ibid.*
123 Interview, C. E. Lartey; also, C.S.O.1324/31, sub-file 9, Ghana National Archives, Accra.

124 Born in about 1913 at Elmina, Bankole Awoonor-Renner, whose father was Capt. Peter Awoonor-Renner from Sierra Leone, and mother was of Dutch ancestry, had his early education at Cape Coast and the Tuskegee Institute in America. From 1922–24, he served as Secretary of the African Students Union of America and was joint editor of the College Magazine from 1924–25. He was admitted into the Institute of Journalists in Great Britain in 1925, the first West African to attain this distinction; he also studied law in Britain. Renner, who openly considered himself a Bolshevik, attended the International Conference of Writers and Artists held in 1927 in Moscow where he studied at the Moscow Eastern University. On his return home in 1930, Renner edited the *Gold Coast Leader* from 1931–32 and also served as assistant editor of Danquah's *The Times of West Africa*. He was elected Councillor of the Accra Town Council from 1942 to 1944, and a member of the continuation Executive Committee of the GCYC. For further details se B. Awooner-Renner, *This Africa*, Watford, 1943.

125 C.O.96/731/31230, minute by H. F. Downie, 27 March 1936.

126 *Provincial Pioneer*, 14 December 1935.

127 *Wallace Johnson Papers*.

128 *Comet*, 23 September 1935.

129 *Ibid.*, 30 November 1935.

130 *Nigerian Daily Telegraph*, 10 December 1935.

131 *African Morning Post*, 9 May 1936.

132 C.O.96/732/31255, Encls. 1 and 3, Gold Coast No. 433, 24 July 1936.

133 C.O.583/109/28194, Conf. Memo. on UNIA in Lagos prepared by G. H. Walker, Deputy Inspector-General of Police, Southern Provinces, Lagos, 26 March 1922.

134 Peter Kilby, *African Enterprise: The Nigerian Bread Industry*, pp. 7–8.

135 C.S.O.26/30468, Vol. 1, Nigerian National Archives, Ibadan. For full text of the appeal, see *Comet*, 2 May 1936.

136 *Ibid.*, Whiteley to Bourdillon, 15 June 1936.

137 *Ibid.*, Whiteley to Mrs Shackleford, 19 June 1936. He added that the deputation should not exceed 6 in number, and on no account should any sort of procession or public demonstration be organised.

138 *Ibid.*, Prominent Lagos Women Society to Bourdillon, 24 June 1936.

139 *Ibid.*, Bourdillon to Ormsby-Gore, 26 June 1936.

140 *Ibid.*, Vol. II, Ormsby-Gore to Bourdillon, 8 July 1936.

141 *Ibid.*, Ormsby-Gore to Bourdillon, Nigeria No. 1036, 28 July 1936.

142 *Ibid.*, Whiteley to Mrs Shackleford, 21 August 1936.

143 *African Morning Post*, 14 May 1936.

144 The resolution is enclosed in F.O.371/20155.

145 An original copy of this resolution entitled, 'Gold Coast Ex-Servicemen's Union Will Not Fight For Europe', was discovered among the few papers of C. E. Lartey, Accra.

146 Conf. C.S.O.361/38, Ghana National Archives, Accra.

147 Parliamentary *Debates* 5s, House of Commons, 1938; also F.O.371/22397.

148 *Gold Coast Spectator*, 26 February 1938. For details about Eden's resignation, see Anthony Eden, *Facing the Dictators*, pp. 586–7.

149 Encl. in C.O.267/666/32216, 28 November 1938.

150 Azikiwe, *Renascent Africa*, p. 239.

151 *Sierra Leone Weekly News*, 24 August 1935.

152 ACC.70/64, *Aborigines Papers*.

CHAPTER FIVE

In defence of Ethiopia

Boycott and Volunteer Campaigns

As an expression of their indignation and resentment against the people of Italy, the militant groups among the Nigerian Youth Movement, Macaulay's National Democratic Party, and the West African Youth League in the Gold Coast advocated the boycotting of Italian merchandise in West Africa. The first indication of boycott action was given at a meeting of the staff of the Ijebu Muslim School in Western Nigeria. Four days after the Italian attack on Ethiopia, it was unanimously resolved by this school that, apart from prayer which in itself was a dynamic force, another way in which the people of Nigeria, and West Africa as a whole, could help Ethiopia was to boycott Italian goods, for:

> . . . the more Italian goods you buy the more money you put into the pockets of Italians and Benito Mussolini to buy their guns and ammunitions. . . . We should be quick to seize this weapon to defeat Mussolini in his ruthless programme by means of an intensive, relentless, intelligently, organised crusade against Italian merchandise. [1]

Boycotting Italian-made goods, therefore, became a popular subject for discussion both in the press and at the protest meetings organised by the nationalist movements in Nigeria and the Gold Coast respectively. Both the NYM and the Gold Coast WAYL appeared to believe that they would be fighting for the Ethiopians physically, morally and financially by means of boycott calculated to weaken the finances of Italy. In their opinion, patronising Italian goods in West Africa would be another way of replenishing Mussolini's exchequer. The boycott was also intended to make the Italian residents in West Africa economically insecure. It was with such objectives in mind that the youths in the Gold Coast, for example, persistently urged the government and the Unofficial Members of the Legislative Council to stop offering contracts to Italians as a protest against the belligerent action of their government in Ethiopia. They urged that Italian builders and contractors in the country be 'ostracised and boycotted'. Italians should not be employed, and should not be allowed to trade in cocoa, minerals or any other commodities within the jurisdiction of the Gold Coast. [2] The Youth League's campaign was supported by the Executive Council of the West African Youth Co-operative Association which had been established in 1931 'to bring the youths of West Africa together in the bond of comradeship and to help one another'. The Executive Council of this association comprised John Buckman, a surveyor (Chairman), A. J. Ocansey (Vice-Chairman), E. O. Asafo-Adjaye (Treasurer) and L. T. Hammond (Secretary). Other influential members included Richard Akwei and Mark Hansen.[3]

Evidently, the boycotting campaign was one of the emotional manifestations of the period for, to imagine that application of sanctions against Italian goods in West Africa could have an appreciable effect on Mussolini or compel him to loosen his grip on Ethiopia was to indulge in wishful thinking. Available evidence would point to the conclusion that not much trade was done between Italy and Colonial West Africa in the mid-thirties.[4] Nevertheless, the campaign was vigorously pursued, urging Italians in the Gold Coast to 'take their exit from the shores' of the country without 'violent measures being resorted to against them'. Some Italian residents responded to this by launching underground propaganda to explain the 'true' state of affairs between Italy and Ethiopia. On 20 April 1938, for example, the Chief Commissioner of Ashanti despatched to the Colonial Secretary in Accra four documents detailing Italian propaganda in the Gold Coast in relation to the Italo-Ethiopian dispute. These voluminous documents were discovered by the Acting District Commissioner of the Ashanti Akim District among the personal effects of G. E. Nessi, a deceased Italian contractor.[5] The hostile attitudes of the people of the Gold Coast towards the Italian residents in the country – particularly building contractors and those working on manganese ore at the Prestea mines – and the intensity of the agitation for the boycott of Italians in all fields of employment, coupled with the League of Nations' sanctions against Italy, compelled the Executive Council to discuss the matter at length at its meeting held on 2 December 1935. The Council considered the question whether any embargo should be laid on the grant of contracts for public works to Italian nationals. It was, however, finally decided that the government be advised not to make such a prohibition.[6]

On the whole, as would be expected, the West African agitation against Italian residents and Italian merchandise did not have any appreciable effect on the progress of the attack on the Ethiopians. It succeeded, only in some way, in embarrassing the local colonial administrators on the West Coast. This is evidenced in the confidential report of Miss Hebe Spaull of the League of Nations Union staff in Britain on her seven-week West African tour in July and August 1938. Giving her impressions on the tour, and on the fifty addresses which she gave to the nationalist groups in Nigeria and the Gold Coast, Miss Spaull concluded that: 'Naturally Abyssinia was the chief matter upon which I was heckled,' adding, 'and I was forcibly reminded on many occasions of what Sir Sidney Barton [the British legation in Ethiopia] had told the Executive Committee [of the League of Nations Union] about the effect of Abyssinia on Africa as a whole. . . .' She said that in both the Gold Coast Colony and Ashanti she was confronted with questions about the local government's continued engagement of Italian contractors.[7] On her return to London, Miss Spaull wrote to ask Sir Arnold Hodson, Governor of the Gold Coast, for an explanation of his government's attitude to this question of the Italian contractors.[8] George London, the Deputy Governor, wrote to explain that the Public Works Department in the Gold Coast had been employing contractors of Italian nationality for at least the previous twenty years. When the League of Nations imposed sanctions on Italy, the government instructed that no further contracts were to be granted to Italian nationals. However, this policy was found 'to be impossible of application, since Government had a very heavy programme of road work to complete and could call upon very few reliable contractors of other nationalities'. Furthermore, London contended that the Italians to whom contracts were granted during the sanction period were 'in no way connected with any companies incorporated in Italian territory, nor were they residents of Italy'. Despite the government's discovery of documents on Italian propaganda in the country, the Deputy Governor concluded that the Italians in the Gold Coast 'are regarded as trustworthy people and we have no reason to suspect them of undesirable activities'.[9] This telling of 'a one-sided story' in their official despatches, as Christopher Fyfe has rightly described it,[10] was not uncommon among colonial administrators during much of the period of the Italo-Ethiopian crisis.

Meanwhile, the boycotting of Italian merchandise and Italian nationals was accompanied by a more positive and practical expression of resentment which took the form of recruitment of volunteers to Ethiopia in defence of the African empire. The nationalist leaders firmly believed that the Emperor would welcome African volunteers; and so shortly after Mussolini's forces had crossed the frontiers of Ethiopia, groups of ex-servicemen in certain parts of West Africa staged rallies to recruit soldiers to defend the 'motherland'. The recruiting activities were more noticeable in the more advanced colonies of the Gold Coast and Nigeria than in those where groups of radical politicians had not yet emerged. In the Gambia, for example, there does not seem to be any evidence of recruiting activities. Although there was a branch of Harold Moody's League of Coloured Peoples in Bathurst, the members preferred organising lectures on the Ethiopian crisis rather than attempting a costly adventure to Ethiopia. Explaining the Sierra Leone situation, a correspondent who styled himself 'A Practical Youngman' stated, among other things, that the majority of his countrymen, because of their 'beautiful wives', their 'affectionate mothers' and their 'promising careers' found it extremely difficult to pack up and go to Ethiopia to fight 'as we should for the imprescriptible rights of man which Italy seems bent on violating'.[11] This, however, appears to be a hollow reason for the Sierra Leoneans' aloofness from volunteering for service in Ethiopia. It would seem that, as indicated elsewhere, it was not until Wallace Johnson established the Sierra Leone Section of his Youth League that the sense of African solidarity and pan-African consciousness in that colony became pronounced. The conservative Congress men who constituted the political leadership of the country were less interested in such radical pan-African ventures as recruiting volunteers for embattled Ethiopia.

In the Gold Coast, on the other hand, the first days of the invasion of Ethiopia stirred up such high feelings that many young men from Wallace Johnson's Youth League, the Ex-Servicemen's Union and the labour organisations came up in favour of forming a regiment and proceedings to fight for Ethiopia, for the 'triumph of Abyssinia is the triumph of Africa'.[12] In Accra, the house of the editor of the Gold Coast Spectator, R. B. Wuta Ofei, was reportedly besieged by war enthusiasts when the news of the 'outrageous and cowardly attack of Italy on Ethiopia flashed out on Thursday, 4 October 1935'. Enquiries, including those from schoolboys and illiterates, lorry drivers and mine-workers, were made about enlistment in the Ethiopian forces amid traditional 'Asafo' war songs. Three schoolboys from the Volta District came to see Wuta Ofei with a letter stating, 'We beg to go by all means, and so do not forget us during the time. . . . If you have any form concerning it [enlistment] you may please send it to us for our signatures. . . .'[13]

The recruitment of volunteers to fight in Ethiopia was thoroughly discussed at the second mass meeting of the WAYL and the Ex-Servicemen's Union held at the Palladium in Accra on 9 October 1935. Sergeant Major J. Q. Allotey, a veteran, and member of an Ethiopia Defence Committee, disclosed at this meeting that 500 persons had applied in Accra for enrolment for the Ethiopian war.[14] This was confirmed by Prince Mohamed Eket in a passionate address in which he related his experiences in the British Navy, and also declared his preparedness, in spite of his advanced age, to fight and die for Ethiopia.[15] An ex-police Royal Navy and ex-police officer, Prince Eket who was then resident in the Gold Coast, was once a member of the Nsit Council and Native Authority in the Eket district of Calabar, Nigeria. Those who spoke at the meeting in support of the issue of recruitment of volunteers included Wallace Johnson, B. E. A. Tamakloe, R. T. Dodoo and Bishop Victor Pratt. The meeting ended with a resolution which stated that the government be approached and acquainted with the intention of those prepared to leave for Ethiopia. The government was also asked to grant permission for the drilling of the would-be volunteers in certain parts of the country.[16]

It is worth stating that the expression of readiness to fight in Ethiopia was not confined to Accra. It was almost a country-wide affair, for the branches of the Ex-Servicemen's Union and the Youth League in the provinces and districts also took up the issue seriously. Many declared, especially the veterans among them, that if no barriers were placed in the way of their obtaining arms, then they would readily fight for the cause in Ethiopia as cheerfully as they did when, over twenty years earlier, the safety and the independence of Belgium and France were threatened by Germany. It was with such a determined posture that the Youth League branch in the Keta District of the former British Togoland wrote to Wuta Ofei, declaring, 'We want to know the time of enrolment as auxiliaries in the Abyssinian war with Italy. We want to shed our blood for our suffering brothers of our dear Africa. Yes, we are ready. We will fight and die on the battlefield'.[17] Similarly, in the historic town of Cape Coast, Azikiwe reported at this time that the youth had become politically and racially conscious to a remarkable degree, judging from the effect which regular news of the Italo-Ethiopian conflict seemed to have taken on them. All over the town, in every nook and corner, he said, young people were to be seen together in groups of different sizes lamenting on what they considered 'the sorrowful plight of our brothers far away in Abyssinia'. Many of the young men began to explore the possibilities and prospects of enlistment for the Ethiopian army. He concluded that they were ready to spill their blood, if necessary, for the freedom of Africa.[18]

But it was in the Ashanti Province of the Gold Coast that this expression of readiness to fight in Ethiopia was said to be most vigorous, positive and practical. The Ashantis generally believed that there was a kind of 'kinship' between them and the Ethiopians, and that they could detect some common superstitions, customs and arts existing between themselves, Egypt, and Ethiopia. Furthermore, it was held that migration took place at one time when the Ethiopians settled in ancient Ghana of which Ashanti was a part. Besides, both the *Comet* and the *Morning Post*, either by design or accident, devoted a series in their respective editorials at various dates in early 1935 to this nineteenth-century thesis of T. E. Bowdich on the cultural and historical connection between Egypt, Ethiopia, and the Ashantis.[19] Perhaps it was against this remote background of Ashanti beliefs, together with their past history as warriors of the Gold Coast, that the intensive preparation for war in Ethiopia in this province can be understood. From this territory came the news that an 'Ashanti Abyssinian Expedition' force had been organised by a captain Kofi Kyei. Kyei was an Ashanti warrior and a veteran of the First World War, who, although illiterate, was captain of his native militia. The 'Ashanti Abyssinia Expedition' force, which reportedly consisted of 250 men, was composed of highly trained Ashanti warriors and fighters, some of whom had served in World War I with the British.[20] Although the activities of Captain Kyei and his expedition force received wide coverage in the foreign press,[21] there is no evidence as to how far the would-be volunteers trained and prepared themselves for war in Ethiopia.

Similarly, although a number of West Africans declared their preparedness at enthusiastic public meetings to sail to Ethiopia 'at a moment's notice', it is difficult to conclude that they were actually ready to implement their objective. Moreover, the fact of their being British subjects would have made such an expedition legally impossible. This was made evident in Nigeria when an ex-serviceman, E. C. Badger of Catholic Street, Onitsha, Eastern Nigeria, applied to the Chief Secretary in Lagos on 5 October 1935, for permission to 'volunteer myself as a soldier and fight on behalf of the Ethiopians'.[22] Badger was to lead a group of Eastern Nigerian ex-servicemen to Ethiopia. Quite apart from the embarrassment which the West African volunteer campaigns caused the colonial governments, there were also the legal implications, for which in Nigeria the Chief Secretary sought the advice of the Attorney-General, as to the legal position of British protected persons who wanted to enlist in the Ethiopian Army.[23]

To combat this development, the British Protectorates Order-in-Council of 1904, the provisions of which were similar to those of the Foreign Enlistment Act of 1870, was invoked.[24] The Act forbade British subjects and 'natives' of a British Protectorate to join forces of countries – in this case, Italy and Ethiopia – which maintained friendly relations with Britain. Accordingly, West Africans were informed that their applications could not be entertained.[25] This was reinforced by a Foreign Office circular marked 'Pressing', signed by Robert Vansittart on behalf of the British Foreign Secretary, Sir Samuel Hoare, addressed to British Consul Officers authorised to issue or renew passports. This was a clear and positive attempt on the part of the British Government to prevent persons desiring to proceed to Ethiopia or seeking employment in a military capacity in that country, from getting their passports issued or endorsed.[26] The circular further stated that persons seeking employment in other capacities apart from military might be granted facilities provided a deposit of £50 was paid to cover the possible necessity for repatriation. Facilities were to be refused to all women except nurses belonging to an organised 'nursing unit or regularly engaged to join one'. The fact that a woman followed the profession of journalist should not be regarded as a ground for ignoring this ruling. There should be no objection to the grant of facilities to male journalists whose bona fides was not in doubt.[27]

Despite these restrictions, a Nigerian in the former Turkish army, Mohamed Tarig Bey, who was at Port Said at the time of the crisis, left for Ethiopia, and was offered the command of Ethiopian troops against the invading Italians in one of the fronts by the Emperor of Ethiopia. He left Port Said on 2 November 1935 for Djubouti en route to Addis Ababa to respond to an invitation which he looked upon as a call to duty.[28] Tarig Bey had served during the First World War with distinction in the Turkish army, attaining the rank of major and being awarded numerous distinctions for bravery.[29]

From the available evidence it is not clear whether the West African volunteers could really have found adequate financial resources to enable them sail to far-away Ethiopia to put their 'noble object' into practical expression. From what can be determined from the various sources about the impact of the economic depression on the people one is inclined to a conclusion that, like many of the passionate endeavours characteristic of the period, the cries about volunteering to Ethiopia would appear to have been more of an emotional gesture than anything else. Mohamed Tarig Bey was able to reach Ethiopia only because he was resident at Port Said within measurable distance from that country. Company Sergeant-Major Lartey who was himself to lead the Accra contingent of volunteers, has confirmed that the problems in the way of volunteering to Ethiopia were immense. No financial assistance could come from either the Ethiopian Government or the imperial power in Britain. Efforts made to communicate 'our plans and objects' to Emperor Haile Selassie proved to be of no avail.

Secondly, the ex-soldiers who offered to volunteer to Ethiopia were seriously concerned about the general aloofness of the local colonial government from the whole exercise. The suspicion of the government of 'our motives' had been aroused by the fact that the volunteer campaigns and its ramifications were accompanied by blatant appeals to race consciousness and, more significantly, by the solid support of 'our programme' by radical nationalists like Wallace Johnson, Kobina Sekyi, Wuta Ofei and Awonoor-Renner who were known as 'link subversives' and anti-European extremists. All this discouraged not a few would-be volunteers.[30] That the whole matter did not advance beyond the stage of proclaimed intention is also substantiated by the lack of evidence of definite agency set up within the Youth League or Ex-Servicemen's Union circles designed to co-ordinate or plan the activities for that purpose. The vounteering 'fever heat', although it was almost a country-wide affair, and received much encouragement from such organisations as the West African Youth Co-operative Association, the Cape Coast clique of the Aborigines' Society, the Motor Drivers' Union and the Carpenters' Union, was, in the circumstances of the time, an impossible idea. Nevertheless, it was a concrete demonstration of the feelings of the pan-African-conscious West Africans about the Italo-Ethiopian question. Thirty years later in 1965, in another bid to pursue a pan-African cause, Ghanaian soldiers and volunteers were to repeat this type of demonstration when Ian Smith of Rhodesia announced the 'Unilateral Declaration of Independence'.[31]

Prayers and Relief Funds

The campaign for recruitment of volunteers went side by side with the organisation of a series of mass prayers for Ethiopia. Many churchmen in West Africa took a great interest in the developing war situation and occasionally warned against the rising tide of hostility between the black and white races. Special religious services were held in many parts of West Africa to enable the people to offer their prayerful support for Ethiopia in her hour of need. Some churches remained open all night, and pedestrians entered, kneeled, and prayed for the safety of Ethiopia. Pamphlets and handbooks containing prayers for the Emperor and his people were freely distributed to the people, and these were made a regular part of the service. It would seem that, in this aspect of the West African reaction to the Ethiopian crisis, so far as it can be gleaned from the available evidence, Sierra Leone excelled her sister colonies. For it was in this colony that church services on a national scale were particularly in evidence.

The United Christian Council and the All-Muslim Congress of Sierra Leone were quick and vigorous in their response to the appeal of the Archbishop of Canterbury and the Moderator of the Federation of Evangelical Free Churches for universal prayer in respect of the 'historic' meeting of the eighty-eighth session of the Council of the League of Nations scheduled for 4 September 1935. The 'fateful' meeting was to undertake a general examination of all aspects of the Italo-Ethiopian relations and to take a final decision under Article 15 of the League Covenant. Already in England daily prayers had begun in Westminster Abbey on 24 August for the holy guidance of British statesmen during the crisis. The *Sierra Leone Daily Guardian* counselled that the United Christian Council and the Muslim Congress should offer a fervent prayer not only on Sunday, 1 September 1935, as contained in the Archbishop's appeal, but also during the whole of September 'so that in case of failure by the League to do anything effective to avert war, by our ceaseless prayer, other causes might intervene to save the world from unnecessary bloodshed'.[32]

It was in the light of this that the following special prayer was prepared in Freetown for use in all the West African Methodist Churches both in the morning and the evening on 1 September and at other times during the crisis between Italy and Ethiopia:

> Almighty God . . . With troubled hearts we bring before thee the crisis which has arisen between Italy and Abyssinia, and the situation which is becoming acute every day, and the threatening dangers which have filled us with fear and anxiety. We implore Thy gracious help in connection with the efforts of the Council of the League of Nations meeting on Wednesday next. Thou, O God our Lord, alone givest wisdom and understanding, inspire we pray Thee, the minds of all who shall take part in the work of the Council. Give to them Thy Divine guidance, also the vision of truth and justice, that by their counsels they may arrive at a wise and just settlement of the dispute between the two nations, and so avert this threatening war.[33]

Other prayers were specially prepared to inspire the Emperor Haile Selassie and to give him 'the same wisdom and understanding' as God gave to Solomon his ancestor. 'The King of Kings' should be given sufficient strength to enable him to bring about the speedy 'redemption of all Africa'– and the whole black world. Added to this was the special religious service organised by the Ethiopia Relief Fund Committee in Freetown on Sunday, 12 January 1936, at the Holy Trinity Church. This service was 'well attended and fully representative of the citizens of Freetown' under whose direction the Committee was functioning. As would be expected, the choir repeatedly chanted the oft-quoted 68th Psalm – 'Ethiopia shall Rise . . .,' and the sermon was delivered by the Ven. Archdeacon T. S. Johnson, M.A., B.D.[34]

But the most powerful and the most inspiring and thought-provoking sermon delivered for Ethiopia during the period of the crisis was the one from the Samaria Church of Freetown entitled, 'Jehovah and Mussolini' by the Rev. G. O. Gabbidon, a West African Methodist preacher. This sermon was delivered in two parts, the first on the 22 September and the second on 20 October 1935. Gabbidon, a race-conscious reverend minister and pan-Africanist, was an enthusiastic follower of Wallace Johnson and his West African Youth League in Sierra Leone. In January 1939 he wrote to explain that he was a 'Comrade' of the Youth League, because he believed in the sincerity of Wallace Johnson and the 'great indescribable possibilities of the Youth League in Sierra Leone', and also, because, 'I can associate myself with Comrade Johnson, whom God has appointed and chosen as our modern Moses'.[35] Like the Rev. Orishatuke Faduma of Chief Alfred Sam's 'Back to Africa' movement of 1914–15,[36] Gabbidon was the ideologue and prophet of Wallace Johnson's Youth League in Sierra Leone.

The text of Gabbidon's widely publicised sermon was apt and revealing: 'Look not upon me because I am black, because the sun has looked upon me . . . they made me the keeper of the vineyards; but mine own vineyard have I not kept.'[37] After expatiating on this theme, Rev. Gabbidon told his crowded congregation that Mussolini was reckoning without God and prophetically declared that 'God's judgement must come however long delayed'. He recalled that at the commencement of the First World War, the Kaiser Wilhelm II of Germany entertained ideals of possible world conquest. To achieve this end, Germans used brute force in Belgium and at other places. But what was the result of all that?

> Brethren, nations like men were made not for unholy competition, but to work together – because God is always on the side of righteousness, and because He has created all men and determined the bonds of their habitation with peculiar and suitable climates. He will answer the world-wide prayers that have been and are being offered for Abyssinia everywhere and will fight their battles, plead their cause. . . . Jehovah must declare to Mussolini and his wonderful cabinet: 'Thus far shalt thou go and no further.'[38]

Until the white man acknowledged the rights of weaker nations, and realised that 'God hath made of one blood all nations of men' there never could be peace on earth. He assured his audience that the black man would sooner or later tell his anxious white brother that he had a just right to 'live in God's universe as himself'. Like Casely Hayford, Gabbidon felt that it would be through the 'blameless Ethiopians' that Africa, East, West, North, and South would be emancipated and freed from persecution forever. The inspiring idea of the future independence of African countries ran through the two sermons he gave in September and October.

On the question of colour, the Rev. Gabbidon argued that the colour of a man's skin did not matter. What counted was unity and co-operation and possible achievement. He advised Sierra Leoneans, and in effect Africans all over the world, to eschew hypocrisy and treachery and begin, as never before, to develop the 'art of mutual love, honour, and respect for your own colour'. After tracing the ancient history and civilisation of Ethiopia, the minister dwelt at length on his anti-imperialist feelings. The black man's destiny, he said, was certainly not to be 'server for ever'. Gabbidon recounted some recent happenings in the world which to him were 'demonstrative proofs' of the great achievements of Negroes everywhere. Furthermore, he expressed the confidence that when the black man came to himself, or, in other words, attained independence, he would be able to take charge of 'his own vineyard' without any European supervision.[39] In support of such themes, the Rev. Gabbidon occasionally cited extracts from *Christianity, Islam and the Negro Race*, the *magnum opus* of Edward Blyden, the 'Pan-Negro Patriot'. To him, the Ethiopian crisis was the Negroes' greatest opportunity and the start of a revolution in racial and world affairs. Africans should therefore grasp firmly 'this opportunity with both hands and make as much use of it as possible'.[40]

These two great sermons of the Rev. G. O. Gabbidon were indeed the most comprehensive and lucid exposition of the impact of the Ethiopian crisis on West Africans, and were also one of the most convincing and persuasive appeals ever made for supporting the Ethiopian Relief Fund Committees which were set up in many parts of West Africa. It should be pointed out, however, that the two sermons were not strikingly original in their conception of the capabilities and the future of the black man. They were to a large extent a repetition of the inspiring words of such early West African nationalist preachers and pan-Africanists as Bishop James Johnson, Mojola Agbebi, Orishatukeh Faduma, Casely Hayford and Edward Blyden. However, Gabbidon's frequent references to, and criticism of, imperialism and colonialism, as well as his call for an urgent need for African independence, must have greatly gladdened the hearts of the anti-colonial nationalists at the time of the Italo-Ethiopian conflict. Above all, his evident belief in the efficacy of prayer was significant. In his opinion, it was prayer that would rescue the Ethiopians in particular and Africans in general from the oppression and exploitation of the white man. On the whole, the two sermons, which were entitled 'Jehovah and Mussolini', stand out distinctly as an interesting piece of work reminiscent of Mojola Agbebi's oft-quoted *Inaugural Sermon* of 1902.

Similar sermons were delivered in the Gold Coast and Nigeria. In the former colony a 'prayer circle' was established in some of the churches in the provincial and district capitals. In Accra, the activities of the circle included regular prayers for the people of Ethiopia, and singing in praise of the role of Ethiopia in the history of the black race.[41] The daily prayer entitled, 'The Blackman is the Alpha and Omega of the World: Africa for Africans at Home and Abroad' called on the Almighty God to 'cause all enemies to be rooted and flee from our Fatherland Ethiopia'.[42] In Nigeria, also, one minute 'universal silent prayer' was observed for the peace of Ethiopia at every signal of the 'Apapa gun' at midday.[43] There is, however, no evidence as to whether this was strictly observed, as repeatedly pressed for by C. Olayemi Blaize ot Lagos. On the whole it would appear that the church services devoted to Ethiopia reached a far wider section of the populace, notably women and school children, than did press or political rallies. For one thing most of the services, particularly those in the villages, were conducted in the vernacular. Secondly, the services were usually accompanied by a procession of singing bands, choristers or bands playing musical instruments.

Organisation of mass prayer was not the only practical demonstration of the anxiety of the articulate nationalist politicians to defend the Ethiopian cause in West Africa. In order to add their quota towards the preservation of the sole African empire, the political movements, as well as a number of benevolent societies, established Ethiopia Relief Fund Committees at various centres in West Africa with a view to helping Ethiopians to acquire proper means of defending themselves and of fighting on equal terms with their 'fully armed and condemned aggressor'. As will be seen, although the nationalist leaders and their radical newspapers made serious efforts in their campaigns and propaganda for funds for Ethiopia, the achievement was, on average, sadly below expectation. Nonetheless, the political organisations would appear to have created the impression that their efforts were matched by some positive achievements. In this section, as in the previous ones, our interest should perhaps be more on the efforts made than on results achieved.

In Sierra Leone, the question of an Ethiopia Relief Fund became a serious preoccupation of both the distinguished politicians of the colony – the African Elected Members of the Legislative Council – and the militant anti-colonialists headed by C. D. Hotobah During. Before the Elected Members met in October to think about the problems of Ethiopia Relief Fund, Hotobah During's radical group had already formed an Abyssinia Relief Fund Committee which the established politicians criticised as being unconstitutional and stigmatised as a 'Self Appointed Committee', in view of the fact that the elected representatives of the people had not been consulted or informed of its existence.[44] Nevertheless, this appeared to be a more serious body than the organisation which was later set up by the Elected Members for the purpose of raising funds for Ethiopia. During's Abyssinia Relief Fund Committee organised dances and many forms of entertainment in aid of Ethiopia both in Freetown and principal towns and villages in the Colony and Protectorate. The Committee members who designated themselves as a 'Committee of Gentlemen', included C. D. Hotobah During (Secretary), E. H. Cummings (Treasurer), Councillor Dr I. C. Pratt (President of the Sierra Leone Railway Workers' Union), Boisy Davies (President of Carpenters' Defensive Union), Councillors Eleady Cole and M. M. Frazer.[45] These were among the nationalist politicians who had lost interest in the National Congress, and were therefore opposed to what the local branch stood for. When Wallace Johnson established the Sierra Leone Section of the Youth League in April 1938, most of the members of the Committee of Gentlemen, led by Hotobah During, joined forces with the League to oppose both the old leadership which composed the Congress, and the local colonial administration.

As indicated above, the problem of the Ethiopia Relief Fund was also taken up by the conservative African Elected Members of the Legislative Council. On 18 October 1935, a great mass meeting, attended by representatives of all sections of the colony and protectorate, was convened in Freetown for a discussion of 'ways and means of assisting our Abyssinian brothers in their hour of need'.[46] The chairman of the meeting was H. C. Bankole-Bright, the Vice-President of the local branch of NCBWA. Bankole-Bright said that the meeting had been called because the Elected Members, as leaders duly appointed by the people, felt called upon to do something to aid Ethiopia, and the 'object of the meeting was for us to give them a mandate to act for and on our behalf'. This was followed by an address by another elected member, E. S. Beoku Betts, also a Congress man, who traced the history of the Italo-Ethiopian dispute and showed how Sierra Leoneans were connected with Ethiopia.

One interesting aspect of Beoku Betts's address which throws light on the ignorance or immaturity of thought among some of the established conservative leaders in West Africa at the time was his detailed reference to the public speeches of South African leaders on the Italo-Ethiopian dispute which he seemed to think were in support of the African stand on the Ethiopian question. Betts recalled, for example, the statement of General Smuts that if Italy attacked Ethiopia serious repercussions would result in black Africa. The Elected Members did not appear to appreciate the real motive behind such statements of South African leaders who were mainly concerned with the fate of the minority white government of the Union, in the event of a general uprising of the black peoples in their country in response to the Italian aggression in Ethiopia. Throughout, the considerations influencing South African reaction to the Ethiopian crisis – her vehement condemnation of the Hoare-Laval pact of December 1935[47] and her uncompromising stand on the question of sanctions against Italy – were quite different from those we have noted in the case of West Africa. For to the leaders of the Union the Italo-Ethiopian conflict was an issue which involved South Africa's own national security and political stability. Both General Smuts and te Water, the Union High Commissioner in London, were of the opinion that if Italy was allowed to conquer and own Ethiopia she would of necessity proceed to follow the French example and militarise the whole population. The same policy would then be forced on governments to the south, till in no great time the whole population of Africa would be trained and accustomed to modern methods of warfare. This militarisation of Africa would, in their view, deal a direct and fatal blow to South African interests.[48]

The less informed nationalist groups in Sierra Leone, on the other hand, took the forthright policy pursued by South Africa in relation to the Ethiopian crisis at its face value. Thinking that South African reaction was motivated by the same racial feeling, the Sierra Leone leaders showered praises on the public speeches of the Union's leaders on the Italo-Ethiopian question. For example, the courageous stand of te Water on the maintenance of sanctions was welcomed in Sierra Leone as having given 'a pleasant surprise to Africans and their friends'. It was described as 'honest and vigorous support of continued sanctions against Italy'.[49] Te Water's speeches at the League of Nations had revealed that South African 'whites are not the Negro-haters they are painted', for they had given evidence that they 'possess larger minds and a higher sense of rectitude than was disclosed by Great Britain' and other dominion countries.[50] It was even argued that if the public tone in South Africa was so healthy, black people within the Union 'need have no fears for their future lot; and those of the neighbouring Protectorates would be well advised not to resist incorporation'.[51]

After this appreciation of South Africa's reaction to the conflict, the Elected Members resolved 'That in order to demonstrate their practical sympathy with the cause of Abyssinia, funds be raised locally to assist Red Cross work in Abyssinia'.[52] They subsequently appointed a body known as the 'People's Committee' to be responsible for finding ways and means of raising funds for Ethiopia. The committee comprised the three elected members (H. C. Bankole-Bright, E. G. Beoku Betts, J. G. Hyde), two ex-Mayors (S. J. S. Barlatt and T. J. Thompson), A. E. Tuboku-Metzger, Canon R. S. Kawaley, the Reverends W. B. Marke and J. B. Nicholas, S. Benka Coker, A. Lisk Carew, Councillor A. F. Renner-Dove, the Imams of Fourah Bay and Fourah Town, Alfred Cole, S. Adole Hughes, C. Dunstan-Williams, Mrs Beoku Betts, Mrs J. G. Hyde, Mrs A. C. May, Mrs W. Ojumiri Bright Taylor, Mrs S. Benka Coker and Miss Edna Elliot. It will be observed that most of the committee members were among the officers of the conservative local branch of the NCBWA and, as usual with the attitudes of the Creole elite, the programme drawn up for raising funds was confined to Freetown. Although the ladies' branch of the Congress and other female societies in Freetown staged plays and fetes in an effort to raise funds, the result was hardly substantial, despite the claims of the press.[53]

On the whole, compared with those in Nigeria and the Gold Coast, the results of the campaigns for raising funds in Sierra Leone were disappointingly limited. The reason for this, according to Hotobah During, was that the Paramount Chiefs whose strategic location as tax collectors, coupled with their strong appeal as the 'fathers of their people', enabled them to tap a substantial share of the cash which flowed in an increasing stream into the protectorate, were not educated enough about the Ethiopian question. The effort made by the Committee of Gentlemen to involve them in the campaign for funds was only a partial success. In the Colony, too, the Creole elite, who expressed concern about the plight of 'the Ethiopians, were not too prepared to part freely with donations and subscriptions of this type'.[54] As confirmed by Henry Moore, the Governor of Sierra Leone, the local Creole was always much more 'ready to open his mouth than his purse, and I am informed that the response for public subscriptions (for Ethiopia) has been disappointing'.[55]

Similarly in the Gambia, the approach to the problems of the Ethiopia Relief Fund was perfunctory and unimpressive. Although after the failure of the 1934 petition to the House of Commons, a number of aggrieved radical Gambians identified their position with that of the oppressed Ethiopians, they were too poor to subscribe lavishly to the relief fund appeal. Also, such influential politicians as Sir Samuel T. Forster or Dr Tom Bishop held themselves aloof from the fund raising campaigns in the country. Consequently, the only Abyssinia Red Cross Fund committee, which was established with Councillor H. Darlington Carrol as honorary treasurer had by February 1936 collected only a meagre sum of £11 16s. 4d.[56] A highly incensed and pan-African conscious correspondent to the *Gambia Outlook and Senegambian Reporter* who wrote under the pseudonym 'Candidus', described in detail the disappointing attitude of his countrymen to the Ethiopia Relief Fund in an article headed 'Abyssinia and We':

> Many do not seem to realise their obligation to Abyssinia in this her hour of crisis; they are not proving themselves worthy of the example of leading in all parts of the civilized world. Excitement to support the Abyssinian forces financially and otherwise is rife in the three West African Colonies, and almost everywhere that African races are to be found pan-Africanism, or African race-consciousness is remarkably pronounced even in South Africa, where Africans boycott Italian trade. . . . It seems to be the idea of some that the Abyssinia crisis does not concern us. I even understand that collectors of the Fund have been confronted with the suggestion that the money being collected for Abyssinia could be given to the poor. I wonder if those who think so really care for the poor. They subscribe liberally to Earl Haig's Fund and they do well. But should not their charity begin at home?[57]

On the other hand, the business of raising funds for the Ethiopian cause was in the advanced colonies of Nigeria and the Gold Coast more than a national affair. It was tackled with all the seriousness that the Ethiopian question deserved. Elaborate and special programmes were drawn up and numerous fund-raising activities were organised. Like Sierra Leone, the Elected Members of the Legislative Council were involved in the Ethiopia Relief Fund campaigns. But, whereas the nationalist newspapers in Sierra Leone and the Gambia contented themselves with the reporting of the events connected with the Ethiopia Relief Fund movement, those in Nigeria and the Gold Coast actually participated in the fund-raising campaigns; they set up their own Ethiopia relief fund committees and took a lively interest in the movement as a whole.

The first Ethiopia Relief Fund Committee in Nigeria was established in Lagos in September 1935 by some leading figures of the NYM, including J. C. Vaughan, Ernest Ikoli, and E. O. Moore of NNDP. It was formally inaugurated as the Lagos Ethiopia Defence Committee at a mass meeting at the Glover Memorial Hall on 10 December 1935. The organisers declared 14 December as 'Ethiopia Day'. Collection boxes were hung up at a number of prominent centres in towns and villages where people could drop in their pennies or shillings. In addition, ladies went round with collection boxes. Advertisements such as the following were boldly printed many times in the local press:

ETHIOPIA DEFENCE FUND

SONS OF AFRICA

SHOW YOUR LOVE OF RACE

NOT BY TALK BUT BY ACTION

Ethiopia is engaged today in a mighty struggle the result of which may mean a turning-point in the history of Black Race. Your Help is needed in this Hour of Trial. Send Your Quota However Small to the DEFENCE FUND.[58]

Branch centres of the Lagos Ethiopia Defence Committee were set up in ten important towns in different parts of Nigeria to work in conjunction with the central committee in Lagos. Among the most important branches where the fund-raising appeal received greater response were those at Ibadan, Ife, Abeokuta, Jos and Kano. By May 1936 the parent body at Lagos had received £54 10s. 6d. from the Ife branch, £60 5s. 0d. from Kano, £111 from Ibadan, £30 from Jos, and £25 from Oshogo. The parent body at Lagos bagged a little over £200, excluding a special donation of £50 from a Lagos businessman, J. Aleshinloye Williams.[59] The Ebute Meta branch had A. S. Wynter Shackleford, the one-time president of the Lagos branch of Garvey's Universal Negro Improvement Association, as its chairman. By May 1936, this branch had collected an amount of £42.[60] In the same month the Benin Provincial committee for the Relief of Ethiopia also paid in £10 to the relief fund headquarters at Lagos.[61]

The women section of the Lagos Ethiopia Defence Committee was known as the Save Abyssinia Society under the inspiration and leadership of the indomitable Mrs G. S. Wynter Shackleford. It was one of the most colourful Ethiopia relief fund committees set up at the time. The leaders of the society moved about market places, commercial houses and government departments soliciting aid for Ethiopia amidst traditional dancing and drumming. In May 1936, the leader of the society, Mrs Shackleford, made the following moving appeal in the name of the Empress of Ethiopia:

Lift up your heads with pride oh men of my race. Think of your past deeds and valour – the American Civil War, the Boer War, the recent War of 1914–18 for England and France . . . Brothers! Men of Africa, you have bled and died for others . . . Yes, but all we ask is not this extreme test – We ask

J. Casely Hayford

Marcus Garvey

T. Ras Makonnen

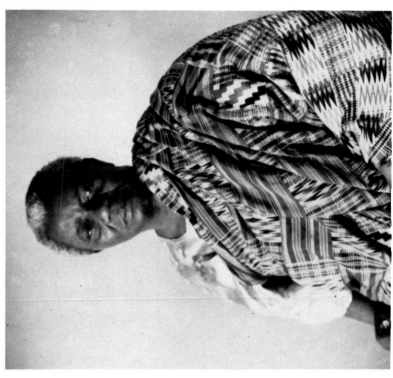

J. B. Danquah

for your MORAL AND FINANCIAL SUPPORT. These can reach us much easier than yourselves. SEND HELP SPEEDILY. . . . Give and Give and Give! even as you did in the World War. Give us some encouragement. We die not for ourselves alone but for you too. You who have fought, bled, and died for OTHERS.

This touching appeal, which was to a large extent a reproduction of the Empress's own appeal to the 'Mothers of the World', also described how innocent women and children in Ethiopia were being mercilessly 'slaughtered by bombs and poison gas – unrecognizable, maimed, and blind'. It recalled the activities of Italian women in support of the Italian warriors in Ethiopia and invited the women of Africa to do the same for the beleaguered people of Ethiopia.[62]

After this widely publicised appeal, Mrs Shackleford led the women in Lagos and the neighbouring towns in organising concerts, dances, fetes and carnivals to raise funds. Once more she approached the Lagos colonial administrators for their co-operation. In an exclusive interview, Mrs Shackleford requested G. C. Whiteley, the Acting Chief Secretary to the Nigerian Government, to 'relax the order prohibiting room to room' collection of Ethiopia funds in government offices. Furthermore, in order to popularise the Ethiopia fund committees in Nigeria, she passionately appealed to Whiteley to 'assist her and the movement by becoming a member of the Save Abyssinia Society' or by presiding at some meeting or other money raising function. Alternatively, Whiteley could make a donation to her fund. [63]The Acting Chief Secretary later confessed that he was persuaded to make 'a strictly anonymous donation'.[64] By the end of 1936, the Save Abyssinia Society had collected a little over one hundred guineas.

Other Ethiopia relief fund committees, which were not connected with the Lagos Committee, were established in some of the provincial capitals of Nigeria. The most important among these was the Enugu Ethiopia Relief Fund Committee under the chairmanship of Colonel Grimes of the Salvation Army, assisted by E. O. Wey, an ex-serviceman, A. Alakija (later Sir Adeyemo Alakija) of Macaulay's NNDP, also an Unofficial Member of the Legislative Council (1933–41), and S. Bentum-Obrigya, Secretary of the Committee. Tribal unions in Eastern Nigeria such as the Ogidi Tribal Union, the Bende District and the Owerri Union Society, became associate members of the Enugu Ethiopia Relief Fund Committee. In May 1936, an amount of £15, which was collected solely from government departments on the day the committee was launched, was remitted to the Ethiopia Minister in London 'for transmission to Abyssinia as the Enugu first series of instalments'.[65] Dr Martin acknowledged receipt of this amount, adding that he highly appreciated 'the kindness of you and your Committee in sending us a donation of £15 (fifteen pounds) subscribed in the town of Enugu towards assisting our suffering people'.[66]

One of the most successful fund-raising committees that sprung up in Nigeria at this time was the 'Comet Abyssinia Relief Fund' under the management of Duse Mohamed Ali. In April 1936, Duse Mohamed Ali received on behalf of the *Comet* a strong and urgent appeal for help from the Ethiopian Minister in London. This was a copy of Dr Martin's special 'Abyssinia Appeal' of March 1936 already circulated throughout Great Britain and Ireland. Its purpose was to raise a 'Private Loan' in order to 'enable us to purchase urgently needed equipments to resist the Aggressor'.[67] In a covering letter to the original appeal, Dr Martin urged Duse Mohamed Ali to 'kindly have the appeal published in the local papers, with necessary alterations, in order to give your readers an opportunity of kindly helping in the matter'. He further requested the *Comet* editor to 'prepare the people to protest strongly' against any unjust peace terms that might be imposed on Ethiopia. The Ethiopian Minister took the opportunity to thank Duse Mohamed Ali for the practical help given 'to my distressed country' and hoped that the editor would be successful in this matter of raising a private loan. [68] Dr Martin's letter to Duse Mohamed Ali is a clear indication of Ethiopia's appreciation of West African contribution to the defence of the beleaguered country. It was also indicative of the significance of West African protest against the Italian attack on Ethiopia. Such protest demonstrations by colonial subjects might bring pressure to bear on the imperial powers to take a much more serious view of the Ethiopian question. The general tone of Dr Martin's letter shows his firm belief in the potency and effectiveness of world public opinion, not least that of the African world.

Encouraged by Dr Martin's note, the *Comet* quickly published the full and original text of the special 'Abyssinia Appeal'. Commenting lucidly on the 'Appeal', the pan-Africanist *Comet* editor urged Africans all over the world to contribute lavishly to it. In his opinion, this was primarily the business of Africans. For 'our honour's sake we have no right to expect others to perform a work which is really ours'. It was high time the indigenes of the continent of Africa awoke from their lethargy in order to demonstrate their practical sympathy with their natural brothers in Ethiopia. [69] The *Comet* subsequently opened an 'All-Nigerian Shilling' subscription list explaining:

> We say ALL-NIGERIAN. By this we include Europeans and Syrians doing business in this section of Africa. Europeans will lose nothing by helping Abyssinia. Africans the world over assisted the Allies in the late war with both blood and treasure. The Africans may be weak but their help will be needed in the next war. . . . As far as the Syrians are concerned their revenue is mainly derived from African support. [70]

Duse Mohamed Ali further stated that the appeal was also the business of Islam. Citing some historical evidence in support of this, the Egyptian *Comet* editor explained that it was an Emperor of Abyssinia who, by granting succour to the Muslims who fled from Arabia during the persecution of the Prophet's followers, prevented Islam from being exterminated. In his view, Muslims had never paid that debt to Ethiopia, and he urged, 'Now is their opportunity'. [71] Finally, Duse Mohamed Ali declared: 'Time is, however, the essence of the contract. Ethiopia bleeds and it is the duty of every African to stop her wounds.' [72]

Thenceforth every issue of the *Comet* throughout 1936 mounted not only the photographs of Emperor Haile Selassie and the Royal Family but also published the gist of the special appeal stating:

Ethiopia Stretches her hands to God for Help through
His People.
HELP!   HELP!   HELP!
YE just and generous People of Nigeria please stop the murder, massacre and slaughter of innocent defenceless PEOPLE OF ETHIOPIA
by helping them to acquire proper means of defending themselves . . .
Let Bravery and Justice have a chance against Brute Force through YOU.

The appeal of Duse Mohamed Ali was forceful, and boldly and widely printed in the Nigerian papers. It was persistent, all-engaging and demanding. Above all, it was business-like. To many Nigerians, the appeal was nothing short of the crying voice of 'Mother Africa' calling 'her teeming sons and daughters to run to her assistance'. It was not surprising, then, that the response was immediate and encouraging. On reading the appeal, a correspondent to the *Comet*, Zambuzza by name, suggested that the hoarded 'National School Fund' in Nigeria be conceded to the people of Ethiopia for 'this pre-emptory need', adding that the 'money will surely not fail to live up to its national aims'.[73] Duse and his wife made initial donations of five pounds each. By October 1936, the *Comet* special appeal fund had amounted to £80, but thereafter collection began to dwindle considerably. This was a disappointment to Duse who wrote that 'Instead of £80 we should have been able to send £8,000' to the Ethiopian Minister in London.[74] When in late 1936 Dr Martin made another strong and urgent appeal for help the Comet Abyssinian Relief Fund had only £18 4s. 6d. in its coffers. Duse Mohamed Ali again appealed to Nigerians to top this up to ' £50 by the next outgoing mail', but there is no evidence that this target was achieved. Duse, however, need not have been so pessimistic about the outcome of his appeal for funds for Ethiopia. For, as we shall see, although the immediate fruits of his *Comet* Relief Fund were small, it played a part, together with his many editorials on Ethiopia in 1935–36, in awakening a new generation of Nigerians.

Some anxious Nigerians preferred to send their contribution direct to Ethiopia, and consequently bombarded the Nigerian administration with letters to this effect. Believing that it would be quicker to pass their donation through the government, many persistently approached the Lagos administration on this subject. The most spectacular among these was Joshua A. Ricketts of Brickfield Road, Ebute Meta. In October 1935 Ricketts sent to the Chief Secretary to the Nigerian Government a cheque for £30 to be forwarded to the Emperor of Ethiopia 'for the purpose of carrying on the war against Italy or caring for the wounded enemies and friends'. Ricketts added in a covering note that his 'ambition' was not for having white men slain or conquered by black men but only to assure the imperialist powers that there was a 'Black King' in Africa.[75] This donation was, however, rejected by G. C. Whiteley, the Acting Chief Secretary to the government, on the grounds that, as the British Government was at peace with both Italy and Ethiopia, the Nigerian Government was precluded from taking the action Ricketts wished in regard to the supply of ammunition: 'You are not, however, precluded from sending money to assist in the care of the wounded and I am to suggest that you should send your cheque, which is returned herewith, to one of the public funds which, it is understood, are being started for this purpose'.[76]

Although the beginning was halting and slow, judged in the light of the prevailing economic distress, coupled with communication problems at the time, the result of the Nigerians' campaigns for funds for Ethiopia was encouraging. As we have observed, relief fund committees were formed in Nigerian cities which had never before engaged in modern political protest. Leading Nigerians of all political factions were involved in the campaigns. The general response which was shown in several parts of the country to the various appeals for funds to help the Emperor and his subjects was a clear indication of how very deeply touched most Nigerians were. It was a matter which affected the whole African race, and the Nigerians were determined not to lag behind. Reports from Abeokuta, Ibadan, Kano, Jos, Enugu, and Calabar showed great enthusiasm for support for the Ethiopians. Like those in the Gold Coast, even Nigerian school children donated to the fund. As one newspaper claimed, the proposed celebration of 'Ethiopia Day' and 'Ethiopia Sunday' on 14 and 31 December 1935 respectively, was a genuine attempt to show the world the 'stuff of which Africans were made'. It was also an attempt to erase once and for ever the galling remark that Africans 'can bark but cannot bite'.[77]

In the Gold Coast, the main effective body for the organisation of an Ethiopia relief fund was Wallace Johnson's West African Youth League. In collaboration with the Ex-Servicemen's Union, the Youth League established in October 1935 an Ethiopia Defence Committee. Among the prominent officers of the Committee were Prince Robert Thomas Dodoo, President of the Ex-Servicemen's Union (Chairman): Nnamdi Azikiwe (Vice-Chairman). Wallace Johnson and Barnaby E. Tamakloe, General-Secretary of the Ex-Servicemen's Union, were appointed Joint Secretaries; J. J. Ocquaye and E. W. Note-Dowuona, both of the Youth League, joint publicity secretaries. The patrons of the committee included A. W. Kojo Thompson, Kobina Sekyi, Rev. Bishop Pratt of the African Church of Accra, Nee Tackie Oblie, Ga Mantse, A. J. Ocansey and A. M. Akiwumi of the Gold Coast branch of the West African Students' Union of Great Britain; Chief Sotomey of Ewe and Togoland, and E. A. Bossman, an eminent barrister in Accra.[78]

As joint secretaries, Wallace Johnson and B. E. Tamakloe wrote to inform the government of the formation of an Ethiopia Defence Committee under the auspices of the Youth League and the Ex-Servicemen's Union. They stated that the main aim of the committee was to get members of the various communities of the Gold Coast to interest themselves in the present Italo-Ethiopian dispute from 'a racial point of view and to render whatever assistance, morally and financially as may be possible to Ethiopia in her present struggle against Italian aggression'. They also indicated that it was the desire of the organising bodies that the committee should remain as a permanent establishment during and after the Italo-Ethiopian crisis for the 'purpose of educating the masses on matters of racial and national importance'. The committee therefore looked to the government for such co-operation and assistance 'as may be deemed necessary to further its human duties'.[79] Evidently, another objective of Wallace Johnson was to use the Ethiopia Defence Committee to rally the masses in support of both Ethiopia and his Youth League. G. C. du Boulay, the Acting Colonial Secretary, acknowledged receipt of this correspondence on behalf of the Acting Governor of the Gold Coast, but the government took no further action.[80] The establishment of the Ethiopia Defence Committee was similar to an earlier effort by Wallace Johnson, the protest over the trial of the Scottsboro Boys in 1934. In both cases an external issue was pursued in order to sensitise the people of the Gold Coast to racial and political injustice.

The first meeting of the Ethiopia Defence Committee was held on 16 October 1935 at the office of the *Vox Populi* to discuss the organisational problems of the committee. As the Youth League was a large organisation with branches at the important towns in the Gold Coast Colony, the meeting agreed that communication be sent to the Executive of the League soliciting the assistance and co-operation of the League branches in whatever way they could to further the work of the committee. On 30 October 1935, the establishment of the Ethiopia Defence Committee was announced in the various nationalist papers. Subscriptions and contributions to the Ethiopia relief fund were invited from the public and the account for the fund was opened at Barclays Bank in Accra and its branches in the other parts of the Colony, Ashanti and the then Northern Territories. The Ethiopia Defence Committee was officially inaugurated with a celebration of an 'Ethiopia Week' from 1 to 9 November 1935. In connection with this, the government was notified that certain ladies of the community would visit 'government offices on 2 November for the purpose of selling rosettes which would continue till 9 November'.[81] The activities during 'Ethiopia Week' included special services for Ethiopia by both the Muslim and Christian communities, dances and processions by singing bands and some youth organisations, sale of rosettes and special public addresses by Kobina Sekyi, Azikiwe, Kojo Thompson, A. M. Akiwumi, Richard Akwei and the Ga Mantse, Nee Tackie Oblie. Badges bearing the photograph of Emperor Haile Selassie were freely distributed to children who 'proudly wore them' throughout 'Ethiopia Week'.

Although there is no evidence that copies of the special 'Abyssinia Appeal', which the Ethiopia Minister in London forwarded to the *Comet*, reached the shores of the Gold Coast, the Ethiopia Defence Committee on its own accord issued a comprehensive appeal which was no less significant and noteworthy:

> Fellow Members of the Negro Race and all patriotic Sons and Daughters of Africa and of the Gold Coast in particular, Greetings. To you this solemn, appeal on behalf of our dear Mother-land is directed. This is the most critical period of our existence as a race and people of one parental origin. This is the period when each and everyone is expected to show to the world at large that he has in him the germ of patriotism and deep feeling of national Consciousness. At the moment, the foundation of our Alma Mater is seriously threatened. The only hope of regaining our pristine glory is now being shaken to the very root. . . . Now is the time to act. Now is the time to show our patriotism. . . . Ethiopia is calling. Mother Africa is shedding bitter tears against European aggression and she is appealing to you. Will you sit still?[82]

This pan-African conscious appeal, which was signed by Wallace Johnson and B. E. Tamakloe, was no less than a re-statement of all that the Youth League stood for: 'the progress and liberty of the African race'. Armed with this appeal, selected members of the Ethiopia Defence Committee toured certain areas of the country, for the purpose of collecting relief funds for Ethiopia. According to the programme of the Committee, Prince R. T. Dodoo, Wallace Johnson and Miss Mary Lokko, organiser of the women's section of the Youth League, toured the main political centres of the Central, Western and Ashanti Provinces. The tour thus took them to Winneba, Kwanyaku, Saltpond, Cape Coast, Sekondi, Takoradi, Elmina, the mining districts of Tarkwa, Aboso and Prestea, as well as Kumasi, the Ashanti capital. At Kwanyaku, the delegates announced that the 'sum of £75 had been cabled to Ethiopia' as the first instalment.[83] The Eastern Province and the then British Togoland were visited by Prince Mohamed Eket and Barnaby E. Tamakloe, who organised fund raising rallies at Koforidua, Mangoase, Odumase, Akuse, Keta and Ho.[84] The activities in Accra were assigned to A. W. Kojo Thompson, whose recent Legislative Council election victory had made him popular in the capital, especially among the Ga community. Supported by the *Mambii* Party, the Ga Young People's Literacy Club and the Muslim community in Accra, Thompson organised dances, mass meetings and lectures about Ethiopia.

Apart from the Ethiopia Defence Committee, a few non-political bodies also organised activities to raise funds for Ethiopia. Among these was the Gold Coast Christian Council. Founded on 30 October 1929, the Christian Council 'is a free association of some of the larger bodies of Christians' in the Gold Coast to 'confer and to take concerted action on matters of common interest to them all'.[85] Its foundation was inspired by an International Conference on African Missions organised by the International Missionary Council in Belgium in 1926. It was this Conference which emphasised the value of Christian Councils. From 1930 onwards, the government tended to deal with the Council rather than individual member churches. At the outbreak of the Ethiopian crisis, the Secretary of the Council circulated the various missions including the English Church Mission, the Methodist, Scottish and Basel Missions requesting them to bring the matter to the notice of their several communions so that in every parish throughout the length and breadth of the country collections could be made for the relief of Ethiopia.[86] Commenting on this, one newspaper suggested that to make the collection a real nation-wide effort both Mohammedan and the heathen elements be asked to co-operate.[87] Both the Youth Committee and the Women's Committee of the Christian Council took up the issue of raising funds for Ethiopia, although the actual amount collected was not specified. Entries for the confidential diaries of the District Commissioners in Cape Coast and Winneba for the period 1935–36 refer to fund-raising activities of the Christians in the two districts,[88] although no mention is made in the quarterly reports to the Commissioner for Central Province.

Another organisation in the Gold Coast which contributed to the Ethiopia relief funds was the Society of African Patriots under its 'Chief Patriot', P. Ofori, a politically-minded merchant at Nsawam in the Eastern Province. Formed in 1930, the objectives of the society included, among other things, the conversion of the African to become a 'patriot to the land that gave him birth', the improvement 'on modern lines of the system of municipal government already existing before the advent of European civilization', and research into the 'mysteries of nature and science' with a view to improving 'upon the latent possibilities of the African'. The society also aimed at selecting some competent and knowledgeable persons 'to go out lecturing in the villages, schools, market-places, churches and open places' in an effort to educate the people about their 'full responsibilities, politically, agriculturally, industrially'.[89] The secretary of the society, H. S. Akrofi, circulated the local branches of the society in the country asking them to organise rallies in aid of Ethiopia.[90] There is no evidence, however, as to how much the society was able to contribute to the Ethiopia relief funds in the country. Similarly, although the *Mambii* Party in Accra vigorously campaigned on behalf of Ethiopia, nothing is known about its actual financial contribution towards the Ethiopian cause. Unlike the Society of African Patriots, this was, as we have noted, a political party which, like Wallace Johnson's Youth League, stood for the masses, the young and the underprivileged in the local politics of Accra. According to Edward O. Asafu-Adjaye, the first Ashanti lawyer and member of the 1934 Gold Coast Colony and Ashanti Delegation, the young, who were shut out of the tribal councils and not represented by any spokesman on the Legislative Council, responded favourably to the 'appeals which their elders resented'.[91] Among the members of the Executive Committee of the *Mambii* Party was Nnamdi Azikiwe who thought that the time had come for the old-guard of compromising nationalists to give way to more forceful leaders who cultivated a youthful attitude. Other members included A. M. Akiwumi, a solicitor of the party, who later became the Deputy President of the Gold Coast Youth Conference. Many of the adherents of the *Mambii* Party later gravitated to Kwame Nkrumah's banner in the 1950s. On the whole, however, despite the enthusiastic demonstrations generated in the Gold Coast towards the cause of Ethiopia, it would appear that not much financial aid was realised from the Ethiopia campaigns.

Poverty of Protest and Protest of Poverty

Although as we have seen, the West African nationalists had the will, they did not have the power to stem the tide of Fascist aggression in Ethiopia. Their protests, therefore, in terms of its influence on the actual events in Ethiopia accomplished little, if anything at all. The French and British Governments, to whom they made their strongest appeals, had resolved to appease Italy in an attempt to retain it as an ally against Germany. They had, therefore, virtually given Italy a free hand in Ethiopia. Thus the great colonial powers and the white world in general which had the power to stop Mussolini lacked the will to do so. Besides, at the time of the crisis, there were exceedingly few in West Africa who possessed the means to contribute financially to the Ethiopian war effort. It was not surprising therefore that the protests of the West African nationalists did not have any appreciable impact on the war generally. In this section, we shall attempt to analyse the problems which confronted the nationalists in their campaigns for relief funds to aid Ethiopia.

An objective appraisal of the efforts of West Africans to raise funds for Ethiopia should take into account several factors, the most important of which was, as mentioned elsewhere, the economic distress and the hardships of the times. The Great Depression made it inordinately difficult, indeed impossible in perhaps most instances, for aroused but impoverished nationalists to assist materially the beleaguered Ethiopians. For example, in spite of the fact that the 1934 Gold Coast Colony and Ashanti Delegation to England was whole-heartedly supported by the Provincial Councils and led by such wealthy Paramount Chiefs as Nana Sir Ofori Atta, it was with great difficulty that money was collected for the despatch of the delegation. Sir Shenton Thomas even doubted whether, in the economic circumstances of the times, the Gold Coast people would 'be able to collect the money' to send a delegation to England, adding, 'at least, I shall be very surprised if they do'.[92] Similarly, without the great financial support of Chief J. E. Biney of Cape Coast, on ex-president of the ARPS and one of the wealthiest merchants and businessmen in West Africa, the rival deputation of the Aborigines Society to England in 1934 would have been impossible. Chief Biney alone donated £3,150 out of the total sum of £3,773 8s. 0d.[93] Through lack of funds the Gold Coast Youth Conference was unable to publish the results of its first session held at Achimota in April 1930, and did not meet again until 1938 at Mfantsipim, Cape Coast.

The situation was the same in the other West African colonies. A confidential report during this period discusses in detail how the Sierra Leone Section of the NCBWA was 'always hard up financially' and consequently was unable to send an 'annual contribution of £25 to the parent body'. The report went on to say that the Gambia 'certainly does not forward any money to the general fund as required by the constitution of the Congress'. Concluding, the report stated: 'It seems that it is impossible during this period to raise sufficient funds in the West African Colonies to pay the expenses of the various delegations' to any Congress session.[94] In the view of the Government of Sierra Leone, the financial problems of the 1930s were one of the factors which contributed to the inactivity of the Congress 'which was designed by its creators to express the united opinion of the four colonies'.[95] The *Sierra Leone Daily Guardian* consoled itself with an editorial that:

> ... even in this poor community where in spite of the hardness of times, pennies, three pennies and six pences have been voluntarily contributed towards the Abyssinia Relief Fund till it has reached such a high sum, is sufficient evidence of the fact that the Sierra Leonean too, like everybody else, has realised that liberty is a thing worth sacrificing money, talent, situation, and even life itself for . . ..[96]

Indeed, the negligible financial achievements of the West African campaigns must always be seen against this larger background of the economic hardships of the period.

Besides this general economic factor, the fund-raising campaigns in the Gold Coast faced a particular problem. Both organisations – the Ex-Servicemen's Union and the West African Youth League – which led the campaigns did not count financially. An official at the Colonial Office commented that only about 'a dozen members are said to have contributed towards the funds' of the League.[97] A more accurate appraisal of the financial position of the League is given in a letter, intercepted by the police, to Wallace Johnson from a Youth League activist which complained that 'the last League meeting raised only 2/- in donations'.[98] Shortage of cash proved a very serious constraint on the success of the League, because the Organising Secretary and other travelling agents were forced to spend inordinate amounts of time badgering the branches for funds. This constant search for money had a dual effect. It diverted crucial energies from the primary endeavours of the League and eroded the sympathy and support of the membership which was primarily composed of persons of extremely moderate, if not inadequate means. As A. M. Akiwumi, an influential member of the League, told me, none of the Youth League's enthusiastic supporters or patrons, not even such notable barristers as Kojo Thompson, Kobina Sekyi, K. A. Bossman and himself were 'well to do financially' during this period. In terms of wealth, he added, the Gold Coast lawyers of the 1930s were significantly different from their counterparts in the 1920s who composed the National Congress movement.[99]

Above all, the personality of Wallace Johnson proved to be a contributory factor to the failure of the campaigns to raise sufficient funds in the Gold Coast. Johnson's uncontrolled enthusiasm for the Ethiopian cause and his leadership of the campaigns turned out to be a liability instead of an asset to both the Youth League and the Ethiopia Defence Committee. An outstanding agitator, he was, nevertheless, unable to work with others well enough to build up a solid organisational foundation of the league. His close associates like Kojo Thompson, Nnamdi Azikiwe, A. J. Ocansey, and even the Gold Coast Ex-Servicemen's Union with which he had established the Ethiopia Defence

Committee, later became hostile to him.[100] In January 1936, certain members of the Ex-Servicemen's Union charged Wallace Johnson 'with misappropriation of the funds of the Ethiopia Defence Committee'.[101] This incident seriously threatened the stability and unity in the membership of the committee. The hitch was occasioned by the failure of the Wallace Johnson delegation to declare proceeds of their tour of the provinces to the committee on their return to Accra. Commenting on this episode, a radical newspaper which had been a staunch supporter of the Ethiopia Defence Committee lamented:

> It is a truism that success in any undertaking depends upon the MIND or personality behind it; we are therefore led to believe that were there such a personality behind the local Ethiopian affairs the present unpleasantness which is manifesting itself amongst the accredited members of the Ethiopia Defence Committee could have been obviated.

To save the situation, as well as the reputation of the African, this paper suggested that a financial committee be set up by the Ethiopia Defence Committee to audit the accounts of the Ethiopia relief fund collectors both in Accra and in the provinces.[102] The alleged financial misappropriation of the relief funds created such a storm that Wallace Johnson was constrained to tender his resignation as joint-secretary of the Ethiopia Defence Committee.[103] The misappropriation story, together with the expenses incurred in the various tours of the Ethiopia Defence Committee delegates, the printing of posters, the organisation of lectures, fetes and concerts, might have greatly eaten into the funds raised by the committee.

Furthermore, it would seem that Wallace Johnson carried his racial feelings about the Ethiopian affair too far to the ultimate detriment of the Ethiopia Defence Committee itself. Under his leadership the Committee arrogated to itself the sole authority for the collection of the Ethiopia relief funds in the Gold Coast. Hence it ridiculously resented the decision of the Central Council Branch of the British Red Cross Society in the Gold Coast to set up its own Ethiopia Relief Fund. In the view of Wallace Johnson, the use by the society of the same name and the same bank as used by his committee implied that the only motive behind the move of the society was to 'boycott the progress of the Ethiopia Defence Committee in its efforts to raise funds for the defence of Ethiopia against Italian aggression by exploiting the foundations already laid by the Committee'. In spite of the apparent triviality of this issue which could easily have been settled amicably, Wallace Johnson compelled his Committee to pass a hostile resolution on the matter on 13 January 1936, and also adopted a policy of non-co-operation with the other relief fund agencies in the country.[104] This attitude of Johnson's alienated not only the British Red Cross Society in the Gold Coast but also the Christian Council, both of which were seriously engaged on raising funds for Ethiopia.

Besides, probably because of his studies in Russia and his involvement in international leftist causes and also the nature of his participation in local politics, Wallace Johnson's leadership of the Ethiopia Defence Committee was resented by the established elite such as F. V. Nanka Bruce and the Rate-payers' Association in Accra, and also by J. B. Danquah, who had earlier spoken on the same platform with Johnson on the Scottsboro Boys case and had thought of establishing a new political movement in the Gold Coast with him.[105] Danquah told the Watson Commission in 1948 that Wallace Johnson's

Youth League was not by itself objectionable, but he happened to know that Johnson was 'in touch with the Communist organisation in Great Britain. . . . I came to the conclusion that he was a Communist'. Furthermore, Danquah said that Wallace Johnson was not directed to 'bringing chiefs together', but to 'getting what he called the working classes together', a policy of which he was not in favour.[106] Wallace Johnson was indeed a firebrand who called everybody 'Comrade', and was thus thought by some to be a Communist.[107] 'Comrade' became the regular mode of address between members of the Youth League. The League's officials and members constantly referred to 'the masses' and their needs and desires. Although neither Johnson nor his colleagues attempted to inculcate scientific Marxism as a way of life or politics, through the agency of the League, 'simplified Marxist ideas and symbols were incorporated into West African political thought'.[108]

Apart from Wallace Johnson's open declaration for Communism, the character of the whole agency, under which the relief funds were being operated, very adversely affected the progress and success of the Ethiopian Defence Committee. The fund-raising rallies appealed only to the youth and the dissident groups in Gold Coast society who formed the support-base of the Wallace Johnson Youth League. No real, conscious effort was made to involve the established elite who, in any case, were fundamentally antagonistic to Johnson and his Youth League. This situation puzzled the *Vox Populi* which painfully remarked that the 'older generation in our midst have not been displaying equal ardour touching the [Ethiopian] crisis in question. . . . Our chiefs seem not in any way affected by the present plight of members of our own race in the far East Africa of this continent.' The editorial attributed the passivity and aloofness of the 'Natural Rulers' to the failure on the part of the youth to acquaint them with the true state of affairs relating to Ethiopia.[109] This, however, seems to be too much of an oversimplification of the real issues at stake.

For it was not that the chiefs were unaware of the plight of the Ethiopians nor were they unconcerned about the urgent need to raise funds for their war effort. They had even in a private audience with Governor Sir Arnold Hodson gone to the extent of expressing their dissatisfaction with the British handling of the Italo-Ethiopian affair.[110] But they were reluctant to support the Ethiopia Defence Committee openly mainly because it was composed of 'all the elements in the country which were violently opposed to the traditional elite and the Provincial Council system'.[111] In other words, the indifference of the 'Natural Rulers' to the fund-raising campaigns was due largely to their utter dislike for the politics, the objectives and aspirations, of the WAYL which organised almost by itself the Ethiopia Defence Committee. They could certainly not be expected to contribute to a fund operated by a Youth League which was openly threatening their political status in the country. It was this hostile attitude of the 'Natural Rulers' to the WAYL which eventually spelt doom for the Youth League, and with it, the Ethiopia Defence Committee. But this is hardly surprising when viewed against the background of the nationalist politics of the inter-war years.

The Aborigines' Rights' Protection Society owed its inception and initial success to the backing of the 'Natural Rulers' of the Gold Coast. When the Society kicked against the Native Administration Ordinance and the Provincial Council system in 1927, and thus incurred the displeasure of the influential and powerful chiefs, led by Nana Sir Ofori Atta I, who strongly supported the

Provincial Council system, and, in fact, inspired its establishment, the heyday of the Society came to an abrupt end. A similar fate was met by the National Congress of British West Africa when it attempted to disregard the chiefs in the politics of the 1920s. This was evidenced in the speech of Nana Sir Ofori Atta I at the Legislative Council on 30 December 1920 which Governor Guggisberg forwarded *en bloc* in a telegram to the Colonial Office.[112] The Secretary of State, Lord Milner, relying on information received from the governors in West Africa refused to believe that the NCBWA and its delegation to London represented 'the native communities on whose behalf it purports to speak'.[113] Lord Milner was firmly convinced that as far as 'the most authoritative exponents of native opinion' – especially the chiefs of the Gold Coast – were concerned, the proposals made by the NCBWA were 'inimical to the best interests of the community'.[114]

Like the NCBWA, the WAYL, under whose auspices the Ethiopia Defence Committee largely functioned, was avowedly political. Here was a movement which completely declared for the masses, the 'toiling masses', 'the working class', as they were usually described by, say, the *Gold Coast Observer*, disregarding the position of the 'Natural Rulers' in the political structure of local and central institutions of the Gold Coast. Its insistence on new ideas and new visions meant that the chiefs had no place under its political umbrella. In a more profound way than the NCBWA, the success of the League might have spelt doom for the chiefs. Moreover, the Youth League took up the Ethiopian question as another means of popularising its teachings and political ideology. Wherever the members of the Ethiopia Defence Committee toured to raise funds for Ethiopia, they took the opportunity afforded them to either inaugurate or organise the Youth League. The Ethiopia Defence Committee made overtures only to places where the Youth League was popular. Hence the relief fund campaigns were mainly confined to the Colony. In Ashanti and the Northern Territories where the WAYL had no great impact, the committee did not achieve any appreciable success. Indeed, the Ethiopia Defence Committee was the handmaid of the West African Youth League. The chiefs would have contributed to their own doom if they had supported the committee. It was not surprising, therefore, that the chiefs held themselves aloof from such cries of the *Gold Coast Spectator* as 'Now is the time for chiefs to donate aeroplanes'.[115] Similarly, the earlier appeal on 13 October 1935 by E. Y. Becr Boni of the Ethiopia Defence Committee to the Presidents of the Eastern, Central and Western Provincial Council of chiefs was quietly ignored by the 'Natural Rulers'.[116]

More significantly, even before the outbreak of the Italo-Ethiopian war, Wallace Johnson had seized every opportunity to heap ridicule on the established educated elite, condemning the position of the chiefs in the political structure of the Gold Coast, and criticising the 1934 Gold Coast Colony and Ashanti Delegation which had the support of the Provincial Councils.[117] At the height of the Ethiopian crisis when he was leading the Ethiopia Defence Committee to put the case of Ethiopia before the people of the Gold Coast, Wallace Johnson invariably declared his opposition to the 'Natural Rulers' of the country, particularly those connected with the Provincial Councils and the Legislative Council.[118] At its first annual conference in March 1936, the Youth League passed resolutions against the Provincial Council system and its relationship with the Legislative Council, and also called upon the government to consider the 'advisability of discontinuing the policy of appointing chiefs to the Legislative Council'.[119] Furthermore, Wallace Johnson alienated the chiefs in the Colony by his support of the sub-stools of Asamankese (a League stronghold) and Akwatia against Nana Ofori Atta I and the colonial government. Cramped seriously by financial disabilities, Wallace Johnson and the Youth League looked to the royalties of the stools as a potential *deus ex machina* to put the Youth League on a sound footing. Thus on 18 April 1935, the Youth League sponsored a mass protest against the Asamankese Division Bill and against the treatment of the Asamankese people arrested by the native police of Ofori Atta.[120]

This sustained attack and hostile criticism of the 'Natural Rulers' just at the time when the Ethiopia Defence Committee was campaigning for funds was not confined to the Colony. In a bid to extend the influence of the Youth League to Ashanti, Wallace Johnson involved himself in the intricacies of Ashanti politics, and thus succeeded in estranging a good number of the Ashanti chiefs who were prepared to respond favourably to the appeals of the Ethiopia Defence Committee. Although he does not appear to have opposed restoration of the Ashanti Confederacy in 1935 and had written a favourable pamphlet on the subject,[121] Johnson strongly attacked the deportation of the Youth members, O. S. Agyeman, Atta Kwadwo, E. C. Bobieh-Ansah, and Akofo Dampare, who had become involved in internal politics and had come under the wrath of the Asantehene and consequently the colonial government.[122] Before then the Executive Committee of the Youth League had on 31 January 1936 protested against the local government's Ordinance which sought to remove and detain Kofi Sechere, an ex-Dadiasuabahene of Kumasi, who was 'involved in certain acts committed by a small group of persons in Kumasi against the Asantehene and the Golden Stool'.[123]

The despatch of a copy of the resolution on Kofi Sechere by the Youth League to the Secretary of the Eastern Provincial Council incensed the 'Natural Rulers' who expressed 'surprise at the attitude of the youth of the country, whose mentality was apparently entirely controlled by a man like Wallace Johnson', and recalled the wisdom of passing on 14 February 1936 the resolution in respect of the 'Undesirable Conduct of Non-Gold Coast Africans'. This resolution had urged that the existing Immigration Ordinance be amended to cover 'Africans not natives of the Gold Coast'.[124] But it was at the joint session of the Provincial Councils held at Dodowa in the Eastern Province in November 1936 that the activities of Wallace Johnson, the Youth League and the Ethiopia Defence Committee were closely studied and discussed. The chiefs unanimously and vehemently disapproved the behaviour of a stranger like Wallace Johnson who, 'as the result of the hospitatility of the people, insult the chiefs'. The 'Natural Rulers' emphasised that it was important for the states to see that Wallace Johnson's 'humbug did not persist'. On the Youth League, the Council declared that there was no difference between the League and Wallace Johnson for 'Wallace Johnson is the West African Youth League and the West African Youth League is Wallace Johnson'. The Ethiopia Defence Committee was similarly identified with Wallace Johnson. In the view of Nana Ayirebi Acquah, Paramount Chief of Winneba, the most painful part of the matter was the determination with which their children were flocking 'under the nefarious banner of the Youth Leagues'. The general feeling at the meeting was that non-Gold Coast Africans, as the directors of the Youth League, posed so much 'as the Protectors or saviours' of the country through the youth of the Gold Coast that the latter had 'assumed and were assuming such refractory conduct and attitude towards their chiefs and every lawful authority that in a few years more there was sure to be a reign of anarchy unless all those imported irregularities were stemmed'.[125] It was in the light of all this that the chiefs demanded the deportation of 'these strangers'.[126]

The effectiveness and tension generated by the activities of the Youth League, despite the fact that such activities were confined mainly to the Colony, created for Wallace Johnson the open opposition and hatred of both the government and the influential chiefs. The Legislative Council election results had surprised the colonial officials and the African elites and convinced them that the Youth League was a powerful force to reckon with. Sir Arnold Hodson's 'broadcast propaganda and other devices' initiated with a view to nullifying the 'efforts of Wallace Johnson and other subversives' proved to have had little or no effect on Wallace Johnson's activities.[127] The Gold Coast officials were in a quandary because they could discover no legal means of dealing with Wallace Johnson. The governor had earlier written to enquire whether the Colonial Office could suggest some plan whereby he could get rid of Wallace Johnson, adding, 'he is in the employ of the Bolsheviks and is doing a certain amount of harm by getting hold of the young men for his Youth League'.[128] Sir Arnold was disappointed by the fact that Wallace Johnson 'just keeps within the law, but only just'. He was obviously disturbed by the law officers' persistent argument that although Wallace Johnson at many of his meetings uttered 'outrageous and criminal things', it was almost impossible to get a conviction on the spoken word. The governor found this insupportable, and in utter desperation, told Sir Cecil Bottomley in confidence: 'There is something wrong in our Constitution which allows these sort of people to be at large. The French would not tolerate this for one second'.[129]

While the officials in London were discussing the possibility of deportation, the opportunity for which Hodson had been waiting presented itself in Accra, when Wallace Johnson's 'outrageous and criminal things' appeared in print in an editorial of the *African Morning Post* of 15 May 1936, entitled 'Has the African a God?' In this article Wallace Johnson, who wrote under the pseudonym 'Effective', condemned European civilisation, Christianity, and imperialism in no uncertain terms. The administrators were outraged by the assertions of Wallace Johnson, who alleged that the European

> believes in the God whose name is spelt *Deceit*. He believes in the God whose law is 'Ye strong, you must weaken the weak. Ye "civilized Europeans", you must "civilize" the "barbarous" Africans with machine guns. Ye Christian Europeans, You must 'Christianise" the pagan Africans with bombs, poison gases, etc.' In the Colonies, the Europeans believe in the God that commands: 'Ye Administrators, make Sedition Bill to keep the Africans gagged. Make Forced Labour Bill to work the Africans as slaves. Make Deportation Ordinance to send the Africans to exile whenever they dare to question your authority'.

Johnson also denounced the government for sending detectives

> to stay around the house of any African who is nationally conscious and who is agitating for national independence and if possible round him up in 'criminal frame-up' so that he could be kept behind the bars.

Ethiopia obviously provided the text for the first part of the article, while in the other paragraphs unpopular local legislation was clearly specified.

These strong words were considered seditious by the colonial government, and in June 1936 Wallace Johnson and Azikiwe, the editor-in-chief of the *African Morning Post*, were arrested and charged under the Criminal Code Ordinance of 1934. This was the first trial under the Gold Coast Sedition Ordinance, and it provoked one of the most sensational events in the nationalist politics of the thirties. Interested individuals and groups in Britain such as Reginald Bridgeman of the League Against Imperialism,[130] and Ronald Kidd of the National Council for Civil Liberties, vigorously intervened on behalf of Wallace Johnson. Kidd contended that the article was, in his view, certainly indiscreet, but it merely expressed the bitterness which 'all our African fellow subjects are feeling at the cynical betrayal of Abyssinia at the hands of European powers'.[131] He agreed that although the article spoke strongly and sarcastically, it was very questionable whether it could properly 'be called seditious'. Kidd finally considered it deplorable that in a great colonial empire as that of Britain's the only way of dealing with a 'patriot should be by means of a seditious prosecution'.[132] Even some of the officials in London who viewed matters more dispassionately from their vantage point at the Colonial Office, thought the Gold Coast Government had overreacted, as 'the article hardly amounts to what we regard as sedition'.[133] Others who felt that a better opportunity had not been found in which to unlimber the 'big gun' argued that the article was 'not so very much worse than what the *African Morning Post* usually publishes'.[134] Similarly, in their application for government funds to finance Wallace Johnson's appeal, Sir Stafford Cripps, Norman Wiggins, and Julius Lewis maintained that Johnson, as a British subject, had been merely addressing himself to 'the broad issue of European-African relations in the light of the Italo-Abyssinian War. . . .'[135] All this shows how seriously Wallace Johnson took up the defence of the Ethiopian cause in West Africa.

Meanwhile, much to the dismay of Sir Arnold Hodson, Wallace Johnson was fined the sum of £50 and not imprisoned. Hodson immediately wrote to inform Sir Cecil Bottomley:

> I wired you about the Wallace Johnson case. It was a great surprise to us all that he was not imprisoned without the option of a fine. . . . We cannot allow Wallace Johnson to remain in this Colony and I hope to insert a clause in the new bill we are drafting to the effect that anyone who has been convicted under the Sedition Ordinance can be forced to leave this Colony and returned to his own country.[136]

The Immigration Ordinance of the Gold Coast was accordingly amended and Wallace Johnson, who had left for Europe in March 1937 in order to 'solicit financial and political aid' in Great Britain to enable him to carry his appeal to the Privy Council, was not allowed to return to the Gold Coast. His departure was a great relief to the Provincial Councils, and especially to Sir Arnold, who informed Bottomley that Wallace Johnson, 'the organiser and main beneficiary' of the West African Youth League, had now left the Gold Coast 'and it is hoped that the League will follow the Society [of Ashanti Freedom] into oblivion'.[137] The governor correctly assessed the situation, for, in the absence of Wallace Johnson, the mainstay of the radical movement in the Gold Coast, the Youth League became moribund in nationalist politics. Similarly, the campaigns for relief funds for Ethiopia lost its appeal and momentum. For Johnson's departure took away much of the dynamism of the Youth League and created substantial difficulties. The loss of Johnson's dynamic leadership plus the financial burdens involved proved too much for the League. The remaining work-horses of the WAYL, F. A. Bruce and Willie Davidson, found that financial incapacity and inability to produce mass benefits eroded support for the league. Even though thousands of persons affiliated with the league, they had done so in the hope of tangible rewards. When those rewards failed to materialise and were replaced by ever-increasing demands for financial contributions, the eager attendants of inaugural meetings were impossible to find for subsequent meetings.

An influential member of the Youth League in Accra, Richard Akwei, has confirmed that the reaction of Wallace Johnson to the chiefs and the colonial government greatly affected the campaigns of the Ethiopia Defence Committee, and 'even alarmed many of us'. He maintains that although they knew that their 'drive for £200,000' for Ethiopia[138] was only a 'political ramp', it was unfortunate that the personality of Wallace Johnson, coupled with the mismanagement of the funds of the Ethiopia Defence Committee, made it difficult for them to realise 'even a tenth of this amount'. Richard M. Akwei, who was an Executive member of the *Mambii* Party and later the vice-President of the Gold Coast Youth Conference and Councillor of the Accra Municipal Council, also disclosed that, so far as the Colony was concerned the campaigns of the Ethiopia Defence Committee spread very widely. That it had little or no response in Ashanti and the Northern Territories, he explains, was due to the rigid administrative separation between Ashanti and the Colony, which was maintained until the Burns Constitution of 1946 under which Ashanti representation on the Legislative Council was achieved. As for the North, he continues, it was difficult to break through its isolation, because of the considerable social and administrative differences which then separated it from the rest of the country.[139] With the sole exception of the Gold Coast Youth Conference, all the major political organisations and youth movements before the late 1940s were centred mainly on the Colony.

Apart from the lack of economic and political power, as well as unity of purpose among the West African nationalists, the other factors which seemed to have contributed to the limited impact of the West African protest on the policy-makers in London was the general unwillingness on the part of the West African colonial governments to show in their confidential despatches the true nature and intensity of this protest. For not only did the despatches on the West African reaction to the Italo-Ethiopian struggle tell a 'one-sided story'; they were also too fragmentary to have had any possible impact on the members of the British foreign policy-making elite. Although, it is true, that no British Government would have been prepared in any matter affecting its own assessment of its vital interests to defer in the least to the views of the West African nationalists, there is evidence that, in spite of the precautions taken against native volunteers who applied for enlistment in the Ethiopian forces, British official circles were apprehensive of the possible repercussions of the conflict on their race-conscious West African subjects.

British fears about such developments were made evident in various official conversations and despatches in 1935. On 9 July, for example, Sir Samuel Hoare, the British Foreign Minister, told the American Ambassador in Britain,

Robert Bingham, of a further reason for seeking a peaceful settlement of the Italo-Ethiopian despute: 'Mussolini has now put the issue in the shape of a contest between the black and white races which had had already unfavourable effect in Egypt, in Great Britain's African colonies and in British Dominions where there is a population of blacks'.[140] In his view it was absolutely wrong for Mussolini to glorify a war between Ethiopia and Italy as a war between blacks and whites.[141] Although on 31 July Mussolini specifically denied that Fascism was making the conflict an issue of race,[142] his 'civilising' arguments had all the tone of nineteenth-century racist imperialism.

The most comprehensive expression of British apprehension is contained in a confidential despatch which Hoare sent to the British Ambassador in Paris in late July. In this despatch Hoare requested Sir George Clerk to draw the attention of the French Government to the serious consequences which 'must or may flow from an Italo-Abyssinian war', and to the necessity for Anglo-French co-operation in order to 'avert some of the serious consequences'. Apart from the consequences on the general European situation, Hoare said that hostilities between Ethiopia and Italy would have grave repercussions 'on native opinion in their colonial possessions'. The French Government would have observed that in a recent demonstration in Addis Ababa the dispute was 'characterised as one between the white and black races', and it appeared that the recent outburst of interest in the quarrel shown by public opinion in Japan in a greater degree assumed a racial character.[143] Hoare contended that generally speaking, it could not be doubted that Italian aggression against Ethiopia would have an unsettling effect upon all 'native' populations. But he was of the opinion that this effect would be spread when the situation in Europe could not but cause the gravest preoccupation of all 'Governments eager for the preservation of peace'. Even if immediate disturbances in colonial possessions 'need not be anticipated', Hoare felt that it should be expected that nationalist feeling, temporarily perhaps quiescent, but still ardent beneath the surface, would receive fresh stimulus. He therefore urged Sir George Clerk to make it clear to Laval that any failure on the part of France and the United Kingdom to show their disapproval of the conduct of Italy must surely arouse the resentment of the coloured races; while a failure to make effective by successful restraint of Italy any disapproval which the two governments 'may publicly express may well bring them not only ill-will but also disrepute'.[144]

The Foreign Secretary then outlined the consequences on the colonial subjects in the event of Italian failure or success in Ethiopia. In his view if Italian military measures should encounter serious difficulties, and still more if the Italian measures should meet with a reverse, the effect could hardly be other than to create or encourage among 'native races' a spirit which might assume unfortunate forms and greatly increase the difficulties of administration. The effects in the special circumstances of an Italian victory over Ethiopia could hardly be less unfortunate. In this case, wrote Hoare, there must arise extensive feelings of resentment among 'native peoples', and it would, in the opinion of the British Government, be unsafe to assume that such feelings would not receive early expression in varying degrees of activity and form. France should not entertain the belief that the consequences of a war between Italy and Ethiopia would only be seen in Italian possessions, for 'they would probably not be confined to those areas'. He stressed that apart from wider repercussions, the neighbouring territories consisted largely of French possessions and of countries under British and French influence. It was therefore incumbent on the two governments to leave nothing undone to prevent the outbreak of hostilities which might well result in the imposition upon Ethiopia of unjust demands or even the extinction of her independence. Finally, Sir George Clerk was asked to make it unmistakably clear to Laval that the Governments of France and the United Kingdom, owing to their position in Europe and their close relations with Italy, were best placed for using their influence with her; and they might well, if unjustly, be 'deemed by native opinion in two continents, particularly responsible', if they failed to forestall a situation which by its influences upon racial, nationalistic and religious sentiment must add a further measure of unsettlement to an already unsettled world.[145]

This confidential despatch by Sir Samuel Hoare, together with his conversations with the American Ambassador, clearly disclose the official British perception of the colonial implications of the Italo-Ethiopian dispute. In the first place, they disclose one of the major reasons for the British decision to prevent an outbreak of war between 'white' Italy and 'black' Ethiopia. Secondly, they are expressive of the anxiety which the British Government felt about the possible impact of the crisis on their colonial subjects. This was seen to be a matter of grave importance to both the British and French Governments, who were between them responsible for the administration of so many large territories throughout the world. Thirdly, Hoare's despatch seems to confirm the fact that the conflict had great significance to the non-white peoples of the world. For, if Italy won, despite the principles of the League of Nations which offered protection equally to all members, it would be proof that the spirit of imperialism, of the subjugation of races, was still condoned by Europe. If Italy lost, 'the spell of Europe' would be jeopardised. Whatever the result of the Italo-Ethiopian conflict might be, the British saw the danger to the old colonial world.

It is interesting to note that in the eyes of the articulate and radical groups in West Africa it was not Mussolini alone who had made the conflict assume a racial character, as Hoare painfully remarked to Robert Bingham. For, in their opinion, it was the conflicting and hesitant policies of the British and the French Governments, their apparent lack of swift, clear and positive action and their involvement in the abortive Hoare-Laval episode, which confirmed them in the view that the crisis was a racial one. This view was reinforced by their experience of the colonial past. Thus, to the politically-minded West Africans, Hoare's statement to the American Ambassador was nothing more than an attempt on the part of the Foreign Secretary to plead *alibi* in the conduct of international diplomacy.

As the British Government was not receiving any official information about the possible repercussions of the Italo-Ethiopian war on their West African subjects, the Secretary of State for the Colonies wrote to the governors in West Africa to ask for a brief report indicating what effect, if any, the conflict (and the action taken by the League of Nations in regard to it) had had on 'native' and local opinion in the territories under their administration.[146] MacDonald disclosed that while he had no doubt that at any rate among the more advanced sections of 'native opinion' in certain African Dependencies, the war had been followed with much interest, he had received no reports indicating that the crisis had aroused in West Africa the same degree of excitement as it had in certain West Indian Dependencies. The Secretary of State added that the governors were already aware that the British Government had been criticised in certain quarters on the grounds that they failed to take action with the object of averting an outbreak of hostilities between Italy and Ethiopia until it was too late to prevent war between the two countries. In particular, he pointed out that it had been alleged that the British Government failed to make clear to the Italian Government at any early stage of the dispute the fact that an Italian attack on Ethiopia would be viewed in the gravest light in Britain as a breach of the Covenant of the League of Nations. In view of the possibility that such criticism might be voiced in the territories under their administration, MacDonald told the West African governors that it might interest them to see a strictly confidential Foreign Office memorandum (a copy of whch he enclosed) summarising the diplomatic action taken by the British Government throughout the period from the beginning of the dispute until the outbreak of war.[147]

Not only did the confidential replies of the West African governors not cover much of what was happening in West Africa, they were also not altogether accurate. Quite rightly, however, each of them stated that the Italo-Ethiopian war, and the action taken by the League of Nations in regard to it, had been followed 'with the keenest interest' particularly by the educated groups in West Africa, and had been 'the subject of continuous comment both in the press and from the pulpit and the public platform'.[148] Governor Bourdillon added that there were a number of Nigerians who 'hold that no real help to Abyssinia' was forthcoming from the League of Nations. Secondly, all the governors indicated in their reports that the struggle was popularly regarded in their respective administering territories as being 'fundamentally an issue of Black versus White'. Thirdly, the reports referred to the attempts being made in West Africa to collect funds for the benefit of Ethiopia. On the question of the attitude of Great Britain to the conflict, the governors of Nigeria and Sierra Leone emphasised that their colonial subjects had been highly critical of the British policy, which in the eyes of the Africans 'was tardy, and might have assumed a more vigorous form'. While Bourdillon accurately stated that Nigerians had expressed hostile criticisms and misgivings about the Hoare-Laval peace plan, Governor Henry Moore showed his ignorance not only of the feeling of the people of Sierra Leone about the Hoare-Laval fiasco, but also of the general trend of the international situation at that time. Writing on 30 December 1935, after the abortive Hoare-Laval peace proposals, Moore said that 'so long as His Majesty's Government' did not become party to any settlement which would in African eyes be regarded as a surrender to Italian aggression, he considered that local Creole opinion 'will continue as at present to be generally appreciative of the policy which His Majesty's Government is pursuing'.[149] And yet by her association with the Hoare-Laval peace plan of 10 December 1935, Britain had already 'become party' to a proposed settlement which was 'a surrender to Italian aggression'. Similarly, in his comparatively brief report, the Deputy Governor of the Gold Coast, George London, went so far as to stress that there had been 'no popular excitement and no evidence of definite ill-feeling against Italian residents',[150] even though, as we have noted, this had been a subject for serious discussion by the Gold Coast Executive Council in December 1935. It had also constrained the Italian residents to launch an underground propaganda campaign to establish their non-involvement which was brought to the notice of the government. Also, this subject formed part of the police confidential reports of 1935 and later of the

'Note of Impressions' which Miss Hebe Spaull of the League of Nations Union staff submitted to the government.

It is important to stress, however, that the confidential reports under discussion were written between December 1935 and February 1936, and therefore could not have embodied the militant outlook which the reaction to the crisis took after this period. The interest which market-women, sailors, school-children, and the little known bodies later showed in the conflict was not clearly evident during the first few months of the Italo-Ethiopian war. As evidenced in an interesting address by Lord Hailey, Director of the African Research Survey, who toured West Africa during this period: 'At the outset of the crisis, there was no striking evidence of general interest; a few meetings were held in the Union and the West Coast, and a few subscriptions collected.' But as the Italian troops penetrated deeply within Ethiopian territory, and it became clearly evident that the white powers were not prepared to take any decisive action against Italy, 'African interest in the conflict quickened and attained larger proportions'.[151] These later events were nowhere detailed in official reports to the British policy-makers in London.

On the whole, on the basis of the evidence it can be argued that the replies to MacDonald's secret enquiry were perhaps a deliberate effort on the part of the West African governors to avoid communicating anything that might embarrass their home government or complicate matters in that trying period of international crisis. But to report that there was no cause for anxiety because the 'position could be described as normal',[152] is certainly most inaccurate. Furthermore, to contend that before February 1936, there was a general appreciation in West Africa of the 'efforts made by the British Government to put an end to hostilities'.[153] is to over-simplify the realities of the West African situation. For there is sufficient evidence that the British refusal to supply arms to Ethiopia, followed by the Hoare-Laval deal, provoked the nationalist groups who vehemently denounced the British conduct of the Ethiopian affair, a denunciation which was frequently reflected not only in the press but also in the police and district commissioners' despatches to the government.

It is evident from the foregoing that the British officials in the colonies did not, in fact, write down all that they believed to be true about the world in which they lived or the regions they governed. Beyond the world of despatches, there was also a world of unstated assumptions. Many of the articulate West African nationalists were very much acquainted with this policy of 'the man on the spot' when it came to furnishing reports to the Colonial Office with regard to conditions in the colonial empire. It was because of this that Azikiwe once advised that the Secretary of State for the Colonies and the British leaders of opinion 'should be in a position to understand the temperament of the African from the tone of the West African press'.[154] Kobina Sekyi also referred to this situation in his critical analysis of the Guggisberg administration in the Gold Coast when he wrote:

... as matters now stand, there can be no doubt that the head of the Colonial Office knows very little of what takes place here, and the British public knows less. ... It is easy to conceive now much mischief can be done here by any administrator who takes it into his head to do harm to the interest of the people of this country, and at the same time sends to the Secretary of State for the Colonies, despatches representing things to be totally different as far as the feelings and the rights of the people are concerned. ...[155]

We have sought to discuss the main organisational aspects of the attitudes of West Africans to the Italian attack on Ethiopia. It has been noted that although many militant nationalists expressed their preparedness to enlist in the Ethiopian forces, the Foreign Enlistment Act of 1870, in their opinion, prevented the realisation of this objective. It seems doubtful, however, whether in view of the economic and financial crisis of the period, these volunteers would have been able to provide themselves with sufficient funds for such a noble pan-African inspired venture. This would appear to have been confirmed by the inadequacy of the relief funds realised for the Ethiopian cause. Indeed, laudable but expensive schemes, such as a journey to far-away Ethiopia, were, to say the least, another instalment of the utopian dreams characteristic of most nationalist leaders at the time. To some extent, therefore, the invocation of the Foreign Enlistment Act of 1870 appeared to have provided the nationalist groups with a most respectable and desirable excuse. The relief fund committees and the organisation of prayers were in fact a practicable substitute for volunteering to Ethiopia. To the governors in West Africa, however, most of these were extraneous issues not worth reporting on in official despatches. But that they were not fully aware of the significance of the impact of the Italo-Ethiopian conflict on the politics of their colonial subjects is the story of the next chapter.

1 *Nigerian Daily Telegraph*, 7 October 1935.
2 *African Morning Post*, 30 October 1935.
3 C.S.O.1324/31 Sub. File 4, Ghana National Archives, Accra.
4 In the Gold Coast, where there was much agitation about boycotting, percentage of trade with Italy from 1934–36 was as follows:

Year	Imports from Italy	Exports to Italy
1934	·79	1.43
1935	1·47	1·83
1936	1·18	·52

Conf. C.S.O.340/35, Ghana National Archives, Accra, Ag. Comptroller of Customs to Colonial Secretary, Accra, 2 February 1937. The value of import trade in 1935 was £107,822, and export trade £167,637. In 1936 the import trade was £100,490 and export trade £63,607. *Blue Books*, ADM.7/1/69.
5 C.S.O.25/36, Conf. file 75/36, Sub. file 2, Ghana National Archives, Accra.
6 ADM13/1/13, Executive Council*Minutes*, 2 December 1935, Ghana National Archives, Accra.
7 Conf. C.S.O.361/38, Ghana National Archives, Accra.
8 *Ibid.*, Miss Hebe Spaull to Hodson, 1 September 1938.
9 *Ibid.*, George London to Miss Hebe Spaull, 12 October 1938.
10 Christopher Fyfe, 'The Sierra Leone Press', *op. cit.*, p. 226.
11 *Sierra Leone Daily Guardian*, 27 September 1935.
12 *Gold Coast Independent*, 15 February 1936.
13 *Gold Coast Spectator*, 5 October 1935.
14 *Vox Populi*, 12 October 1935.
15 *Gold Coast Spectator*, 10 October 1935.
16 *Vox Populi*, 17 October 1935.
17 *Gold Coast Spectator*, 26 October 1935.
18 Azikiwe in *African Morning Post*, 10 October 1935.
19 For a detailed reference to this thesis, see Philip D. Curtin, *The Image of Africa: British Ideas and Action, 1780–1850*, London ,1965, p. 257. This is also discussed in Jack Goody, 'The Myth of a State', *Journal of Modern African Studies*, vi, 4, 1968, pp. 465–8.
20 *African Morning Post*, 8 October 1935.
21 See for instance, *Chicago Defender* (Chicago, U.S.A.) 7 December 1935; also *El Ouma* (Paris) August–September 1935 and *Cri des Nègres* (Paris), November 1935.
22 C.S.O.26/30468, Vol. 1, Nigerian National Archives, Badger to Chief Secretary, 5 October 1935.

23 *Ibid.*, minute by Ag. Chief Secretary to Attorney-General of Nigeria, 21 October 1935.
24 *Ibid.*, minute by Attorney-General, 22 October 1935.
25 *Ibid.*, G. C. Whiteley to Badger, 25 October 1935.
26 *Ibid.*, Foreign Office Circular T.10544/378 of 6 September 1935 to British Consular Officers authorised to issue or renew passports.
27 *Ibid.*
28 *Nigerian Daily Times*, 29 November 1935.
29 *Gold Coast Independent*, 25 January 1936.
30 Conversation with author.
31 A. A. Afrifa, *The Ghana Coup*, London, 1967, p. 104.
32 *Sierra Leone Daily Guardian*, 31 August 1935.
33 *Sierra Leone Weekly News*, 7 September 1935.
34 *Ibid.*, 18 January 1936.
35 *African Standard* (Freetown), 13 January 1939.
36 For details about Faduma and Chief Sam's movement, see Langley, *Pan-Africanism and Nationalism*, London, 1973, pp. 41–58.
37 The text was taken from the 'Songs of Solomon', ch. I, vrs. 6.
38 *Sierra Leone Daily Mail*, 28 September 1935.
39 *Ibid.*, 30 September 1935.
40 *Ibid.*, 25 October 1935.
41 *Vox Populi*, 16 October 1935.
42 *Ibid.*, 2 September 1935.
43 *Nigerian Daily Telegraph*, 25 September 1935.
44 *Hotobah During Papers.*
45 *Ibid*
46 *Sierra Leone Daily Mail*, 21 October 1935.
47 Extracts of South African condemnation of the Hoare-Laval plan are provided in F.O.371/20155, G. A. Willinger, Ag. British High Commissioner in South Africa, to MacDonald, 18 December 1935.
48 This was evident in an address by te Water at the League of Nations, *Official Journal*, special supplement No. 18, pp. 66–7.
49 *Sierra Leone Weekly News*, 11 July 1936.
50 *Ibid.*
51 *Ibid.* For details, see my article, 'South Africa and the Italo-Ethiopian Crisis, 1934–36', *Journal of Social Science* (Legon), iii, 1, December 1974.
52 *Sierra Leone Daily Mail*, 21 October 1935.
53 There is no evidence indicating the actual amount collected by the People's Committee.
54 *Hotobah During Papers.*
55 F.O.371/20154, Moore to J. H. Thomas, Secretary of State for the Colonies, 30 December 1935.
56 *Gambia Outlook and Senegambian Reporter*, 13 February 1936.
57 *Ibid.*, 8 February 1936.
58 See, for example, *Nigerian Daily Telegraph*, 9 December 1935.
59 Details supplied by Akisanya.
60 *Nigerian Daily Telegraph*, 12 May 1936.
61 *Ibid.*
62 *Comet*, 2 May 1936.
63 C.S.O.26, file No. 30468, Vol. II, Nigerian National Archives, Ibadan, minute by Whiteley, 4 November 1936.
64 *Ibid.*
65 Bentum-Obrigya to Dr Martin, Ethiopia Minister in London; *Comet*, 16 May 1936.
66 *Ibid.*, Dr Martin to Bentum-Obrigya, 11 July 1936.
67 *Ibid.*, 25 April 1936.
68 *Ibid.*
69 *Ibid.*
70 *Ibid.*
71 *Ibid.* The Indian Muslim sympathy for Ethiopia during the crisis was based on the memory of Ethiopian conduct during the persecution period. It remained a living force. For details, see Royal Institute of International Affairs, *Survey of International Affairs*, Vol. II, 1935, pp. 107–8.
72 *Ibid.*, 16 May 1936.

73 *Ibid.*, 20 June 1936.
74 *Ibid.*, 10 October 1936. For some of the lists of contributors, see *Comet*, 9 May 1936; also, 19 July 1936.
75 C.S.O.26/30468, Vol. I, Nigerian National Archives, Joshua Riketts to Chief Secretary, 19 October 1935.
76 *Ibid.*, G. C. Whiteley to Ricketts, undated.
77 *Nigerian Daily Telegraph*, 26 November 1935.
78 C.S.O.1324/31, sub-file No. 18, Ghana National Archives, Accra.
79 *Ibid.*, joint-secretaries, Ethiopia Defence Committee, to the Colonial Secretary, Accra, 15 October 1935.
80 *Ibid*, G. C. du Boulay to joint-secretaries, Ethiopia Defence Committee, 19 October 1935.
81 *Ibid.*, joint-secretaries, Ethiopia Defence Committee, to the Colonial Secretary, Accra, 31 October 1935.
82 *Wallace Johnson Papers*; also *Ocansey Papers*.
83 *Gold Coast Spectator*, 18 December 1935.
84 *Vox Populi*, 27 November 1935.
85 See *40 years: Ghana Christian Council Anniversary Handbook*, p. 20.
86 This circular was discovered among the Christian Council papers at Osu, Accra.
87 *Gold Coast Independent*, 30 November 1935.
88 D.6254 and 1064, Conf. Diaries, Cape Coast and Winneba Districts respectively, Ghana Regional Archives, Cape Coast.
89 ACC.716/56, Ghana National Archives, Accra.
90 *Ibid.*
91 Interview, E. O. Asafu-Adjaye, Accra, June 1971.
92 C.O.96/714/21639/1934, Thomas to Fiddian, 27 February 1934.
93 ACC.92/65 *Aborigines Papers*, Cape Coast.
94 C.O.267/655/32157/1936, Ag. Governor of Sierra Leone to W. G. A. Ormsby-Gore, Secretary of State for the Colonies, 20 September 1936.
95 *Ibid.*
96 *Sierra Leone Daily Guardian*, 17 January 1936.
97 C.O.96/740/31230/1, minute by C. Lambert, 22 March 1937.
98 C.O.323/1517/7046/3, general, a letter from John Jos Begnaya to Wallace Johnson, 18 April 1937.
99 Conversation with Akiwumi, Accra, 21 June 1971. For example, on the very first day of the Conference of British West Africa held in Accra on 11 March 1920, Thomas Hutton-Mills, who was the President, was able to subscribe as much as £1,050. Langley, *Pan-Africanism and Nationalism*, pp. 125–6.
100 *Wallace Johnson Papers*. For Johnson's inability to work with any of the post-1945 Sierra Leone opposition parties, see Cartwright, *Politics in Sierra Leone*, p. 37, n. 7.
101 *Ibid.*
102 *Vox Populi*, 5 February 1936.
103 *Ibid.*, also, *Wallace Johnson Papers*. In 1937, Wallace Johnson, as General-Secretary of the International African Service Bureau in London, was confronted with a similar allegation about misappropriation of funds. Johnson was 'dismissed from the post of General-Secretary of IASB, because he was suspected of mixing the Bureau's funds with his own'. G.O.96/740/31230/1. For details see O. G. R. Williams to Sir Douglas Jardine, Governor of Sierra Leone, 10 April 1938, despatch No. 7046/3/38, enclosed in Gambia secret M.P. No. 179, 4/73, 22 February 1938, Gambia Records Office, Bathurst.
104 C.S.O.1324/31, Sub. file 18, Ghana National Archives, Accra.
105 *Danquah Papers*.
106 *Proceedings*, Watson Commission, 1948.
107 Interview with Mabel Dove, Accra, 20 June 1970.
108 Spitzer and Denzer, 'I. T. A. Wallace Johnson and the West African Youth League', p. 435.
109 *Vox Populi*, 16 October 1935.
110 A letter from Nana Tsibu Darku IX, Paramount Chief of Assin Atandansu, 21 April 1970.
111 *Ibid.* Enstooled in 1932, Nana Sir Tsibu Darku IX was one of the influential chiefs in the Legislative Council. He was later nominated to the Executive Council after the death of Nana Sir Ofori Atta I in 1943.

112 C.O.554/50, Guggisberg's telegram to Lord Milner, 2 January 1921.
113 *Ibid.*, H. J. Read, Colonial Office, to Bankole-Bright, Secretary to the London Delegation of the NCBWA, 26 January 1921.
114 *Ibid.*
115 *Gold Coast Spectator*, 11 November 1936.
116 ACC.730/1956, Ghana National Archives, Accra.
117 *Wallace Johnson Papers.*
118 *Vox Populi*, 9 November 1936.
119 *Wallace Johnson Papers.*
120 *Provincial Pioneer*, 27 April 1935.
121 See Wallace Johnson, *A Restoration of the Ashanti Confederacy*, Accra, 1935, for details.
122 ADM.12/1/100, Ghana National Archives, Accra.
123 Conf. ADM.12/510, Ghana National Archives, Accra.
124 ACC.805/56, *Minutes* of the 23 Session, Provincial Council, Eastern Province, Ghana National Archives, Accra.
125 S.N.A.212/32, *Minutes*, Joint Provincial Council Meeting, 27 November 1936.
126 C.O.96/738/31189.
127 C.O.96/731/31230 minute by Gerald Creasy, 27 February 1936.
128 *Ibid.*, Hodson to Sir Cecil Bottomley, Secretary of State for the Colonies, 14 January 1936.
129 *Ibid.*
130 Bridgeman wrote on 3 June 1936 to ask for the reasons for the raid of the office of Wallace Johnson on 2 June 1936. Details of Bridgeman's reaction are provided in *Bridgeman Papers*.
131 Mss. Brit. Emp. S.332, ACJ.18/3, *Creech Jones Papers*, Kidd to the Colonial Office, 8 July 1936.
132 *Ibid.*
133 C.O.96/731/31230/1936, minute by Gerald Bushe, undated.
134 *Ibid.*, minute by M. R. Maclennan, 15 June 1936; also, *ibid.*, minute by Alex Fiddian, 5 September 1936.
135 *Times* (London) 24 May 1938, enclosed in H. W. B. Blackhall, the Attorney General, Gold Coast, to Bushe, 13 November 1938. C.O.96/749/31230/2/1938.
136 C.O.96/731/31230, Hodson to Bottomley, 16 October 1936.
137 *Ibid.*, 21 April 1937.
138 A correspondent to the *Nigerian Daily Telegraph*, who styled himself 'Kritikus', referred to the Gold Coast £200,000 drive in aid of Ethiopia in an article, 'Let's Come to Earth Awhile!: Emotion versus Reason', *Nigerian Daily Telegraph*, 23 December 1935.
139 Interview, Richard Akwei, Accra, 29 May 1971.
140 *United States Diplomatic Papers*, 1935, 1, p. 613.
141 F.O.371/20155, Hoare to Dominion representatives in London, 29 July 1935.
142 See Mussolini, *Opera Omnia*, xxvii, pp. 110–11. Cited in Baer, *The Coming of the Italian-Ethiopian War*, p. 127.
143 F.O.371/19149, Hoare to Sir George Clerk, 29 July 1935.
144 *Ibid.*
145 *Ibid.*
146 F.O.371/20154, MacDonald to officers administering the governments of British Colonies and Dependencies, 19 November 1935.
147 *Ibid.*
148 *Ibid.*, Henry Moore to J. H. Thomas, Secretary of State for the Colonies, 30 December 1935; also, Bourdillon to Thomas, 27 February 1936.
149 *Ibid.*, Moore to Thomas.
150 *Ibid.*, George London to Thomas, 17 January 1936.
151 Lord Hailey's address to the Royal Empire Society, 'Nationalism in Africa', *Journal of the Royal African Society*, xxvi, April 1937, p. 143.
152 F.O.371/20154, Bourdillon to Thomas, 27 February 1936.
153 *Ibid.*, London to Thomas, 17 January 1936.
154 Azikiwe, *Renascent Africa*, p. 70. A similar comment by Wallace Johnson to the Colonial Secretary in Freetown is contained in C.O.267/666/32216, 15 July 1938.
155 ACC.539/64, *Sekyi Papers.*

CHAPTER VI

The impact of the crisis on nationalist thought and politics

In her 1961 'Reith Lectures', Margery Perham asserted that the rape of Ethiopia, followed by the German colonial claims, ended what she termed the period of 'colonial honeymoon' or the period of acceptance. For almost the first time in history, she continued, the 'idea of imperialism was put, however mildly, upon the defensive'.[1] There can be little doubt that the Ethiopian conflict was among the main influences in the awakening of racial and political consciousness in West Africa. It aroused the aspirations of most anti-colonial nationalists who were stimulated to question not only their relationship with Great Britain but also those assumptions on which the philosophy of the colonial system itself rested. Hitherto, the doctrines of the 'civilising mission' and 'trusteeship', however distasteful, appeared to have been tacitly accepted by a good number of the nationalists, although, on occasion, they tended to press for a reform of the colonial system so as to remove obstacles to their rapid advancement within its framework.[2] More radical demands were not generally included in their agitation for a share in the colonial administrations. It was not until the Italian invasion of Ethiopia that unequivocal demands for self-determination began to be made and signs of militancy began to appear. Subsequent demands for the reform of the colonial administrations no longer aimed at a modest share in the ordering of imperial affairs. From now such demands ceased to be an end in themselves but were merely a means to a more fundamental end – self-government. Even the moderates' criticisms of the colonial regimes, hitherto tempered with polite phrases, thenceforth assumed a tone of marked harshness and hostility.

It was this rising tide of radicalism which received further impetus from the Atlantic Charter, the temporary collapse of the British colonial empire in the Far East and the anti-imperialist utterances of such leading American politicians as Wendell Wilkie. Scholars of British colonial administrations, such as Professor R. Coupland and Lord Hailey, who closely studied the political forces in West Africa in the late 1930s, began to 'bombard' the Colonial Office with proposals for a grant of 'some measured advance in the direction of self-government'.[3] And by the time the Second World War broke out, Britain 'had both advertised and advanced her promise of greater self-government for her African colonies'.[4]

The main theme of this chapter will relate to how the Ethiopian crisis stimulated the nationalists to subject to a detailed examination certain aspects of the colonial system. This chapter will also show how, under the impulse of the events in Ethiopia, the youth movements and the leagues were able – even if for a comparatively short period – to contest and win the municipal and town council elections, as well as the Legislative Council elections, which had hitherto been dominated by the established elite. Finally, this chapter will atttempt to bring into focus the impact of the Italo-Ethiopian conflict on the political thought and activity of selected post-1945 nationalist leaders, some of whom were critically involved in the protest demonstrations against the Italian action in Ethiopia. The nationalism of these leaders shifted from the idea of working within the trusteeship concept to a more militant anti-white pan-Africanism which culminated in the historic 1945 Manchester Pan-African Congress.

End of the Old Colonial Empire

The long resistance of the Ethiopians to the Italian attack, and the failure of Great Britain to check the aggressive militarism of Italy, stimulated the nationalist leaders and the political organisations to anathematise colonialism and all the appendages of that system. One major concern which preoccupied the attention of the anti-colonialists was the question of Britain's breach of faith to the Ethiopians and, as they viewed it, to the millions of her African subjects. To the nationalist groups, this hampered the relationship between West Africans and their ruling colonial power. For not only did this attitude of Britain strain the loyalty of West Africans which had 'never wavered in the past', but it also shattered their last vestige of hope in their colonial overlord and destroyed their sense of security under British imperialism.[5] The general topic everywhere was whether West Africans could trust Great Britain any longer, for many articulate nationalists were very deeply moved by this display of British insincerity in the Italo-Ethiopian affair. The issue between Italy and Ethiopia therefore constituted a crucial test not only of the 'white man's insincerity' in his dealings with the black man in general, but also, and more significantly, it was the 'acid test' of West Africa's relationship with Great Britain. The belief in the British 'gospel of equity and fair play' had, in the eyes of the nationalist organisations, been destroyed. The lesson was instructive:

> The misfortunes, failures and calamities that befall wise men widen their outlook on life and add more to their stock of experiences than a hundred successes can do. The African is a child and possesses both the praiseworthy and contemptible qualities of a child. Some of the despicable traits of the African are credulity, over-loyalty, sycophancy. His native goodness makes him a prey to others because he thinks that all are as honest, trustworthy and guileless as himself.[6]

It was such 'despicable traits of the African' which in the view of the nationalists formed the basis of Haile Selassie's general attitudes to the white powers, he being a typical African who 'believeth all things, hopeth all things, endureth all things'. Thus, if any fault could be attributed to the Emperor of Ethiopia, it was his 'almost childlike faith in the British pledge', and it was this which had proved the undoing of Ethiopia and betrayed the black race.[7] Africans would therefore never again regard as sacred and inviolate the British word of honour 'spoken or documented'. For not only had the foundations on which their relations with Britain rested been destroyed, but also in their place had sprung up suspicion, lack of confidence and mistrust.[8] Thenceforth, as declared by Olu Ayodele Alakija, one of the successful NYM candidates to the Nigerian

Legislative Council election in 1938, West Africans should no longer be satisfied with talk, reliance on the sanctity of treaties and solemn covenants: 'We want something definite, void of vagaries, concrete.'[9]

One other subject which engaged the attention of the radical organisations was whether there was anything at all to be gained from Western civilisation by colonial subjects. In their view, the means whereby Africans had been kept in subjection under the European nations was religion and civilisation. At the beginning of the Ethiopian crisis many of them believed that civilisation was so potent a factor that not only could it 'meet Mussolini's harangues' with the cool deliberations of collective security and sanctions, but also prevent him from executing his diabolical ambition and condemn his brutalities. On the contrary, however, this belief and confidence in Western society proved in the end to be a delusion and, as it appeared to the members of the Nigerian Youth Movement, 'Western civilization bows before might and colour'.[10] For, if the savage act and immoral conduct of Italy was a true reflection of what Western civilisation stood for and meant, then those who boasted as the bearers of the torchlight of that civilisation had nothing at all to boast of – 'and those they lead have yet to look elsewhere for a worthy example and pattern to follow and adopt'.[11]

This conclusion led such organisations as the West African Students' Union to a detailed analysis of the achievements of Western civilisation. Members of the union contended that, as a people, they were easily taken in by the manifest achievements of Western civilisation. This was because when they compared 'their dug-out with the floating hotel' of the white man; their bow and arrow with his machine gun; their ignorance of the forces of nature with his almost complete knowledge thereof, they could not but admit their 'backwardness' and acquiescence in the lordship of the white man. But, they argued, as the Ethiopian crisis had fully demonstrated, the time had come for West Africans to 'shake off the spell and face reality'. For although Western civilisation had achieved many miracles of which they were proud, they wondered at 'what price these had been achieved'. In their opinion, the nations which met at Geneva to condemn the aggression of Italy subscribed to a form of society which was based on the exploitation of the many by the few for the enrichment of the latter. In such a society, war 'was an integral part'. It was recalled that what Italy was doing in Ethiopia in the mid-thirties, the other great nations had done in the past. When it was not a war of aggression, as in the case of Italy, it was a war (euphemistically called 'struggle') of a more subtle, but none the less ruthless nature between the classes – 'those who exploit and those who are exploited – within the nation'.[12]

Not only did the nationalist leaders reject the political forms of Western civilisation; they also stressed the danger of introducing in Africa free of colonial powers, the same 'struggle' inherent in Western civilisation. The Ethiopian conflict and the outbreak of the Spanish Civil War were for the nationalist groups constant reminders that the white people had nothing to be proud of. The use of poison gas on the Ethiopians by Italian troops constrained the militant anti-colonialists to one conclusion: 'Politically and religiously the West has been weighed in the balance and found wanting'.[13] Thenceforth Western civilisation and all that it stood for became suspect. But the villain of the piece was Great Britain, their ruling colonial power.

The colonial subjects in West Africa took the 'failure of nerve' of Great Britain in the Italo-Ethiopian dispute to be a true measure of her real power which, so they concluded, was not as great as she claimed it to be. They wondered whether Great Britain had still the will-power, the strength and resources to protect her colonial subjects. In their view, the Ethiopian conflict had brought into serious question the often repeated argument that colonial systems were ethically justified by the protection which great powers gave to technologically backward peoples. From then on, they saw their relationship with Britain with new and realistic eyes, and whether rationally or instinctively, they felt that the grasp in which they had been held had been relaxed. This was made evident in some of the secret and confidential despatches to the Colonial Office at this time. In Nigeria, for example, some secret 'Intelligence Reports' disclosed clearly that the nationalist leaders in the colony considered that since Ethiopia had fallen to Italy without any intervention on the part of Great Britain, their colonial power was 'frightened to interfere in any uprising in Africa' because her power was now on the wane.[14] This feeling was reinforced by the knowledge of the Palestine disturbances: '. . . the question why Great Britain sent a whole division to protect the Jews, and did not send a single soldier to protect the Abyssinians, exercises the minds of some members of the populace, who are doubtless unacquainted with the terms of the Balfour Declaration'.[15] The predominant view after the fall of Ethiopia was that either Britain had no longer any interest in her colonial subjects in Africa or her colonial system was fast disintegrating, as a result of the weakness of British power. This view was eloquently expressed in an important public address, 'The Beneficial Effects of the Italo-Abyssinian Imbroglio', delivered by S. L. Akintola, a staunch member of the Nigerian Youth Movement, who was later to become one of the most outspoken nationalists among the leaders of the Action Group, and Premier of Western Nigeria at the time of the 1966 military coup.[16]

This development led to the intensification of the earlier general denunciation of the indirect rule system in West Africa which, in the opinion of the nationalist agitators, was an obstacle to self-determination.[17] According to the nationalists, the facts about indirect rule – the attempt on the part of the British Government to rule her colonial subjects, as far as possible, through the agency of indigenous institutions – did not justify the assertions and hopes of the British administrators. Indirect rule, they said, did not displace 'Rule by Proclamations or Ordinances' and was itself installed by the use of those powers. The experience of the West African territories was that the kind of indirect rule established had largely violated the spirit of 'native institutions, usage and tradition'. They explained that it was a well established principle with the people of West Africa that the power of the chiefs was derived from the people and that their official acts must be performed in the presence of the people and in consultation with the chief's elders and councillors as representing the people. But under indirect rule the chiefs looked to British power and not to their own people for support and authority. Traditional authority was, therefore, undermined insofar as the practice was diametrically opposed to the concept that the chief's power springs from the citizens. Moreover, certain chiefs were installed who did not carry the confidence of the people. For the colonial administration had the tendency to press for the election to the position of chief persons loyal to the British administration, who had little or no title under the customary law and to resist efforts to destool chiefs who had lost the support of their people. These 'imposed' chiefs failed to command the allegiance necessary for sustaining a traditional chief. There were even cases where there was a 'chief gazetted by the government but ignored by the people', and an unofficial chief whom they regarded. It was 'notorious how the knowledge of the backing of the government' encouraged some chiefs to exercise their powers in an authoritarian manner, in a way they could rarely have done in traditional society without deposition.

Briefly, the system of indirect rule in West Africa was denounced by the militant nationalists for three main reasons. In the first place, they argued that most Africans considered indirect rule as a policy of trying to control Africa through a so-called representative of the people, who was in reality merely a puppet in the hands of the government; and as no serious attempt was being made by the government to secure co-operation between the educated and the uneducated Africans, they concluded that the result of the system must be to hinder African progress and destroy African solidarity.[18] Secondly, since under the indirect rule system, the government in practice made no attempt to consult educated Africans, these nationalist agitators found it difficult to reconcile the fact of indirect rule with the government's declared policy of encouraging African development. The European always claimed to know what was good for the African; but he did not consult the educated African, who might be supposed to have ideas on what was good for himself. In any case, to the colonial administration the educated African was 'a worse evil than the primitive savage'.[19] Thirdly, indirect rule was widely accused of reinforcing the power and authority of single chiefs. Voices were raised pointing out that, with the acquisition of personal wealth by the chiefs, indirect rule was increasing their importance and encouraging them to clamour for more power. The influential chiefs, in fact, ultimately acquiesced in British colonial control because there was the virtual guarantee that they would thereby become beneficiaries of further constitutional advances, and heirs to the British Government. In the view of the educated elite and professionals, as the interests of the chiefs were coming to coincide with those of the colonial authorities, the chiefs would be only too glad to slow down the struggle for national independence. Indirect rule therefore became a *bête noire* of the nationalists whose criticism of the system increased tremendously after the Italian conquest of Ethiopia. Officially disinherited and restive, Wallace Johnson and his West African Youth League in Sierra Leone, for example, emphatically declared:

> We stand firmly on the platform of self-determination. . . . If the African is capable of administering his own affairs, he must rule minus the influence of European supervision. He must breathe his own free air in his administrative deliberations. He must say out in his own mind freely and speak in his own terms and not in the terms of 'investors who know next to nothing of his way and mode of living'.[20]

By the close of the 1930s such writers as Meek, MacMillan and Hussey had come to the conclusion that the Gold Coast in particular had already reached a stage where strong and enlightened control of government, in which moreover the people must participate, was essential.[21]

The Gold Coast agitation against the indirect rule system occupied the attention of the permanent staff of the Colonial Office as well as the Colonial Service officials in the Gold Coast, who were beginning to lose their faith in the existing system of indirect rule in the colony. As a result of the disillusionment with the system, a vigorous debate was conducted in London and in the Gold

Coast on the subject of indirect rule. In London a meeting was held on 15 October 1935 at which it was agreed that with the progress of education and the economic development of the country, the time had come when the government would have to contemplate a complete change of policy in the Gold Coast, that was, to get away from the idea of 'bolstering up the native chiefs'.[22] Alex Fiddian, a senior official at the Colonial Office, felt, however, that the substitution of *direct* for *indirect* rule would 'be simply a ghastly confession of failure' in the Gold Coast, as 'all our endeavours at present have been directed to establishing on a sound footing the practice of government through a recognised Native Administration and not directly'.[23]

Yet no one doubted that the political life in the Gold Coast, as described by H. M. Grace, the Principal of Achimota College, in his letter to Dr Meyer Fortes, a young anthropologist and a Fellow of the International African Institute in London, was in a 'precarious position'.[24] Gerald Creasy (later Sir Gerald Creasy, Governor of the Gold Coast, 1948–49), agreed with him, for 'affairs in the Colony have continued to drift' and no attempt was being made to examine the question of native administration as a whole and 'to think out a policy for the future'.[25] This viewpoint was confirmed by Sir Cecil Bottomley, the Under Secretary of State for the Colonies, who confessed to Governor Arnold Hodson that even the Secretary of State was himself somewhat uneasy about the 'present situation in the Colony and still more perhaps at what may develop in the future if nothing is done now. . . . I understand from your letter that you yourself are doubtful whether the Government is on the right lines in its native policy.'[26] The dilemma of the Colonial Office as to whether or not the indirect rule system was still practicable in the Gold Coast was made evident in a report by Lord Hailey on his recent tour of the colony. Lord Hailey, who later in an address to the Royal Empire Society in London referred to the impact of the Ethiopian conflict on nationalist thought and activity in West Africa, had also formed the impression that the administration of the colony was drifting into a form of direct rule which 'the central government endeavoured to undertake, through the agency of departmental officers' work which should properly be carried out by the Native Administrations'. He observed that the administrative officer was being 'pushed into the background and was losing his place as an adviser and helper of native authorities'. Looking to the future, Lord Hailey was of the view that direct rule was not a practicable policy and he saw no alternative to an endeavour to build up in the Gold Coast Colony a system ot indirect administration 'based on existing native institutions, that is, the chiefs'.[27] On the other hand, Governor Sir Arnold Hodson, who was 'not primarily interested in Native Administration, and would not readily move in these matters',[28] strongly opposed the idea of an outside commission to investigate the political situation in the Gold Coast, as suggested by the Colonial Office, on the grounds that there were plenty of experienced and capable officers in the Gold Coast if such a commission were necessary, and that a general debate would in any case be more useful than a commission.[29]

It is pertinent to observe that throughout the debate on the Gold Coast political situation, the Colonial Office officials, Lord Hailey, and the Gold Coast Government itself were of the view that the then militancy of the agitation against indirect rule in the colony had been caused by the local lawyers and anti-colonialists in their search for 'pickings', the opportunity for which had been provided by the British policy towards the Ethiopian question. They asserted that the country suffered from outside agitators of the type of Wallace Johnson who had become incensed by the events in Ethiopia. Consequent upon the violent opposition to the indirect rule system which had been occasioned largely by the Italo-Ethiopian conflict, Governor Sir Arnold Hodson informed the Secretary of State for the Colonies that 'especially in view of the present international political situation' and local reaction to it, any measures that he contemplated with regard to the administration of the country 'should be undertaken by degrees, and not simultaneously'.[30] The general feeling was that the political atmosphere in the Gold Coast was so hostile to official control that the radical re-organisation of local government would be impossible.

The agitation against the indirect rule system, which received impetus from the Italian conquest of Ethiopia, greatly accounted for the failure of the British Government to introduce a classic indirect rule policy in the Gold Coast. Thus, unlike Nigeria, the Gold Coast experienced a peculiar case so far as the policy of indirect rule was concerned. For while development of indirect rule was 'the accepted policy and the administrative officers have been instructed accordingly, no steps have yet been taken to provide by legislation a constitutional framework adapted to the operation of such a system'.[31] The Colonial Service officials in the field described the system of government in the Gold Coast as 'a mixture of direct and indirect rule, with a steady bias towards the latter'.[32] For 'the great needs of the Colony' which would have ensured a proper functioning of the indirect rule system – control of stool funds and control of the occupants of the stool – were 'just the things' which the militant nationalists and groups, especially the ARPS, 'reject so violently'.[33]

It is worth emphasising, however, that to see the Italo-Ethiopian conflict as the sole cause of the opposition against the introduction of indirect rule in the Gold Coast during this period would clearly be an oversimplification of a complex situation. For the establishment and practice of indirect rule in the country was complicated throughout the colonial period by an important legal controversy about the relationship between the chiefs and the British Crown. Appealing to the precedent of the Bond of 1844 and the Legislative Assembly of 1852, the chiefs of the Gold Coast consistently claimed that their jurisdiction was inherent and not derivative. Moreover, it was even held by some officials that the very democratic nature of the colony chiefdoms made indirect rule impossible. Thus, what the Ethiopian question really did was to intensify the agitation against the system, and to make it all the more difficult for the government to implement the policy of indirect rule fully. It was, therefore, a much diluted and modified form of indirect rule that was introduced in the Gold Coast during the 1930s.

In Nigeria, too, the Youth Charter of the Nigerian Youth Movement declared that its members were 'opposed to the term "Indirect Rule" literally as well as in principle. Honest trusteeship implies either direct Nigerian rule or direct British rule. We shall therefore strive for the complete abolition of the Indirect Rule system'.[34] This declaration annoyed Governor Bourdillon who sharply reacted to it in a 'Memorandum on Future Political Development of Nigeria' which he prepared in 1939. Bourdillon held that the NYM declaration contained 'an obvious inconsistency, and I have been quite unable to discover what is at the bottom of it'. He claimed that the Nigerian Youth Movement had so far taken no action to implement this declaration, to which he attached no importance. The governor then disclosed that the Legislative Council, at the end of 1937, unanimously approved the proposal to introduce the indirect rule system into the colony districts, 'a proposal which the African members had unanimously rejected eleven years previously, is now universally approved'.[35] However, as an attempt to meet the renewed agitation against indirect rule, Bourdillon, who believed that the system 'encourages the native to reach political responsibility', proposed that reform of the central legislature, with the object of connecting it more closely with the 'Native Administration', would 'be found necessary at a fairly early date'.[36]

According to H. O. Davies, the Secretary of the NYM in 1938, the question of indirect rule was discussed on many occasions at the executive committee meetings of the Youth Movement, and the government was regularly confronted with this issue. Chief Davies, who claimed to have drafted the 'Youth Charter' for adoption by the executive committee, further disclosed that the NYM attacked the system more violently and uncompromisingly than before when 'we became convinced, after the Italian annexation of Ethiopia, that our liberty "lies in self-determination".' By the early 1940s, he concluded, indirect rule had become 'our main target of attack'.[37] This view of Chief Davies is confirmed by Margery Perham when she says that in the thirties the educated Africans 'showed their discontent with indirect rule', and that whenever she talked to them 'their constant themes were that it led nowhere and had no place in it for them'.[38]

Among the few British politicians, diplomats, and missionaries 'on the spot' at the time of the Ethiopian crisis, it was Sir Sidney Barton, the British Legation in Addis Ababa, and Lord Hailey, director of the African Research Survey, who appeared to appreciate sufficiently the profound effect of the Ethiopian affair on the thought and politics of the subject peoples in Africa. Just before the outbreak of the Italo-Ethiopian war, Sir Sidney Barton wrote to warn Sir Samuel Hoare that in the presence of the growing nationalist spirit among African races, the exhibition afforded by Italy's actions and propaganda methods in the course of the dispute, far from furthering the cause of that 'civilisation of which she claims to be the champion' had done more to lower the reputation of the white race than any occurrence since the 1914–18 war. In his opinion, the success of such actions and methods could not fail to influence that spirit in the direction of enmity against all the Western powers having interests in Africa.[39] Having been in Ethiopia since the beginning of the crisis, Sir Sidney could sense the dangers ahead for Britain in her relationships with her African subjects.

Lord Hailey was more specific in his evaluation of the impact of the crisis; he saw more clearly where the 'political wind of change' in West Africa was blowing. In his address to the Royal Empire Society in London, Lord Hailey observed that psychologically, just as Japan's defeat of imperial Russia in 1905 had served to rekindle Asian, particularly Indian, nationalism so did the Italo-Ethiopian conflict serve as a rallying-point for race-conscious Africans in South and West Africa. For, he declared:

... it may well be that to thinking Africans the fact that its three prominent colonising nations were not competent to check the militaristic aggressiveness of a new arrival, were more striking than the evidence that Europeans could still desire to possess themselves of African lands. But I feel that the Abyssinian campaign may yet be destined to have its effect on African thought, for it breaks harshly into the era of altered attitude towards the African Native which the Mandate policy had seemed to signalise.[40]

Lord Hailey's assessment would seem to give a truer picture of the impact of the Ethiopian question on nationalist thought and activity in West Africa than the colonial governors would have us believe. He rightly observed that there were signs of a movement towards an African consciousness which might everywhere 'challenge the integrity of European authority'. Specifically, he said:

> Turning to the West Coast one encounters movements of a more definitely political nature, for the existence of a number of higher educational institutions on the West Coast, and the emergence of a strong lawyer and journalistic element, had produced at Accra, and to some extent at Lagos, a class which more nearly resembles the Indian politician type than can be seen elsewhere in Africa . . . its ambition is a larger representation in the legislature, and a greater share in Government employ.[41]

It is important to observe that even before wartime development began to influence British colonial policy, such well-known experts of British colonial administrations as Professor R. Coupland and Lord Hailey, who had surveyed the political forces in West Africa in the late thirties, had begun to press the Colonial Office to consider substantial 'revisions in policy', and to give considerable weight to the new forces on the West Coast. Already at this time the issue of self-government for the West African colonies was being regularly discussed by the New Fabian Research Bureau at its weekend conferences on 'Colonial Trusteeship' usually held at Lady Margaret Hall in Oxford.[42] In a private and confidential memorandum to the Colonial Office in September 1939, Professor Coupland observed that the colonies of Nigeria and the Gold Coast 'would be the most fruitful field' in which to start some measured advance in the direction of self-government. Although it was held that no part of West Africa was 'in fact ripe for such a measure of self-government as was enjoyed by an Indian province, say, in 1914', nevertheless Coupland advised that a substantial advance might be much more practicable than 'local official opinion would be ready to admit'. The memorandum made reference to the existence of 'an articulate educated African society at Lagos' and suggested that this could provide 'a quota of reasonably competent and public-spirited politicians'. Professor Coupland then recommended that: 'If a constitutional advance were practicable, it would seem that both at Lagos and Accra we are as much committed as we were in India to Parliamentary institutions'. However, in his opinion, the colony of the Gold Coast was 'probably riper for advance' than the colony of Nigeria.[43] On receiving this memorandum, MacDonald, the Secretary of State for the Colonies, commissioned Margery Perham to 'do some work for the Colonial Office on this question'.[44]

Professor Coupland was not, however, the only expert in this field of study who arrived at this conclusion. For after his visit to Africa in 1940 during which he encountered 'movements of a more definitely political nature' in the Gold Coast, Lord Hailey expressed the opinion in a confidential report that if the ultimate political goal of the Gold Coast was 'dominion status or self-government, progressively to be realised', then the political constitution of the country should 'now be organised with a logical foundation to achieve that end'. He would like to see Africans being appointed assistant district commissioners while the Joint Provincial Council should continue, 'but under a different constitution'. It should be a 'Chamber of the Paramount Chiefs' concerned with

Sylvia Pankhurst

Ladipo Solanke

Jomo Kenyatta

Kwame Nkrumah

the internal administration of their different states, 'and ready to form a second Chamber of Government with the coming of Dominion Status'. Lord Hailey further recommended that there should be a Legislative Assembly for the whole country, with manhood or property qualification, concluding: 'To wait until the general masses are educated before such a measure of constitutional freedom is provided is unnecessary, for the people pay taxes whether they are educated or not. Their representatives would be educated and they would represent their views'.[45]

The confidential assessment of the constitutional advances in West Africa by Coupland and Hailey, together with Professor MacMillan's private conversations with the Colonial Office officials in London on the 'political matters' of Sierra Leone during this period,[46] reflected, to some extent, the achievements of the persistence and fervour of the demands of the radical nationalist groups – demands which, as we have seen, were greatly heightened by the events in Ethiopia. For the Italo-Ethiopian struggle awakened the aspirations of the budding West African nationalist leaders and stimulated organisational activity among the youth movements. These movements not only assumed a more active political and national role but also made it unequivocally clear that they were no longer content to accept the pace of political change laid down by their colonial power. Consequently, they began to question persistently the moral foundations of colonialism. The agitation of the youth movements and leagues was not entirely unrewarded. In the first place, to some extent, the tired elite leadership – particularly in Nigeria and Sierra Leone – was temporarily replaced by a vigorous new elite. Secondly, as a result of the radicalism of the new elite, the Colonial Office began to consider seriously the question of granting some constitutional concessions to satisfy the West African nationalist aspirations. To many of the young and progressive nationalists of the late 1930s, this change in outlook of the politics of the period was due partly to the impact of the Italian rape of Ethiopia. For, as some of them variously argued, 'Nationhood developed out of a consciousness of a common past, a common experience and especially of common sufferings and glories'.[47]

The March Towards Self-Government

The violent criticism of the various aspects of British colonial rule developed into a persistent and unequivocal demand for self-government, which received greater attention at this time than any other subject. It was debated in schools and colleges; it was discussed from political platforms and by the nationalist press; it was a subject of symposia; and above all, it was vigorously put forward in a series of memoranda and resolutions by the youth organisations. Political demands no longer took the form of programmes of limited reforms such as an increase in the proportion of elected African members in local legislatures, Africanisation of the public service and the judiciary, and an accelerated tempo of educational development. Self-government on the whole replaced partnership as a political goal.

In the Gold Coast, the attention of both radical groups like the West African Youth League and the ARPS, and 'semi-political associations' like the Gold Coast Youth Conference was devoted to a more penetrating analysis of the British colonial system and the necessity of self-government. The militant nationalists in particular argued on several occasions that the British colonial policy viewed in the light of the Ethiopian question, had disclosed 'on all hands many defects'. Its tendencies seemed to defeat the noble objects of a policy which professed to safeguard and protect the welfare of the subject races inevitably brought under the tutelage of Great Britain as trustee for the civilisation of her devoted and loyal wards. Everywhere, they observed, was heard the cry of dissatisfaction with a policy which 'has now become obsolete':

> This cry of general dissatisfaction entails a serious indictment of present day Imperial Colonial Policy by the subject races of the Empire who cherish grave misgivings and despondent feeling that successive British governments and British people as a whole, bemused by visionary and unpractical ideas regarding self-government and the universal applicability of democratic institutions, are feebly abandoning their great mission of security to the 'dumb millions' of backward peoples the peace, justice and individual liberty which is *de jure et de facto* theirs by virtue of their status as British subjects and members of the British Empire. This indictment is true in substance and in fact, for it cannot be denied that Great Britain had nowadays been most negligent in the discharging of her obligations of sacred trust towards her loyal and faithful wards scattered all over different outposts of the Empire.[48]

Furthermore, the nationalists lamented that Britain had forgotten her responsibilities and failed in her duty to provide for the welfare and administrative needs of the great masses of her 'backward peoples in Africa'. All that one could see was what appeared to be a total disregard of the duties of the colonial power, her right of trusteeship, of protection, of civilising influence, 'the noble and proud heritage of a governing and directing people'. In the light of all this, the radical political organisations declared that Britain had forfeited her moral right to continue to hold West Africans in subjection. More importantly, they argued that, as had been made evident by the Ethiopian episode, it could 'hardly be seriously contended that the Englishman holds a monopoly of justice and fairplay'. Britain was therefore called upon to devise methods which would enable West Africans to have a definite voice in the management of their own affairs leading to immediate self-government. This was considered to be the just claim and legitimate demand of the West African colonies, 'whose inhabitants are given only the shadow for the substance' by the system of associating the people with the government in a subordinate or advisory capacity, the ultimate power being reserved to the Secretary of State for the Colonies as the instrument of the imperial Parliament. It was made unequivocally clear that there was a growing feeling throughout the British Empire, particularly West Africa, that more extended measures of self-government should be granted to the colonial subjects:

> This is a problem of vital importance which should have the generous attention and consideration of the Powers That Be. It is being urged with consistent insistence because the governed are conscientiously convinced that it is their right and due and that it has been too long delayed and they cannot be indefinitely patient; for there is a point at which patience ceases to be virtue and that point has long since been reached. What is, and what can now be the answer of Great Britain?[49]

The nationalist leaders rejected outright what they described as the 'lame excuse' on the part of Great Britain that West Africans were 'travelling too fast on the road to self-government'. In their view, this was only a 'feeble pretext to brush aside' what was admitted to be a just claim and to evade the prompt attention it demanded. In a mood of impatience, despair and frustration, they declared that the claims of the people in West Africa to self-government 'cannot be denied. That this claim has been too long deferred cannot be gainsaid. It is not true that they are going too fast. It is more true that they have been going too slow and there should now be doubling up of speed. . . .'[50]

Such, then, was the prevailing mood of the nationalists on the question of self-government. The general feeling was that West Africans should no longer be 'content to suffer itself' to be governed by Great Britain. In the Gold Coast the Aborigines' Rights' Protection Society and the West African Youth League were extremely vocal and persistent in their demand for self-government. This demand formed part of the campaigns of the ARPS delegates in Britain in 1935 and 1936. G. E. Moore and S. R. Wood, who, as we have noted, played an important role in the protest demonstrations organised in London by Padmore and C. L. R. James against the Italian rape of Ethiopia, from time to time confronted the Colonial Office with the issue of self-government for West Africa. More specifically, in August 1935, G. E. Moore, leader of the Aborigines' Society deputation in England, questioned Sir Cecil Bottomley about what British policy was in regard to self-government for the Gold Coast. He then referred him to the declaration of the Report of the 1865 Select Committee appointed by the House of Commons on this subject. Although Sir Cecil Bottomley replied that he did not think that British policy on this issue 'had fundamentally changed', the ARPS frequently argued that the Gold Coast was ripe for self-government.[51] William Ofori Atta, then a budding nationalist and son of Nana Sir Ofori Atta, Paramount Chief of Akim Abuakwa, even began to challenge the legitimacy of British rule in West Africa. In an interesting article headed 'Gold Coast Was Made a Crown Colony by Fraud' he argued that, like the Italians in Ethiopia, the foundations of the British West African colonies were 'built on gross injustice and cruelties', adding that it was, for instance, by a 'subtle diplomatic fraud' that the Gold Coast became transferred from an independent state to a Crown Colony.[52]

But it was not the radical organisations alone which in the Gold Coast identified themselves with the struggle for self-government during this period. There were other groups, not strictly political in their aims, which acted as 'carriers' of nationalist ideas, and which played an important part in the building up of public opinion around the issue of self-government. To this class belonged the Gold Coast Youth Conference which, as noted elsewhere, was formed in 1929. Under the leadership of J. B. Danquah, the Youth Conference drew up schemes which pointed to the need for greater social and economic progress as well as for the necessity of self-government. In making the explicit demand for self-government, the Youth Conference had reached a higher level of articulation in comparison with the demands of the twenties and early thirties. Those demands for self-government were not yet backed up by organisational support. But in the late thirties and early forties the intellectual groundwork was laid 'for the behavioural imperatives of the next decade'. Danquah was clear and precise on the demand for political change:

We must as soon as practicable have autonomy or self-government. Our colonial status must be abolished. With self-government we shall be able to speak of our Government as 'Our Government', and any Executive or

Cabinet of the Gold Coast that refused to do the will of the people, could be made to cease to be the Executive or Cabinet in a day's general election. The case for African freedom is a cast iron case.[53]

Danquah, speaking for the intelligentsia, perceived the elite's role in a more advanced framework. The solution was, at least intellectually quite simple. In his own words: '. . . all one would have to do would be to place in power a Cabinet of men who are prepared to carry into effect that policy of raising the status of this country to that of world citizenship industrially and economically'.[54] By the late thirites, the executive committee of the Youth Conference included such radicals as A. M. Akiwumi, Kobina Sekyi and Richard Akwei who had earlier patronised the campaigns of the Ethiopia relief funds. After the deportation of Wallace Johnson from the Gold Coast, the remnants of his Youth League tended to work together with the Youth Conference. At least, both movements were agreed on the demand for self-government, the agitation for which gathered momentum after the fall of Ethiopia in 1936, reaching its climax in 1938 when news reached 'us that Ethiopia had been annexed to Italy'.[55]

The demand for self-government in the Gold Coast at this time was referred to by a *Report on the British Empire* published in London in 1938. This report observed, *inter alia*, that there was 'a very strong demand' on the part of the articulate West Africans for a larger share in the government of their territories. Of the Gold Coast in particular, it specifically stressed that the people had developed such a sense of community that there had been some discussion 'in recent years of a Gold Coast nation'.[56] This view was shared by Meek, Mac-Millan and Hussey, who, in their illuminating study, indicated that the really urgent issues of Gold Coast politics during this period were 'in essence already national rather than "local" ' and that the Gold Coast was 'perhaps the most hopeful of all African colonies'. Concluding, they said, 'Nothing will really satisfy' the people of the Gold Coast 'but unambiguous evidence that the goal towards which they move is representative parliamentary government'.[57]

The agitation for self-government, and the violent criticism of the colonial regime which accompanied it, put the Gold Coast Government in a state of quandary. Evidence would seem to suggest that the Colonial Office in London and the local colonial government in the Gold Coast held different views with regard to the intensity of this agitation in the Gold Coast. In a strongly worded confidential despatch, Sir Arnold Hodson emphatically objected to the view of the Colonial Office that this persistent demand for self-government had created a precarious political position in the Gold Coast. Hodson maintained that the Gold Coast was like 'a dog with a bad name'. He then told the Colonial Office:

> We are cursed with some professional agitators and an anti-government, anti-imperialistic and anti-European press which week after week pours out distorted and exaggerated views on these subjects to their circle of readers. . .
> The result is that the outside world gathers the impression that the country is in a seething state of discontent and dissatisfaction . . . [but] I venture to state . . . that I have never seen a Colony which is more contented, and where the relations between the Europeans and the Africans are better.[58]

Sir Arnold admitted, however, that although the Italo-Ethiopian war had evoked bitter feelings throughout the country, he was 'glad to say, we have had absolutely no trouble, no resolutions and no disturbances'. He added that he had got in touch with all shades of opinion and that he was convinced that, with the exception of a small minority, both the educated and uneducated Africans in the Gold Coast were 'loyal and contented', concluding, 'they are far too comfortable in the Gold Coast'.[59]

Considered in the light of the available documents on the protest demonstrations against the Italo-Ethiopian war, and on the events that led to the Cocoa Hold-Up which soon followed it, Sir Arnold would appear to have oversimplified the feelings of his colonial subjects in the Gold Coast. Barely a week previous to this display of complacency, the governor's deputy, George London, had reported to the Colonial Office that there had been series of mass meetings and protest demonstrations against 'the white races in general' whom the people of the Gold Coast firmly believed were 'conniving at the despoilation of a black race' in Ethiopia.[60] It was also during this period that Wallace Johnson's series of indictments of the white race culminating in his sensational article, 'Has the African A God?' – an editorial which was considered by H. Thomas, the Secretary for Native Affairs in the Gold Coast, as 'a pretty vicious' one written with the object of creating ill-will between African and European[61] – had led the local government to arrest him and Azikiwe. Besides, by this time, the Youth League, the Ex-Servicemen's Union, and the ARPS had systematically pilloried the colonial government in petitions, resolutions and organised protest marches in the streets of Accra, Cape Coast and Sekondi, to which references had been made in confidential police despatches to the government, showing the impact of the Ethiopian crisis on the people of the Gold Coast. That the governor's complacency was a misplaced one, and that the Colonial Office was better informed of the turbulent political situation in the Gold Coast than the 'man on the spot', is evidenced in Sir Arnold's subsequent despatch within a period of less than four weeks after his previous report. Having become disturbed by the widespread criticism of the colonial system, the governor proposed to the Colonial Office that Sir Shenton Thomas's sedition bill be amended so as to enable him to stop press and nationalist agitation for self-government.[62] Not unnaturally, relying perhaps on Sir Arnold's earlier despatch, a meeting of the Colonial Office officials held on 20 March 1936, decided that the governor 'should be warned off his proposed amendment to Sir Shenton Thomas's Bill'.[63]

Although the agitation for self-government by both radical and semi-radical nationalist groups in the Gold Coast was a failure, it was not an unqualified one. The mass movement and the utilisation of modern political techniques like public rallies brought about, as we have noted elsewhere, the victory of the radical Kojo Thompson in a Legislative Council election over Nanka Bruce, a member of the established elite. The agitators organised all segments of Accra society and the neighbouring areas ostensibly for an all-out assault on the colonial regime, but specifically against the 'collaborators' of the British colonial administration. Their tactics made it possible for the *Mambii* Party to become a radical and a revolutionary movement. Apart from the victory of Kojo Thompson, the *Mambii* Party routed the Ratepayers' Association, which formed the hard core of the social elite of Accra society, at subsequent municipal council elections. And so, a new order was established in Accra under the militant leadership of Kojo Thompson.

In Nigeria, too, the claim for self-government was spearheaded by the militant Nigerian Youth Movement. On the assumption by Sir W. Ormsby-Gore of the office of Secretary of State for the Colonies, the Youth Movement pointed out for his immediate consideration the 'necessity for the entire revision of the Crown Colony system' so as to bring it in line 'with modern conditions and intellectual advancement'. Like its counterpart in the Gold Coast, the movement said that an 'excuse has been advanced that the peoples in the Crown Colonies are not yet ripe for accession to those political liberties' which were being enjoyed by the dominions. It then argued that India, with certain reservations, had been advanced to dominion status and 'we have no hesitancy in stating that the inhabitants of the West African Crown Colonies' were at least as enlightened as the inhabitants of India, their cultural background notwithstanding.[64] All through the period of the 'Hands Off Abyssinia' campaigns, the Youth Movement made the British colonial policy its target of attack. By this means, wrote a correspondent, the movement grew popular in stature and became the chief source of the 'clarion call to all the people in Nigeria to hasten the awakening of true national consciousness' by cultivating the spirit of 'real selfless service'.[65]

In May 1938 the Nigerian Youth Movement drew up its official programme, the formidable document, the 'Nigerian Youth Charter', to which reference has already been made. Addressing the country's youth, the Charter stressed the need to unify the different tribes of Nigeria by adopting and encouraging means which would foster better understanding and co-operation between the tribes 'so that they may come to have a common ideal'. This was the first time that a programme cutting across tribal and religious distinctions had been put before the people of Nigeria. The Charter outlined a concrete programme of national reconstruction as a prerequisite to self-government. Indeed, it advocated as its political goal complete self-government:

> The goal of our political activities is a complete taking-over of the Government into the hands of the indigenous people of our country. We are striving towards a position of equal partnership with other member states of the British Commonwealth of Nations, and enjoying complete independence in the local management of our affairs.[66]

The movement accepted the principle of trusteeship 'as the basis of co-operation with the British Government in Nigeria' and pledged itself 'to make that period of trusteeship as brief as possible'. The Youth Charter condemned the official majority of the Legislative Council 'as an inadequate medium for effective articulation of the wishes of our people'. It contended that the Legislative Council as it was then constituted was incompatible with the principle of trusteeship, and therefore demanded a reconstruction of the Legislative Council so that 'all sections of the indigenous population throughout Nigeria will be progressively represented'. The political Charter also aimed at the abolition of the property qualification for the exercise of the franchise and the substitution of universal suffrage 'for every person in Nigeria who is above the age of 21'. It condemned the representation of vested interests on the legislature as opposed to all principles of democratic government. In the view of the movement, this was 'a hindrance to fair and impartial legislation and therefore a challenge to the manhood of Nigeria'. Consequently, the Charter made it clear that the movement would work for the abolition in the Legislative Council of the seats for 'Banking, Mining, Commerce, Shipping and other interests'. Furthermore, as ultimate self-government was the declared aim of the movement, the Charter urged progressive Nigerianisation of the administrative service, the judiciary and town councils. [67]

The Nigerian Youth Charter, which also included pages of the NYM's economic aims and objectives, was indeed a comprehensive document, not unlike the voluminous 1934 Gold Coast Colony and Ashanti Petition to the Colonial Office that preceded it. Both in style, content and aims, the two documents were not dissimilar, although to some extent, the Charter was more idealistic and utopian in inspiration. It was a revolutionary document, and was the first real attempt in Nigeria at expressing disapproval of colonial rule both in theory and in practice. Such fundamental and highly sensitive issues as colour prejudice and racial discrimination in church or state, the necessity of separating the judiciary from the executive and the need for mass education as the 'true pivot of the educational policy' of the government were all given serious attention in the Charter.

What brought the NYM into prominence and made it 'announce their intention of entering the political arena' in full swing was the 'Cocoa Agreement' which led to the 1937 Cocoa Hold-Up, the agitation over the British recognition of the Italian conquest of Ethiopia, and the subsequent rumours that Britain might be disposed to hand over Nigeria or any of her West African colonies to Germany in pursuit of her appeasement policy. In a heated confrontation with Bourdillon on 29 October 1938, a delegation of the movement pressed for an assurance that in the event of negotiations with Germany with regard to her demand for colonies the British Government 'would not do anything affecting the welfare or the interests of the people of Nigeria without first consulting their views'. [68] This was reinforced in the Legislative Council by O. Alakija, member of the NYM, who asked the government to make an unequivocal and authoritative statement on this subject which would 'give all Nigerians a full assurance' that Nigeria was in no danger of being handed over to Germany. [69] Bourdillon's statement that the idea that Nigeria 'should be handed over to any foreign power appeared to be quite fantastic' did not wholly satisfy the members of the NYM who 'expressed the wish that this declaration be reaffirmed' by the Secretary of State for the Colonies. [70] As detailed in the report of Miss Hebe Spaull of the League of Nations Union in Great Britain, there seemed to be a genuine fear of a German or Italian invasion and 'I was constantly asked about the provision of gas masks and a supply of arms to protect the inhabitants in the event of invasion'. [71] Indeed, the general demand for self-government or eventual independence by the West African colonies after the fall of Ethiopia was due partly to the fear that any of them could easily be sacrificed to the Fascist powers in the interest of European peace, in just the same way as Ethiopia had been sacrificed by Britain and France.

As the first step towards the realisation of the goal of self-government, the NYM entered the field of politics in earnest and, at the Town Council elections held in June 1938, secured three out of the four seats, the Democratic Party only getting in one member, Dr Adeniyi-Jones, who topped the poll. [72] The total votes polled were 972 by the Youth Movement candidates and 505 by the Democratic Party candidates. This was followed by the elections for the three Lagos seats on the Legislative Council in which the NYM captured all three seats, thus ending the fifteen years' domination of Herbert Macaulay and his NNDP over Lagos politics. [73] The movement maintained its supremacy in Nigerian politics when its candidate, Jabril Martin, won the Legislative Council election of 1940 to fill the vacancy created by O. Alajija's death. In 1941, however, the NYM split up over the nomination of a candidate to replace Dr K. Abayomi, president of the movement.

The available evidence would seem to suggest that the events in Ethiopia contributed in no small measure to the growth and development of the Nigerian Youth Movement as a radical element in Nigerian politics. The protest demonstrations against the Italian hostilities in Ethiopia, and the attitude of the colonial power in regard to the whole affair, coupled especially with her almost unexpected recognition of the Italian conquest, provided the leaders of the movement with sufficient material to build up the image of their party, as confirmed by Samuel Akisanya, known as 'The Bull Dog of the Movement'. Through its organisation of the Ethiopia Defence Committee the NYM was able to make its influence felt on the Nigerian nationalist front. The Ethiopian meetings gave the leaders of the movement an added opportunity to ventilate their grievances against colonial rule and, as we have noted, to extend their influence to major Nigerian towns and cities which had never before engaged in modern political protest. For example, Ernest Ikoli, later president of the NYM, openly declared at the various 'Hands Off Abyssinia' campaigns that he and his colleagues did not belong to that class of black men who delighted in waving the Union Jack, called themselves British subjects and grew contented that all was well with them and their generation. If the African was to be anything at all, he concluded, he had to fight out his own salvation.[74]

Similarly, Chief H. O. Davies, known as 'The Dynamo of the Movement', has recently confirmed how the idea of 'our being under British rule' was considered as 'a political sting' at the time of the Ethiopian crisis. He has said that when Italy finally conquered Ethiopia, he and the central committee of the NYM had the strongest determination to be free from colonial rule, adding, 'we were against not only the Italians but the whole system of imperialism and colonialism'.[75]

The NYM began to question and contest the legitimacy of colonial rule of African peoples. The question of the legitimacy of colonial government involved it in a range of political activities quite beyond those of the earlier political associations. When exerting its organised influence for alterations in the structure and purposes of colonial government, the NYM utilised various political techniques, and as we have seen, participated in elections to the Legislative Council. For the young leaders of the NYM joined by Azikiwe with his militant racial consciousness and political dynamism on his return from the Gold Coast in 1937, the Ethiopian question remained a sharp and constant reminder of the racial basis of colonialism. For them the era of submission, without constitutional opposition and all the concomitants of 'Uncle Tomism', was gone. The most effective challenge to the legitimacy of British rule in Nigeria had begun. For the first time in the political history of Nigeria, the radical youth, under the impetus of such external forces as the Ethiopian crisis and Cocoa Pool, were able to dislodge the established elite from their seats in both the local and central political structures of the country. These two external events contributed significantly to a wider popular awareness of the existence of the NYM as a national institution.

The agitation for constitutional reform during the mid-thirties was not confined solely to the advanced colonies of the Gold Coast and Nigeria. To a limited degree the conservative NCBWA branches in Sierra Leone and the

Gambia, which organised the Ethiopia relief fund committees, also put forward schemes for greater African representation in central colonial government. Partly because of its stage of development and partly because of lack of radical nationalist organisation throughout the thirties, the Gambia did not agitate for self-government, as was the case in the other colonies. Instead, she continued to press for 'the franchise', and a limited measure of elective representation. In November 1936, M. S. J. Richards, the vice-president of the Gambia section of the NCBWA, complained about the failure of the government to grant a franchise to the citizens of Gambia to place them in line with their sister colonies of British West Africa. He referred to the fact that the constitutional status of the Gambia had not been improved by the government even though it was time 'for Government to appreciate that we are ripe and entitled to enjoy the same privilege of the franchise as our sister colonies'.[76] Richards and a group of nationalists like Councillor H. Darlington Carrol, who established the Abyssinia Red Cross Fund in Gambia, argued that the Ethiopian crisis had awakened the racial consciousness of the people of Gambia and that there was an absolute need for constitutional reform for an effective realisation of their aspirations. Specifically, Richard complained:

> Race consciousness has manifested itself in the people of the Gambia. If yesterday it was said by Government that the people were not ripe, could it be conscientiously said today that they are what they were? On the contrary it would appear that the Government has been keeping the wheels of progress backward and contenting itself with remaining in *status quo* for over a hundred years with the same old constitution.[77]

Nonetheless, until the late forties the political position of the Gambia remained almost the same.

In Sierra Leone, the agitation for self-government was debated not only by the conservative local branch of the NCBWA but also by the radical students of the Fourah Bay College, 'the intellectual pioneer of West Africa'. After registering a protest against Italy's brutalities, the students called 'upon young Africans to observe a day of mourning for the misfortunes of Abyssinia'.[78] The Fourah Bay College subsequently launched a debate on the subject of whether West Africa was ripe for self-government. The consensus of opinion at this debate was that 'no life is worth the living without self-government; and it must be said that self-government is and ever will be the inherent right of West Africa. . . .' since there could be no protection under colonialism. The proceedings of this debate were given wide publicity throughout West Africa.[79] The local branch of the Congress also argued that the 1924 constitution was only a small step toward self-government. It had only provided a new framework for the development of African interests. Animated by the events in Ethiopia, the members of the NCBWA, who also constituted the People's Committee, passed resolutions 'advocating certain Constitutional and Municipal, as well as Legal and Judicial, Reforms'.[80] They reaffirmed the resolution of Congress that the people of British West Africa should be given effective voice in their affairs and specifically resolved: 'That in order to achieve this object the system of elective representation be made universal in the Legislative Council and that nominative representation be done away with.' Like the 1934 Gold Coast Colony and Ashanti petition, the local branch of the Congress further resolved 'That the unofficial members of the Legislative Council do form a majority of that body'.

Besides, the Municipal Corporations with full local self-government should be established in each Municipal town in British West Africa. In particular, the resolution expressed the opinion that the time had come that the City Council of Freetown, which had been taken from the control of the people of Freetown as a temporary 'measure for the purpose of reformation be restored to them'.[81] Other resolutions bearing on medical reforms, agricultural problems, and matters affecting the educational system of Sierra Leone were passed.

These resolutions were neither new nor revolutionary, for they were a reaffirmation of the earlier resolutions of the Sierra Leone Congress movement in the 1920s. Neither Bankole-Bright nor Beoku Betts, the two urban members of the Legislative Council who dominated the local branch of the Congress, was prepared to go further than moderate resolutions. The former remained all through the thirties a true disciple of the basic principle of the Congress and would hardly tolerate any radical approach to the Sierra Leone political situation which might 'so flagrantly violate' the basic aims of the NCBWA.[82] In spite of the comparatively moderate tone which characterised the resolutions, the government made it clear that it saw 'little hope in the present state of the development of Sierra Leone of meeting the desires of Congress in the matter of Constitutional and Municipal reforms'.[83] The revolutionary Wallace Johnson directed his attention to organising a challenge to this uncompromising attitude of the local colonial administration after the British recognition of the Italian conquest of Ethiopia.

Ethiopia and the New West African Nationalists

To a great extent the Ethiopian question played a part in awakening a new generation of West African nationalists whose growing awareness of the inequities of colonialism and disenchantment with the British connection led to their progression towards liberation. For not only did the Italian attack on Ethiopia help to create an awareness, hitherto lacking, of events in other parts of Africa; it also contributed to the creation of a new awareness of Europe's growing stranglehold on Africa which sowed the seeds of nationalism. The political memories of the post-1945 West African political leaders who had lived through the Ethiopian crisis were coloured by the events of this period which may be considered a period of political incubation; their ideas were formed and the basis of their policies was laid during this period.

Among the new West African anti-colonialists who reacted to the Italian invasion of Ethiopia, Wallace Johnson's role was unique. We have noted how in the Gold Coast Johnson was the central figure, 'life and health', of the Ethiopia relief fund campaigns and protest demonstrations organised in that country. We have also seen how the Ethiopian question served his purposes admirably as a unique means by which consciousness of the evils of racial imperialism could be aroused. The Ethiopia Defence Committee which he organised provided valuable organisational and propaganda impetus to the forces of anti-imperialism in the Gold Coast. After his ejection from the colony in March 1937, Wallace Johnson went to the United Kingdom where he was determined to set up an organisation capable of rendering services to the cause of Ethiopia and all the African peoples under the domination of colonial governments.

Originally, Johnson's idea had been to create a Central Bureau in Europe for coloured peoples, which would be free from interference from colonial governments. This Bureau was to be established in the first place in Paris. He thus visited Paris from 19 to 22 March doubtless with the intention of seeking assistance there and generally exploring the field. It did not appear, however, that Wallace Johnson received much encouragement in the French capital. He therefore returned to London where in May 1937 he and George Padmore between them succeeded in founding the International African Service Bureau (IASB)[84]. Padmore became the chairman and Wallace Johnson the general secretary. Johnson's association with the IASB was short-lived, for, on 23 April 1938, he returned home to Freetown to establish, as we have noted above, another major branch of the Youth League.

In an amazingly short period of time, Wallace Johnson was to construct the beginnings of a mass political organisation for Sierra Leone. He drew upon a number of sources of appeal to attract members to the League. First, he was a native Sierra Leonean and hence had family and community ties and an intimate knowledge of local attitudes. Second, Johnson came from middle elite status for which a highly developed sense of consciousness existed in Sierra Leone. To a greater degree than in the Gold Coast, the Sierra Leone middle elite was keenly aware of not belonging to the upper elite. Thirdly, the foremost representatives of the upper elite, led by H. C. Bankole-Bright and Cornelius May in the NCBWA, had for two decades enjoyed tenure as the spokesmen of educated opinion. By 1938 they were tainted with extended collaboration and were separated from the mass of the population not only by social and economic status but also increasingly by age. Wallace Johnson was able to draw on neglected inclinations toward anti-colonialism as well as to engage the participation of groups previously unconsulted because of youth and lower social status. As in the Gold Coast, he was able to enlist the support of teachers, clerks, small traders, and wage labourers.

It would be a mistake to overlook the importance of the excitement and enthusiasm aroused by Johnson. Being a flamboyant character, he was able to relieve some of the humdrum monotony of life in the colony. In many regards, he was more successful as an entertainer than as a politician. Johnson's efforts were greatly enhanced by a libel suit brought against him by Bankole-Bright in November 1938. The suit made him the *cause célèbre* of Sierra Leone and the trial was as much of a standing-room-only performance as were his speeches at Wilberforce Hall. During 1938, Wallace monopolised the attention of the masses in Sierra Leone, and the League prospered accordingly.

The growth and development of the Youth League was also greatly stimulated by Wallace Johnson's consistent fostering of racial awareness. For not only did he mercilessly expose the illegal and immoral basis of European imperialism but he also focused on such dramatic examples of racial injustice as the Scottsboro Boys' Case and, especially, Italy's cruel aggression in Ethiopia. We have already noted how, to heighten racial hostility, in September 1938 Wallace Johnson mobilised the Youth League against the celebration of Earl Haig's Poppy Day fixed for 11 November as a fitting reprisal for the British recognition of the Italian annexation of Ethiopia in that year. Johnson's Youth League activists frequently viewed the Sierra Leone situation in the light of the events in Ethiopia, and on many occasions made it clear in their platform speeches that there was a similarity of treatment of Africans by the British and the Italians. In somewhat exaggerated language, they claimed that like Ethiopia, Sierra Leone was 'being swallowed up by Fascist influence'. For the British Government, for all its professions of defending the cause of justice, humanity, and freedom had failed to 'realise the importance of good colonial government'. To the more radical elements, despite the fact that 'iron links' were not round their necks, the 'all undisputable fact remains that politically, mentally, economically and otherwise we are enslaved like our brother Ethiopians'.[85] Perhaps as a result of the popularity of Sylvia Pankhurst's *New Times and Ethiopia News*, the contents of which were frequently referred to at Youth League meetings and reproduced in Youth League organs as an inspiration to Johnson's followers, the Colonial Secretary in Sierra Leone, H. R. R. Blood, listed this weekly in May 1939 as one of the papers to be banned in Sierra Leone under 'An Undesirable Literature Bill'. The banning of the *New Times and Ethiopia News* was viewed by members of the Youth League as a direct attempt on the part of the local colonial government to 'cut us off from receiving communications about activities in Ethiopia' which had been throughout 'a source of inspiration to us and our movement'.[86] C. A. Davies, a leading Youth League activist and the agent of this weekly in Freetown, then wrote to inform Sylvia Pankhurst about the banning in Sierra Leone of 'your very esteemed paper which is the only paper in Britain that champions the cause of our distressed brothers in Abyssinia'. He disclosed that the police had confiscated all the past copies of this weekly found in his possession and that a 'warrant of arrest' would soon be issued against him, or any other person who possessed them. Davies added that although the *New Times and Ethiopia News* had been banned in Sierra Leone, the editor should 'not forget us, but keep us informed by way of letter as to how our brothers in Ethiopia are faring on', so as to inspire members of the Youth League in their similar struggle against colonial rule. Concluding this letter, Davies declared, rather desperately:

> Colonial administrators, I am afraid, are a means of grave danger to the British Empire. Let the Colonial Office change its policy and avoid a catastrophe. The peoples of the colonies are groaning under capitalist and imperialist yoke. We know you will not leave this matter to lie dead. . . . God bless your efforts on behalf of humanity, justice, and freedom. We do hope that other people like yourself in Britain will follow in your wake by fighting for us, the oppressed people. [87]

This letter provoked Sylvia Pankhurst, Arthur Creech Jones and Reginald Bridgeman respectively to bombard the Colonial Office with serious protest notes, enquiring about the 'real justification of this legislation'. Creech Jones protested that he had difficulty in appreciating why ordinances involving such danger to the elementary civil and political rights should become necessary and why 'these extraordinary powers' should be given to a government which had no accountability and which could use them with scarcely any provocation.[88] Later on 21 November 1939, he introduced a deputation composed of Ladipo Solanke of WASU, Bridgeman of LAI, Ronald Kidd of the Council for Civil Liberties in Great Britain and Harold Moody of LCP to MacDonald. Each member of the deputation addressed the Secretary of State in turn on the newly enacted legislation in Sierra Leone.

But the most serious protest came from the indomitable Sylvia Pankhurst who since the Walwal incident of December 1934 had devoted herself fully to the Ethiopian cause and fought Fascism bitterly. Following in the steps of her mother, Mrs Emmeline Pankhurst, Sylvia Pankhurst, who was born in Manchester on 5 May 1882 ,was throughout her life the advocate of all human beings who were refused their rights. A devoted and acknowledged Africanist, Sylvia Pankhurst had founded in the spring of 1936 the *New Times and Ethiopia News* through which she championed the Ethiopian cause against heavy odds and strong obstacles. This was to supplement her already extensive publications about the Italo-Ethiopian conflict in British newspapers. In a ten-page confidential protest despatch to Malcolm MacDonald, Sylvia Pankhurst, who settled in Ethiopia permanently from 1956 until her death on 27 September 1960,[89] told the Secretary of State for the Colonies that Davies's correspondence (a copy of which she enclosed) was the 'third intimation' which she had received from unrelated sources about the banning of her weekly, the *New Times and Ethiopia News*. She said that, according to the sources, the legislation banning the paper was introduced ostensibly to deal with unrest in Sierra Leone and to cope with anti-British propaganda. The renowned suffragette then argued that the *New Times and Ethiopia News* had not in any way dealt with local conditions in Sierra Leone or in any other British colony. It had concerned itself with questions of international justice and opposition to the 'Fascism of Italy and Nazism [National Socialism] of Germany'. If, in pursuit of this objective, her weekly had criticised the British policy towards Ethiopia and had thereby inspired the activities of the Wallace Johnson Youth League, societies, and other various groups in Sierra Leone, as contended by Governor Jardine, this should not 'bring our paper within the definition of seditious publications'. She therefore requested MacDonald to 'get into immediate touch' with the Sierra Leone Government and ascertain whether any action had been taken or was being contemplated against the *New Times and Ethiopia News*. Miss Pankhurst finally urged the Secretary of State to prevent any such dangerous development in Sierra Leone, as such action would be 'wholly unjustifiable and unreasonable' in the case of her paper.[90]

For many months the impact of the Ethiopian conflict on the Sierra Leone political situation became a subject of embarrassing confrontation between Reginald Bridgeman of the League Against Imperialism, Arthur Creech Jones, Labour Member of Parliament, Harold Moody of LCP, and the Colonial Office.[91] It excited much apprehension among British officials both in London and Freetown and caused many lapses of judgement on their part.

There can be no doubt that although the economic exploitation, racial discrimination and political dissatisfaction in the late 1930s accounted for much of Wallace Johnson's success in rallying anti-colonial sentiment in Sierra Leone, the Ethiopian question heightened this sentiment and helped stimulate the growth and emergence of militant nationalism in the country. Both the Youth League activists themselves and the colonial administrators variously alluded to this fact in speeches and official confidential despatches. In a private conversation with O. G. R. Williams, for example, Governor Jardine admitted that the discontent among the Creole elite which Wallace Johnson was engaged in exploiting, was due not so much to a genuine sense of economic grievance as to racial antagonism which had been provoked by the Italo-Ethiopian conflict, adding that there 'was a certain amount of racial feeling'.[92] Police reports had earlier confirmed that colour prejudice and racial injustice had been Wallace Johnson's chief weapons.[93]

By the early part of 1939, Wallace Johnson had successfully established him-self as an avowed non-collaborator of British colonial rule in Sierra Leone, pursuing a 'positive action' line of unrelenting criticism of the government, the heightening of racial and territorial awareness, and organisation of all dissident groups. More specifically, he was determined to form a united front of non-collaboration to threaten the very security of colonial rule and development in Sierra Leone. Johnson was violently against such 'collaborators' of British colonial administration in Sierra Leone as Bankole-Bright, the first urban elected member of the Legislative Council. In the view of the colonial ad-ministrators, therefore, Wallace Johnson's presence in Sierra Leone would be 'a continual source of danger'; he was even believed to be 'rendering signal service to any power hostile' to the British empire or to its system of govern-ment. Charles Abbot, the acting Attorney-General, painfully admitted that Wallace Johnson had successfully 'contrived to exercise a mischievous influence' over the African civil service, the soldiers of the imperial garrison, the work-men employed on the defence fortifications in Sierra Leone, and upon African labour generally. Besides, he was reported to have focused his attention on the police, and was said to have been undermining the loyalty of the soldiers of the Royal West African Frontier Force.[94] He was a disruptive force, and pro-nouncedly anti-colonialist and anti-British.

In both Freetown and London, therefore, a series of consultations was held on how to put Wallace Johnson 'out of harm's way'. For already H. W. B. Blackhall, the Attorney-General in the Gold Coast, had written to warn his counterpart in Sierra Leone, I. J. F. Turbett, that Wallace Johnson was a 'most dangerous agitator and demagogue' and that any apprehension felt against him was fully justified.[95] Wallace Johnson had by this time become the *bête noire* of British officials in Sierra Leone. They saw him as a man 'inimical to good govern-ment' who used the press and the public platform 'to bring . . . white people into contempt among the black people', a powerful individual with a large and enthusiastic following who had managed to purloin confidential government despatches, and in the aftermath had not only publicly embarrassed the governor but also made a government-appointed commission of inquiry look foolish. Although more cautious in their dealings with Wallace Johnson, the officials at the Colonial Office in London were of the opinion that Johnson's movement was more than legitimate labour agitation, for it had a political and tendentious character.[96]

In February 1939, H. R. R. Blood, the Colonial Secretary in Freetown, and Charles Abbott, the acting Attorney-General, initiated the offensive against Wallace Johnson. Abbott suggested, with the consent of Blood, now the acting governor while Jardine was in England on leave, that the Colonial Office be urged to approve an introduction of legislation which would provide for the deportation of Wallace Johnson from Sierra Leone. Charles Abbott indicated that he should be deported to either the Faulkland Islands, St. Helena, or Cyprus. Blood suggested the United Kingdom or some other part of the empire.[97] London was not, however, in favour of this proposal which 'seemed to be going much too far', especially as no case had been made for such an extreme step. Since Johnson was a native of Sierra Leone, it was for the administration to deal with him locally. Moreover, Wallace Johnson's de-portation would give him a fine 'advertisement for the time being', and provide ample ammunition for attacking the government.[98] As an alternative, however, the Secretary of State, Malcolm MacDonald, suggested to the acting governor of Sierra Leone that, 'in view of the potentialities for mischief in Mr Wallace Johnson's activities', he explore the possibility of strengthening the powers of the Sierra Leone Government by the enactment of an ordinance on the lines of the United Kingdom Incitement to Disaffection Act of 1934.[99]

In order to deal effectively with Wallace Johnson, who had by this time so conducted himself as to be 'dangerous to peace, good order and good government', the Colonial Office permitted the Sierra Leone Government to introduce 'a web of restrictive legislation which went far beyond the explicit requests of Blood and Abbott in severely curtailing individual freedom'. As a result of the Colonial Office suggestions, six bills were more or less simultaneously introduced: the Undesirable British Subjects Control Bill; the Sedition Bill; the Undesirable Publications Bill; the Incitement to Disaffection Bill; the Trade Union Bill; and the Trade Disputes (Arbitration and Inquiry) Bill. The activities of Wallace Johnson were the prime stimulus for the introduction of these bills.

Public indignation against these bills reached such a peak that the governor convened a special meeting of the Unofficial Members of the Legislative Council on 19 May 1939 to explain the action of the government. Jardine explained that Sierra Leone had changed greatly during the previous twelve months, for events had obtruded themselves on the normally peaceful life of the Colony. Reminding the Unofficial Members of the extremely tense international situation and of the Colony's strategic importance to the empire, the governor specifically stressed that during the period in question there had 'risen up in our midst' organisations whose methods were definitely subversive of law and order. These associations, he said, obviously had as their main objects the 'undermining of authority, the vilification of those in authority and the eventual frustration, if not the downfall of British rule' in Sierra Leone.[100] The government action was supported by the key established Africans or such collaborators of British rule as Bankole-Bright and the press, notably, the *Sierra Leone Weekly News*, which 'seized on the introduction of the bills as an opportunity to score against Wallace Johnson'.

The opportunity which the government had been seeking came on 1 September 1939 when Wallace Johnson was arrested and charged with criminal libel. Johnson had written an article in the *African Standard* of 11 August 1939 entitled 'Who Killed Fonnie?' and alleging that the district commissioner at Bonthe, John Henry de Burgh Shaw, had murdered an African youth named Fonnie.[101] But in view of Wallace Johnson's previous record, the colonial officials were not fully confident that he would be convicted or imprisoned, as they had wished. They remembered how in June 1936 Wallace Johnson had been able to escape imprisonment on a similar charge in the Gold Coast, much to the annoyance of Governor Sir Arnold Hodson. It was for this reason that the government seized upon the declaration of war between the United Kingdom and Germany as 'a pretext for additional action against Wallace Johnson, this time certain that he had no possibility of escaping'. Accordingly, under Regulation 18 of Defence Regulations of 1939, Jardine ordered Wallace Johnson's detention and internment on 6 September 1939. On 20 June 1940, the West African Court of Appeal under the presidency of Donald Kingdom, the Chief Justice of Nigeria, dismissed Wallace Johnson's appeal filed by his solicitor, Otto I. R. Oyekan During, on the grounds that the sentence was not unduly severe.[102] In a confidential despatch about Wallace Johnson's future, Governor Jardine made it clear to London that he had every intention of detaining Wallace Johnson as long as the war lasted. Not only was he a most dangerous character, anti-British and determined to undermine British rule in Sierra Leone; he was also utterly unscrupulous in all matters, so that any undertaking from him to abstain from political intrigue for the duration of the war would be quite valueless.[103]

Wallace Johnson therefore spent the duration of the war at the detention camp on Shebro Island under the watchful eye of a British district commissioner, and was not released until the latter part of 1944. After his release, Johnson renewed his efforts to construct a mass movement through the Youth League but achieved little success. The League lasted until the early 1950s but only as a rump movement. Wallace Johnson continued to affiliate with various parties but was viewed increasingly as a respected eccentric, now co-opted into the Creole elite. He joined with Bankole-Bright against the Sierra Leone People's Party, branding it as the stooge of the colonial government. Although Wallace Johnson retained many of his socialist, anti-colonialist beliefs, he was unable to recover the personal eminence and attention that he had enjoyed throughout the 1930s. It was his fate, like that of many another has-been, to be forgotten as younger men came on the scene.

Evidently none among the West African anti-colonialists of the inter-war period was paid as much attention in Colonial Office records as I. T. A. Wallace Johnson. He was much in the news throughout this period. From October 1933, when his premises in Lagos were searched for seditious literature, to June 1946, when he briefly touched Bathurst on his way to Moscow to attend a meeting of the World Federation of Trade Unions, every activity of Wallace Johnson was closely watched and weighed in London with the greatest suspicion. For any kind of grievance against the colonial governments in West Africa was grist to his mill. In consequence, he was generally referred to as the 'notorious Wallace Johnson', who, having graduated in Moscow in the art of subversive propaganda, had returned to West Africa as a professional agitator.[104] When Johnson was in Nigeria he was reported to have made such 'a nuisance of himself' that the people and government of that colony were 'glad to get rid of him'. And when he was deported from the Gold Coast, London expressed a serious concern over the affairs of Sierra Leone should Wallace Johnson decide to 'take refuge there'.[105] To prevent his return to Nigeria after his ejection from the Gold Coast, London immediately advised the Government of Nigeria to quickly amend the Immigration Ordinance of the colony so as to exclude Wallace Johnson.[106] It is not surprising, then, that on Johnson's arrival in Sierra Leone, R. J. Craig, the acting commissioner of police, described him as a rascal who had found that the career of a professional agitator provided an easy living.[107] In the Gambia, the flying visit of Johnson *en route* for Moscow, and the prospect of his return to that colony stirred Bathurst to action. The government immediately thought of amending the Immigration Restriction Ordinance (1940) so as to prevent Johnson's return to the colony. Although the Executive Council of the colony decided against taking an action which might create some unrest among the nationalist groups, nevertheless, the names of the nationalists who attended a party organised by J. L. Mahoney for Johnson were listed for the government.[108] Besides, E. R. Ward, the Colonial Secretary, warned the superintendent of police at Bathurst to notify his office without delay of the 'impending visit to Bathurst by this gentleman' whose movements should be carefully watched.[109]

Wallace Johnson, however, cannot simply be dismissed as a 'professional agitator', 'rabid confusionist', or an 'aimless firebrand', as the colonial administrators used to describe him.[110] From a historical standpoint Wallace Johnson was an outstanding figure in the nationalist awakening in Sierra Leone. Even such critics of Johnson's as J. Ade Sawyer could admit that the Youth League was a panacea for the 'healing of wounds' which Sierra Leoneans had been suffering as a result of their 'being in mental, economical, moral and political slavery'.[111] To many others in Sierra Leone, it was Wallace Johnson who broke the 'awful spell' in the country: he was 'a god-send'. He had aroused his compatriots to action and impressed upon them the necessity of their 'rolling with the world'.[112] Even in the Gambia, where he neither lived nor formed a section of his Youth League, Wallace Johnson's influence on the nationalists like J. L. Mahoney, Sam Sylva, Garba-Juhumpa, T. R. Roberts, Downes Thomas and Henry Carrol of the *Gambia Echo* was tremendous. He was known to them as the 'African labour leader and political giant', and one of the most outstanding figures of the negro race, champion and defender of human rights and liberties. The brief visit of Johnson to the colony was welcomed by the Gambian nationalists as an event which should inspire 'the revival of the social, economic and political activities of this country which seem to lie dormant'.[113]

Moreover, it was not only the mass elements in Sierra Leone – the poorer urban wage-labourers, the small traders and a few struggling journalists – who were attracted to Johnson's Youth League as contended by certain writers such as Martin Kilson and John Cartwright.[114] Although at the beginning of his political activities in 1938 Wallace Johnson did not have the co-operation of the middle-class Creoles, as evidenced by police reports,[115] the position changed dramatically during the course of the year. Many influential Creole elite, such as O. T. V. Tubeku-Metzger, E. D. Morgan, Constance Agatha Cummings-John, F. A. Miller and Edmund Collingwoode Davies, who were staunch members of the local branch of the National Congress, later gravitated to the cause of such a non-collaborative organisation as the Youth League. Tubeku-Metzger, for instance, was a lawyer and vice-president of the Sierra Leone National Congress in 1924 while Mrs Constance Cummings-John was the founder and organising secretary of the Sierra Leone Women's Movement and a vice-president of the Sierra Leone People's Party. The legal adviser of WAYL was C. D. Hotobah During, and its assistant secretary, Mrs Edna S. Elliot Horton, a graduate formerly employed in the Education Department in Freetown. Besides, most of the members of the Bar (precisely 18 out of 21) were adherents of Wallace Johnson's. It was because of this that in his libel case with Wallace Johnson Bankole-Bright had to conduct his own case while as many as sixteen members of the Bar represented Johnson.[116] That the Youth League effectively split the leadership of the established Creole elite collaborators is evidenced in a correspondence by Bankole-Bright who, in a mood of despondency, bitterly complained:

In the advent of the West African Youth League to this country, one of the vice-presidents of Congress, in the person of Mr F. A. Miller, J. P. . . . . joined forces with the League, attending and taking part in its deliberations where violent and distasteful insults were proclaimed from the platform against the representatives of His Majesty – the King in this country, as well as Congress and its Representatives. I raised a protest at our meeting pointing out that Mr Miller and other members of Congress associating themselves with such a body, were deliberately violating the principles of Congress, but my protestations received no support.[117]

Wallace Johnson broke through the self-imposed barriers of decades of separation between the Creole elite and the educated Protectorate men. He combined the Creoles with the Temne and Mende of the Protectorate. The statement of Professor MacMillan, a contemporary observer, that the 'ventilation of constitutional or labour grievances' by the Youth League began to 'bridge the old deep cleavage between the Creoles and the peoples of the Protectorate' and that the Creole leaders were not uninfluenced by the 'ideologies' of the new age,[118] was not too far off the mark. By the end of the 1930s the Creole elite would seem to have come into their own as the 'natural leaders of discontent wherever it may happen to show itself'.

Also, in spite of the unfavourable political environment of the late 1930s, as well as the nature of the colonial context in which he had to operate, Wallace Johnson successfully split the Creole elite by setting one elite group against another. This enabled him to install his supporters into dominant political positions, when the Youth League contested and gained all the seats of the Municipal Council of Freetown.[119] Even Douglas Jardine, of whose administration he was the greatest critic, could not but admit the impact of Wallace Johnson's activities on the political situation in Sierra Leone. The governor disagreed with the view shared by the Colonial Office that the propaganda of Wallace Johnson's League would 'diminish in acrimony'. Jardine contended that such a hope was not likely to be realised so long as Wallace Johnson was the League's organising secretary. For the man had 'considerable personal magnetism for the masses, some sense of humour, unbounded conceit, and an unblushing disregard for the truth'.[120] In June 1938, barely two months after Johnson's return to Freetown, Jardine confessed to the Secretary of State for the Colonies:

> It may be said at once that Johnson has succeeded far beyond our expectations and far beyond what his previous experience led us to anticipate. His achievement in attracting about 800 people to his 'West African Civil Liberties and National Defence League' is a not inconsiderable one. His audience has been drawn from all sections of the community. . . .[121]

The emergence of a radical 'left wing' in the country's politics had a great impact on Jardine. For Johnson's agitation not only jolted the governor out of the easy-going days of the early thirties; it also precipitated and, in a sense, caused to be granted constitutional concessions in 1938 and 1943. A 'Standing Committee' of the Legislature consisting of two official members and all the unofficial members (7 Africans and 3 Europeans) was established in November 1938. The committee thus became the first organ of central colonial government to have an unofficial majority as well as an unofficial African majority. Another constitutional concession was the appointment in 1943 of two Africans to the Executive Council. Thus, as a result of the intensity of Johnson's Youth League agitation, the colonial government was 'inclined to accommodate some of the moderate post-1924 demands of the more established colony elite'.[122]

Although like Sierra Leone, the Gold Coast section of the West African Youth League never had a chance to test the potential offered by its novel political methods, as Wallace Johnson was forced out of the colony, it however achieved the first rudimentary base for a mass political movement that the country had seen. For in its short existence between 1935 and 1937, the Youth League broke into new realms of political activity in the country. Whereas other organisations had tended by personnel and identity to be highly elitist, the league sought mass participation, especially among labour and sub-elite groups. It had very little in common with the Congress which concentrated on elite problems like a West African Court of Appeal, a West African University, or property-based franchise. It was quite unlike the ARPS which manipulated the chiefs to protect lawyer and entrepreneur interests in mining rights or cocoa trading and to safeguard the position of a handful of Cape Coast leaders to articulate their own interests in the name of the masses of the Gold Coast. The WAYL was also not heavily dependent on traditional identity or support of the chiefs as was the Kotoko Society. As we have indicated above, the league sought mass membership, particularly from the sub-elites and from potentially organisable labour. It articulated all available grievances against the European ruling system of missions, firms, and government. It was consciously racial and anti-colonialist in tone. But rebellion was not possible, given the moderate nature of grievances, the absence of rebellious tradition, and the socio-economic differentiation in the Gold Coast. Unable to overthrow the system but also unwilling to lobby politely through normal channels of constituted authority, the league utilised Wallace Johnson's connections with the socialist, anti-imperialist fringe of the British Parliament to lobby through parliamentary questions, informal contacts, and resolutions of *ad hoc* committees to heckle, coax, and cajole the colonial system into making concessions. In this regard Wallace Johnson was forced by circumstances to lobby well within the colonial system rather than to destroy it.

Not until after the Second World War when people could see that the days of the colonial system were numbered did mass participation become possible. Wallace Johnson's WAYL had laid the foundation by stimulating broader opposition to the colonial system; moreover, the league had encouraged the desire of sub-elites to take over governing from the chiefs and the ratepayer elites. When Kwame Nkrumah's Convention People's Party was formed, Youth League leaders like Bruce and Pobee Biney were available as trained cadres.

Evidently, Wallace Johnson made a remarkable impact on the West African nationalist movement of the 1930s. The unfavourable international political and economic situation at the time, and the colonial powers' attitude to it, particularly during the period of the Italo-Ethiopian war, stirred up Wallace Johnson who bitterly criticised the colonial system and centred his journalism and trade union activities on the theme of racial inequalities and injustices. Thus, for the first time in the history of West African nationalist movements, a concrete and determined attempt was made to interest the people in matters of importance to black peoples as a whole. Johnson's exposure of the 'tricks' of 'colonial imperialism' in many of his public speeches to social and literary clubs, especially during his Ethiopia relief fund campaigns, was more emphatic and uncompromising than that of the moderate nationalists of the 1920s. The boldness, daring, and sometimes shocking directness of his articles and platform speeches radically differentiated them from those of the old leadership. His emphasis on the need for the colonies to control their own finances, together with his constant theme that the people of West Africa were ripe for 'Self-government Now', stirred the hearts of the anti-colonialists. By means of such activities, Wallace Johnson also introduced a new dimension, an element of radicalism, into the nationalist struggle in West Africa which found full expression in the nationalist parties that emerged after the war. In this sense, Wallace Johnson can be said to have signalled the birth of modern nationalism in West Africa, especially in Ghana and Sierra Leone. On the whole, then, judged in the light of his nationalistic activities along the West Coast, it can also be said that Wallace Johnson's mission, like that of Casely Hayford, was the regeneration of West Africa.

Another crucial figure in the West African nationalist struggle was Nnamdi Azikiwe, who was emerging as a nationalist leader at the time of the Italian invasion of Ethiopia. We have already referred to Azikiwe's involvement in the activities organised in the Gold Coast in connection with the Ethiopian question, and the impact which the conflict appeared to have had on his political thinking and nationalist activity, as illustrated in his study, *Renascent Africa*. In a confidential despatch, Governor Bourdillon of Nigeria devoted attention to Azikiwe as a prominent member of the Nigerian Youth Movement and, significantly, to his attitude towards the Ethiopian question. After giving a brief biographical sketch of Azikiwe, Bourdillon said that this Ibo-born editor of the *West African Pilot* believed that it was his duty to explore and publish African grievances, particularly such as those engendered by the Italo-Ethiopian conflict.[123] Azikiwe was indeed greatly disillusioned with the British attitude towards the Italian conquest of Ethiopia, and also with the subsequent British policy of appeasement. He became highly apprehensive of the possible reper-cussions of such a policy on the colonial system. His suspicions and fears were strengthened by Britain's readiness to offer Zeila in East Africa to Ethiopia in June 1935 in return for territorial concessions to Italy in Ethiopia. Azikiwe's agitation against another 'rape of Africa', probably on the West Coast, became a dominant strand in his pan-Africanism.[124]

Other young future Nigerian leaders such as Chief Obafemi Awolowo, then the Secretary of the Ibadan branch of the Nigerian Youth Movement, Chief Enahoro and the late S. L. Akintola had in various ways shown in their memoirs and other writings how the Ethiopian crisis inspired their nationalism. For example, just before the outbreak of the conflict, Akintola, destined to be one of Nigeria's most powerful political figures before the military coup of January 1966, wrote a worried letter to the *Comet* asking its editor to enlighten his readers on the situation, taking into account the League of Nations' supposed dedication to collective security.[125] Akintola was bluntly told that Mussolini would annex Ethiopia should victory attend the armed invasion of Ethiopia by Italy.[126] After the Italian invasion, Akintola sent the *Comet* a further letter, in which he observed among other things, that the war had shown that 'the partitioning of Africa makes our political and intellectual emancipation re-mote'.[127] Chief Enahoro, recollecting his school days, has written:

> I was fairly well informed about those matters which occupied the attention of the Lagos press of those days. . . . Our favourite newspaper, the *Comet*, was a weekly publication by an Egyptian emigré domiciled for many years in

Lagos. From it I followed the fortunes of the Italo-Abyssinian war, about which Father and my teachers appeared considerably agitated. Fellow-feeling with other Africans was a newly awakened sentiment, much disappointment was felt about England's failure to go to the aid of the Ethiopians, and collections were taken for a 'Help Abyssinia Fund'. The seeds of nationalism were being sown in me.[128]

But nothing is more instructive than the immediate reaction of the young Kwame Nkrumah, the future theoretician and leader of the pan-African and colonial liberation movement, just arrived in London, when he saw the placard, 'Mussolini Invades Ethiopia'. To Nkrumah, who was then a student passing through England from the Gold Coast to the United States of America, the news of Italy's invasion of Ethiopia 'was all I needed'. He was immediately seized by emotion. 'At that moment', he wrote, 'it was almost as if the whole of London had suddenly declared war on me personally', and he glared at each impassive face, wondering if those people could possibly realise the wickedness of colonialism: 'My nationalism surged to the fore: I was ready and willing to go through hell itself, if need be, in order to achieve my object', the end of colonialism.[129]

Kwame Nkrumah's political activities during his student days in America, his leadership of the African nationalist struggle after his return from America in 1945, and his uncompromising stand against colonialism and imperialism up to the time of his overthrow as President of Ghana in February 1966 need no repetition.[130] Perhaps all these show how seriously he might have taken the lesson of Mussolini's 'civilizing mission' in Ethiopia. For the Italian action strengthened his conviction that a crime of enormous proportions was being committed against Africans, and that colonialism had to be terminated across the continent, as a matter of the greatest urgency. Revulsion from the attack on Ethiopia persuaded him that a free and independent Africa was more than a mere desideratum: it was a necessity to be brought into reality by a determined leader. Thus the white man's folly in the Italo-Ethiopian war partly contributed to Nkrumah's desire to play his part in bringing about the downfall of colonialism. Italian brutalities probably inflamed his ambition. But these developments were not confined to West Africa. They also had a significant impact on the pan-African movement at the time.

Ethiopia and pan-Africanism

We have mentioned how the Italian attack on Ethiopia stirred the intellectual activities of the few West Indian and African agitators resident in Britain, who studied the existing political and social systems critically. We have also noted the manifestation of their reaction in such pan-African organisations as the International African Friends of Abyssinia, West African Students' Union and the League of Coloured Peoples. It was this response to the Ethiopian question which did much to keep the spirit of pan-Africanism from becoming dormant during the years immediately before the outbreak of the Second World War. For throughout the period of the Italo-Ethiopian conflict, pan-Africanism became the rallying slogan, the springboard, the ideological vehicle for the common efforts of the exiled Africans and West Indians to advance the cause of Africa and of Africans. The period was, therefore, 'one of the most stimulating and constructive in the history of pan-Africanism'.[131] It was an important period of transformation of pan-African ideas, a period in which African students gave pan-Africanism a thorough revision and put on it the stamp of their experience. Significantly, it was also the period in which intellectual leadership of pan-Africanism was taken over from American Negroes by ambitious and politically disillusioned young West Indians and Africans. Moreover, it was a period of transition. The new pan-African intellectuals such as Wallace Johnson, Nnamdi Azikiwe and Jomo Kenyatta became the practical men of politics.

What has hitherto not received much attention is the fact that this sense of black solidarity which was stimulated by Mussolini's conquest of Ethiopia was not confined only to the blacks in Britain, France, and America. It also became a major theme for discussion among nationalists in West Africa. In the Gambia, for instance, E. F. Small's *Gambia Outlook and Senegambian Reporter* frequently referred to the Italo-Ethiopian affair as an event which had forced Africans and all other coloured races of mankind to think together, and heightened their 'sentiment for Mother Africa'.[132] Discussing this sentiment, a nationalist newspaper in Sierra Leone wrote:

> Much as Mussolini's name is in bad odour amongst them just now, peoples of the African group will admit that the Italian dictator has done a distinct service in giving them the fillip that was necessary to rouse them up to a lively sense of race-consciousness and brotherly love. Never before have dark-skinned people shown such a united front as they have done during the past few weeks. Religious differences and prejudices, political demarcations and geographical distance have been swept away by the magic touch of kinship – the only thing that matters to them.[133]

This opinion was shared by the Gold Coast nationalists who claimed that Ethiopia had served to bring all Africans and peoples of African stock 'into an indissoluble bond of racial oneness', and compelled them to think of 'race and not grace', and to take pride 'in country rather than cliquish circles'.[134] The nationalists once more realised that their colour was all that counted in a world in which there was 'no universal ethical norm', and that no matter whether they were under the British, the French, or the German, they knew that they were one and 'racially form an inseparable whole'. African political consciousness erupted as never before on a continental scale. Richard Pankhurst rightly sees this as 'the birth of pan-Africanism as far as the ordinary African was concerned'.[135]

Evidently, the Italian brutalities in Ethiopia fully convinced Africans and peoples of African descent everywhere that 'black men had no rights which white men felt bound to respect' if they stood in the way of their imperialist interests. In West Africa, the progressive nationalist leaders noted with surprise the earlier attempts of the League of Nations to shelve the appeals of Ethiopia. They noted also the annoyance shown by some European states at the idea of such a minor African independent state as Ethiopia being allowed to jeopardise the peace of Europe, even though she was a full member of the League. They watched with greater interest still the progress of the attempt to persuade Ethiopia to stand down from her place in the League of Nations in order that Italy might despoil her of territory without disturbing the sweet amity which prevailed within the League. As they began carefully to scrutinise the situation throughout the African continent, they were confronted with the same picture: black men being exploited by white. This picture, when coupled with the realisation that opinion in the twentieth century still regarded the African as a 'creature with imperfect human rights', not only intensified fledging nationalist aspirations but also added impetus to a growing feeling of racial solidarity. For, with the realisation of their utter defencelessness against the new aggression from Europeans in Africa, the blacks felt it necessary to look to themselves, and not to any other power, for their own protection. Thus, responding to the provocation of Mussolini, the West African nationalists were reiterating a *raison d'être* for pan-Africanism.

However, while the central theme of the discussions among the nationalist leaders during and after the Ethiopian episode was unity in West Africa and of the coloured races, this remained only a dream. It was not given any organisational form, as witnessed in the 1920s when the National Congress of British West Africa became a kind of regional branch in Africa itself of the pan-African movement. Apart perhaps from Wallace Johnson, who through his Youth Leagues, appeared to be positively committed to political action for the realisation of the goal of West African unity, the other nationalists like Kobina Sekyi and his dissident ARPS colleagues, or even Nnamdi Azikiwe, remained mere advocates of pan-Africanism during the 1930s. On the other hand, however, the West Indian and African agitators in Britain seriously attempted a revival of pan-African organisations as institutional carriers of pan-African ideas and as rallying points for race conscious Africans and peoples of African extraction. George Padmore, who, since the mid-thirties, had become disenchanted with the sincerity of Communism's support for colonial freedom and had in consequence resigned from the Communist Party, was seeking a basis for unity among Negroes of Africa, America, the West Indies, and other lands. Padmore and his group in Britain clearly saw the Italian aggression as the right opportunity not only of drawing the blacks together, but also of emancipating coloured peoples from the 'oppressive' imperialist governments of foreign countries.

Thus, in order not to be caught again in a state of unpreparedness, the group resolved to form a pan-African organisation known as the International African Service Bureau (IASB) on 17 May 1937.[136] This was in fact an outgrowth of C. L. R. James's International African Friends of Abyssinia. Padmore became the chairman of this organisation and Wallace Johnson its general secretary. The executive committee included Christ Jones, the Barbadian trade unionist (organising secretary); Jomo Kenyatta (assistant secretary); R. T. Makonnen (treasurer); J. J. Ocquaye (Gold Coast); Louis Mbanefo and N. Azikiwe (Nigeria); K. Sallie Tamba (Sierra Leone); Timeko Garan Kouyate (Sudan); Gilbert Coker (South Africa); and the West Indian Trotskyist, C. L. R. James (editorial director). Among its patrons were the editor of the *New Times and Ethiopia News*, E. Sylvia Pankhurst; Nancy Cunard, Arthur Creech Jones, Dorothy Woodman, D. N. Pritt, Noel Baker, F. A. Ridley and Victor Gollancz.[137] Like the WASU or the LCP before it, the IASB provided itself with an organ called the *International African Opinion* which was launched in July 1938 under the editorship of C. L. R. James assisted by the Afro-American William Harrison. The motto of this monthly journal was 'Educate, Co-operate, Emancipate: Neutral in nothing affecting the African Peoples'.[138] More familiar with the problems of Negroes in the British Empire, the IASB appealed to all

Negroes for support in the columns of its mouth-piece. The attention of the Colonial Office was immediately drawn to the existence of the IASB by Wallace Johnson.[139]

What the IASB was, and what it stood for, was lucidly explained by Wallace Johnson in a release entitled: 'What is the International African Service Bureau?' In this release, the IASB was described as 'a non-party' organisation which owed 'no affiliation or allegiance' to any political party, organisation or group in Europe. As an organisation, the release claimed that the IASB represented the 'progressive and enlightened public opinion' among Africans and peoples of African descent. It supported the demands of Africans and other colonial peoples for democratic rights, civil liberties and self-determination. Active membership was 'open to all Africans and peoples of African descent', regardless of their political persuasions or religious beliefs. Europeans and members of other races who sympathised with the aspirations of the Bureau and desired to demonstrate in a practical way their interest in Africa and peoples of African descent were permitted to be associate members. Briefly, the Bureau aimed at agitating for constitutional reforms such as the granting of freedom of the press, speech, assembly and movement, and other democratic rights, which were denied to millions of black subjects. Another chief function of the organisation was to enlighten public opinion in Great Britain as to true conditions in the various colonies, protectorates and mandated territories of Africa, the West Indies and other colonial areas. Its third function was to expose and combat 'child labour, forced labour, colour bar acts' and other forms of legislation directed against Africans and peoples of African descent in the colonies. In order to explain the existing conditions of subject races in various parts of the British Empire, the Bureau supplied speakers to Labour Party branches, Trade Unions, Co-operative Guilds, League of Nations Union branches, Peace Societies and religious organisations.[140] In sum, as Padmore, the movement's most articulate spokesman put it, members of the Bureau 'orientated themselves to pan-Africanism as an independent political expression of Negro aspirations for complete national independence from white domination – Capitalism or Communist',[141]

In spite of the available evidence to the contrary, some recent scholars in this field of study have tended to underestimate the impact of the Italo-Ethiopian conflict as being the immediate and sole cause of the formation of the IASB. For example, Imanuel Geiss in his comprehensive study of *The Pan-African Movement* does not even mention the Ethiopia crisis in relation to the establishment of the IASB.[142] On the other hand, although Dr Peter Esedebe devotes some attention to the crisis in his unpublished doctoral dissertation, he argues rather surprisingly that to see the Italo-Ethiopian conflict as the sole cause of the establishment of the IASB 'would be an oversimplification of a complex situation'. For, in his opinion, the 'growth of articulate racialism' even in Britain 'and the protracted debate on the German and Italian colonial demands' should be considered as a strong compelling motive which inspired the creation of the Bureau,[143] but the facts hardly seem to warrant this view.

In the first place, discussing the reason for the formation of the IASB, Wallace Johnson, the secretary-general of the Bureau, clearly explained that from the time of the trans-Atlantic Slave Trade period down to the 1930s, the black peoples of the world had been victims of the most ruthless forms of oppression and exploitation. But, he went on:

. . . Never since the emancipation of the slaves have Africans and other subject races been so awake to a realisation of the wrongs and injustices inflicted upon weak and defenceless peoples as since the brutal Italian fascist war against Abyssinia. This cold-blooded organised act of imperialist aggression against a people who had been led to place their security in the League of Nations and the Kellogg Peace Pact, demonstrated as never before that the world is still dominated by the philosophy of might over right. It has also opened the eyes of Africans the world over, that they have no rights which the powerfully armed nations are bound to respect. And precisely because of this they have decided to close their ranks and place their hopes for the future, not in imperialist statesmen, but in the organised forces of all lands who are passionately devoted to the cause of peace.

Johnson then emphasised that it was 'with this object in view' that representative leaders of Africans and peoples of African descent had organised the International African Service Bureau 'in order to co-operate with all peace-loving, democratic, and working-class forces who desire to help the advancement of Africans'.[144] The editorial of the maiden issue of the Bureau's journal, the *International African Opinion*, reinforced this view, stressing that the Ethiopian struggle had awakened black 'political consciousness as never before'. It had shown that although 'problems differ from country to country', yet there was a common bond of oppression and, because of this, Negroes everywhere had begun to see the necessity for international organisation and the unification of their scattered efforts, as exemplified in the formation of the IASB.[145]

It is significant to note that this view is also fully shared by both Padmore, the chairman and chief ideologist of the Bureau, and Ras Makonnen, an executive member and one of the only three surviving members of the IASB (the other two being Jomo Kenyatta and C. L. R. James). Stating the motive behind the revival of pan-African movements in the thirties, Padmore wrote:

> The betrayal of Ethiopia and the hopes of hundreds of millions of coloured peoples in Asia, Africa, and the islands of the seas, who had been led to place their faith in the League of Nations and collective security had forced upon Africans and peoples of African descent the resolve that they must not agzin be caught in a state of unpreparedness. In this mood, some members of the erstwhile International African Friends of Abyssinia Society . . . met in London . . . to form the International African Service Bureau. . . .[146]

T. Ras Makonnen, the veteran pan-Africanist, has confirmed in his recently published memoirs that the whole movement towards the establishment of the Bureau 'derived directly from the Ethiopian crisis. . . .'[147]

In the light of the available evidence, therefore, Dr Esedebe's contention would appear not to be convincing. Secondly, his attempt to distinguish between the Italian rape of Ethiopia and the 'protracted debate on the German and Italian colonial demands' would seem to be equally untenable when closely studied against the background of the international politics in the thirties and of the response of the pan-Africanists to it. For it was the Italian invasion of Ethiopia and the ease with which this was accomplished – following Japan's forcible seizure of Manchuria in 1932–33 – which whetted the appetite of the Axis powers, and led almost directly to the re-opening of the question of redistribution of colonies. This was made evident by Padmore in his correspondence of October 1938 to the Gold Coast ARPS in which he warned Kobina Sekyi and his articulate group to be on their guard and also asked for their closest collaboration with the newly established IASB.[148]

Earlier in June 1937, Wallace Johnson, as general secretary of the IASB, had similarly written to John Parker, M.P., stating that, as he was undoubtedly aware, as a result of the Italian annexation of Ethiopia, the colonial situation had 'come so sharply' before the British public as a vital issue in international politics that suggestions were being made in certain sections of the press for a 'return of the former German colonies to Hitler, while others propose the alternative of placing all African territories under the Mandates system'. Johnson asked for Parker's moral and material support in IASB's 'carrying out a campaign of enlightenment of the British public as to the views of Africans'.[149] Still not satisfied, Wallace Johnson and T. Ras Makonnen emphasised at their meeting with the Labour Party Commonwealth Group of the House of Commons held on 29 November 1937 the relationship between the Italian annexation of Ethiopia and the demand of Germany for the return of her ex-African colonies.[150] Throughout, the West African nationalist politicians took the view that 'this talk about redistribution of colonies is doubtless caused by the Italo-Ethiopian conflict'.[151]

After the conquest of Ethiopia, Italy shifted gradually to the German camp, a shift which ultimately resulted in the formation of the 'Rome-Berlin Axis' in October 1936. It was this, stigmatised by F. W. Deakin as 'The Brutal Friendship',[152] of Hitler and Mussolini which intensified the claim for colonies and set the world astir as to how to meet the Axis challenge. Hence began in 1935 and 1936 conferences on 'Peace and Colonial Problems' and a series of lectures on 'Economic Policies and Peace'. All the evidence would seem to point to the conclusion that the Italian attack on Ethiopia, and the subsequent annexation of that black empire, greatly transformed the international scene. Thenceforth, colonial questions and the League of Nations' mandates system increasingly claimed attention on the international stage.[153] As a conscientious observer of the then African contemporary scene remarked in 1938, 'at no other moment in history has the colonial theme come forward as it does now to occupy the attention of England, France, Germany, Italy, all at once and the same time' than the period following the Italian aggression in Ethiopia.[154] This inevitably stimulated discussion and activity among such coloured organisations as the LCP, WASU, and particularly the IASB.

Of some significance is the fact that, apart from Padmore's IASB, the Italian conquest of Ethiopia caused the formation of a number of pan-African associations and societies in 1937 and 1938. In the United States, for instance, two pan-African organisations were established in early 1937. The first was the United Aid for Peoples of African Descent, and the other, the Congress of the African Peoples of the World. While the former was short-lived, the latter which, like the WASU, was a students' organisation, was radical and pervasive.

One of the main objects of the Congress was 'to make Liberia one of the Great Powers of the world'. Secondly, it declared its intention 'to help in the hard fight for Ethiopian independence'.[155] The Congress announced that plans were 'under way for a general conference to be held in Africa' some time in late 1937, but there is no evidence that this materialised. Another organisation which was formed in New York City in early 1938 was the militant but little

known pan-African body, the United African Front. This organisation sometimes referred to itself as the Ethiopia Young People's League. Its main aim
was to bring together 'the millions of black peoples throughout the entire
world for a united and free Africa'. It also declared that Lagos in Nigeria should
be made the headquarters of the organisation. To this end, the organisation
wrote to the British Secretary of State for the Colonies in May 1938, stating
among other things the following:

> We, as Black People, have fought in every known war large or small, and
> have given also our 'Blood', not for the protection of our peoples but for
> others. . . . We are now united as African Brothers . . . and are prepared to
> make it possible for our people to be free; we hereby respectfully request all
> the Powers of the world, to give the Black Man a place in the world for him-
> self. We are forced to request you to give up Africa to the Black People, who
> are the rightful owners of that land. We are determined to take Africa and
> will stop at nothing until we are free, free from all powers of the world.[156]

The organisation then listed a catalogue of events to highlight how Africans
had been exploited by the white for centuries culminating in the recent conquest of Ethiopia. About Marcus Garvey, it recalled that the Negro leader, who
tried 'throughout every way to bring happiness, peace, and freedom to the
people of Africa', was denied recognition and the right to be heard by the white
representatives in the League of Nations. He was even branded as 'an outcast
and denied the right to justice'.[157] The declared intention of the United African
Front about Lagos seriously disturbed the officials of the Colonial Office,
especially at this time when the Neville Chamberlain administration was being
distracted by fresh Hitlerite threats in Austria and Czechoslovakia.

While the pan-African associations and societies which emerged as a result
of the Italian conquest of Ethiopia were of comparatively short duration, the
IASB remained for about seven years, 1937–44, as the rallying point of radical
coloured groups in Britain. The members of the Bureau recognised that their
position in the metropolitan capital of London made them more immediately
aware of the problems of the Negroes in the British dependencies. Their appeal
was directed to Negroes everywhere – in the colonial empires, South America
and the United States. As later reported by the Colonial Office, the IASB
'interested itself in the affairs of Negro populations all over the world'. The
platform of the Bureau was said to have received considerable sympathy and
response 'from all sections of the public'. The subject in greatest demand was
the question of the colonies in relation to the 'Have' and 'Have Not' struggle in
Africa. There was also 'a large demand for speakers on Abyssinia'.[158]

Of particular interest was the very prompt action which was taken by the
Bureau in connection with the Cocoa Pool organised by European merchants in
the Gold Coast and Nigeria. Correspondence on the subject was opened with
Members of Parliament and the Colonial Office, and questions raised in the
House of Commons led to the appointment of a Commission of Enquiry into
the activities of the pool. The Colonial Office was alarmed by the keen interest
which the IASB took in the Cocoa Pool; it immediately made enquiries as to the
'possible connection between the International African Service Bureau and the
strike of the cocoa workers and farmers in the Gold Coast'. Subsequent in-
vestigations, however, revealed that there was no direct evidence that the
strikers were in contact with the Negro community in London led by Wallace

Johnson. Nevertheless, the Colonial Office continued to entertain the view that Wallace Johnson and the Bureau would 'certainly support and encourage strikes in West Africa, or elsewhere'. It was, however, anticipated that such support and encouragement would not 'go much beyond expressions of sympathy and possible protest meetings', as the resources of the Bureau were extremely limited.[159]

Until late 1944 when it merged into the Pan-African Federation, the body which was responsible for planning the 1945 Pan-African Congress in Manchester, the International African Service Bureau, as Wallace Johnson recalled in 1964, was one of the more effective pan-African organisations that emerged from the experience of the Ethiopian episode. It established a 'procedure whereby colonial matters were brought before Parliament weekly'.[160] Branches of the Bureau were established in France, Belgium and the United States. The IASB appeared to be popular among the West African nationalist groups. For instance, in their detailed instructions to Ashie Nikoi, the ARPS representative at the 1945 Pan-African Congress, the Gold Coast Aborigines recommended Padmore and Kwame Nkrumah, the organisers of the Congress, to 'revive the good work' of the IASB, and urged the necessity of establishing, in addition to the IASB, a Pan-African Council with offices in London, New York, Paris, Geneva, Moscow and New Delhi with a central press in London.[161] The programme of the Bureau in 1938 included the calling of a world congress of Negro progressive organisations, particularly among colonial peoples; the establishment of Trade Union Movements in the colonies and bringing these into contact with the British Labour Movement; the carrying on of a propaganda campaign against war and fascism, and imperialist aggression. Lack of sufficient funds, however, militated against full implementation of this comprehensive programme which required 'no less than £500'.[162] Nevertheless, through regular contacts the Bureau was able to co-ordinate and centralise, though to a limited extent, the activities of some of the various coloured organisations existing in different parts of the black world, in particular those of the West Coast, such as the Aborigines' Rights' Protection Society.[163] In this way, not only did it attempt to bring the cause of the coloured peoples to the 'better understanding of the universe', but it also stimulated in no small measure an 'intellectual understanding and co-operation among all groups of Negro descent'.

Briefly stated, then, there is much evidence to warrant the conclusion that pan-Africanism – as a reaction to European imperialism, as a moving expression of deeply felt emotions, and as an intellectual and political movement among Africans and peoples of African descent – was very much in evidence during the 1930s. The whole phenomenon would seem to have received tremendous impetus from the Ethiopian experience, and gained additional political momentum. Although it did not express itself in congresses of the Henry Sylvester Williams -W. E. B. DuBois's type, pan-Africanism, as a recognisable movement, was active and vigorous, 'stimulating and constructive', owing largely to the italian invasion of one of the last citadels of African independence.

1 M. Perham, *The Colonial Reckoning*, pp. 34 and 35.
2 For example, the 1934 Gold Coast Colony and Ashanti Delegation asked no more than that, in order to play an 'effective part in the government', African members of the Legislative Council be allowed to elect among themselves 'two to take seats on the Executive Council', and also that the representation of the African population on the Legislative Council should 'be brought up to one half the whole number'. C.O.96/717/21750/3/1934.

3 C.O.554/122/33632, R. Coupland to A. J. Dawe, 16 December 1939.
4 M. Perham, p. 49.
5 O. A. Alakija, 'Great Britain and West Africa', *West Africa*, 31 August 1935.
6 *Vox Populi*, 20 May 1936; also, *Gambia Outlook and Senegambian Reporter*, 11 July 1936.
7 *Ibid.*
8 *Service*, June 1936; also, *Gold Coast Independent*, 2 May 1936.
9 O. A. Alakija, 'Great Britain and West Africa'.
10 *Service*, September 1936.
11 *Gold Coast Independent*, 'Western Civilization in the Crucible', 9 May 1936.
12 *Wasu*, iv, 5, November 1935, pp. 70–1.
13 *Ibid.*
14 C.O.583/220/30159, 'The External and Internal Intelligence Reports of the Year Ending 31 December 1936'.
15 *Ibid.*
16 *Comet*, 30 November 1935.
17 It is not my intention to discuss the system of indirect rule which has received wide attention from scholars. For a very interesting analysis of the system in Ghana see especially R. L. Stone, 'Colonial Administration and the Rural Politics in South-Central Ghana, 1919–1951, unpublished thesis, p. 61ff. Our main purpose here is to outline briefly the increasing objection to the system following the fall of Ethiopia.
18 P. D. Quartey, 'Education and African Political Thought', *West Africa*, 29 August 1936.
19 John H. Harris, *Dawn in Darkest Africa*, London, 1968, p. 107.
20 *African Sentinel*, March–April 1938, enclosed in Sierra Leone secret despatch C.O.267/665/32208/1938, 30 September 1938.
21 C. K. Meek, W. M. MacMillan and E. R. J. Hussey, *Europe and West Africa: Some Problems and Adjustments*, London, 1940, p. 94. Also, P. S. Gupta, *Imperialism and the British Labour Movement, 1914–1964*, Cambridge, 1975, p. 264.
22 C.O.96/723/31135/2.
23 *Ibid.*
24 C.O.96/730/31228/36, H. M. Grace to Dr M. Fortes, 9 November 1935.
25 *Ibid.*, memo by G. Creasy, 20 January 1936.
26 *Ibid.*, Bottomley to Hodson, 12 April 1936.
27 *Ibid.*, Note of a meeting between Lord Hailey and Colonial Office officials, 14 December 1936.
28 *Ibid.*, minute by I. M. R. Maclellan, 20 March 1936.
29 *Ibid.*, Hodson to Secretary of State, Conf. despatch of 31 August 1936; C.O.96/739/31228/37, Hodson to Secretary of State, Conf. despatch of 13 November 1937.
30 *Ibid.*
31 C.O.96/749/31228, Hodson to Ormsby-Gore, 19 July 1938.
32 *Annual Report on the Central Province for the Year 1938–39*, prepared by A. F. E. Fieldgate, Commissioner for Central Province, 5 July 1939 (copy in Foreign and Commonwealth Office Library, London JS 7649. G6. 3. A8). Cited in Stone, p. 147.
33 C.O.96/730/31228/36, I. M. R. Maclellan to G. Creasy, 8 January 1938.
34 'The Nigerian Youth Charter', enclosed in C.O.583/234/30386, 7 November 1938.
35 C.O.583/224/30453.
36 *Ibid.* For further views of Governor Bourdillon on the indirect rule system, see his article, 'Guiding the Native Towards Home Rule', *The Listener* (London), xvii, 419, 20 January 1937.
37 Interview with H. O. Davies.
38 M. Perham, *Colonial Reckoning*, p. 59.
39 F.O.371/19122, Barton to Hoare, 10 July 1935.
40 Lord Hailey, 'Nationalism in Africa', p. 143.
41 *Ibid.*
42 ACJ.17/2, *Creech Jones Papers*.
43 C.O.554/122/33632, 'Constitutional Advances in West Africa: Professor R. Coupland's Proposal', Coupland to A. J. Dawe, 16 September 1939.
44 *Ibid.*
45 Lord Hailey, 'Native Administration and Political Development in British Tropical Africa', Confidential Report, 1940–42. Further details are provided in Mss. Brit. Emp. S.334–337 and 342, 'Lord Hailey Papers', Rhodes House Library, Oxford.

46 C.O.267/671/32245, 'Note of Points About Sierra Leone Made by Professor W. M. MacMillan in Conversation with A. J. Dawe', prepared by O. G. R. Williams, 20 January 1939.

47 *W.E.A. Ofori Atta Papers.*

48 *Gold Coast Independent*, 18 April 1936.

49 *Ibid.*

50 *Ibid.*

51 C.O.96/723/31135/2.

52 *African Standard* (Freetown), 10 February 1939; enclosed in ACJ.18/7, Creech Jones Papers.

53 J. B. Danquah, *Self-Help and Expansion*, Accra, 1943, p. 20.

54 *Ibid.*, p. 23.

55 Interview, A. M. Akiwumi, Accra, 22 May 1971.

56 Royal Institute of International Affairs, *The British Empire: A Report on its Structure and Problems*, p. 153.

57 Meek, MacMillan and Hussey, pp. 106 and 108. See also, Norman Ley's address to the Labour Party Advisory Committee on Imperial Questions, 'Politics in the Gold Coast', in ACJ.18/3, Creech Jones Papers.

58 C.O.96/730/31228, Hodson to J. H. Thomas, 26 February 1936.

59 *Ibid.*

60 F.O.371/20154, London to J. H. Thomas, 17 January 1936.

61 C.O.96/731/31230, Encl. in Gold Coast No. 740, 8 December 1936.

62 C.O.96/729/31205, Hodson to Thomas, 10 March 1936.

63 *Ibid.* The Meeting was attended by Sir Cecil Bottomley, Sir Gratton Bughe, Downie and Gerald Creasy.

64 'The Claim for Self-Government,' *Comet*, 6 June 1936.

65 A. T. Ariori, 'The Significance of "Youth Day" 1935', *op. cit.*

66 Nigerian Youth Charter, p. 1.

67 *Ibid.*, pp. 2–3.

68 C.O.583/234/30386, Bourdillon to MacDonald, 1 November 1938.

69 Nigeria Legislative Council *Debates* 16th Session, 1938.

70 C.O.583/234/30386, Bourdillon to MacDonald, 1 November 1938.

71 Conf. C.S.O.361/38, Ghana National Archives, Accra, Miss Hebe Spaull to Hodson, 1 September 1938. For the Gold Coast reaction to this fear of Germany claiming any of the West African colonies see S.N.A.212/32, Ghana National Archives, Accra, *Minutes* of the Joint Session of the Provincial Council held on 8 November 1938. The views of the inhabitants of the Gambia on this subject are provided in C.O.87/245/33124 (Gambia) 1957. Sierra Leone expressed similar fears as reported in *Sierra Leone Weekly News.* 25 December 1937.

72 C.O.583/234/30386, Bourdillon to MacDonald, 7 November 1938.

73 *Ibid.*

74 See for example, *Nigerian Daily Telegraph*, 5 November 1935.

75 Conversation with H. O. Davies.

76 M. S. J. Richards, 'The Franchise', *Gambia Outlook and Senegambian Reporter*, 26 November 1936.

77 *Ibid.*

78 *Sierra Leone Daily Guardian*, 9 May 1936.

79 See for example, *Gambia Outlook and Senegambian Reporter*, 19 September 1936.

80 C.O.267/655/32157/1936, S. Adole Hughes and T. J. Carew, joint secretaries of the Sierra Leone Section of the Congress, to Colonial Secretary, Freetown, 9 June 1936.

81 *Ibid.*

82 C.O.267/669/32157, Bankole-Bright to the joint secretaries of the local branch of the Congress, 8 August 1939. Encl. No. 11 of Sierra Leone despatch No. 537, 21 August 1939.

83 C.O.267/655/32157/1936, A. B. Mathews, Ag. Colonial Secretary, Sierra Leone, to joint secretaries, NCBWA, Sierra Leone Section, 13 August 1936.

84 Gambia 4/73, Colonial Secretary's Office, File No. 179, secret despatch 7046/3/38 entitled, 'Wallace Johnson and the International African Service Bureau', O. G. R. Williams to Sir Thomas Southorn, Governor of the Gambia, 27 January 1938, Gambia Records Office, Bathurst.

85 Mss. Brit. Emp. S.332, ACJ.18/7, *Creech Jones Papers.*

86 *Ibid.*
87 *Ibid.*, C. A. Davies to Sylvia Pankhurst, 28 May 1939.
88 *Ibid.*, Creech Jones to MacDonald, 23 June 1939.
89 For a brief biographical sketch of Sylvia Pankhurst, see *Ethiopia Observer*, v, 1, pp. 13–60.
90 Mss. Brit. Emp. S.332, ACJ.18/7, *Creech Jones Papers*, E. Sylvia Pankhurst to Mac-Donald, 12 June 1939.
91 For example, see Bridgeman's letter to MacDonald, dated 28 June 1939 in *Creech Jones Papers*.
92 C.O.267/671/32245, Jardine to O. G. R. Williams, 17 February 1939.
93 C.O.267/665/32208/1938, Report by R. J. Craig, Ag. Commissioner of Police, Sierra Leone, 20 June 1938.
94 Memorandum on Wallace Johnson prepared by Charles Abbot, Ag. Attorney-General in Sierra Leone, 5 February 1939, encl. in C.O.267/670/32210/2.
95 *Ibid.*
96 C.O.267/666/32216, minute by O. G. R. Williams, 18 August 1939.
97 C.O.267/670/32210/2, memorandum by Abbot, 5 February 1939.
98 *Ibid.*, minute by O. G. R. Williams, 15 February 1939.
99 C.O.267/670/32210/2, 1 (1939), MacDonald to Blood, 6 March 1939.
100 'Statement Made On 19 May by His Excellency the Governor to Unofficial Members Regarding Certain Bills', printed by Government Printer, Freetown, 1939.
101 C.O.267/677/32303; also, *Sierra Leone Weekly News*, 2 and 16 September 1939; *Daily Mail*, 2 and 4 September 1939.
102 *Ibid.*
103 *Ibid.*, Jardine to O. G. R. Williams, 22 October 1940. Wallace Johnson's prison life and experiences are published in his small but informative panphlet, *Prison In the Muse*.
104 C.O.96/736/31088/2A, minute by C. Lambert, 21 August 1937; also, C.O.96/736/31230/2, observations by Blackhall, 13 November 1938.
105 C.O.96/738/31189/1937, minute by Downie, 27 February 1937.
106 *Ibid.*, minute by Lambert, 6 March 1937.
107 C.O.267/665/32208/1938, police report, 20 June 1938.
108 Gambia 4/73, File No. 179, 'Wallace Johnson and the International African Service Bureau', Gambia Records Office, Bathurst.
109 *Ibid.*, Ward to superintendent of police, Bathurst, 27 July 1947.
110 See, for example, C.O.267/666/32216, minute by O. G. R. Williams, 18 August 1938.
111 J. Ade Sawyerr, 'The Sierra Leone Youth League – As I see It: Present and Future', *Sierra Leone Weekly News*, 16 July 1938.
112 H. Ade Morrison, 'An Awakening', *ibid.*, 13 August 1938.
113 Extract from the *Gambia Echo*, 10 June 1946 encl. in Gambia 4/73, File No. 179.
114 Kilson, *Political Change*, pp. 143–5; Cartwright, *Politics in Sierra Leone*, pp. 36–7.
115 C.O.267/665/32208/1938, report by R. J. Craig, 20 June 1938.
116 C.O.267/666/32216, Jardine to MacDonald, 28 November 1938.
117 Encl. in despatch No. 537, 21 August 1939, C.O.267/669/32157, Bankole-Bright to joint secretaries, Sierra Leone Branch, National Congress of British West Africa, 8 August 1939.
118 Meek, MacMillan and Hussey, p. 76.
119 C.O.267/673/32254.
120 C.O.267/666/32216, Jardine to MacDonald, 28 November 1938.
121 C.O.267/665/32208/1938, Jardine to MacDonald, 30 June 1938.
122 Kilson, *Political Change in a West African State: A Study of the Modernization Process in Sierra Leone*, Harvard, 1966, p. 145.
123 C.O.583/234/30386, Bourdillon to MacDonald, 7 November 1938.
124 See J. A. Davis, ed., *Pan-Africanism Reconsidered*, p. 48.
125 Letter from S. L. Akintola on the Ethiopian question, the *Comet*, 20 July 1935.
126 *Ibid.*, 27 July 1935.
127 *Ibid.*, 30 November 1935.
128 Enahoro, *Fugitive Offender: The Story of a Political Prisoner*, London 1965, p. 45. For a similar reaction of Awolowo to the crisis, see Obafemi Awolowo, *Path to Nigerian Freedom*, London, 1947, p. 28.
129 Kwame Nkrumah, *Ghana: The Autobiography of Kwame Nkrumah*, p. 27.

130 For details, see my article, 'Kwame Nkrumah and Pan-Africanism: The Early Pbase 1945–1961', *Universitas* (An Inter-Faculty journal, University of Ghana, Legon), iii, 1, October 1973.
131 George Padmore, *Pan-Africanism or Communism?*, London, 1956, p. 151.
132 *Gambia Outlook and Senegambian Reporter*, 12 October 1935.
133 *Sierra Leone Weekly News*, 9 October 1935.
134 *Vox Populi*, 14 September 1935; also, *African Morning Post*, 27 April 1936.
135 Richard Pankhurst, 'Ethiopia and Africa: The Historical Aspect', *Ethiopia Observer*, viii, 2, 1964, p. 159.
136 *African Sentinel*, March–April 1938 enclosed in Sierra Leone secret despatch, C.O.267/665/32208/1938, 30 September 1938.
137 The full list of patrons and executive committee members is provided in Gambia 4/73, File No. 179, secret despatch 7046/3/38, 27 January 1938.
138 *International African Opinion* (London), i, 1, July 1938. Copies of this very rare journal can be seen in an unmarked file of Padmore's newspaper cuttings in Research Library of African Affairs, Accra, Ghana.
139 C.O.96/733/31230, Wallace Johnson to the Secretary of State for the Colonies, 22 June 1937.
140 'Why Such A Bureau?' in IASB Broadsheet, enclosed in C.O.96/736/31088/2ᴬ.
141 George Padmore, *Pan-Africanism*, p. 148.
142 Geiss, *The Pan-African Movement*, p. 355.
143 Peter Esedebe, 'A History of the Pan-African Movement in Britain', unpublished thesis, p. 137.
144 IASB Broadsheet, enclosed in C.O.96/736/31088/2ᴬ.
145 *International African Opinion*, i, 1, July 1938.
146 George Padmore, *Pan-Africanism*, p. 146.
147 T. R. Makonnen, *Pan-Africanism from within*, London, 1973, p. 120.
148 ACC.156/65, *Sekyi Papers*, Padmore to Sekyi, 4 October 1938.
149 ACJ.17/2, *Creech Jones Papers*, Wallace Johnson to John Parker, M.P., 17 June 1937.
150 The proceedings of the meeting, which was chaired by Tom Johnstone, M.P., are provided in *Sierra Leone Weekly News*, 25 December 1937.
151 For example, *Gold Coast Spectator*, 16 November 1935. Marcus Garvey made a similar remark in *Black Man*, ii, 2, July–August 1936.
152 *The Brutal Friendship* is the title of F. W. Deakin's fascinating study of Hitler and Mussolini published in London in 1962.
153 This has been analysed in Rayford W. Logan, *The African Mandates in World Politics*.
154 Nancy Cunard, 'The African Claims His Responsibility', *African Sentinel*, March–April 1938.
155 *New Times and Ethiopia News*, 6 March and 7 April 1937.
156 C.O.554/114/33539, the United African Front to Malcolm MacDonald, 2 May 1938. The letter was signed jointly by George Phillips, Thelma Dixon, F. M. Walkes, A. B. Rama, Stanley Davis, and S. Washington.
157 *Ibid.*
158 O. G. R. Williams to Sir Thomas Southorn, Governor of the Gambia, 27 January 1938, 7046/3/38, Gambia 4/73, File No. 179. See also, *African Sentinel*, March–April 1938, 'A Brief Review of the Activities of the International African Service Bureau for the period May to December 1937.'
159 *Ibid.*
160 *Wallace Johnson Papers*.
161 ACC.187/65, File No. 100, 'Pan African Congress', *Aborigines Papers*, Ghana Regional Archives, Cape Coast, Sekyi to Ashie Nikoi, 8 October 1945.
162 *African Sentinel*, March–April 1938.
163 The *Aborigines Papers* include copies of the IASB correspondence to the ARPS and also to such nationalist movements as the Kikuyu Central Association, Kenya.

Conclusion

This study has sought to contribute to the growing literature on the development of African nationalism during the inter-war period. It has stressed the view that West African nationalism cannot be said to be a product of recent manufacture. Its roots go farther than is usually appreciated, and are complex in character. It draws its strength and inspiration from many sources, external as well as internal. This study has attempted to focus attention on one of the most significant but relatively neglected external factors that impinged upon imperial policy and the West African nationalist movements of the 1930s.

Imperial occupation, and especially experience of aggression, helped to sharpen the outlook of the West African colonial subjects. The Italo-Ethiopian conflict, as we have seen, had a significant impact upon the thoughts, aspirations, and activities of both the illiterate and literate West African. It constituted a peg on which the nationalist movements of West Africa and the articulate anti-colonialists hung their grievances which ante-dated the Italian attack on Ethiopia itself – their opposition to Christian missions, their disillusionment with the indirect rule system, their profound distrust and suspicion of the expatriate companies, their attitudes to European civilisation and racism, and the challenge to the whole colonial situation. For the Ethiopian question provided an unrivalled opportunity for West African nationalist politicians to view themselves in the mirror of European opinion, and what they saw was not only unflattering but saddening. They became convinced that the policy of submission and dependence upon the goodwill of Great Britain would never ensure autonomy and economic justice in West Africa. This realisation awakened in them a rebellion and determination to recapture the control of their own lands and the desire to shape their own destiny.

Thus the late 1930s marked the beginning of a new era in which the nationalist movement was destined to be of an entirely different order from that of the 1920s and the early 1930s. The idea of an immutable empire underwent some rude shocks during this period. The forceful proddings of West Africa's vigorous nationalist movements forced officials into a gradual reconsideration of Britain's colonial policy in Africa. It is worth stressing, therefore, that our understanding of the forces and trends shaping up during the latter part of the 1930s throws considerable light on the events of the post-war years, making them appear less sudden than they would otherwise seem.

We have briefly sketched the impact of the Italo-Ethiopian struggle on the nationalist thoughts and politics of some of the pioneers of post-war West African nationalism. Much more attention has, however, been focused on Wallace Johnson whose opposition to the West African colonial establishment was undoubtedly reinforced by the events in Ethiopia. Wallace Johnson had a much clearer idea than most other West African leaders at the time of the ways in which the Ethiopian cause could be used to create organisations, both within the colonies and on a pan-African basis, for the anti-colonial campaign which was his chief concern. Hitherto, Johnson's many-sided nationalist activity, his attempt to introduce militant racial consciousness into the West African nationalist struggle and thereby broaden the popular base of discontent against colonialism, and the challenge which his multi-dimensional roles posed to the colonial governments, the traditional elite and the conservative old leadership, have been neglected or minimised by students of the West African nationalist movements of the 1930s. We have concluded that from a historical standpoint Wallace Johnson was an outstanding figure in the rise of West African nationalism. His sphere was the whole of British West Africa rather than merely his native country of Sierra Leone; he thus fits very well the usual model of an early twentieth century-Western-educated West African. We have also noted that, among the leading nationalists in the 1930s, it was Wallace Johnson who broke into new realms of political activity, at least in the Gold Coast and Sierra Leone. Under the impact of the Italo-Ethiopian struggle, Johnson attempted to introduce the techniques of mass agitation and organisation and to increase political awareness in the towns and countryside. He ceaselessly urged West Africans to unite and recognise their common nationality: this was exemplified in the foundation and leadership of his movement, the West African Youth League, which was suggestive of his expansive and universalist orientation. Whereas the other political organisations in West Africa were generally confined to the elite of a few large urban centres, Johnson's Youth League, as we have seen, attempted to mobilise mass support by incorporating the sub-elite groups – farmers, small traders and wage-earners – into its political programme. Although the Youth League was short-lived, it was able to discredit the gradualist approach of moderate Africans towards the all-engaging issue of self-government. By the close of the 1930s the traditional political leadership of the established elite, especially in Sierra Leone, had temporarily given way to the radical Wallace Johnson Youth League activists. To Johnson, as to the emerging leaders of the post-1945 West African nationalist politics, as well as the dreamers of a united West Africa, the long resistance of the Ethiopians to Italian imperialism was a source of inspiration and hope for a West African struggle for emancipation.

Another view which has emerged from this study is the significance of the racial overtones of the West African nationalist thought and activity. We have seen that the tendency to see things in terms of race had for long been part of the consciousness of the West African colonial society, and that the question of race was an important factor in the nationalist politics. This was not only on account of its importance as a social phenomenon, but also, and in some cases, principally, of what in this semantically vague word stood for emotional, psychological, economic, religious suggestions or implications. Thus, throughout the period of agitation against colonialism, the nationalist movements tended to share a feeling of fraternity, of racial brotherhood, of a common history of oppression and exploitation and of attachment to 'Mother Africa'. It was because of this that the Italian invasion of the sole black empire of Ethiopia readily supplied the race-conscious West Africans with a focus. It stimulated among them an awareness of belonging to a wider cause.

Thus during the period of the Italo-Ethiopian crisis loyalty to the British Empire was replaced by identification with a kindred, if distant, African people. For the West African reaction to the conflict was directed towards the awakening of a racial, not a territorial consciousness. Although Ethiopia at that time did not herself provide sufficient inspiration as touch-bearer of pan-Africanism the picture of Ethiopia loomed large in the minds of the nationalist politicians, and struck deep chords of racial awareness.

This same prestige and recognition gives Ethiopia a special place in the contemporary African political scene. Ethiopia's true racial identity is no longer a controversial issue, as it was in the 1930s; neither is she any longer surrounded by peoples with whom she could make no direct contact because they were still under colonial rule. Addis Ababa is now regarded as the headquarters of Africa, politically and economically, with the bureaucracies and regular meetings of the Organisation of African Unity and the United Nations Economic Commission for Africa. The 'Addis Ababa Charter' of the OAU has become the embodiment of all the aspirations of the African people.

In retrospect, therefore, the special role of Ethiopia in the politics of independent Africa has gone a long way to justifying the intense and varied response of the West Africans to the Italian aggression on a country which then represented the only spark of glory on the vast continent of Africa.

Another theme to which we have devoted attention is the dramatic change of outlook on the part of the nationalist leaders in West Africa to the international diplomacy of the great powers, and especially to the League of Nations as an international organisation designed to promote international peace and security. We have stated that prior to the outbreak of the crisis, external affairs attracted little attention in West Africa. Although the nationalist press occasionally carried news about the treatment of the black peoples by the white in other parts of the world, it was very much a local press concerned chiefly with local affairs and open to the accusation of being somewhat parochial in outlook. The nationalist organisations were mainly taken up with the sorting out of their relationship with the colonial establishment. It was the Italo-Ethiopian controversy which provided a testing-time for the articulate nationalist groups, broadened their horizons, and intensified their nationalism, which took on a more pan-African perspective. Thenceforth, the colour bar and allied questions in almost all parts of the world received greater attention and interest among the nationalist leaders than previously. In an important sense, the profound interest shown by the nationalists in the League of Nations' handling of the Ethiopian affair would seem to have foreshadowed West Africa's present vigorous involvement in the activities of the United Nations in such matters as decolonisation, racial discrimination and oppression, and minority rule.

The full meaning and significance of the Italo-Ethiopian dispute for pan-Africanism during the second half of the 1930s has been briefly stated. The conclusion towards which the closing chapter of this study tends is that the Italian rape of Ethiopia marked a vital step in the growing unity and determination of the pan-Africanists of the Padmore school to change world realities. The conflict provided the spark needed to sustain the pan-African movement even in times of acute crisis. That it created an effective external dynamo of black racialism was evidenced by the revival of the pan-African organisations which culminated in the convening of the all-important 1945 Pan-African

Congress in Manchester, where pan-Africanism was said to have attained its maturity. Unlike the West African Students' Union and the League of Coloured Peoples which were dominated by moderate lawyers and doctors, the International African Service Bureau, whose creation was inspired principally by the Italo-Ethiopian conflict, was dominated and led by radical professional politicians, veteran agitators and experienced trade unionists who were bent on achieving concrete results. Their ambitions and aspirations were far more intense, positive and urgent. The reaction of the blacks resident in Britain and France, as well as those in America and the West Indies, to the Ethiopian question illustrated the international character of pan-Africanism. It also demonstrated that pan-Africanism was a plea for international black unity and concerted action to meet common problems faced by blacks. Africans and many persons of African descent were brought into close touch with one another and endeavoured to map out common policies and to give a picture of unanimity to the world. To a great extent this also would appear to have foreshadowed present-day African responses to white 'aggression', as was evidenced in the protracted Congo crisis and the current Rhodesian issue. As in the 1930s, Africans today believe that what happens to Africans in one part of Africa affects Africans living in other parts.

It is of considerable importance to note that the tendency to rely mainly upon the white colonial administration for an appraisal of nationalist sentiment and activity leaves much to be desired. There is indeed the likelihood that certain information bearing on nationalism is locked up in classified files. Besides, circumstances tended to place the colonial administrators too close to events or too far removed from the people. As we have seen, both in the Gold Coast and Sierra Leone the colonial governors of the second half of the 1930s refused to have anything to do with such nationalist organisations as Wallace Johnson's West African Youth League, the Aborigines' Rights' Protection Society, and its radical leaders like Kobina Sekyi, Samuel R. Wood or George Edward Moore. There was thus a total lack of rapport or confidence between nationalists and administrators, and this gave the latter many blind spots. Indeed, had not Malcolm MacDonald, the Secretary of State for the Colonies, written to enquire about the responses of the West African colonial subjects to the Ethiopian crisis, the colonial officials would have preferred to remain almost unconcerned, despite the impact of the Ethiopian conflict on the nationalists and the nationalist movements. And even when they did officially report, their despatches were a miscalculation of nationalist strength and trends. It is worth noting that the attitude of the colonial administrators to the expression of nationalist agitation in West Africa in the 1930s deserves to be the object of another study. Their fears, their adjustments, and their efforts to suppress, retard, or manipulate, nationalism are all relevant in a complete study of the many interacting factors present in the nationalist situation in West Africa. It is hoped that a more encompassing study of this nature will reveal more elements in this intriguing political history.

Appendix

A Poem on Ethiopia

> Ethiopia! rugged land, the Black man's pride,
> For you our forefathers fought and died –
> Fought that this land ever might be
> Died that its children in it would be free.
> The hills and valleys have ever been thine
> Since handed down from that Royal line
> Of Sheba, that Queen in days of old
> Who matched wits with Solomon, the story's told
> Now comes man with greed of gain,
> To take that land, through blood and pain
> Regarding not the Black man's right,
> But will pillage by the power of might,
> Black man will you stand and see
> Your home land taken, your life and liberty
> By those, who, of our fathers made slaves
> Beaten, chained, tortured, they filled alien graves?
> No! Ethiopia to us means far more,
> And as our forefathers died of yore;
> And so shall we with loyal swords
> Ne'er give up what our fathers won
> Haile Selassie, to thee honour is due
> Ethiopians are proud to acknowledge you
> Our leader, upright, courageous and brave
> Who'd lay down thy life thy country to save
> At thy call we will rally forth
> From East and West, South and North
> To Ethiopia we'll come, a fighting band
> To drive imposters out of the Black man's land;
> If we win not, we will die trying
> To keep our land, and freedom flag flying
> Greedy man, let your war madness cease
> The Ethiopian wants his land, and peace.[1]

1 Vox Populi, 21 September 1935.

Bibliography

A. *Manuscript Sources*

I *Public Record Office, London*

Volumes covering despatches to and from London, together with enclosures and Colonial Office minutes and reports on the African Progress Union and the National Congress of British West Africa; effects of sanctions against Italy on colonial trade; proposals on constitutional advances in West Africa; and the United African Front response to the Italo-Ethiopian crisis: C.O. 554/54/2760, C.O. 554/57/2760, C.O. 554/114/33539, C.O. 554/122/33632, C.O. 852/56/57

Report on UNIA activities in Nigeria, activities of Wallace Johnson in Nigeria, despatches on the Nigeria Youth Movement, Intelligence Reports on impact of the Italo-Ethiopian conflict on Nigeria, etc: C.O. 583/109/28194, C.O. 583/195/21029, C.O. 583/220/30159, C.O. 583/224/30453, C.O. 583/234/30386

Despatches on the 1934 Gold Coast Delegations to the Colonial Offices, with enclosures and Colonial Office minutes: C.O. 96/714/21639/1934, C.O. 96/717/21750/2/1934, C.O. 96/717/21750/3/1934, C.O. 96/723/31135/2

Confidential despatches on the control of the Gold Coast press: C.O. 96/707/21613/1933, C.O. 96/729/31205

Despatches on the political and economic situation in the Gold Coast: C.O. 96/696/6835, C.O. 96/696/6844, C.O. 96/699/7050A, C.O. 96/730/31228

Correspondence on misuse of Italian National flag in the Gold Coast: C.O. 96/732/31255

Confidential despatches on Wallace Johnson in the Gold Coast, the Gold Coast section of the West African Youth League, and the Italo-Ethiopian question: C.O. 96/731/31230, C.O. 96/736/31088/2A, C.O. 96/738/31189, C.O. 96/738/31189/1937, C.O. 96/739/31228/1937, C.O. 96/740/31230/1, C.O. 96/749/31228/1938, C.O. 96/749/31230/2/1938, C.O. 96/759/31230, C.O. 323/1517/7046/3

Report on the nature and activities of the Sierra Leone section of the NCBWA in the 1930s: C.O. 267/655/32157/1936, C.O. 267/669/32157

Volumes covering Sierra Leone confidential despatches to and from London; police reports, activities of Wallace Johnson and the Sierra Leone Section of the West African Youth League, with special reference to the Italo-Ethiopian crisis: C.O. 267/655/32210, C.O. 267/665/32208/38, C.O. 267/666/32216, C.O. 267/670/32210/2, C.O. 267/671/32221, C.O. 267/671/32245, C.O. 267/671/32216, C.O. 267/672/32254/1939, C.O. 267/673/32254, C.O. 267/677/32303

Despatches on the Gambian petition for constitutional reform in 1934; also, reports on possible cession of the Gambia to Germany: C.O. 87/240/33010, C.O. 87/245/33124

'Intelligence report on the Ethiopian Movement' prepared by Major R. H. Massie, Johannesburg, South Africa, December 1903: C.O. 537/513

Despatches on British official policy towards the Italo-Ethiopian dispute: F.O. 401/9, F.O. 371/19106, F.O. 371/19114, F.O. 371/19170, F.O. 371/19175, F.O. 371/19184, F.O. 371/19122, F.O. 371/19125, F.O. 371/19127, F.O. 371/19142, F.O. 371/19149, F.O. 371/19235, F.O. 371/20185, F.O. 371/22397

Confidential despatches dealing with the Vatican and the Italo-Ethiopian conflict: F.O. 371/19135, F.O. 371/19155, F.O. 371/19164, F.O. 371/19166, F.O. 371/19227, F.O. 371/20179

Official despatches on the reaction of British subjects in East and West Africa to the Italo-Ethiopian crisis: F.O. 371/20154

Reaction of Eastern Nigeria to the Italian invasion of Ethiopia: F.O. 371/20155

Re-establishment of Ethiopian independence: F.O. 371/27516

Confidential despatches dealing with the Union of South Africa and the Italo-Ethiopian conflict: F.O. 371/19125, F.O. 371/19127, F.O. 371/19170, F.O. 371/19175, F.O. 371/19222, F.O. 371/20155, F.O. 371/20156, F.O. 371/20185, F.O. 371/22397

Egypt and the Italo-Ethiopian crisis: F.O. 371/19064, F.O. 371/19073, F.O. 371/19116

Haitian, West Indian and the American Negro responses to the Italo-Ethiopian dispute: F.O. 371/19125, F.O. 371/19142, F.O. 371/19147, F.O. 371/19164, F.O. 371/20154

II *Rhodes House Library, Oxford*
1. Mss. Brit. Emp. S.332, Box 17 (Files 2 and 4) and Box 18 (Files 3 and 7), *Arthur Creech Jones Papers.*
2. Mss. Brit. Emp. S.334–7 and 342, *Lord Hailey Papers.* These papers contain numerous addresses and notes on visits to West Africa, as well as correspondence with the Colonial Office between 1939–42.

III (A) *Ghana National Archives, Accra*
Membership, nature and activities of such organisations as the Gold Coast branch of the WASU and the Society of African Patriots: ACC. 716/56

Resolution by the Provincial Council, Eastern Province, on Wallace Johnson and Azikiwe: ACC. 805/56

The Ethiopia Defence Committee appeal to Presidents, Eastern, Central and Western Provincial Council of Paramount Chiefs to support the Ethiopian cause: ACC. 730/56

Correspondence Relating to the National Congress of British West Africa: ADM. 7/1/67, 68 & 69, Blue Books. ADM. 5/4/19, ADM. 11/1427, ADM. 1344/26

Gold Coast Colony and Ashanti Cocoa Federation (1930): ADM. 11/1070

Papers Relating to the Petition of the Delegation from the Gold Coast Colony and Ashanti, 1934: ADM. 12/1/68

Governor's Despatches on Gold Coast nationalists: ADM. 12/3/103, 12/510, 12/1/100, 12/1/82, 5/1/111, 11/1/974

Details about imports from and exports to Italy, 1933/36: C.S.O. 340/35

Confidential reports by Governor-General of French West Africa at Dakar on the Gold Coast Press and its impact on neighbouring French colonies: C.S.O. 400/35

'Notes of Impressions of Miss Hebe Spaull of the League of Nations Union Staff in Great Britain on her visit to the Gold Coast and Nigeria, with regard to the West African reaction to the Italo-Ethiopian conflict', C.S.O. Conf. 361/38

Details about Wallace Johnson's educational background: C.S.O. Conf. 25/36

Italian underground propaganda in the Gold Coast: C.S.O. 25/36, Conf. file 75/36, sub. file 2

West African Youth Co-operative Association: C.S.O. 1324/31, sub. file 4

Gold Coast Ex-Servicemen's Union: C.S.O. 1324/31, sub. file 9

Ethiopia Defence Committee and the Gold Coast Section of the West African Youth League: C.S.O. 1324/31, sub. file 18

Gold Coast Youth Conference: C.S.O. 1324/31, sub. file 36

J. B. Danquah and the *Times of West Africa*: C.S.O. 1243/30, sub. file 7

Demonstrations against Income Tax Bill, 1931: C.S.O. 1403/31

Minutes of the Joint Provincial Council Meeting on Wallace Johnson, the West African Youth League, the Ethiopia Defence Committee and alleged German claim of some West African colonies: S.N.A. 212/32

III (B) *Cape Coast Regional Archives, Ghana*

ARPS Papers, ACC. 109/65, File No. 22.

ARPS Papers, ACC. 187/65, File No. 100, 'Pan African Congress'.

Volumes dealing with the nationalist activities of the ARPS and their contacts with coloured organisations and anti-imperialists abroad: ARPS Papers, ACC. 70/64; ARPS Papers, ACC. 72/64; ARPS Papers, ACC. 73/64; ARPS Papers, ACC. 74/64; ARPS Papers, ACC. 75/64; ARPS Papers, ACC. 77/64; ARPS Papers, ACC. 89/65; ARPS Papers ACC. 91/65; ARPS Papers ACC. 92/65; ARPS Papers, ACC. 145/65; ARPS Papers, ACC. 154/65; ARPS Papers, ACC. 179/65, File No. 92, 'American Negro Immigrants'; ARPS Papers, ACC. 183/65, ARPS, the West African Youth League, and the Ethiopian question; ARPS Papers, ACC. 583/64, 'Papers of Farmers' Association'.

(B2) Kobina Sekyi (W.E.G. Sekyi) Papers

(C) *Institute of African Studies, University of Ghana, Legon.* Transcript copy of some Wallace Johnson papers and memoirs.

IV (A) *Nigerian National Archives, Ibadan*

C.S.O. 26/30468, Vols. I and II: These volumes contain detailed reports on the Nigerian reaction to the Italo-Ethiopian dispute.

C.S.O. 1/36, Padmore's 'Pan-African Brotherhood' and the resolution on Ethiopia.

(B) *Ibadan University Library*

1. The Herbert Macaulay Papers.
2. Jacob Akinpelu Obisesan Diary, 1920–1960.

V *The Gambia Records Office, Bathurst*

Gambia 4/38 (1930), 'Activities of George Padmore'.

Gambia 4/73, File No. 179, 'Wallace Johnson and the International African Service Bureau'.

VI *Other Private Papers Consulted*

Bridgeman's Papers, in owner's possession, Middlesex.

Catholic Church Papers, Cape Coast, Ghana.

Christian Council Papers, Offices of the Christian Council, Osu, Accra, Ghana.

J. B. Danquah Papers, in possession of Mrs Elizabeth Danquah, Kanda Estate, Accra, Ghana.

Hotobah During Papers, in private possession, Freetown, Sierra Leone.

A. J. Ocansey Papers, in private custody, Accra, Ghana.

W.E.A. Ofori Atta Papers, in owner's possession, Accra, Ghana.

B. *Printed Primary Sources and Sessional Papers*

Publications of the Abyssinia Association
  i. *Memorandum on the Policy of His Majesty's Government toward Ethiopia*, London 1941.
  ii. *Nemesis*, London 1939.
  iii. *Treaties Broken by Italy in the Abyssinian War*, London 1937.

Publications of the Gold Coast/Ghana Government:
  i. *Correspondence Relating to the National Congress of British West Africa*. Sessional Paper VII of 1920.
  ii. *Executive Council Minutes, 1934–1938*.
  iii. *Legislative Council Debates, 1920–1938*.
  iv. *Ghana Parliamentary Debates*, Official Report, January 1965.
  v. *Judgement Book, Supreme Court, Accra, Vol. 13, February 1936*.
  vi. *Papers Relating to the Petition of the Delegation from the Gold Coast Colony and Ashanti*, Sessional Paper XI of 1934.
  vii. *Proceedings of the Watson Commission, Accra, 1948*.
  viii. *Report on the Police Department, 1929–1939*.
  ix. *Report on the Eastern Province of the Gold Coast Colony for the Year 1933–1934*.

Publications of the League Against Imperialism (Bridgeman Papers):
  i. *Abyssinia*, London 1935.
  ii. *The Anti-Imperialist Review*, Vol. 1, No. 1, September–October 1931.

Publications of the League of Coloured Peoples (British Museum):
  i. *The Keys*, July 1933–September 1939.
  ii. *Impressions of Liberia, November 1934: A Report to the League of Coloured Peoples*, by Charles Roden Buxton, n.d.

Publications of the League of Nations (British Museum):
  i. *Dispute between Ethiopia and Italy. Request by the Ethiopian Government*, Official No. C.230(1), M.114(1), 1935. VII, Geneva, 1935.
  ii. *Dispute between Ethiopia and Italy. Memorandum by the Italian Government on the situation in Ethiopia*, Official No. C.340.171.1935.VII, Geneva, 1935.
  iii. *Document*, C.49, M.22, 1935, VII.
  iv. *Document*, C.482, M.258, 1935, VII.
  v. *International Commission of Enquiry in Liberia*, Official No. C.658, M.272, 1930, VI, Geneva, 1930.
  vi. *Official Journal*, 1923–38.

vii. *Records of the Sixteenth Ordinary Session of the Assembly*; Plenary Meetings.

viii. *Treaty Series*, 1929, Vol. 94, No. 2158.

Publication of the League of Nations Union:
   The Tragedy of Abyssinia: What Britain Feels and Thinks and Wants, London, 1936.

Publication of the New Statesman and Nation:
   Abyssinia: The Essential Facts in the Dispute and an Answer to the Question – 'OUGHT WE TO SUPPORT SANCTIONS?'

Publication of the Nigerian Youth Movement:
   Nigerian Youth Charter: The Official Programme of the Nigerian Youth Movement, Africana Library, University of Ibadan, Nigeria.

Publication of the Government of Nigeria:
   Legislative Council Debates, 1920–1938.

Publication of the Government of Sierra Leone:
   Statement Made on 19 May by His Excellency the Governor to Unofficial Members Regarding Certain Bills, Government Printer, Freetown 1939.

Publications of the United Kingdom Government:
   i. *British Admiralty Handbook of Abyssinia*, London, 1917.
   ii. *Correspondence Respecting Abyssinia Raids and Incursions Into British Territory*. Cmd.2553(1925), Abyssinia, No. 1(1925).
   iii. *Correspondence Respecting the Agreement Between the United Kingdom and Italy of December 14–20, 1925, in Regard to Lake Tsana*. Cmd.2792(1927), Abyssinia, No. 1 (1927).
   iv. *Report of the Commission of Enquiry into Disturbances in the Gold Coast* (Chairman, A. Watson) Col. No. 231, London 1948.
   v. *Parliamentary Debates* (Hansard): House of Commons, Official Reports, 1929–38.
   vi. *Parliamentary Debates* (Hansard): House of Lords, Official Reports, 1929–38.
   vii. *Statement of Policy on Colonial Development and Welfare*, Cmd.6175, 1940.
   viii. *The Colonial Empire (1939–1947)*, Cmd.7167, 1947.

Publication of the United States, Department of State:
   U.S. Diplomatic Papers, 1935, I: The Near East and Africa.

Publication of the Government of the Union of South Africa:
   House of Assembly *Debates*, Vol. 26, January 1936.

Publication of the Universal Negro Improvement Association and African Communities League:
   The Case of the Negro for International Racial Adjustment, Before the English People, Speech Delivered by Marcus Garvey at Royal Albert Hall, London. 6 June 1928, London 1928.

Publications of the West African Students' Union (British Museum):
   i. *Wasu*, No. 1, March 1926 – Vol. XII, No. 3, Summer 1947.
   ii. *The Truth About Aggrey House: An Exposure of the Government Plan for the Control of African Students in Great Britain*, London 1934.

C. Printed Secondary Sources

AFRIFA, A. A. *The Ghana Coup*, London, 1967

AGBEBI, MOJOLA. *Inaugural Sermon*, Lagos, December 1902

AHUMA, ATTOH, S. R. B. *Memoirs of West African Celebrities*, Liverpool, 1905
— *The Gold Coast Nation and National Consciousness*, 2nd edn, London, 1971

AINSLIE, ROSALYNDE, *The Press in Africa: Communication Past and Present*, London, 1966

AKYEAMPONG, H. K. (compiled), *Historic Speeches and Writings on Ghana by J. B. Danquah*, Accra, 1966

ALLEN, C. & JOHNSON, R. W. eds, *African Perspectives*, Cambridge, 1970

ANANABA, WOGU, *The Trade Union Movement in Nigeria*, London, 1969

APTER, DAVID, *Ghana in Transition*, New York, 1963

ARENDT, HANNAH, *The Origins of Totalitarianism*, London, 1958

ARNDT, W., *The Economic Lessons of the Nineteen Thirties*, London, 1944

AUSTIN, D., *Politics in Ghana, 1946–1960*, London, 1964

AWOLOWO, OBAFEMI, *Awo: The Autobiography of Chief Obafemi Awolowo*, Cambridge, 1960
— *Path to Nigerian Freedom*, London, 1947

AWOONER-RENNER, BANKOLE, *West African Soviet Union*, London, 1946
— *This Africa*, Watford, Herts, 1943

AYANDELE, E. A. *The Missionary Impact on Modern Nigeria, 1842–1914: A Political Analysis*, London 1966
— *Holy Johnson: Pioneer of African Nationalism, 1836–1917*, London, 1970
— *A Visionary of the African Church: Mojola Agbebi (1860–1917)*, Nairobi, 1971.

AZIKIWE, N., *Renascent Africa*, 2nd edn, London, 1968
— *Liberia in World Politics*, London, 1934
— *The Development of Political Parties in Nigeria*, London, 1957
— *My Odyssey: An Autobiography*, London, 1970

BAER, GEORGE W. *The Coming of the Italian-Ethiopian War*, Harvard University Press, 1967

BAETA, C. G., ed., *Christianity in Tropical Africa*, London, 1968

BARKER, A. J., *The Civilizing Mission: The Italo-Ethiopian War, 1935–36*, London, 1968

BARTELS, F. L., *The Roots of Ghana Methodism*, Cambridge, 1965

BAXTER, P., & SANSON, B., eds, *Race and Social Difference*, Middlesex, 1972

BINCHY, D., *Church and State in Fascist Italy*, London, 1941

BITTLE, W. & GEIS, G., *The Longest Way Home: Chief Alfred Sam's Back to Africa Movement*, Detroit, 1964

BONTEMPS, A. & CONROY, J, *Anyplace but Here*, New York, 1966

BOURRET, F. *Ghana: Road to Independence*, Oxford, 1960

BOWEN, J. W. E., ed., *Africa and the American Negro: Congress on Africa*, Atlanta, Ga., 1896

BUCKMAN, P., *The Limits of Protest*, London, 1970

BUXTON, C. R., *The Race Problem in Africa*, London, 1913

CALVOCORESSI, P., 'The Politics of Sanctions: The League and the United Nations', in Segal, R., ed., *Sanctions Against South Africa*, London, 1964

CARTWRIGHT, J. R., *Politics in Sierra Leone*, Toronto, Canada, 1970

CARY, JOYCE, *The Case for African Freedom*, London, 1944

CECIL, VISCOUNT, *A Great Experiment*, London, 1941
— *All the Way*, London, 1949

CHARLES-ROUX, F., *Huit ans au Vatican, 1932–1940*, Paris, 1947

CHAMBERLAIN, W. H., *Appeasement: Road to War*, New York, 1962

Chicago Commission on Race Relations, ed. *The Negro in Chicago: A Study of Race Relations and a Race Riot*, Chicago, 1922

CHIN SHENG-PAO, *The Gold Coast Delegations to Britain in 1934*, Taipei, Taiwan, 1970

COLEMAN, J. S. *Nigeria: Background to Nationalism*, Berkeley, 1958

COOPER, DUFF, *Old Men Forget*, London, 1957

CROCKER, W. R., *Self-Government For the Colonies*, London, 1949

— *Nigeria: A Critique of British Colonial Administration*, London, 1936

CRONON, E. D., *Black Moses*, Madison, 1955

CROWDER, M., *West Africa Under Colonial Rule*, London, 1968

CUNARD, N., *Negro Anthology*, London, 1934

CURTIN, P., *The Image of Africa: British Ideas and Action, 1780–1850*, London, 1965

DANQUAH, J. B., *Liberty: A Page from the Life of J.B.*, Accra, 1960

— *Liberty of the Subject: A Monograph on the Gold Coast Hold-Up and Boycott of Foreign Goods, 1937–1938*, Accra, n.d.

— *The Constitutional History of Ghana in the Past Fifty Years*, Accra, 1961

— *Self-Help and Expansion*, Accra, 1943

DAVIS, J. A., ed. (for the American Society of African Culture), *Pan-Africanism Reconsidered*, Berkeley, 1962.

DEAKIN, F. W., *The Brutal Friendship*, London, 1962

DEBRUNNER, HANS W., *A Church Between Colonial Powers: A Study of the Church and State in Togo*, London, 1965

DELANO, ISAAC O., *One Church For Nigeria*, London, 1945

DEMANGEON, A., *The British Empire: A Study in Colonial Geography*, London, 1923

DENIGA, ADEOYE, *The Necessity for a West African Conference*, Lagos, 1919

DESAI, RAM, ed., *Christianity in Africa As Seen by Africans*, Denver, 1962

DU BOIS, W. E. B., *The World and Africa*, 3rd edn., New York, 1967

EDEN, A., *Avon Memoirs: Facing the Dictators*, London, 1962

EDWARDS, A., *Marcus Garvey, 1887–1940*, London, 1967

ENAHORO, A. E. O. *Fugitive Offender: The Story of a Political Prisoner*, London, 1965

ESSEIEN-UDOM, E. U., *Black Nationalism: The Search For Identity in America*, Chicago, 1962

FANON, F., *The Wretched of the Earth*, New York, 1968

FEILING, KEITH, *The Life of Neville Chamberlain*, London, 1947

FERMI, LAURA, *Mussolini*, Chicago, 1961

FREYRE, G., *The Racial Factor in Contemporary Politics*, University of Sussex, Herts, 1966.

GAILEY, H. A., *Road to Aba: A Study of British Administrative Policy in Eastern Nigeria*, London, 1971

GARVEY, AMY JACQUES, *Garvey and Garveyism*, Kingston, Jamaica, 1963

— *Black Power in America: Marcus Garvey's Impact on Jamaica and Africa*, Kingston, Jamaica, 1968

GARVEY, MARCUS, *Philosophy and Opinions of Marcus Garvey or Africa for the Africans*, ed. Amy Jacques-Garvey, New York, 1923 and 1925

Ghana Christian Council. *40 Years: Ghana Christian Council Anniversary Handbook*, Accra, 1971

GEISS, I. *The Pan-African Movement*, trans., Ann Keep, London, 1974

GILBERT, M., *The Roots of Appeasement*, London, 1966

GILBERT, M. and GOTT, R., *The Appeasers*, London, 1963

GINSBERG, MORRIS, *Nationalism: A Reappraisal*, Leeds, 1963

GUPTA, P. S., *Imperialism and the British Labour Movement, 1914–1964*, Cambridge, 1975

HAILEY, WILLIAM, MALCOLM, LORD, *An African Survey*, rev. ed., London, 1957

HALPERIN, W. S., *Mussolini and Italian Fascism*, Chicago, 1964

HANCOCK, W. K., *Survey of British Commonwealth Affairs*, Vol. ii: *Problems of Economic Policy, 1918–1939*, London, 1942

HARDIE, F., *The Abyssinian Crisis*, London, 1974

HARRIS, BRICE, Jr, *The United States and the Italo-Ethiopian Crisis*, California, 1964

HARRIS, JOHN H., *Dawn in Darkest Africa*, London, 1968

HAYFORD, J. E. CASELY, *Ethiopia Unbound: Studies in Race Emancipation*, London, 1911

— *Gold Coast Native Institutions*, London, 1903

— *William Waddy Harris: The Man and His Message*, London, 1916

— *The Truth About the West African Land Question*, London, 1913

— *United West Africa*, London, 1919

— *The Disabilities of Black Folk and their Treatment with an Appeal to the Labour Party*, London, 1929

HAYFORD, MARK C., *West Africa and Christianity*, London, 1900

— *The Baptist Church and Mission and the Christian Army of the Gold Coast*, London, 1913

HIBBERT, C., *Benito Mussolini*, London, 1962

HODGKIN, THOMAS, *Nationalism in Colonial Africa*, London, 1962

HOOKER, J. T., *Black Revolutionary: George Padmore's Path from Communism to Pan-Africanism*, London, 1967

HOPKINS, A. G., *An Economic History of West Africa*, London, 1973

JAMES, C. L. R., *World Revolution 1917–1937: The Rise and Fall of the Communist International*, London, 1937

— *The Black Jacobins*, London, 1937

— *Why Negroes Should Oppose the War*, New York, n.d.

JEMOLO, A. C., *Church and State in Italy 1850–1950*, Oxford, 1960

JESMAN, CZESLAW, *The Ethiopia Paradox*, London, 1963

JOHNSON, J. W. DE GRAFT, *Towards Nationhood in West Africa*, 2nd edn, London, 1971

JOHNSON, WALLACE, I. T. A., *A Restoration of the Ashanti Confederacy*, Accra, 1935

JULY, ROBERT W., *The Origins of Modern African Thought*, London, 1968

KILBY, PETER, *African Enterprise: The Nigerian Bread Industry*, Hoover Institution Studies No. 8, Stanford University, 1965

KILSON, M., *Political Change in a West African State: A Study of the Modernization Process in Sierra Leone*, Harvard University Press, 1966

KIMBLE, DAVID, *A Political History of Ghana: The Rise of Gold Coast Nationalism, 1850–1928*, London, 1963

KOHN, H. and SOKOLSKY, W., *African Nationalism in the Twentieth Century*, Princeton, N.J., 1965

KWAANSAH, KOBINA, *The Gold Coast Politics with Particular Reference to the Gold Coast Aborigines' Rights' Protection Society*, Kumasi, Ghana, 1947

LANGLEY, J. A., *Pan-Africanism and Nationalism in West Africa 1900–1945*, London, 1973

— *Introduction to Kobina Sekyi: The Blinkards*, London, 1974

LAURENS, F. D., *France and the Italo-Ethiopian Crisis, 1935–36*, The Hague, 1967

LEGUM, C., *Pan-Africanism: A Short Political Guide*, rev. edn, New York, 1965

LEWIS, W. A., *An Economic Survey: 1919–1939*, London, 1949

LOCKE, A. and BERNHARD J. STERN, eds, *When Peoples Meet: A Study in Race and Culture Contacts*, New York, 1959

LOGAN, R. W., *The African Mandates in World Politics*, Washington, 1948

LYNCH, H. R., *Edward Wilmot Blyden: Pan-Negro Patriot 1832–1912*, London, 1967

MACMILLAN, A., *The Red Book of West Africa*, London, 1920

MAIR, LUCY, *Native Policies in Africa*, London, 1930

MAJEKE, NOSIPHO, *The Role of the Missionaries in Conquest*, Johannesburg, 1952

MAKONNEN, T. RAS, *Pan-Africanism From Within*, London, 1973

MAUNIER, RENÉ, *The Sociology of Colonies: An Introduction to the Study of Race Contact*, 2 vols ed. & tr., E. O. Lorimer, London, 1949

MAZRUI, ALI A., *Towards A Pax-Africana: A Study of Ideology and Ambition*, London, 1967

MEEK, C. K., MACMILLAN, W. M., and HUSSEY, E. R. J., *Europe and West Africa: Some Problems and Adjustments*, London, 1940

METCALFE, G. E., ed., *Great Britain and Ghana: Documents of Ghana History, 1807–1957*, London, 1964

MOSLEY, L. *Haile Selassie: The Conquering Lion*, London, 1964

NKRUMAH, KWAME, *Ghana: Autobiography of Kwame Nkrumah*, Edinburgh, 1957

— *I Speak of Freedom*, New York, 1961

OFOSU APPIAH, L. H., *The Life and Times of J. B. Danquah*, Accra, 1974

OLUSANYA, G. O., *The Second World War and Politics in Nigeria, 1939–1953*, Lagos, 1973

OMONIYI, BANDELE PRINCE, *A Defence of the Ethiopian Movement*, Edinburgh, 1908

ORIZU, NWAFOR, A. A., *Without Bitterness*, New York, 1944

PADMORE, GEORGE, *How Britain Rules Africa*, New York, 1936

— *Africa and World Peace*, London, 1937

— *Pan-Africanism or Communism?*, London, 1956

— ed., *History of the Pan-African Congress*, London, 1963

PAREKH, BHIKHU, ed., *Colour, Culture and Consciousness*, London, 1974

PERHAM, MARGERY, *The Colonial Reckoning*, London, 1962

— *Colonial Sequence, 1930–1949*, London, 1967

PIUS XI, *Discorsi di Pio XI*, Domencio Bertetto, ed., 3 vols, Turin, 1960

— *The Pope and Catholic Action* (addresses), London, 1930

RHODES, A., *The Vatican in the Age of the Dictators, 1922–1945*, London, 1973.

ROTBERG, R. I. and MAZRUI, ALI, A., eds, *Protest and Power in Black Africa*, New York, 1970

Royal Institute of International Affairs, London, *Abyssinia and Italy*, Information Department Papers, No. 16, London, 1935

— *The British Empire, A Report on its Structure and Problems*, London, 1938

— *Documents on International Affairs, 1934–1938*
— *Survey of International Affairs, 1934–1938*
RUBENSON, SVEN, *Wichale xvii: The Attempt to Establish a Protectorate Over Ethiopia*, Addis Ababa, 1964
SALVATORELLI, L., and GIOVANNI, M., eds, *Storia d'Italia nel periodo fascista*, 3rd edn, Rome 1959
SAMPSON, M., *West African Leadership*, 2nd edn., London, 1969
SEGAL, RONALD, ed., *Sanctions Against South Africa*, London, 1964
SHEPPERSON, G. and PRICE, T., *Independent African*, Edinburgh, 1958
SITHOLE, N., *African Nationalism*, London, 1959
SOLANKE, L. *United West Africa (or Africa) at the Bar of the Family of Nations*, London, 1927
SPILLER, G., *Papers on Inter-Racial Problems*, London, 1911
SPITZER, LEO, *The Creoles of Sierra Leone: Responses to Colonialism, 1870–1945*, University of Wisconsin Press, 1974
STEER, GEORGE, *Caesar in Abyssinia*, Boston, 1937
STRANG, LORD, *Home and Abroad*, London, 1956
SUNDKLER, B. G. M., *Bantu Prophets in South Africa*, reprinted, London, 1964
TAMUNO, T. N., *Nigeria and Elective Representation 1923–1947*, London, 1966
TEMPLEWOOD, VISCOUNT, *Nine Troubled Years*, London, 1954
THOMPSON, V. B., *Africa and Unity: The Evolution of Pan-Africanism*, London, 1969
THWAITE, DANIEL, *The Seething African Pot: A Study of Black Nationalism, 1882–1935*, London, 1936
TORDOFF, W., *Ashanti Under the Prempehs, 1888–1935*, London, 1965
ULLENDORFF, E., *Ethiopia and the Bible*, London, 1968
VAUGHAN, D. A., *Negro Victory: The Life Story of Dr. Harold Moody*, London, 1950
WALLBANK, T. WALTER, *Documents on Modern Africa*, New York, 1964
WALLERSTEIN, I., *Social Change: The Colonial Situation*, New York, 1966
WALTERS, F. P., *A History of the League of Nations*, London, 1960
WEBSTER, J. B., *The African Churches Among the Yorubas*, London, 1964
WEISBORD, R. G., *Ebony Kinship: Africa, Africans, and the Afro-Americans*, Westport, 1973
WELBOURN, F. B., *East African Rebels*, London, 1961
WIGHT, M., *The Gold Coast Legislative Council*, London, 1946
WILLOUGHBY, W. C., *Race Problems in the New Africa*, Oxford, 1923
WILSON, HENRY S., ed. *Origins of West African Nationalism*, London, 1969

D. *Articles and Unpublished Papers*

AFIGBO, A. E., 'The people and the introduction of Direct Taxation in 1928', seminar paper, Institute of African Studies, University of Ibadan, Ibadan, 26 November 1964
AJAYI, ADE J. F., 'Nineteenth Century Origins of Nigerian Nationalism', *Journal of the Historical Society of Nigeria*, ii, 2, pp. 196–210, December 1961
AKIWOWO, A., 'The Place of Mojola Agbebi in the African Nationalist Movements: 1890–1917', *Phylon*, xxvi, 2, pp. 1965 122–39,
ANON. 'Appeasement Re-considered: Some Neglected Factors', *Round Table*, 212, September 1963 pp. 358–71,

ASANTE, S. K. B., 'The Aborigines' Society, Kwame Nkrumah and the 1945 Pan-African Congress', *Research Review*, Institute of African Studies, University of Ghana, Legon, 7, Lent Term 1971, pp. 46–72

— 'Kwame Nkrumah and Pan-Africanism: The Early Phase, 1945–1961', *Universitas*, University of Ghana, Legon, iii, 1, October 1973

— 'South Africa and the Italo-Ethiopian Crisis, 1934–36', *Journal of Social Science*, University of Ghana, Legon, iii, 1, December 1974

— 'The Catholic Missions, British West African Nationalist and the Italian invasion of Ethiopia, 1935–36', *African Affairs*, 73, 291, April 1974, pp. 204–16

— 'The Afro-American and the Italo-Ethiopian Crisis, 1934–36', *Race*, xv, 2, 1973, pp. 167–84

— 'Pan-Africanist: C. L. R. James', *Africa*, 30, February 1974

ASHANIN, C. B., 'Christianity and African Nationalism', *Universitas*, iv, 3, June 1960, pp. 85–7

ASKEW, W. C., 'The Secret Agreement between France and Italy on Ethiopia, January 1935', *Journal of Modern History*, xxv, March 1953, pp. 47–8

AYANDELE, E. A., 'An Assessment of James Johnson and His Place in Nigerian History, 1874–1917', Part I, 1874–90, *Journal of the Historical Society of Nigeria*, ii, 4, December 1963, pp. 486–516

AZIKIWE, N., 'In Defence of Liberia', *Journal of Negro History*, xvii, 1, January 1932, pp. 30–50

BELL, PHILIP, H. M., 'Great Britain and the Rise of Germany, 1932–34', *International Relations*, ii, 9, April 1964, pp. 609–18

CONTEE, CLARENCE G., 'The emergence of Du Bois as an African Nationalist', *Journal of Negro History*, lix, 50, 1969

DALZELL, CHARLES F., 'Pius XII, Italy and the Outbreak of War', *Journal of Contemporary History*, ii, 4, 1967, p. 137

DIDDIS, D. 'The Universal Races Congress of 1911', *Race*, xiii, 1, 1971, pp. 37–46

DRAKE, ST. CLAIR, 'The International Implications of Race and Race Relations', *Journal of Negro Education*, xx, 1951, pp. 261–78

DUFFIELD, IAN, 'The Business Activities of Duse Mohamed Ali: An Example of Economic Dimension of Pan-Africanism, 1912–45', *Journal of Historical Society of Nigeria*, iv, 4, June 1969, pp. 571–600

— 'Duse Mohamed Ali, Pan-Africanism, Islam and the Nile Valley', a paper read at the International Conference at the University of Khartoum, February 1968

ELLIS, G. W., 'Liberia in the Political Psychology of West Africa', *Journal of the Royal African Society*, xii, 1912–13, pp. 52–70

ELUWA, G. I. C., 'Casely Hayford and African Emancipation', *Pan-African Journal*, vii, 2, Summer 1974, pp. 111–18

FYFE, C. H. 'The Sierra Leone Press in the Nineteenth Century', *Sierra Leone Studies*, new series, 8, June 1957, pp. 226–36

GARIGUE, PHILIP, 'The West African Students' Union: A Study in Culture Contact', *Africa*, xxiii, 1, January 1953, pp. 55–69

GEISS, I., 'Notes on the Development of Pan-Africanism', *Journal of the Historical Society of Nigeria*, iii, 4, June 1967, pp. 719–40

GIGLIO, CARLO, 'Article 17 of the Treaty of Uccialli', R. Caulk, trans, *Journal of African History*, vi, 2, 1965, pp. 221–31

GWAM, L. C., 'Dr Mojola Agbebi', a seminar paper, Institute of African Studies Library, University of Ibadan, Nigeria

HAILEY, WILLIAM MALCOLM, LORD, 'Nationalism in Africa', *Journal of the Royal African Society*, 36, April 1937, pp. 134–47

— 'Native Administration and Political Development in Tropical Africa', Confidential Report, London, 1940–42

HARLAN, LOUIS R., 'Booker T. Washington and the White Man's Burden', *American Historical Review*, lxxi, 2, January 1966

HESS, ROBERT I., 'Italy and Africa: Colonial Ambitions in the First World War', *Journal of African History*, iv, 1 1963, pp. 105–26

HIETT, HELEN, 'Public opinion and the Italo-Ethiopian Dispute: The Activity of Private Organisations in the Crisis', *Geneva Special Studies*, vii, 1, February 1936, pp. 3–38

HODSON, SIR ARNOLD W., 'An Account of the part played by the Gold Coast Brigade in the East African Campaign, August 1940 to May 1941, Part I – The Defence of Kenya', *Journal of the Royal African Society*, xi, October 1941, pp. 300–11

— 'Part II – The Invasion of Italian Somaliland', *Journal of the Royal African Society*, xii, January 1942, pp. 14–28

HOPKINS, A. G., 'Economic Aspects of Political Movements in Nigeria and the Gold Coast 1918–39', *Journal of African History*, vii, 1, 1966, pp. 133–52

HUGHES, A., 'The Nationalist Movement in the inter-war period: 1923–1938', seminar paper, Institute of African Studies, University of Ibadan, November 1964

HUTCHINSON, LESTER, 'Abyssinia – The Thieves Fall Out', *Labour Monthly*, 17, 9, September 1935, pp. 542–3

IRERE, ABIOLA, 'Negritude or Black Cultural Nationalism', *Journal of Modern African Studies*, xiii, 3, 1965, pp. 321–48

— 'Leopold Sedar Senghor As Poet', *Odu*, new series, 1, April 1969, pp. 3–27

ISAACS, HAROLD R., 'Du Bois and Africa', *Race*, ii, 1, November 1960, pp. 3–23

JONES-QUARTEY, K. A. B., 'Kobina Sekyi: A Fragment of Biography', *Research Review*, 4, 1, 1967

KENYATTA, JOMO, 'Hands Off Abyssinia', *Labour Monthly*, xvii, 9, September 1935, pp. 532–6

KIERAN, J. A., 'Some Roman Catholic Missionary Attitudes to Africans in Nineteenth Century East Africa', *Race*, x, 3, January 1969, pp. 341–59

KILSON, MARTIN, 'Nationalism and Social Class in British West Africa', *Journal of Politics*, xx, May 1958, pp. 368–87

— 'African Political Change and the Modernisation Process', *Journal of Modern African Studies*, i, 4, 1963, pp. 425–40

LANGLEY, J. A., 'Garveyism and African Nationalism', *Race*, xi, 2, October 1969, pp. 157–72

— 'Modernisation and Its Malcontents: Kobina Sekyi of Ghana and the re-statement of African political theory (1892–1956)', *Research Review*, vi, 3, 1970, pp. 1–61

LOUIS, ROGER, 'Great Britain and the African Peace Settlement of 1919', *American Historical Review*, 71, April 1966, pp. 875–92

— 'The United States and the African Peace Settlement of 1919: The Pilgrimage of George Louis Beer', *Journal of African History*, iv, 3, 1963, pp. 413–33

LYNCH, HOLLIS R., 'Pan-Negro Nationalism in the New World before 1862', *Boston University Papers on Africa*, ii, 1966, pp. 413–33

— 'Edward W. Blyden: Pioneer West African Nationalist', *Journal of African History*, vi, 3, 1965, pp. 373–88

MACDONALD, R. J., 'Dr. Harold Arundel Moody and the League of Coloured Peoples, 1931–1947', *Race*, xiv, 3, January 1973, p. 291

MARCUS, H. G., 'A Background to Direct British Diplomatic Involvement in Ethiopia, 1894–1896', *Journal of Ethiopian Studies*, i, 2, July 1963, pp. 121–132

— 'A Preliminary History of the Tripartite Agreement of December 13, 1906', *Journal of Ethiopian Studies*, ii, 2, July 1964, pp. 21–40

— 'The Last Years of the Reign of the Emperor Menelik 1906–1913', *Journal of Semitic Studies*, 9, Spring 1964, pp. 229–34

MARKOWITZ, M. D., 'The Missions and Political Development in the Congo', *Africa*, x, 3, July 1970, pp. 234–6

MAZRUI, ALI A., 'On the Concept "We are All Africans" ', *American Political Science Review*, 57, 1963, pp. 88–97

OMU, F. I. A., 'The Dilemma of Press Freedom in Colonial Africa: The West African Example', *Journal of African History*, ix, 2, 1968, pp. 275–98

PADMORE, G., 'Ethiopia and World Politics', *Crisis*, xlii, 5, May 1935

PANKHURST, R., 'Ethiopia and Africa: The Historical Aspects', *Ethiopia Observer*, viii, 2, 1964, p. 155

— 'The Ethiopian Slave Trade in the Nineteenth and Early Twentieth Centuries: A Statistical Inquiry', *Journal of Semitic Studies*, 9, Spring 1964, pp. 220–8

ROHDIE, SAMUEL, 'The Gold Coast Aborigines Abroad', *Journal of African History*, vi, 3, 1965, pp. 389–411

— 'The Gold Coast Cocoa Hold-Up of 1930–31', *Transactions of the Historical Society of Ghana*, ix, 1968, pp. 105–18

RUBENSON, SVEN, 'The Protectorate Paragraph of the Wichale Treaty', *Journal of African History*, v, 2, 1964, pp. 243–83

— 'Professor Giglio, Antonelli and Article xvii of the Treaty of Wichale', *Journal of African History*, vii, 3, 1966, pp. 445–57

SANDERSON, G., 'The Foreign Policy of the Negus Menelik, 1896–1898', *Journal of African History*, vi, 1964, pp. 87–97

SHACK, WILLIAM A., 'Ethiopia and Afro-Americans: Some Historical Notes, 1920–1970', *Phylon*, Vol. xxxv, 2, 1974, pp. 142–155

SHALOFF, STANLEY, 'Press Controls and Sedition Proceedings in the Gold Coast, 1933–1939', *African Affairs*, lxxi, 284, July 1972, pp. 241–63

— 'The Press and Politics in Accra: The Accra Legislative Council Election of 1935', *Societas*, i, 3, Summer 1971, pp. 213–19

SHEPPERSON, GEORGE, 'Notes on Negro American Influences on the Emergence of African Nationalism', *Journal of African History*, i, 2, 1960, pp. 299–312

— 'External Factors in the Development of African Nationalism, with Particular Reference to British Central Africa', *Phylon*, xxii, 3, 1961

— 'Pan-Africanism and "Pan-Africanism": Some Historical Notes', *Phylon*, xxii, 4, Winter 1962, pp. 346–58

—— 'Ethiopianism and African Nationalism', *Phylon*, xiv, 1, 1953, pp. 9–18

SPITZER, LEO and DENZER, LA RAY, 'I.T.A. Wallace Johnson and the West African Youth League', *International Journal of African Historical Studies*, vi, 3, 1973, pp. 413–52

— Part II: 'The Sierra Leone Period, 1938–1945', *International Journal of African Historical Studies*, vi, 4, 1973, pp. 565–601

SUYIN, HAN, 'Race Relations and the Third World', *Race*, xiii, 1, 1971, pp. 1–20

ULLENDORF, EDWARD, 'The Anglo-Ethiopian Treaty of 1902', *Bulletin of School of African and Oriental Studies*, xxx, Part 3, 1967, pp. 283–317

VOEGELIN, ERIC, 'The Growth of the Race Idea', *Review of Politics* ii, July 1940, pp. 283–317

WATT, D. C., 'The Secret Laval-Mussolini Agreement of 1935 on Ethiopia', *Middle East Journal*, xv, Winter 1961, pp. 69–78

WEISBORD, R. G., 'British West Indian reaction to the Italian-Ethiopian War: An Episode in Pan-Africanism', *Caribbean Studies*, x, 1, April 1970, pp. 34–41

— 'Black American and the Italian-Ethiopian Crisis: An Episode in Pan-Negroism', *Historian*, xxxiv, 2, February 1972, pp. 230–41

— 'Marcus Garvey: Pan-Negroist: The View from Whitehall', *Race*, xii, 4, April 1970, pp. 419–29

WESTERMAN, D., 'Ein Kongress Westafrikaner', *Kolonial Rundschan*, Berlin, 1920, pp. 114–18

WOOD, S. R., 'West Africa and the Sedition Ordinance', *Labour Monthly*, xvii, 8, August 1935, p. 494

E. *Newspapers*

African Church Chronicle, Lagos
African Mail London
African Morning Post, Accra
Africa and Orient Review, London
African Sentinel, London
African Standard, Freetown
African Times & Orient Review, London
Chicago Defender, Chicago
Colonial & Provincial Reporter, Freetown
Comet, Lagos
Cri des Nègres, Paris
Daily Telegraph, London
El Ouma, Paris
Ex Service, Accra
Gambia Outlook and Senegambian Reporter, Bathurst
Gold Coast Aborigines, Cape Coast
Gold Coast Independent, Accra
Gold Coast Leader, Sekondi
Gold Coast Observer, Accra
Gold Coast Spectator, Accra
Gold Coast Times, Cape Coast
Lagos Daily News, Lagos
Lagos Standard, Lagos
Lagos Weekly Record, Lagos
Liberian Herald, Monrovia
Liberian Patriot, Monrovia
Manchester Guardian, Manchester

News Chronicle, London
New Times & Ethiopia News, London
New York Times, New York
Negro World, New York
Nigerian Catholic Herald, Lagos
Nigerian Daily News, Lagos
Nigerian Daily Telegraph, Lagos
Nigerian Daily Times, Lagos
Nigerian Pioneer, Lagos
Pittsburgh Courier, New York
Periscope Africaine, Dakar
Provincial Pioneer, Koforidua, Ghana
Service, Lagos
Sierra Leone Daily Guardian, Freetown
Sierra Leone Daily Mail, Freetown
Sierra Leone Weekly News, Freetown
Times, London
Times of Nigeria, Lagos
Times of West Africa, Accra
Voix des Nègres, Paris
Vox Populi, Accra
West African Mail, London
West African Pilot, Lagos

F. *Journals*

African World, London
Black Man, London
Crisis, New York
Ethiopia Observer, London and Addis Ababa
International African Opinion, London
Keys, London
Labour Monthly, London
Listener, London
Round Table, London
Universitas, Legon, Ghana
Wasu, London
West Africa, London

G. *Unpublished Theses*

DENZER, LA RAY, 'The National Congress of British West Africa: Gold Coast Section', M.A. thesis, University of Ghana, Legon, 1965
DUFFIELD, IAN, 'Duse Mohamed Ali and the Development of Pan-Africanism, 1866–1945', Ph.D. thesis, Edinburgh University, 1971
EDMONDS, W. D., 'The Newspaper Press in British West Africa 1918–1939', M.A. thesis, University of Bristol, 1951–52
ESEDEBE, P. O., 'A History of the Pan-African Movement in Britain, 1900–1948', Ph.D. thesis, University of London, 1968

GARIGUE, P., 'An Anthropological Interpretation of Changing Political Leadership in West Africa', Ph.D. thesis, University of London, 1953

HELLERSTEIN, W., 'J. B. Danquah', Honors thesis, Harvard University, 1967

HOLMES, A. B., 'Economic and Political Organisations in the Gold Coast, 1920–1945', Ph.D. thesis, Department of Political Science, University of Chicago, 1972

MARSHALL, MARY J., 'Christianity and Nationalism in Ghana', M.A. thesis, University of Ghana, Legon, 1965

SCOTT, W. R., 'The American Negro and the Italo-Ethiopian Crisis, 1934–36', M.A. thesis, Howard University, 1966

SPIEGLER, J. S., 'Aspects of Nationalist Thought Among French-Speaking West Africans, 1921–1939', D. Phil. thesis, University of Oxford, 1968

STONE, R. L., 'Colonial Administration and the Rural Politics in South-Central Ghana, 1919–1951', Ph.D. thesis, Cambridge University, 1974

Index

Aba Riot (1929), Nigeria, 31, 32
Abayomi, Dr Kofo, 100, 188
Abbot, Charles, 194, 195
Abomire, J. Adebayo, 28
Aborigines' Rights' Protection Society
  (ARPS), Gold Coast, 12, 18, 21, 26, 32,
  46, 51, 64, 74, 101–4, 105, 106, 109, 110,
  112, 113, 114, 123, 124, 141, 208, 216;
  split within, 101–2; and Provincial
  Councils, 102, 103; and anti-colonialism
  of, 103–4; 'Natural Rulers' attitude to-
  wards, 158–9; demands for self-govern-
  ment in Gold Coast by, 181, 183, 185
Abyssinia Association, Britain, 42
Abyssinia Red Cross Fund committees in
  Gambia, 119, 147, 189
Abyssinia Relief Fund Committee, Sierra
  Leone, 145, 156; see also Ethiopia Relief
  Fund Committees
Accra, 31, 109, 110; National Congress
  conference (1920), 48; Kojo Thompson
  wins seat in 1935 Legislative Council elec-
  tions, 112–14, 124; mass meetings at
  Palladium, 122, 123–4, 139; 1st Annual
  Conference of WAYL (1936), 124–5;
  anti-Italian protests in, 125, 128; re-
  cruitment of volunteers to Ethiopia in,
  139; and prayers for Ethiopia, 144; and
  fund-raising, 153–4
Acquah, J., 124
Acquah, Nana Ayirebi, 160
Addis Ababa, 46; treaty of (1896), 40; fall
  of (1936), 42, 125; as political and econo-
  mic headquarters of Africa, 215
Addo, Glover, 113
Ademola, Prince Adetokunbo, 62
Ademola, Omoba Remi, 50
Adeniyi-Jones, Dr, 187
Adigrat, Italian aerial bombing of (1935),
  40, 63
Adjei, Ako, 82–3
Adowa, battle of (1896), 11, 19, 39; Italian
  aerial bombing of (1935), 40, 63
Afigbo, Dr, 32
African and Orient Review, 53
African Bethel Church, Lagos, 13
African Church Chronicle, 92
African Communities League, 6
African Methodist Episcopal Zion Church,
  Cape Coast, 13, 18
African Morning Post, 51, 52, 53, 58, 61, 63,
  73, 93, 114, 161, 162

African Progress Union, 53, 64
African Sentinel, 116
African Standard, 118, 195
African Times and Orient Review, 53
African Welfare Committee of the Federal
  Council of the Churches of Christ in
  America, 42
Afro-American, 54
Afro-Americans in Ethiopian Imperial Army,
  56
Agbebi, Mojola, 12–13, 14, 18, 144
Agence Metromer, 52
Aggrey, J. E. K., 49
Aglionby, Rev. Dr John O., Bishop of Accra,
  122
Agusto, L. B., 19
Agyeman, I. K., 124
Agyeman, O. S., 160
Akintola, S. L., 175, 200
Akisanya, Oba Samuel, 101, 188
Akiwumi, A. M., 152, 153, 155, 156,
  184
Akiwumi, S. O., 28
Akrofi, H. S., 154
Akwei, Richard, 137, 153, 163, 184
Alakija, Chief C. A. A., 121
Alakija, Olu Ayodele (later Sir Adeyemo
  Alakija), 149, 173–4, 187
d'Alberto, Messrs Cupp, mass demonstra-
  tion in Lagos against, 125
All India Congress Committee, 22
All-Muslim Congress of Sierra Leone, 142
Allotey, Sergeant Major J. Q., 128, 139
Allotey, Thomas B., 65, 92
Amery, L. S., 49
Amoah, R. W., 110
Angell, Norman, 42
Angola, 64
Ansa, Winifried Tete, 29
Apter, David, 104
Arbleh, J. A., 110
arms embargo into Ethiopia, 72–3
Asafu-Adjaye, E. O., 137, 154
Asamankese, 103, 160
Asante Kotoko Society, 124
Ashanti, 15, 104, 110, 111, 130, 137, 139–
  140, 154, 160, 163; see also Gold Coast
Ashanti Abyssinian Expedition force, 140
Ashanti Freedom Society, 124
Ashie-Nikoi, G., 19
Association for the Study of Negro Life and
  History in New York City, 24